Blues *for* America

A CRITIQUE, A LAMENT, AND SOME MEMORIES

Blues *for* America

A CRITIQUE, A LAMENT, AND SOME MEMORIES

Doug Dowd

MONTHLY REVIEW PRESS
New York

Grateful acknowledgment is made to the following for permission to quote: Alkatraz Corner Music Company: California, for Country Joe and the Fish, "Feel-Like-I'm-Fixin'-To-Die-Rag" (words and music by Joe McDonald), 1965, renewed 1993; Farrar, Straus, and Giroux Inc.: New York, for Mark Hertsgaard, *On Bended Knee: The Press and the Reagan Presidency*, 1988; HarperCollins Publishers: New York, for Allen Ginsberg, *HOWL*, 1955; Harcourt Brace and Company: New York, for T.S. Eliot, *The Complete Poems and Plays, 1909-1950*, 1952; Hougton Mifflin Company: Boston, for Walter Russell Mead, *Mortal Splendor: The American Empire in Transition*, 1987; The Macmillan Publishing Company (a division of Macmillan Inc.): London, for John Maynard Keynes, *The Economic Consequences of the Peace*, 1921; Pantheon Books/Schocken Books (a division of Random House Inc.): New York, for Joyce Kolko, *Restructuring the World Economy*, 1988; Vintage Books (a division of Random House Inc.): New York, for W.H.Auden, *Selected Poems*, 1989; and Michael Yeats for W.B. Yeats, "The Second Coming," 1994.

Copyright © 1997 by Douglas F. Dowd
Book design by Akiko Ichikawa
Cover photographs courtesy of (bottom left and top right) Division of Rare and Manuscript Collections, Cornell University; Zirel Sweezy

Special thanks to Mervyn R. Dowd, Jr., Zirel Sweezy, and Bruce Dancis for additional interior photographs

Library of Congress Cataloging-in-Publication Data

Dowd, Douglas Fitzgerald, 1919-
   Blues for America : a critique, a lament, and some memories / Douglas F. Dowd
      p.   cm.
   Includes bibliographical references and index.
   ISBN 0-85345-981-9 (cloth : alk. paper). — ISBN 0-85345-982-7 (paper : alk. paper)
   1. United States—History—20th century—Anecdotes. 2. United States—Social conditions—Anecdotes. 3. United States—Economic conditions—Anecdotes. 4. Dowd, Douglas Fitzgerald, 1919-   —Anecdotes. I. Title.
E741.D69 1997
973.9—dc20
                                                                96-30891
                                                                CIP

Monthly Review Press
122 West 27th Street
New York, NY 10001

Printed in the United States of America
9 8 7 6 5 4 3 2 1

For my children Jeff and Jenny,
in love and admiration,
as they carry on the good fight.

CONTENTS

PREFACE AND ACKNOWLEDGMENTS

The blues of the book's title, like that quintessentially "American" music, mixes sorrow with anger with hope with love. Our country has been aptly seen as "a marriage of all that's admirable with all that's appalling"[1]—unlike a marriage, however, the country cannot be dissolved; it must be understood and dealt with lest all that is appalling smother and destroy all that is admirable. My hope is that what follows will contribute to that essential effort.

For the purposes of this book, it is more than happenstance that I was born in 1919, and that my life span coincides with the decades in which the United States moved toward and then became the new global "hegemon"—its way paved by the physical and social breakdown of all major nations but our own by the end of World War II.

Further, for those of us who teach about society, all too many of us have discovered that the first half of this century is very much *terra incognita* for those under thirty. So, in fact, are all but the most recent years: FDR? Ike? Abbie Hoffman? the depression? Korea? Vietnam? The Mobe? Puzzlement. What follows seeks to bring some of that within easier reach.

Most who read this will know that the name "American," when it is used by the people of the United States to describe themselves but in reference to no others, is very much resented by those many tens of millions of Americans to the north and to the south of us. In this usage, "America" has also often had a silent exclamation mark following it: America! It has had a dream associated with it—not least for me. But the "dream" has been betrayed by two persisting and deepening characteristics of our society: we have allowed and encouraged natural human selfishness to be transformed into bottomless greed; and, although we by no means invented racism, we have allowed and caused it to become always more deep-seated in our lives, despite recurrent attempts to lessen or end it.[2] These two patterns have been our undoing as a society; an analysis of their interaction and consequences will constitute the core of the book's critique and my lament.

I shall also adopt a device, adapted from a work of fiction, namely *U.S.A.* by John Dos Passos. It was a huge novel, a trilogy—*The 42nd Parallel, 1919,* and *The Big Money* (published, respectively, in 1930, 1932, and 1936, and reissued last year in its entirety)—tracing out the lives of several people over many decades. In doing so, Dos Passos added muscle and nerve to his story by interrupting it from time to time with "Newsreels" (poetic treatments of significant events), "Camera Eyes" (stream-of-conscious-ness musings), and portraits of figures who reveal something of their times (e.g., Thorstein Veblen, Sacco and Vanzetti, Woodrow Wilson).[3]

As mine is a work of history rather than fiction (although some might argue otherwise) I shall do something similar. Portraits will be called "Snapshots," the journalism will come under the heading of "News Flash," and personal recollections will be prefaced by "Story."

The prologue will seek to explain (all too hastily!) the nature and interac-tions of the main socioeconomic currents of the epoch before 1919 that created the United States of this century and the world over which, ultimately, it came to preside: capitalism, colonialism, industrialism, and nationalism. The energizing core of that "big four" was capitalism.

The history that follows leads to the somber conclusion that we cannot hope to rid ourselves of the human, natural, or social damages caused by any of the shapers of our lives unless we recognize their interdepend-encies, and recognize also that to move ahead for the better we must seek to work away on all four "clusters." That should keep us busy.

All along the way, for everyone, there is much to learn, and most of it must be learned outside a classroom. My fond hope is that this book in all its parts and references can be a useful part of that learning in itself and, more importantly, in leading to further reading (and perhaps discussions).

But there is also much else besides reading to do, not least in the political realm—in which we all can both learn and teach. We the People of the United States do not much have the habit of participating in the political process, except as voters—choosing between alternatives set in front of us like a cafeteria lunch at grammar school, and just as tasteless, the menu put there by those who preside over the status quo. That habit is just as bad for us as smoking, and just as hard—and just as possible—to break.

To start, we need to turn material self-interest around into profound introspection. As Hillel (who lived about the time of Christ) taught, we must ask ourselves "If I am not for myself, who will be for me?" And the questions that follow are perhaps more crucial for Americans: "And if I am for myself alone, what am I? And if not now, when?"

Hence this book.

There are some I wish to thank very much, my own Gang of Four. Anna Hilbe, who has graced my life in so many ways for a dozen years, began some time ago to urge that I write a book such as this. The die was cast when compatible suggestions arrived from two other sources, first from Barbara Thayer, who had edited and produced my economic history, *U.S. Capitalist Development Since 1776: Of, By and For Which People?* Barbara proposed that I write another kind of history, a deeply personalized memoir aimed at the current generation. Meanwhile, Bruce Dancis of the *Sacramento Bee* (whose good works are noted in chapter 4) was urging me to write an autobiography, recounting the many stories he had endured from me over the years.

Their prodding and my ego finally combined to cook up this pastiche of personal and social history. Several drafts ensued, each a response to the abundant if friendly criticism of Anna, Barbara, and Bruce. The task of Akiko Ichikawa, my editor at Monthly Review Press, was to slim down (by more than 40 percent!) and edit it for readability by an audience closer to her age than mine. She did all of that (with the generous assistance now and again of Barbara).

Thanks, Gang; now it's back to work on the film version.

PART I

FROM CHAOS AND CONVULSION TO THE GOOD WAR

PROLOGUE: INTRODUCING 1919

Writing in January 1919, as the wreckage of the Great War still smoldered, the Irish poet W.B. Yeats saw that the worst was yet to come:

> Turning and turning in the widening gyre
> The falcon cannot hear the falconer;
> Things fall apart; the centre cannot hold;
> Mere anarchy is loosed upon the world,
> The blood-dimmed tide is loosed, and everywhere
> The ceremony of innocence is drowned;
> The best lack all conviction, while the worst
> Are full of passionate intensity.

And, after a few more lines, the poem concludes:

> The darkness drops again; but now I know
> That twenty centuries of stony sleep
> Were vexed to nightmare by a rocking cradle
> And what rough beast, its hour come round at last,
> Slouches towards Bethlehem to be born? [1]

What Yeats saw as falling apart was European civilization, its apogee not much more than a tumbled memory as the twentieth century began. The "rough beast ... slouching towards Bethlehem" that inspired his dread was very rough indeed: the horrors of the next decades were, by any measure, the bloodiest, most destructive, and most shameful in history.

The twentieth century draws to its end and the twenty-first century is edging over the horizon; but large-scale bloodshed continues, destructiveness takes always new forms and, by our standards of decency, the grounds for shame abound.

All the more reason, therefore, to reflect—necessarily with desperate brevity—on what constituted the "centre" that could not hold; what "things" fell apart and why, and why they did so with such violence; what the connections are between all that and the fearsome realities besetting our present—with their likelihood of persistence and worsening—here, there, almost everywhere.

Such social reflection must be historical if it is to bring understanding, whatever else it must also encompass. But in the United States, as the playwright Clifford Odets pointed out in 1935, "We cancel our experience. This is an American habit." [2] It is the kind of habit to which a society can become accustomed when it lives with the boundless optimism that until recently characterized our country.

The Big Four

The "centre" began to take modern shape no later than the seventeenth century, when capitalism, colonialism, industrialism, and nationalism— the four shaping clusters of the modern world—were embryonic, and growing unevenly in both geographic and functional terms. Their subsequent histories soon became ever more tightly coiled in a process of mutual transformation and dependence, an interaction that has brought out the worst in all of them—and in us. Such an unkind assertion begs for at least some elaboration, if only to show how "worst" is meant.

First to be examined is capitalism, that "cluster" of institutions and processes that had come to dominate the other three by the mid-nineteenth century. Bless capitalism for having freed up economic and political possibilities previously choked by the tangles of medieval and dynastic powers; but damn it for having bent or broken a multitude of valuable traditions—most painfully and harmfully those concerning and protecting labor and the land.

Among capitalism's several and always more urgent tendencies is one that moves all aspects of social existence toward commodification: all goods and services are to be bought and sold, their life histories to be set by the play of market forces and, "ideally," by nothing else—tendencies already too well realized even as they gain strength: it is now difficult indeed to find *anything* that does not have, as we say, a price on it, and plain to see that its price becomes its most commanding feature. For ships and shoes and sealing wax, for VCR's and tennis rackets and restaurant meals and pottery. . . . OK. But for health? for education? for safety? for the preservation of the planet? for political office? That is the short list; its contents and those of a justifiably much longer list would of course be very controversial. But for capitalism *any* listing is, finally, *verboten*. (Just ask Prof. Milton Friedman, if you think I'm kidding.)[3]

One unavoidable consequence of the tendency to commodify all the dimensions of existence is that the whole of life comes to be thought of increasingly in *quantitative* terms. A by-product of that is our daily abiding with social tragedies—which, when they entail great numbers of people dying for lack of adequate food, clothing, shelter, and medical care, might more reasonably be called crimes;[4] but because we are human, we find ways to novocaine ourselves against what might otherwise be painful. (And, all too many of us, to blame, hate, and fear the victims of our social carelessness.) In letting all this happen, we lose sight of the *qualitative* "side" of life—and even have trouble knowing what that might mean. Such developments have been just as much an outcome of capitalist development as its extraordinary productivity.

When Adam Smith (1723-1790) argued for freeing up the economy, it was not because he thought the result would be a perfect world; just the best possible one. He saw business people as being selfish to the point of greed.[5] But he also thought that free markets, by which he meant markets in which *no* seller could in any way control or influence either supply or demand, would transform individual self-seeking into social well-being, "private vice into public virtue"—dross, as it were, into gold.

Smith and his most eminent and influential follower, David Ricardo (1772-1823), took the exploitation of labor as a given, but hoped it would diminish as industrialization proceeded; instead, the century after *The Wealth of Nations* saw exploitation spread and deepen—glossed over by the philosopher Jeremy Bentham (1748-1832) who, noting the role of four to five-year-old children's tiny hands in tying up the spindles' loose ends in the new cotton mills, cheerfully observed that "infant man, a drug at present so much worse than worthless, may be endowed [now] with an indubitable and universal value." The new factories making this possible were seen by his contemporary William Blake as "dark" and "satanic."[6]

Smith's manual for economic freedom assumed the abolition of any and all forms of social power—rooted in either religious or civil traditions—while assuming that capital's control over the means of production (that is, the means of life) would be neutralized by incessant competition. So transfixed was he by the entrenched and pervasive corruption and associated inefficiencies of his era, emanating principally from the great power of the State (and its beholden private companies), he failed to see that the very industrialization process he advocated would yield the growth of large-scale production and business baronies which would use their uncontested social power to construct a State after their hearts' desires. That's what happened: and always more so as we approach the present—successfully demanding always more of people's lives and of nature's bounty.

What about colonialism, the second of our Big Four? What "worst" in it has been brought about by its interaction with the other powerhouses of modern history? There is nothing good to be said of colonialism, nothing at all, so we may be mercifully brief. Colonialism was bad enough in the pre-industrial centuries, so bad—not least in its achievement of a wholesale slave trade—that it could scarcely become worse.[7] But it did.

As industrialization took hold, colonialism became imperialism, and nascent industrial capitalism was energized by high-tension nationalism. Horrendous and destructive though colonialism had been—the native populations of many areas reduced by 90 percent from the sixteenth to the eighteenth century, for example—its effects were mild by comparison with the impact of the imperialism of the nineteenth century; and the latter were to pale by comparison with the human and natural damage dispensed in this century. In the beginning, lives were lost and cultures warped; later, whole societies were taken over, their populations disrupted or pressed into highly exploited labor; in our epoch it has been necessary and possible to continue all that has gone before and to add to it the capture of "the hearts and minds" of the native populations.

But surely there is little of fault to be found with industrialism? Of course there have been and, even more, could be large advantages from industrialism. But the *kind* of industrialism we have had has of course been definitively shaped, harnessed, driven, and directed by capitalist and nationalist drives—drives that have always had profits and power, never human, natural, or social needs as their starting point: and let the devil take the hindmost. Which the devil has done.

To be sure, industrialism has required and enabled widespread education, improved health care, and brought all sorts of other good things; and to add that it has done so at a steep price is not saying enough. Education has been all too much deformed and abused in its customary (if seldom admitted) service of capital and nation; improved health care, most especially in the United States, has been accompanied by large areas of neglect and deteriorated health; our air is dangerously foul; we use up too much of time, energy, talent, and resources to produce junk, some of it very dangerous junk; and so on. Industrialism *could be* an unqualifiedly beneficial development. It hasn't been, and it couldn't have been, not with those sleazy partners it has always hung out with.[8]

By now you will have guessed that nationalism, our fourth honcho, is not going to come off well, either. Precisely because it *is* nationalism under scrutiny it is difficult to see or to think clearly. Nationalism and the nation are not the same thing, although one could argue that without the former there would be many fewer of the latter; and that the world would not be the worse for it. Nationalism may be understandable and hard to criticize when it is a small country trying to get a larger one off its back, where it has been for too long. Some years ago it might have been less difficult than now to get behind the mask of nationalism and find a human face; not today.[9]

The foregoing brusque treatment of the immensely complicated processes and relationships of "The Big Four" will not be seen by you, nor is it by me, as more than the barest minimum of an introduction. To understand the behavior of each, to say nothing of all four together, has required many, many volumes. Tacitly or explicitly present in the foregoing notes on capitalism, for example, has been the view that for capitalism to persist and to flourish it must find ways to satisfy three imperatives: it must expand, it must exploit, and it must achieve and maintain oligarchic rule—a generalization as controversial as it is suggestive of complexity. Much the same can be said of colonialism, industrialism, and nationalism. Some, but by no means all, of those complexities will be dealt with as the book moves along. But this Prologue will now end with another set of generalizations, concerning the tortuous and increasingly volatile interaction between the Four that inexorably culminated in what became, up to then, the most destructive war in history.

The Big One

As the Civil War in the United States drew to its bloody conclusion, the industrialization process had begun to spread swiftly outside Britain—most forcefully in Germany and the United States, less so in the Low Countries and Scandinavia, France, Italy, Japan, and Russia.

As industrialization proceeded and nation-states became more voracious and better-armed, both the needs and the stakes rose. Industrialization meant steamships and railways, tying continents together while
allowing and requiring hinterlands to be penetrated. Bulkier, lower-value
commodities were needed to supply growing industry and industrial
populations with raw materials and foodstuffs. (By 1900, Britain depended
upon imports for at least half of such goods.) These meant long-term
investments overseas—in harbor facilities, railroads, mines, and planta-
tions. It also meant imperialism rather than colonialism, and a different
political resolution to match the deeper economic commitments,

> a large measure of political control over the *internal* relations and structure of
> the colonial economy . . . ; a movement from "economic penetration" to
> "spheres of influence," [thence] to protectorates or indirect control, [thence] *via*
> military occupation to annexation. [10]

The period did not so much end as blow apart, in a war seemingly
without limits or conclusion. When the shooting stopped on November
11, 1918, it was as the result of an "armistice"—a formal cessation of
shooting, but nothing more than that: anything more required a peace
treaty, done at Versailles.

In January of 1919 (as Yeats was composing "The Second Coming"),
the Versailles Peace Conference began. John Maynard Keynes (1883-1946),
Britain's chief economic representative at the conference (and a leading
economist of that time), wrote a savage critique shortly after its conclusion—in which, among other matters, he made it clear that the Versailles
Treaty guaranteed that the armistice would be only that: an armed truce.
In the elegant statement that opens his book, Keynes, perhaps as much
sardonically as descriptively, is in any case expressing the smug views of
what was then the "establishment" of Britain (and which, by 1960, and with
appropriate alterations, was that of its subsequent counterpart in the United
States):

> What an extraordinary episode in the economic progress of man that age was
> which came to an end in August 1914! The greater part of the population, it is
> true, worked hard and lived at a low standard of comfort, yet were, to all
> appearances, reasonably contented with this lot. But escape was possible, for any
> man of capacity or character at all exceeding the average, into the middle and
> upper classes, for whom life offered, at a low cost and with the least trouble,
> conveniences, comforts, and amenities beyond the compass of the richest and
> most powerful monarchs of other ages. The inhabitant of London could order
> by telephone, sipping his morning tea in bed, the various products of the whole

earth, in such quantity as he might see fit, and reasonably expect their early delivery upon his doorstep; he could at the same moment and by the same means adventure his wealth in the natural resources and new enterprises of any quarter of the world, and share, without exertion or even trouble, in their prospective fruits and advantages; or he could decide to couple the security of his fortunes with the good faith of the townspeople of any substantial municipality in any continent that fancy or information might recommend. He could secure forthwith, if he wished it, cheap and comfortable means of transit to any country or climate without passport or other formality, could despatch his servant to the neighbouring office of a bank for such supply of the precious metals as might seem convenient, and could then proceed abroad to foreign quarters, without knowledge of their religion, language, or custom, bearing coined wealth upon his person, and would consider himself greatly aggrieved and much surprised at the least interference. But, most important of all, he regarded this state of affairs as normal, certain, and permanent, except in the direction of further improvement, and any deviation from it as aberrant, scandalous, and avoidable. The projects and politics of militarism and imperialism, of racial and cultural rivalries, of monopolies, restriction, and exclusion, which were to play the serpent to this paradise, were little more than the amusements of his daily newspaper, and appeared to exercise almost no influence at all on the ordinary course of social and economic life, the internationalisation of which was nearly complete in practice.[11]

The "projects, politics, and rivalries" that played "the serpent to this paradise" were, of course, the bone, meat, and gristle of a world shaped by social institutions and processes that simultaneously depended upon and feverishly increased both conflict and competition, whatever more positive meanings they might have had. War could not be avoided in that process except by continuous economic and geographic expansion: but that need could not be fulfilled because of the very basis for it.

That basis was and largely remains a complex composed of capital accumulation driven by profit, and supported in diverse ways by competing national states. In turn, this encourages a steady increase in productive capacities which become duplicative and excessive.

Thus, every "major power" had, by definition, its own steel industry, its own machinery industry, its own arms industry, etc. So by 1910, for example, Germany alone could satisfy the capital goods needs of *all* of Europe. Those markets being closed, Germany used its heavy industries to produce its excellent armaments; all of this intensified, and then. . . .

Capitalism's intrinsically unequal distribution of income assures that an inadequate percentage of productive capacity can be absorbed by consumption. To this poisonous stew, there must be stirred in the need by each nation to seek and to gain assured access to colonial/imperialist possibilities to meet their production needs (and to prevent others from doing so). Taken together, the question then is not would international war result, but how could it possibly be avoided?

As the twentieth century opened, "small" wars had already begun—in Asia, the Middle East, Africa, and Latin America—involving most of the major and many of the minor powers. When a young man in Sarajevo in a moment of nationalist rage shot and killed a symbol of the imperialism stifling his people, it was just one of many sparks that sooner or later would serve to ignite the fuse for "The Great War."

The surprise was not the war, which had begun to be anticipated as early as the mid-1890s, but its depth, its spread, its duration—and its seemingly unparalleled (and at the same time, banal) savagery. Except for our Civil War, the first industrial war, there had never been an intimation that war could be so destructive on such a large scale, and that would endure for what seemed like forever to those who fought it.[12]

The damage done by that war could not be measured only in (at least) ten million lives lost in the fighting, nor in the destruction of resources and equipment. The considerably more lasting damage was social: the war's effects were those of a massive earthquake, followed by seemingly endless aftershocks—which, in an important sense, have yet to cease, may never cease.

The struggles the world daily tries with little hope to end—the bloody tangles in the Balkans, the Middle East, and Central and Eastern Europe—although their origins usually antedate the war, were given their current intractability by the "solutions" consequent upon the "peace."

To the various leaders of Germany—business, military, intellectual—it was clear already in 1915 that the war could not be won; as early as then it had come to be called "the endless war." But in ways to which we became accustomed in the Vietnam war, it was just as clear to those leaders that surrender was to be averted. So the war ground on and on until, in 1917, the United States entered—fresh in mood and body, innocent in spirit and bursting with matériel. Already in our industrialized Civil War it had been learned that victory was on the side which, as one general famously put it, "gets there fustest with the mostest." By the time we entered the hostilities, Germany's soldiers and civilians had begun to experience starvation; Russia had arrived at the breaking point earlier, and had its way much eased toward revolution as one result; and the French and the British could continue only because of the strength given to them by their new ally.

Of the many problems that had produced the war, not least those that were economic, all were exacerbated and none resolved by it. That was clear to Keynes and to the many others who warned that the end of World War I was merely the prelude to a second world war. As will be discussed later, perhaps the major problem of the Great War was not that it was destructive, horrendously so though it was, but that it was not destructive *enough:* not destructive enough to weaken the principal contenders sufficiently to deter them from further social lunacy, to defang them. As will be seen, that "sufficient destruction" was accomplished by World War II, which left only the United States able to fend for itself—even, for a few years, to feed itself.

Thus was the stage set for the chaos and convulsion, the revolutions and counterrevolutions, the economic cataclysms, and vast cultural and social transformations that ensued in the next twenty years, and that ended with a new world war. From my own considerably narrower perspective, however, the fateful year 1919 drew to its close with a positive event, worthy of our first

News Flash

San Francisco, December 7: Sybil Elizabeth Dowd gave birth this day to Douglas Fitzgerald Dowd. Mother and child are both well. (Some years later, President Roosevelt informed the Congress of the United States that "December 7 is a day that shall live in infamy.")

1 PROSPERITY AND ALL THAT JAZZ, AND TOWARD THE BLACK HOLE: 1919-1929

i.

The Making of a Skeptic

The 1920s were called "roaring" by the journalists of the time. Those who experienced the 1960s would see the Twenties more as snoozing than roaring; but the decade was turbulence incarnate when compared with all earlier years—rupturing the boundaries of personal and social behavior, morality, and taste, while broadening the range of pleasurable activities. Here began the flood of intoxication with all that was earlier held illegal and immoral.

I was a child in those years, and my family was close to the cutting edge of the social changes belonging in the category of "ruptures." Recounting diverse aspects and episodes of my childhood may shed some light on that—and on me.

It is not difficult to find a starting point: my mother's family was Russian-Jewish, my father's Irish Catholic. They were married in 1915. From as far back as I can remember, there was a cacophony of bigotry issuing from both sides of the family—"in front of the children," though not, usually, when both our parents were present. After I was six, they never *were* present at the same time.

My father, good Catholic that he was, married three times. I remember his second wife with a certain poignancy.

Story: Aussie Flapper

She was the first Aussie I ever knew. I've forgotten her name, but not her appearance. She must have had more than the one dress I remember, a slinky black number, and the little cloche hat on her well-shaped head; and probably she did not always paste that black beauty spot on her left cheek. She was the classic "flapper," or "John Held girl." She and my father both tended to drink too much, which soured more than sweetened their relationship—at least in my infrequent observations. I remember one occasion in his financial district office (he was an attorney), when I was to meet him in order to go to the Stanford/Cal track meet. As I entered, they were yelling strenuously at each other, struggling over a bottle of booze—this, of course, during Prohibition, when booze was illegal. But what I remember most vividly was a quasi-insane vacation my father insisted he and she and my brother (Merv Jr.) take together. For three weeks we lived in a large tent on the shore of Lake Tahoe. My stepmother couldn't cook, or anything else that had to be done in the great out-doors; and my father expected his wife to do everything. My father, true to his Irish background, was a potato zealot. That meant building a fire on the ground and finding ways to boil, bake, or whatever, lots of potatoes: completely beyond my stepmother, who was close to a total breakdown just being out there in the country, and at 6,000 feet yet. I felt very sorry for that poor woman, and relieved for her when not much later she signed up for my pop's second divorce.

From all the divorces on the Catholic side of the family, one might deduce that religion was taken with something less than seriousness by them; nor was it practiced much, if at all, on my mother's side. I don't remember anyone in her family—grandparents, uncles, aunts, cousins, least of all my mother—ever attending a synagogue or speaking of religion—except against Catholics.

So much for religion, so much for marriage. From developing a suspicious eye looking at those two sacred institutions, it is not surprising that other sacred institutions have also had much trouble getting through my door, as will be abundantly confirmed as this book goes on.

Small War Story

I was in the army for four years in World War II, most of the time overseas. My mother wrote worried letters to me once a week, religiously, one might say. And she *always* closed the letter this way: "Douglas dear, take care of yourself. I pray to our Lord Jesus Christ for you every night. And fly low and slow." Oh well.

Until the war, I had spent all my life in San Francisco, and so had two generations or more of my familial predecessors. My father's grandfather came to San Francisco in 1846, among the first of the million or more Irish to flee the potato blight. My mother's father and mother arrived in New York in the 1880s, fleeing the pogroms of Russia. "Pops" was a carpenter, and he brought the whole family to San Francisco in 1906, where work was easy to get after the earthquake. The subsequent histories of members of both families ranged wildly between the not quite customary and the bizarre. I begin with the Irish, who got here first.

Grandpa Dowd, who died before I was born, was one of four sons, all born in San Francisco. Their lives were as different from each other as could be. Grandpa became Sheriff of the City and County of San Francisco. Grand Uncle Cleophas was ordained as a Jesuit priest when he was twenty-one. That very day, the story is written, he strapped on his gun, took the boat to Sausalito, killed a man against whom he had long held a grudge, fled to the Wasatch mountains of Utah, and began to raise horses—sold to among others, the train robbers Butch Cassidy and the Sundance Kid. Cleophas soon became a federal marshal for the region, but in 1896 was murdered by a horse rustler.[1] Not much later, showing that symmetry is not entirely lacking in the social process, his brother was hanged for stealing horses, a bit south of San Jose, CA.

The law affected the Dowd family in seminal ways. After the divorce, I seldom saw my father. He was an attorney, as noted. After graduating from Berkeley, he had gone on to Columbia and Harvard to study law, and at one time or another he expressed a passing interest in whether I was ever going to college. His brother Gerald had become a biologist, on the faculty at Cornell, where he specialized in studying tuberculosis—from which he died in his thirties. Which brings me to another

Story: Filial Ties

While I was overseas, my father's interest in me grew. I was a pilot and all that, and he would write to me asking for photos and the like, presumably to show around the office: my son, the hero. I went along with it, until that letter in which he got carried away with passages against Jews, blacks, unions, etc. I responded by reminding him that, apart from any more general concerns, my mother was a Jew and that if the war was being fought for anything it was against his kind of arguments, etc. And that he must write and apologize, whether he meant it or not, and never again write or speak in such ways in my presence. I didn't see him until 1946, when he came to S.F. on a business trip. He invited my brother and me and our wives to a dinner at a tony restaurant. Dad brought up the matter of my education, which had disappointed him. (I had gone to S.F. Junior—now Community—College and one semester of Berkeley before the army.) He offered to pay for my college education *if* I would go to Cornell and major in biology—like Uncle Gerald. By 1946 I was already well on my way toward radicalism and wanting to study the social process, but even if that hadn't been so, I didn't want his help, let alone his guidance or control. (The new GI Bill strengthened my resolve, of course.) The dinner from that point on became an imbroglio, and before long anti-semitism and the like filled the air. My then wife and my brother's wife were both Jewish, and before much time had passed the management asked us to leave. Just about that time, the Committee for Constitutional Government was founded in New York, Dad one of the founders. Even Governor Dewey, a staunch conservative, branded it as a "fascist-type organization." You could conclude that my left-leaning politics were largely an Oedipal (or something of that sort) response; perhaps, but my brother—whose attitude toward Dad was even more negative than mine—couldn't see much wrong with McCarthy in the 1950s, was a Goldwater supporter in 1964, and stayed pretty much in that groove until the Vietnam war days.

Over time, the Dowds have continued to straddle the law. My cousin Gil Dowd I never knew, but Gil knew me, or was supposed to. He was head of the San Francisco Red Squad in the 1940s, when I was achieving a modest infame in Bay Area politics (if only with the FBI, which was busy accumulating 2,500 pages about me). Gil's duties included surveillance of his cousin Douglas.

My mother's side of the family wasn't quite so spectacular, but it played its part in making me into a doubter. "Muh" was born in Brooklyn in 1893 (so was Mae West, in case you didn't know), her sister Mary likewise, three years earlier. Neither of them finished grade school, it being the Jewish way then that the two boys in the family should go to collitch, aided by their sisters going to work. Martin became an M.D., Eddie a pharmacist.

Sybil, my mother, worked in offices as a clerk, and became a specialist in the "Comptometer"—a manually operated calculating machine. After the divorce, she sought and got a job as a high school teacher of comptometry, despite never having attended either high school or college, a requirement for such a job. When asked for documents credentialling her, she—though a prim and conscientiously honest person *almost* all the time—replied that her documents had been destroyed in the earthquake and fire of 1906. Which occurred, however, when she was thirteen. She was also very small, only 5'1", and quite lovely, and perhaps that distracted the bureaucrat from his arithmetic.

Older sister Mary, on the other hand, was neither prim nor petite. Her first husband (she always called him, simply, "Hartman") was a gambler and a gangster, and he was shot dead in the street. Mary was beautiful in the same way as Mae West—flamboyant, *zaftig* (a Yiddish term for a Rubens-type figure), straight out of Damon Runyon. Her last husband, Harry Jenkins (she always called him "Jenks"), was also a professional gambler. Together they ran a bookie joint and poker game in downtown San Francisco. As a kid I often dropped in to the joint after school, just to watch. (I won at least $5,000 at poker from my fellow heroes during the war.) One afternoon the doorbell rang, and I opened the door only to see a cop. I shut the door quickly, ran to Mary and told her the cops were at the door. "Give the nice man this envelope, Sweetie," she said. I did, returned, and asked what was going on. "Every business has to pay taxes, Douglas," she said. "Some of us pay them in the mail, others pay them at the door." My first civics lesson.

My mother taught at what was called Continuation High School, out in the Mission District (a relatively poor part of the city). Most of its students were kids who had never finished high school. This, along with her own deprivation, heightened my mother's valuation of an education and led her to seek out the very best public school for her two sons: Grant Grammar School, in the richest part of the city. But that was three years after the divorce. In those three years, with my mother very much lost in her life and dependent on advice and some financial help from her brother Martin, we were sent to military school.

We went to two: the first, run by two emigré Spaniards across the bay in Alameda, was all spit and polish, cross and sword, but with little or no education. Uncle Martin had been an army surgeon in France in the war and loved it. While we were at the Spanish place, two of his army buddies opened up a military school outside of Palo Alto. It had a laundry, a kitchen, a barracks, and some fields surrounding it. I don't remember any classrooms. I worked in the laundry, my brother in the kitchen, and we played in the fields. No classes, no discipline, and terrible food. In the middle of its and our second semester, the school was shut down, as its two owners were found guilty of fraud and embezzlement and marched off to San Quentin.

By then, our clothes consisted entirely of uniforms. Though it was in mid-semester Muh had been able to enroll us in Grant Grammar School, and off we went—in our military uniforms. As we entered the school yard, it was as though the script of "The Lord of the Flies" was being shot: dozens of boys immediately descended on us and, back to back, we fought them off as well as we could. By the time the teachers stopped the fracas, we were bloody and our uniforms were in ribbons. And I had become an anti-militarist.

But I digress—anticipating myself a bit.

ii.

"How Ya Gonna Keep 'em Down on the Farm, after They've Seen Paree?" [2]

The 1920s began with the sharpest and shortest inflation in our history; as they ended, our and the world's deepest, longest, and most pervasive depression was well under way. Of the developments discussed in the prologue, the most momentous was the war. Its economic consequences were devastating for Europe, but, for the United States, the war was manna from heaven.

For the preceding half century or so, the U.S. economy had been verging toward primacy among industrial nations; the war accelerated that process and strengthened its foundations. U.S. industry and agriculture were very much stimulated and transformed by the war-connected needs of Europe: greatly increased exports and loans changed us from a debtor to a creditor nation with stunning suddenness; our own military needs with their assured markets paved the way for major technological advances; wartime private and public spending and private and public (including military) employment gave us a rising and prevented what almost certainly would have been a falling economy after 1914 and into the 1920s; and, among other matters, the war's needs and possibilities were responsible for creating our first governmental structures suited to a complex industrial capitalist society—soon to be dismantled in the boyish economic euphoria to follow.[3]

With all the many stimuli provided by the war it is not difficult to understand the buoyancy of the war years and of the 1920s. But what brought it to an end? And, more to the point (for under capitalism expansions always come to an end), why was the depression of the 1930s so deep? Why did the worst ever of hard times last for a dozen years or so? And why, on a different level of analysis, was a World War II required to lift us out of that depression?

One way to begin to answer such questions is to dwell for a moment on the word "prosperity." Like so many other pleasing terms we find to describe our history, it must be viewed with an eye to who uses it. Until very recently, almost all of those who have informed us about our society—historians, economists, sociologists, journalists, politicians, et al.—have been in or from the upper ranks of society. They have thought, spoken, and written from the vantage point of the comfortable beneficiaries of what are seen as the society's achievements. But, as Thorstein Veblen (1857-1929) noted when speaking of professors of social science, "their intellectual horizon is bounded by the same limits of commonplace insight and preconceptions as are the prevailing opinions of the conservative middle class." Thus, for the university to be corrupted in keeping with business—or any other—ideologies was a profound and crippling tragedy.[4]

In short, the term "prosperity" was corrupt by definition. What was worse, it derived from narrow-minded infatuation with technologically-driven consumption.

The political economy of the 1920s functioned within a larger social process. Science and technology surged forward by leaps and bounds in the 1920s. The ways and means of consumers struck ahead on new paths, whether as regards products, debt, style, taste, almost everything; advertising and the media made their first large dents on our consciousness: what we now take for granted had its roots and flowering then.

iii.

New World A-Borning

The first time one could tune in on a private (commercial) radio broadcasting station was in December 1920—if one had a radio, which few did. My family was middle-income in the first half of the decade; not until its second half did we have a radio. Before then, and like many others, my brother and I struggled with a homemade (at school) "crystal set": a piece of crystal mounted on a simple wooden stand with a connected thin wire that one poked around on the crystal to find sounds from one of the few radio stations—recorded music, religious talks, a political convention, a prize fight. Radio sales began to be significant in 1922; by 1929 sales had risen more than fifteen times, very much lubricating the emerging new era.

A good deal of both reality and symbolism were contained in radio's beginning. Radio's first practical use was as an instrument of communications and propaganda during the Great War; then, in the 1920s, radio became an instrument of advertising and entertainment—then as now, its fate determined by the amount of radio advertising and the number of listeners. This is another way of saying that commercial radio was born in, and helped to accelerate the processes of, what is now called "consumerism."

The mass purchase and use of industrial products such as radios (and appliances, autos, telephones, etc.) of course implies their mass production; and vice versa.[5] The Twenties were the first time in history that mass industrial production and mass consumption of its products were joined, and the United States the first—and until after World War II, the only— nation where it could and did happen, on any substantial basis.

It is worth noting that industrial mass production began in the United States with Eli Whitney's processes for producing muskets for the War of 1812. The key elements of the process were standardization of the product and the interchangeability of parts. Since then, nothing much has changed in those respects—except that there are always more advanced techniques and always more products, and always more changes, taking place always more rapidly in the social setting in, by, and for which all that happens—come hell or high water, both of which keep coming, always more. A bit of reflection suggests that standardized products also require a proportionate degree of standardized responses among interchangeable consumers—and which, like the products, must be produced: the Age of Advertising's time had come to be in the 1920s.

Advertising of many sorts had existed well before, of course, but both its scope and its purposes were markedly different. Almost always, early advertising was merely informative (where, what, when, how much); modern advertising can be informative also; but its function is to mold minds and feelings—or, as Paul Baran put it, "to make people want what they don't need, and not to want what they do." And of course what sells products can sell ideas and politicians and wars and just about anything else some one or some group can pay for. In the 1920s, lots of products were bought by people who a bit earlier had no idea they wanted them, from oranges to cigarettes, from vacuum cleaners to automobiles—and, of course, all sorts of other things. The purchase of durable and expensive commodities was also facilitated by the introduction (first, in the auto industry, in 1923, by GM) of consumer credit. And what a many-headed change *that* was to become! [6]

All the foregoing took place in a sociopolitical process equally as dramatic, varying from the foolish to the joyous to the dreary to the cruel. The 1920s were a most peculiar decade in the United States if for no other reason than the manner in which so many diverse, even conflicting extremes lived side by side: from 1919 until 1933 the Eighteenth Amendment to the Constitution ("Prohibition") made it illegal to buy or drink an alcoholic beverage. In 1933, the Twenty-first Amendment "repealed" the earlier amendment. In the years between, the United States was among the most fervently moralistic and probably the most law-breaking nation in the world—and surely the most fertile ground for gangsterism, racketeering, extortion, kidnapping, etc. Al Capone (born not far from my mother's house in Brooklyn, a few years later) symbolized the latter; and it is generally acknowledged that the transformation of the so-called Mafia from a long-standing band of Sicilian outlaws of local power and substantial positive meaning[7] into today's nationally and internationally powerful group with entirely negative meaning is linked to the era of Prohibition and gangsterism in the United States: the chickens have come home to roost, but have become a plague of locusts with insatiable appetites and much social corruption and decay upon which to feed.

The "roaring" 1920s were the very years of the "Jazz Age." That term referred to a spreading "loose" lifestyle as much as to music. A very large number of those who went to nightclubs to listen to jazz and to dance went there also—or only—to have a nip or more of the forbidden "booze." They were the years of religious fundamentalism *and* the worship of science, of puritanism *and* of suddenly very short skirts, of galloping divorce rates and some early attempts at a new level of social freedom, most controversially for women. Accordingly, and among other contrasts, the presidents of the 1920s made a motley group: Wilson, Harding, Coolidge, and Hoover—in that same order, a Protestant idealist; an easy prey for corrupters, and whose main interests were far from puritanical; a prim, almost lifeless man; and an efficiency engineer.

It was an age of great disillusionment, not least because of the horrors of the Great War; and, perhaps for the same reasons, it was a decade in which many heroes of all sorts were found or created, the age in which the cult of the celebrity began in the United States: from athletes such as Babe Ruth and Jack Dempsey to film stars such as Douglas Fairbanks and Mary Pickford and Charlie Chaplin to, among others and most deified of all, the man who in 1927 flew from New York to Paris non-stop: Lucky Lindy, the Lone Eagle.[8]

Within such a tumultuous and uncertain decade there was much fear, of all kinds and on all levels. In the very years in which Einstein and Freud became household names and science a popularly revered discipline, fervent evangelistic religion "sold like hotcakes" (which, along with hot dogs, were the pizza of the era).

Standing out among the evangelists, and influencing all who have followed, were Billy Sunday and Aimee Semple McPherson. Sunday had been a professional ballplayer and acrobat before he became a spectacularly successful traveling "bunkshooter" (as the poet Carl Sandburg called him). Like Sunday, McPherson had begun her career before the war but really struck it rich in the lush years of the Twenties. In 1923, McPherson built her Pentecostal "Angelus Temple" along with her own radio station and Bible College. And, like so many Fundamentalist ministers then and since, she was caught up in numerous sexual and financial scandals.[9]

Among the leading notions of Fundamentalism (then and still) was its "creationist" interpretation of human history, which led to "the monkey trial"; in the same years the campaign to protect the United States from alien influences (especially "Bolshevism") led to the trial and execution of Sacco and Vanzetti.

The Scopes trial—which was even more a trial of Bryan and his beliefs—was a passionate concern of those who adhered to the Fundamentalist position; for the larger part of the population, it was a matter of indifference or laughter. By that time—the mid-Twenties—the people were at least equally concerned with the doings of Jack Dempsey, the stock market, crossword puzzles, or mah jongg.

And, in a crescendo of controversy beginning in 1920 and rising throughout the 1920s, excruciatingly so in 1927, much of the nation and a noticeable part of Europe (especially Italy and France) had their attention riveted on the Sacco-Vanzetti case.

The case began in early 1920, when the "Red Scare" and the "Palmer Raids" were at their height. The Soviet Revolution was very fresh in people's (especially business people's) minds; U.S. (and various European) troops were involved in the fighting of the ongoing civil war in the Soviet Union; trade unionism was riding on the strength it had gained during the war; the immigrant population as a percentage of the total population since 1900 had increased at something like one million a year up to 1917 or so; and the Socialist Party, both despite and because it had opposed the war, was a focus of strong feelings. In this context, the "Palmer Raids" and the "Red Scare" had taken hold; and in this context there was a factory payroll robbery eventuating in murder in Boston—for which two well-known Italian anarchists, Nicola Sacco and Bartolomeo Vanzetti, were arrested, charged, convicted, and sentenced to death.

The 1921 verdict made few headlines in the United States; but when the story was spread in France, Italy, and Spain, it soon bounced back to the United States to inflame passions, to lead to repeated appeals, and to a very large-scale involvement of the legal, intellectual, and political establishment of the time.

The trial was marked by what amounted to legal scandal. Neither of the defendants spoke English well, and the weakness of their English and consequent misunderstandings should by themselves have been cause for a mistrial. In addition, the prosecution's witnesses were unconvincing and contradictory in themselves, and even more so when compared with the dozens of witnesses for the defense. Much more could be said, and there is a large literature one can consult (some of it to be noted later). Suffice it here to reproduce excerpts from the conclusions reached by Felix Frankfurter:

> By systematic exploitation of the defendants' alien blood, their imperfect knowledge of English, their unpopular social views, and their opposition to the war, the District Attorney invoked against them a riot of political passion and patriotic sentiment; and the trial judge connived at—one had almost written, cooperated in—the process. . . .
>
> I assert with deep regret, but without the slightest fear of disproof, that certainly in modern times Judge Thayer's opinion stands unmatched for discrepancies between what the record discloses and what the opinion conveys. His

25,000 word document cannot accurately be described otherwise than as a farrago of misquotations, misrepresentations, suppressions, and mutilations. [10]

Vanzetti was quoted in an interview (with mispronunciations spelled out) just after his death sentence was handed down, precursing the profound historic effect of the injustice done by that court in 1927:

> If it had not been for these thing, I might have live out my life talking at street corners to scorning men. I might have die, unmarked, unknown, a failure. Now we are not a failure. This is our career and our triumph. Never in our full life could we hope to do such work for tolerance, for joostice, for man's onderstanding of man, as now we do by accident. Our words, our lives, our pains—nothing! The taking of our lives—lives of a good shoemaker and a poor fish peddler—all! That last moment belongs to us—that agony is our triumph. [11]

As the Twenties ended the worst depression in history had begun.

iv.

Depression Was Just Around the Corner

There are at least two important matters requiring explanation for the period from 1914 to 1929: a) the sustained quality of the expansion, and b) the manner in which that long expansion connects with the unprecedented collapse after 1929. The prosperity of the fifteen years preceding 1929 was quite unusual in our history; drastically more so was the depression—in its severity, its duration, and its pervasiveness. Something new was going on; it probably began before (and was obscured by) World War I, in a process that can be called "semi-stagnation." We now take a closer look.

First, in the years just before the war, the United States had reached the limits of economic complexity then allowed—by extant technology, real income and purchasing power, and business conditions—whether the reference is to productivity, the balance between consumer and capital goods production, the total of all production, or the scale of individual plant production.

Second, although the years after 1909 were conventionally seen as a period of recovery from the panic and depression of 1907-1908, that recovery was quite uneven and feeble. The uncertainty and rocky quality of the U.S. economy was matched or worse by Europe's. For the two strongpoints of the world economy to have such weaknesses was an ominous portent of the disaster that exploded in 1929. [12]

Much of the talk about the causes of economic difficulty in the United States in the decade before 1914 pointed to the inadequacies of the financial system. Attention was however diverted from deeper problems (as is true once more today). Faulkner portrays the situation usefully:

> An inefficient and inelastic credit system, however, was by no means the only cause for the unstable condition of American economic life between 1907 and 1914. High finance had overloaded the railroads and other corporations with fantastic capital structures; industrial "trusts," as in the case of United States Steel after the panic of 1907, were reluctant to adjust prices to decreasing demand. Wages were barely keeping up with the increased cost of living, whereas unemployment in manufacturing and transportation amounted to 12 percent or over in 1908, 1914, and 1915.... [Despite] a vigorous speculative advance.... in the early months of 1914 on both the London and New York stock exchanges..., the world saw no revival in trade and industry. In the United States the recession of 1913 sank into a depression in 1914 with an increase in gold exports, a decline in foreign trade, a weakening of commodity prices, and an increase in unemployment. [13]

What Faulkner saw as a condition of substantial instability, Baran and Sweezy later saw as the onset of *stagnation*—a condition in which, in the absence of "external stimuli" such as war, the economy tends to limp along with underutilized productive capacities, depressed businesses, and high unemployment. This was true of much of the world throughout the 1930s and could again be true, although to a lesser degree (one trusts) for the 1990s. [14]

It may be said once again that the outbreak of war in August 1914 entirely altered the prospects of the U.S. economy—in terms of its strengthened position in the world economy, expanded industrial and agricultural productive capacities, many technological improvements, and the strengthening of purchasing power. Taken together with developments not directly tied to the war, the foundations had thereby been laid in the United States for what came to be called "the new era." [15]

For reasonably but not adequately informed people in the 1920s the "system" could seem to be doing very well indeed, despite serious and deepening problems in a broad range of industries and most of agriculture: as auto and truck production and road construction expanded briskly, but the railroads had begun their prolonged process of decline (most especially for passenger traffic); as electricity and petroleum were used increasingly for fuel and power, but coal mining shrank; as synthetic textiles were growing, but cotton textiles suffered; as fruits and vegetables and dairy and meat products became more a part of food consumption, but staple agriculture (grains and cotton, especially) fell into depression.[16]

That is, the activities where much of industrial labor and most of the farm population worked—relatively inefficiently, perhaps—were all in serious trouble, all declining, so of course those whose jobs depended upon them were in even more serious trouble.

In this connection, it is pertinent to examine a key finding regarding the distribution of income—and therefore of purchasing power—in the 1920s. The data show that the following percentages of families received the following income in the years indicated:

Income Level	1929	1947	1962
Under $3,000	51%	30%	21%

The dollar figures are in 1962 values. In 1964, when President Johnson declared his "war on poverty," he asked his advisors for a dollar figure for annual family income, beneath which a family would be deemed to be living in poverty. The figure was set at $3,000—a figure, as we shall see later, that very much understated the severity of the situation. Even so, when applied to the 1920s, it places half of the population as living in poverty.[17]

In the Twenties, as in recent years, part of the reason so many were poor is that so many had lost relatively well-paying jobs and, both despite and because of the new technologies, could not find other jobs that were as good, or could not find jobs at all. (It may be added that, then as now, as commodity production jobs were decreasing, service jobs—in finance, distribution, city and state governments, etc.—were increasing.) And there were many who were working for very low wages indeed, because they were children, among them yours truly.

Story: Worthwhile at Last!

I was one of those counted as employed just as 1930 began and who, by 1938, could not have worked legally because of the new "Child Labor Law"—before which there were no restrictions at all in the United States. I wasn't one of Jeremy Bentham's newly-made worthwhile four-year olds; I was already ten, had been worthless for six years. In 1930, my schoolteacher mother (along with all other teachers) was given the choice between taking a 50 percent cut in wages or, although she had tenure, losing her job. She kept working, but it wasn't enough for us to get by, so my brother and I went to work for the *San Francisco Examiner*. There were two parts to the job: we had to complete delivery of the papers before 6 a.m. and we had to "collect"—not an easy matter in those hard times, even if one went the rounds fifteen nights a month. And the carriers—all kids— had to foot the bill for those who never paid. My "route" was in North Beach, where it was fragrantly obvious that a high percentage of the Italians, incredulous regarding "Prohibition," made their own wine—against the very law regularly broken by President Harding! Thus did my learning accumulate about the definitions of both morality and unemployment, in both high and low places.

Unemployment statistics before the 1930s are notoriously unreliable as, for different reasons, they remain today. In 1933, when there *was* substantial unemployment, the economics profession said it was "voluntary"—that is, workers were *choosing* unemployment instead of taking wages too low for their tastes. Besides, the economics profession at that time almost unanimously believed that a depression is impossible.[18] Estimates however for the years 1920-1929 range from an average of 5 to about 13 percent unemployed.[19]

At the same time, the income of "labor" grew in the 1920s, but it is vital to remember that "labor income" includes not only the wages of the hamburger flipper but also the salary of the CEO: the wages and salaries of *all* manual and white collar workers. So, when we note that labor income for the bottom 93 percent of the population grew by 6 percent, 1920-1929, the significance of the figures can be gleaned only if we recognize that the destination of that increase was quite disproportionately directed to those whose "labor income" was made up of fees and salaries, rather than wages. And then there is the remaining top 7 percent of the population, whose income (predominantly interest, profits, and rents) rose by double that amount in the same years. Between 1923-29, corporate profits rose by 62 percent as the national income rose by 21 percent, and as tax policies were changed to lower the taxes paid as a percentage of income the *higher* the income (one percent reduction at $5,000, 31 percent reduction for incomes over $1 million).[20]

Income data and inequality are but one aspect—and both partial cause and consequence—of a larger "dualizing" process that had begun to be obvious in the economy of the United States (and the rest of the world) before this century opened, and that has intensified ever since. This process has resulted in what has come to be called "dual economy" which, in the modern world, has become inextricably the basis for and the outcome of a dual society, famously described by Disraeli well over a century ago:

> Two nations, between whom there is no intercourse and no sympathy: who are as ignorant of each other's habits, thought, and feelings, as if they were dwellers in different zones, or inhabitants of different planets. [21]

A further examination of this matter is in order here, if we are to be able to comprehend the extraordinary contrasts of "so much poverty in the midst of plenty," so much misery accompanying phenomenal advances in technology and science, production and wealth; and, among other matters, the almost permanent strife of this century.

v.

Progress and Poverty [22]

As used here, duality signifies the evolution of two systematically diverging paths of socioeconomic change: one path leading to good property incomes (profits, rent, and interest) and wages, whose beneficiaries have lives partaking of all that is deemed desirable in our culture: abundant consumer goods, but also a good education, good health care, recreation and travel, a rich cultural life, an enviable status, some degree of power over their own lives and that of their society, and the morale that attends access to all the foregoing. The other (and retrogressive) dynamic may be seen as the negatives of those positives, lives made not only difficult because material well-being is out of reach, but often disastrous because of accompanying demoralization, the absence of hope and dignity. [23] As duality has proceeded in this century, those trapped in the stagnant category in the United States have amounted to between a third and a half of the population; and the percentages are considerably worse for the peoples of the nonindustrial world. [24]

The excruciating irony, however, is that with the advent of modern industrialism and its great productivities and productive capacities, there has quite simply ceased to be any *natural* reason for anyone to have too little food, clothing, shelter, education, or medical care.

What began to characterize some nations and much of the world by the close of the nineteenth century had never happened before, either quantitatively (numbers and percentages of people) or qualitatively (the kinds of social processes and relationships). Never had so many people in so many places gotten so much better off in as many ways as they did, increasingly, in the nineteenth century; and never had so many had their lives worsened, ruined, or destroyed so much as in that same century. How and why did all that happen earlier, and speed up so very much in our own time, the past half century?

The answer lies in the combined power, influence, and contradictions of the four definitive clusters of capitalism, colonialism, industrialism, and nationalism: it is the very essence, indeed the need, of each of them to be *expansive,* and voraciously so—their appetites increasing as their feeding increases. [25] And because the "big four" must and do interact, their individual needs are stimulated all the more. This insatiability is systemic. Consider:

Capitalism is incontestably dependent upon expansion for its health; and each enterprise must also meet that standard for itself or be absorbed (or crushed) by those who do. There can be no standing still.

Colonialism (and its successors) has a dynamic which, whether propelled by the need to advance or the fear of attack from within or without, leads it always to push on its borders for defensive or offensive purposes, and, more usually, to increase its penetration and sway within its existing areas of control.

Industrialism's dynamic is fueled by ceaseless and uncontrollable technological change, whose advances now take place in an exponential process. "Technological change" once was confined to the realm of *commodity* production (agricultural, industrial, etc.); now its impact knows no "sectoral" boundaries, indeed knows no boundaries at all: technological change is the driving element, in, among other areas, education, entertainment, health care, and the military.

Nationalism, as the daily news confirms, is a beast whose appetite—whether it be for power, more territory, glory, whatever—is contained only by the competing nationalist impulses of others, and, more frequently this century than in the past, by war—every year, large or small, somewhere.

As history has put these four clusters into an increasingly frenetic dance, the consequent social process has become earthquake country. The frenetic dance engenders 1) an always more rapid, virtually kaleidoscopic process of social change which is 2) essentially uncontrollable by any of the existing economic, political, or social powers. But, as well, 3) along this precarious path there are processes of increasingly great gains and increasingly devastating losses: gains to those (an always lower percentage) with power, losses to an expanding majority of the earth's people.

It behooves us to see all this in practice in our own backyard.

vi.
The Bottom Line

Years after he had been rudely ejected from the White House by an angry electorate, Herbert Hoover, with more than a little justice, observed that the depression that had been blamed on him was not his fault at all. Hoover then went on to blame it all on Europe.

It cannot be emphasized too often that no capitalist economy can do well for long unless the world economy of which it is a part is doing well. That has been so for at least a century and a half, and always more so since World War II, as the world economy has become more integrated than ever before. The U.S. economy of the 1920s was heading for a fall even had there *been* a healthy world economy—which there was not, by any means. [26]

The decline that began in 1929 (and also that of 1990, as will be argued much later) was structural. If the problem was structural, it should be clear, any solution to the problem would therefore have to speak to a change in structures and their relationships.

The structures of an economy are many, of course; but those that count most for present purposes are easily identified: the structures of production, of consumption, of foreign trade, of income and wealth, and, not least, of power. How each structure functions is of course very much dependent upon its dynamic relationships with the others. What went wrong in the 1920s, which had to be set aright by the New Deal of the 1930s—to the limited degree it *was* set aright—was due to the substantial and growing imbalance in those structures: something like a building too tall for its foundation.

In a capitalist economy everything is produced for profit, in principle and, in the 1920s, almost entirely in practice as well. [27] But such profit is normally gained only in buoyant markets, in turn dependent upon consumer spending and upon business purchases for working capital (to produce with existing productive capacities) or for new/expanded productive capacity (in expectation of expanding sales in the future). In the 1920s, we can forget about buoyant foreign markets, for the world economy was in a process of an always worsening contraction. Domestic markets were another and different matter, but for both better and worse.

Real investment and productive capacity in manufacturing and in both private (personal and business) and public (mostly road) construction boomed for much of the Twenties: it was that "boom" that gave the period its good name. But, as we have seen, there was a redistribution of income *upward* going on in the same period, aided and abetted by a tax "reform" program that very much favored those at the top and left those at the bottom where they had always been: stuck in the thick bottom mud.

Well, it may be said, someone is always at the bottom, so what else is new? But in the 1920s the bottom was sinking for the worst off; and, something else was happening for the first time: the combination of all those shiny (and expensive) new consumer goods—cars, washing machines, etc.—and the advertising for them began to make a very large percentage of the population *feel* worse off, as if, as most were, they were on the outside looking in at the charmed circle. Some relevant data:

> [Between 1920 and 1929] the top 5 percent of the total population [increased] its share of disposable income from 24 to 34 percent. . . . Personal savings became more concentrated, with 2.3 percent of families with incomes over $10,000 supplying more than two-thirds of all saving [which] constrained mass purchasing power, and it also fueled financial instability as the rich diverted portions of their increasing wealth to real estate and stock market speculation. [28]

In manufacturing, output per labor-hour rose 72 percent and output per unit of capital by 52 percent in the decade. But prices did not fall at all between 1923 and 1929, and manufacturing wages rose only about 8 percent for the entire decade—less than one percent a year. So, corporate profits rose accordingly: by 62 percent. Surely a free market would have assured a different outcome?

Surely, but the free market had been a thing of the past before the Great War, and with the explosive merger movement of the 1920s it had become a political slogan rather than an economic reality. The first great merger movement in industry, 1897-1905, created 318 giant corporations for what had been 5,300 separate and smaller firms. The second great merger movement took hold about 1923 and ended as the depression began. By then, in addition to the "horizontal mergers" of the earlier period (that is, mergers of firms producing and selling the same products), there were "vertical" and "conglomerate" mergers: respectively, the merging forward and backward in the structure of production (an auto company buying up a steel company, for example), and the merging of unrelated companies (an industrial company buying up an unrelated distribution company). [29]

Successive merger movements yield an intensification of duality in the economy—not just that between the small and the giant firm, but as well between their relative earning powers, access to technological possibilities and, among other matters, their strength both in the market and in the halls of government. Their power in the market—what economists call oligopoly power, the ability of a very few dominating sellers to organize (illegal) agreements *not* to compete on price—helps to explain why prices did not go down as productivity went up; the access of the giants to the powers of the State helps to explain their ability to keep unionism down, to achieve tax reforms favorable to property incomes, protective tariffs, and so on. And of course what was true for the Twenties continues to be true today—if anything, given that the concentrations of economic and political power are considerably greater today than earlier, all the more true.

The rest of the landscape, that which comprised the less powerful—whether the weaker businesses in agriculture and industry or that three-quarters or so of the population struggling to make ends meet—might just as well not have been there. But there it was, a critical portion of a dangerously unbalanced economy. We may begin to understand the nature of that imbalance by looking no further than "the automobilization" of the U.S. economy, the dynamic center of the Twenties. [30]

The automobile is vital not only in itself but in terms of all that is required for its production and use: machinery, metals, paint, glass, leather, and rubber (etc.) in the product itself, and a transformed and massive petroleum industry, extraordinary increases in road construction, and service stations, and motels, and suburban housing and . . . . By the time the automobile industry had matured it was estimated that one of six jobs was directly or indirectly dependent upon it.

There are three kinds of car buyers: new owners, those replacing an old with a new car, and used-car buyers. [31] Already by 1924 new car buyers were no longer the prime focus of the auto industry's attention; their numbers had leveled off and were in decline. What was needed was more rapid replacement, and a large used-car market to support it. In turn, this led to the creation of what has since become the hallmark of durable consumer goods production and distribution: deliberate product obsolescence, extensive advertising, and consumer finance. General Motors took the lead in all three: and advertising, yearly model changes, trade-ins, and living in constant debt were thereby elevated to what many take to be "the American way of life." Thus was the day postponed when the auto industry (and other durable goods producers) would find itself with chronic excess capacity—postponed for a short while, but not averted:

> installment buying could not obviate the eventual retardation of expansion. There was certain to come a time when all families who would utilize installment loans were loaded up with all the debt they could carry. In the long run the only possible means of keeping these new industries expanding would have been to augment the cash purchasing power of the consumers through sufficient increases in wages and salaries or through sufficient reduction in retail prices. [32]

And what was true of consumer durable goods was even more applicable to housing, as Soule points out:

> Only a fraction of the population was able to buy or rent new houses or new apartments at the prices charged, and the number which could do so provided an upper limit to the market. After a few years of active building, this limit was being approached [by 1926]. There was still an actual need for better housing in large quantities, but this need could not be converted into a market demand unless either the number of those who could afford the housing was increased by sufficient enlargement of income, or the prices of the new housing could be materially decreased. Neither of these developments occurred. (Ibid.)

But couldn't the State intervene to supplement consumer demand? That was precisely the recommendation of Keynes. But note just how little the State did to intervene in the economy until the New Deal of the 1930s: in 1929, the combined expenditures of federal, state, and local governments were about 10 percent of GNP; in our day they are always above 30 percent (and in Western Europe considerably above that). But those figures do not tell the most important part of the story: in the 1920s neither in principle nor in practice did any level of government in the United States seek to intervene in the economy to supplement private purchasing power. State expenditures on roads and education *did* of course affect the economy, but that was not their intended function.

vii.

Down the Tubes

Not even monetary policy—the only intervention sanction by conservative economists—was utilized in the 1920s. The powers of the Federal Reserve System—through which monetary policies are exercised—have been enlarged and strengthened many times in the eighty years or so since 1913, when it was created; they remain inadequate to counter anything more than a mild recession. In the 1920s, with the euphoria and the power of business and finance, not even its then very limited tools were used. After all, the only way was up.

The stock market certainly made it look that way, and the fixation on the stock market then has allowed the general appreciation of the depression's onset to be fixed on that market's "crash" [33] as either *a* or *the* major cause. More astute heads have since prevailed among most economic historians; but the fact remains that the stock market to this day is given an importance that is wildly beyond the reality, one manifestation of which are the multiple "Dow-Jones" reports on the market's behavior every day. [34]

As it happens, the stock market's great boom—the great "bull market" of the 1920s—began in the same period in which the "real" (that is, the producing sector of the) economy was already showing signs of weakness: from 1926 on, real (as distinct from financial) investment declined. [35] What was booming was not production, but speculation—in securities of one sort or another, and in real estate. Indeed, one of the reasons for the early stages of the Wall Street boom was that in August of 1927 the Fed had acted to cheapen and expand the money supply—in order to stimulate lagging business. The first week in December 1927 saw a vast expansion in trading of shares on Wall Street, the greatest amount in U.S. history. And that was just the beginning.

The decisive jump was made in early March 1928. Fueled by spectacular (some would say conspiratorial) buying of "heavy hitters" the nervous optimism that had been around for months exploded, with key companies' prices doubling and tripling in the next year.

And then came "Black Thursday"—October 24, 1929. By July 1932, stock prices had fallen almost 90 percent from their September '29 levels. More importantly, qualitatively similar drops took place for jobs, profits, sales, etc., in the Thirties.

The sensational rise of share prices of the late Twenties did not happen in a week, month, or year, nor was it without downward interruptions. Nor was it only euphoria that fueled the rise; equally or more important was "margin" buying on a large and growing scale, in an essentially unregulated and crooked market.[36] (This was the same kind of market so strenuously moved toward in the 1980s, when so much vigor and power was used to return to the legalized thievery of the Twenties.)

The market had cracked several times before Black Thursday (beginning in December 1928), but it had recovered and soon soared to new highs. But the explosion of October 24 was both more violent and more encompassing than its predecessors, so much so as to threaten the solvency of the largest number of (especially) New York banks. That this happened as a serious "real" downturn was already well on its way made that downturn even more serious—not only because liquidity dissolved and borrowing became close to impossible, but because the very spirit that had so much marked the "new era" evaporated along with its paper profits. More than any other capitalist economy, that of the United States has had a "boomer and booster" mentality acting as one of its ongoing stimuli; a characteristic much intensified during the rollicking Twenties. With the collapse of the stock market and its horrendous losses—both a psychological and a financial blow for optimism—there was an unavoidable transition to pessimism.

This is not to say that there was anything like a prompt recognition of the severity of the economic situation that lay ahead: how could there have been, for such an entirely unprecedented development? If anything, there was more a feeling of calm than of panic concerning the economic downturn, as there had been when the stock market had its first shocks in December 1928 and subsequently. President Hoover was not alone in believing prosperity to be just around the corner. The economy neither rises nor falls as rapidly as a stock market can; nor are its movements simple to decipher.

Nevertheless, the depression of popular memory is of a sudden Whoosh!, as though production and prices and jobs hurtled toward rock bottom in a matter of weeks and months. But, as Robert A. Gordon pointed out,

> That a depression of unusual severity was developing did not become clearly apparent until the second half of 1930. After the collapse of the stock market and the sharp decline in business activity in the last quarter of 1929, there was a slight abortive recovery in the early months of 1930.... In the early months

of 1931, the American economy again seemed to be attempting to stage a recovery . . . . In the late spring of 1931, the international financial structure collapsed completely . . . . and deepened the depression in the United States . . . . Beginning in the third quarter of [1932], noticeable improvement began to be evident in the United States and other countries . . . . In the United States this recovery was struck a severe blow at the beginning of 1933 by an outbreak of bank closings beginning in the Middle West and spreading through the rest of the country..., and by the end of the first week of March all banks in the United States were closed.[37]

That small piece of history regarding intermittent hopes for "recovery" is well to keep in mind as nowadays the economy is repeatedly seen to "recover" from the recession of 1990—while, in its major characteristics, the economy's sluggishness continues and spreads, both here and abroad.

The roaring, jazzy, prosperous 1920s may now be seen as a bridge between the military horrors of World War I and the ensuing disillusionment at the decade's beginning, and the economic horrors that began to shake even the comfortable portion of the population by its end—the rest of the population having become accustomed to hard times all throughout that "new era."

The unmistakeable marks on our history that the Twenties left were buried as the decade ended, however; except greatly transformed they will not be seen or felt again, for better and for worse. As we turn now to the 1930s, the "depression decade," it will be clear that it certainly was just that; but the Thirties were much more than an economic disaster. Just as the presumably wonderful Twenties had their grim side, so too do the really dreadful Thirties—dreadful in more than just economic catastrophes—have something good to be said of them. Ask anyone who lived through them.

2 DEATH, DESTRUCTION, AND DELIVERANCE: 1930-1945

HARD TIMES [1]

i.

The Making of a Radical

The magnitude of the disasters unleashed in the 1930s must be understood if they are not to be repeated, but they cannot be captured in a paragraph, a page, a chapter—probably not at all through the written word. One assertion is fundamental: had it not been for the depression of the 1930s, World War II would not have occurred when and where and how it did; most of all, its duration, its spread, and its savagery (from all sides) were exacerbated by the national and personal economic desperation that became common in the years after World War I.

We begin with one number, however, and ask that the reader imagine how such a number could have happened: in Europe alone, 60 million people died as a direct consequence of the war that began in 1939 and ended in 1945.

When the depression struck, no sector of the economy was left standing upright; the entire capitalist world underwent the same collapse as did, even more calamitously, the dependent nonindustrial countries. Each nation had its own crisis, and each had its share of a worldwide crisis. Then as now, however, the United States was the leading economy, and, as W. Arthur Lewis says,

It is clear that the center of the depression was the United States of America, in the sense that most of what happened elsewhere has to be explained in terms of the American contraction, while that contraction is hardly explicable in any but internal terms. The slump was also worse in the United States than anywhere else (with the possible exception of Germany, whose severe contraction was a direct result of American events).[2]

The United States and Germany were the two most advanced industrial states of the time: industrial production in both countries fell by 50 percent between 1929 and 1933.[3] But what made for indisputably "hard times" in the United States meant something considerably more devastating for the economy and the society of Germany. Not only was the United States a far richer society than Germany in all relevant ways, but it also had an economic structure considerably more balanced between consumer and capital goods production. Germany's productive capacity in capital goods was hugely excessive for existing markets; and, although its workers were the most efficient in Europe (probably in the world), their real wages were even lower than those of their British and French counterparts. When the German economy contracted, therefore, the always thin margin between subsistence and starvation disappeared. Given its other great tensions— emanating from its ruinous defeat in 1918, the deepest and broadest class struggle in the world, a weak government and a decadent society[4]—it may be seen that Germany was pushed by the economic collapse toward extreme solutions, either of the Left or the Right.[5]

Neither President Hoover nor the Congress did anything substantial or effective to halt the economic collapse in the U.S. from 1929 to 1932, and the political process went on pretty much as though nothing untoward had occurred. Even though Hoover was soundly rejected by the electorate, the newly-elected President Franklin Delano Roosevelt (FDR) was about as conservative economically as had been the beleaguered Hoover, and much the same was true of the new Congress. To be sure, his inaugural address lifted the hopes of the people, and that brought some beneficial consequences; but not until 1935 did his economic policies "liberalize" and begin to stimulate the economy.

In Germany between 1929 and 1932, in sharp contrast, the electorate was polarizing: the numerous "center parties" declined toward the vanishing point, while the votes for the Nazis and the Left (the total for the Communists and the Social Democrats) mounted rapidly and by 1932 had become a neck-and-neck race.[6] In January of 1933, President Hindenburg appointed Hitler as Chancellor. In March—the same month that FDR was inaugurated as U.S. president—Hitler suspended the German Constitution.

In that momentous year I was in my first year of high school, paying more attention to my pimples and how skinny I was than to the rest of the world; willy-nilly, I became involved in a revolution.

Story: Hank and Me

I was *very* skinny: at the age of twelve, I was 6'3" but weighed only 120 pounds. By my second year in high school that height (*very* tall for then) enabled me to become a junior member of the basketball team. I mention this because the guy who a few years later was the best in the country—Hank Luisetti—was on the same team. Some of you will know that shots from the field until the 1930s were *always* made as a two-handed set shot, feet together. Believe it or not, it was on that high school team that Hank began to make running one-handed corner shots, the first in the country to do so. From us (Galileo High), Hank went on to Stanford, became an All-American, took Stanford to NCAA championships, and later became their coach. And the game of basketball was revolutionized. Not by me, however. Our coach used to say to me: "Dowd, if I could stick a lighted firecracker up your bum maybe *that* would get you moving, and then you could be at least mediocre!"[7]

ii.

Brother, Can You Spare a Dime?

In a decade filled with memorable songs, "Can You Spare A Dime" was the most memorable, not only more widely-known but more widely-applicable than any other. Everybody picked it up in '30 and '31. Some Republican-backed network radio people were told to lay low on the song, and in some cases, they tried to ban it from the air. As its composer has said,

> The prevailing greeting at that time [1930], on every block you passed . . . was "Can you spare a dime?" "Brother, Can You Spare a Dime" finally hit on every block, on every street. I thought that could be a beautiful title [for a musical comedy sketch] if I could only work it out by telling people, through the song, it isn't just a man asking for a dime. This is a man who says: I built the railroads.

I built that tower. I fought your wars. I was the kid with the drum. Why the hell should I be standing in a breadline now? What happened to all this wealth I created? [8]

A recession or a depression is a process of economic contraction which, whatever else it means, implies an under-utilization of the society's productive resources: workers and productive assets. Just how far markets contracted in the 1930s is shown by figures for capacity utilization—whose optimum rate is in the neighborhood of 85 percent. Already by 1928 the figures had begun to drop below that desired level, but witness what happened in the Thirties to capacity utilization (and, in parentheses, to unemployment):

1930	66 percent	(8.7%)		1935	68 percent	(20.1%)
1931	53 percent	(15.9%)		1936	80 percent	(16.9%)
1932	42 percent	(23.6%)		1937	83 percent	(14.3%)
1933	52 percent	(24.9%)		1938	60 percent	(19.0%)
1934	58 percent	(21.7%)		1939	72 percent	(17.2%) [9]

The pervasiveness of the depression's tragedies between 1929 and 1933 is suggested by the following data: [10]

- GNP fell from $104 billion to $56 billion.

- Per capita disposable income (after personal taxes) fell from $678 to $360.

- The income of farm proprietors fell from $5.7 billion to (in 1932) $1.7 billion.

- Unemployment rose from 1.5 million to 12.8 million, or 25 percent of the labor force.

- The Dow-Jones dollar average per share of sixty-five stocks (different from their index method of today) fell from $125 to $36.

- The average number of bank suspensions in 1928 and 1929 was 566; in 1930, 1931, and 1932 it was 1,700.

- Merchandise exports fell from $5.2 billion to $1.7 billion.

- The value of building construction of all sorts was $4 billion in 1925, $3 billion in 1929, and $500 million in 1933.

- Farm prices (at wholesale) fell by more than half.

The general impression is that FDR's "New Deal" initiated corrective policies starting in the early 1930s. That impression is made up of a mixture of half-truths, confusion, and the misleading arguments of both opponents and supporters of the New Deal. There were significant social reforms and novel economic policies put in place in that period of course. In addition to being highly controversial, however, the programs were not up to the task at hand even had they been sufficiently financed—which they were not.

iii.

The First and Second New Deals, 1933-1940

FDR was first elected president in 1932 and for the fourth time in 1944. The policies of what has come to be called the "first New Deal" extended from 1933 into 1935. FDR was conservative when he first took office. It was only in 1935 that he was reluctantly persuaded by his advisors (including Eleanor) that to be reelected he had to begin to construct a "second New Deal," one pointed toward raising the rights and living standards of ordinary people rather than, as in the "first New Deal," guarding the power and privileges of the top layers of the society. Then, after 1938, FDR slowly but surely began to place foreign policy and the emerging war at the center of his concerns.

The term "New Deal" covers three sets of policies enacted from 1933 to 1940: relief, recovery, and reform. One of the major "reforms" of the New Deal has been seen as a deliberate use of government spending and taxation to speed recovery and slow inflation. But what marked most of the 1930s was not how much, but how little was done until the approach of war.

But at least the New Deal *introduced* the systematic practice of governmental intervention to get recession/depression off our backs and, as well, other forms of governmental intervention in the economy and in the larger society. Neither the deficit spending nor the institutional reforms of the New Deal had substantial effect before World War II, but the institutional and functional precedents were established, along with the habits and experience of control and intervention. When accompanied by the largesse of a war economy, the stage was then set for the emergence of a new political economy in the postwar years. In the war years, business, labor, and agriculture all learned just how useful and bountiful an intrusive State could be.

Relief, recovery, and reform in some cases of course tended to overlap, as represented particularly in the National Industrial Recovery Act (NIRA) of 1933, which set up the National Recovery Administration (NRA). This institution (declared unconstitutional by the Supreme Court in 1935) is more indicative than any other of the conservative—or better, business-like—bent of the first New Deal. The inspiration for this legislation lay directly in the ideas of Gerard Swope (head of General Electric and then of the U.S. Chamber of Commerce, 1931 and 1932). [11] At the core of the NRA was the notion that recovery would come about if business could be allowed to control its markets—through what was called "self-government in business." This meant that *all* industrial firms must belong to trade associations (dominated by the most powerful firms in each industry, as a matter of course), and that each association's "code authorities" would have the power to fix prices (usually upward), output, and regional quotas; in short, price and production cartels with the power of law behind them. So much for "the free market" as the solution to problems, when it was business' ox that was being gored.

Like it or not, the NRA was a substantial reform. That it might have led to recovery may be doubted: in a time of inadequate purchasing power, raising prices and reducing production seems the opposite of promising. And just what kind of reform it was is suggested by the fact that in 1934 a delegation of economic planners from Nazi Germany visited the United States to study the provisions of the NRA.

By 1935 two matters had become very clear to FDR's inner circle (most notably Harry Hopkins, his closest advisor): first, the economy (unemployment at 20 percent) was languishing still, and second, unrest and political dissent were growing. On the political spectrum by 1935 there could be found a growing Socialist as well as a growing Communist Party; in California, despite its electoral defeat in 1934, was the very popular EPIC movement led by Upton Sinclair; in Louisiana, perhaps most politically threatening of all, was Huey Long—assassinated in that year—and his "Share the Wealth" movement, which combined populist, socialist, and fascist elements in a very hot brew; in Michigan, Father Coughlin and his "Silver Shirts"—racist and fascist—were growingly popular; and there were many other groups growing on both ends of the spectrum, but not in the middle. Nor could the swelling number of industrial strikes be ignored.

It was crystal clear that FDR and the Democratic Party would have great trouble in the forthcoming 1936 election if the proliferation of social and political unrest was not dealt with, and dramatically. The response was the Second New Deal, with its many social reforms and its fiscal stimuli. It was then that so much now taken for granted became institutionalized: social security, unemployment compensation, job, income, and infrastructural projects,[12] and, more broadly, the idea that the government has an obligation to serve *all* the people, not just the most privileged. The ideal was not reached in the 1930s, nor since, though it did reemerge with great vigor in the 1960s, able to do so because of the unrest and political energies of large segments of the population in the 1930s and up into the 1960s. The foundations for much of that were laid by workers' organizing efforts in the 1930s.

Most of the "pump priming" of the Second New Deal was under the aegis of the Public Works Administration (PWA) and the Works Progress Administration (WPA). The PWA was principally concerned with construction projects (bridges, buildings, etc.), the WPA largely (but not entirely) with the funding of projects in the realm of the arts and education. Lasting beneficial effects of many kinds resulted, for those who earned incomes then and who have benefitted from the projects ever since. There was also the Civilian Conservation Corps (CCC), which put unemployed youth to work in the fields and the forests, among other "alphabet soup agencies."

As I already noted in the last words of chapter 1, the Thirties do "have something good to be said of them." Why else would someone like myself—despite having endured its depression and gone off to its war—think back not only grimly but with fondness of those years?

Partly the reason is that one tends to think back fondly on one's youth; but there is more to it than that, and for many more than me. It was not yet the age of consumerism run amok. There was a different spirit to those years. Some of the fun and joy of the music and films, the "feel," was trivial, but much of it was not. I shall soon discuss what was not: the hopes and struggles of workers for "unions of their own choosing"—a struggle which, when it took hold in San Francisco, was a turning point in my life, as it was for many, many others.

What was remarkable about the 1930s was that although the depression and the everpresent threats of war gave rise to dark thoughts and feelings well beyond the norm for our history, a clear strain of hopefulness, even of good cheer, never disappeared. It showed itself in the realms of entertainment and sports, and also in politics. Perhaps FDR was beloved because that strain showed itself so clearly in him. That all this was so can be seen most in the behavior of workers from 1933 into World War II.

iv.

The Bitter with the Better

In his second inaugural address (1937) FDR again spoke phrases that have become part of our remembered history: "I see one-third of a nation ill-housed, ill-clad, ill-nourished." That was a rather significant understatement. Already in the 1920s, it seems clear that a good *half* of the population was in that condition. Thus, when the depression struck and the 1930s began, it seems fair to believe that not one-third but closer to two-thirds of the nation was in dire straits: the ordinary workers and farmers—the largest part of what today is called "the middle class" of the nation. Despite this, the spark of FDR's first inaugural address had become a spreading fire by the close of 1933, despite also the continuation of severe unemployment for all workers, and bitter conditions for farmers. [13]

The economy did not change appreciably for the better in 1933 or begin to do so clearly until 1936. But hopes had risen, and that had happened not just or principally because of FDR's "nothing to fear . . ." but because of Section 7(a) of the National Industrial Recovery Act, which referred to labor. As what was not much more than a sop to the temper of times, there were some timid steps toward outlawing child labor (about time!) and "guaranteeing" workers the right to bargain collectively with employers (about time!). [14]

At least some industrial workers took Section 7(a) at its word. The upshot was a tidal wave of strikes—in coal, textiles, machine tools, steel, autos; by teamsters, longshoremen, journalists, and so on. Almost always, strikes were held with the aim of improving wages and working conditions, of course; but also, throughout the 1930s, more often than not gaining union recognition and security—that is, the very right to have an effective or "red" (as distinct from a company or "blue") union—was the central issue. The Supreme Court did not uphold union security until 1937; the great majority of strikes both before and after that year in the 1930s were ultimately over just that issue: union security.

I shall discuss only three of the most important: the longshore strike in San Francisco, the sit-down strikes of rubber workers in 1934 and later of auto workers in Flint, Michigan, and the "Memorial Day Massacre" of striking steelworkers in 1937. I begin with the strike I lived (and "came to life") through, the 1934 waterfront strike in San Francisco that became a general strike and shut the city down. I've never been the same, and because of the actions, feelings, and institutions generated by that strike and others of the mid-1930s, neither has the country.

v.

Waiting for Lefty [15]

Organized labor had reached its peak of strength during and immediately after World War I. But the 1920s, as was noted earlier, weakened and in many cases simply crushed most unions, at the same time that the "red scare" deported, imprisoned, and even killed radical organizers. What remained as the 1930s began was a fairly large number of unions, but they were either those of the skilled crafts (carpenters, electricians, plumbers, etc.), whose members drew strength from their local monopoly status, or they were unions—such as the International Longshoremen's Association (ILA) and the Rubberworkers—that functioned for all practical purposes as "company unions"—that is, not as unions at all.

Given the rising unemployment of the early 1930s, it might reasonably have been expected that organized labor's weakness would have worsened, but the opposite began to happen in 1933. Most of the drama centered on the numerous, innovative, and usually violent—often deadly—strikes. In the same years, powered by much the same energies and moving along parallel tracks, was the movement to establish the Congress of Industrial Organizations (CIO) federation of unions, to supplement (or supplant) the conservative American Federation of Labor (AFL).

Those who have seen the 1950s film "On the Waterfront" (whose longshoreman hero was the young Marlon Brando) may remember that a chief gripe of the longshoremen was the "shape-up": those seeking work had to appear early every morning and hang around virtually as beggars waiting for a job. Even under the best of circumstances there were always more jobseekers than jobs, with the lordly decision made by the corrupt union official as to which of the crowd would be chosen.

"Corruption" in that context meant that the union hiring boss was on the take from the employer as well as gettting a "slice" from the workers who were chosen daily. I learned a little about that on my own, in 1935.

Story: Max the Knife

After high school, I would go to a teamsters' "shape-up" every day to seek work as a "wagon boy" (a driver's helper) to deliver packages in the afternoon and early evenings. It was before UPS had supplanted delivery truck systems of the big department stores. I was the only kid in the process who was going to school, and pretty much disdained by the others. But I still remember their regular conversations while waiting for the jobs to be handed out by Max (reminiscent both in appearance and morality of nobody more than Dickens' "Fagin the Viper"). When talking of job expectations or plans, it was striking to me how many of these young guys saw their most realistic choice as being between becoming a petty crook or a cop—which were treated as being roughly equivalent (as indeed they often seem to be, still). One of them, Teddy, wound up in the chair at San Quentin. I *know* that *my* shape-up was a vehicle for a variety of forms of corruption. "On the Waterfront" had such corruption as its main theme, and its abolition was the main goal of the strike of 1934 in San Francisco.

The shape-up was replicated every working day in all the seaports of the United States—on both coasts and in the Gulf. Given the generally underpaid, overworked, and dangerous conditions of longshore work, what finally brought the long-seething situation to the point of explosion was the combination of the loathsome shape-up with the depression, the hopes raised by Section 7(a), and a substantial rise in membership in the ILA.[16]

It soon became clear that the officers of the ILA were disinclined to support the grievances of what in numbers had become a very strong union. The result was the emergence of a rank-and-file revolt within the union led by Harry Bridges. Anyone who lived in San Francisco in the Thirties and Forties would agree that, like him or hate him, Harry Bridges became very much the symbol of workers' militancy in those years, as well as being very much at the center of dissenting and protest politics in the Bay Area.[17]

Snapshot: Harry Bridges

Harry Bridges had a great hawkface and was skinny as a rail, looking something like a tall jockey. He was from Australia, and sounded like it. He was instrumental in transforming the ILA into the International Longshoremen's and Warehousemen's Union (ILWU)—"the best union in the capitalist world."[18] Bridges arrived in San Francisco from Australia in 1920. He became a merchant seaman and then sailed with the U.S. Coast Guard. By 1923 he had begun to work as a longshoreman on the San Francisco docks. In those years and until 1934, the ILA dominated the waterfront, and was known derisively as the "Blue Book" union, as a company union. As the depression began, the employers forced a speed-up on top of the hated shape-up. Loading and unloading ships has always been dangerous and literally backbreaking work. With the speed-up, Bridges wrote in 1934, "men have dropped dead from exhaustion. From the time you go to work in the morning until evening you are driven like a slave." (Bridges was injured twice in the Twenties himself.) By 1933-34, at least half the longshoremen were unemployed. Bridges became their spokesman, and led the fight to transform the ILA into a union that would represent the workers rather than either the employers or the "pie cards" (that is, union officials). He was tough, experienced and, it was generally agreed, absolutely incorruptible and honest. He was brought to court six times (and once the House of Representatives even passed a bill to deport him) over twenty years, accused of being a member of the Communist Party (and thus deportable). The accusation never stuck, and was officially rejected by the Supreme Court in 1945 (*Bridges v. Wixon*).[19]

Bridges did involve himself in political activities only indirectly connected with his function as a union leader, and such activities were often in concert or at least in tune with those of the Communist Party. Just as I found myself working to support the ILWU and, from time to time, involved in activities—both knowingly and not—also "in tune" with the C.P.

In the 1930s and up through the 1950s (after which he became controversial *within* the union), it is my considered judgment that Harry did more for San Francisco and the largest part of its population than any other one person, because what became the general strike of July 1934—led superlatively by Bridges—had positive consequences for unions other than the ILWU and for issues going well beyond unionism itself. With Bridges at its head, the ILWU was always to be found in the forefront of movements for social justice, and against war.

Perhaps the key early moment for the general strike was in February 1934, when the militant rank-and-file longshoremen used their already large numbers to call a West Coast convention, at which they forced union officials to accept a program the latter opposed: abolition of the shape-up, its replacement by a union hiring hall, and the threat of a strike within two weeks. It is hard to know which was more ferocious, the conflict between the rank-and-file and the union officials or that between the workers and the Waterfront Employers Association.

The demands were rejected and the fuse was lit; after many weeks of arguments, discussions, proposals, and threats, the whole edifice of traditional ways and means on the docks was in ashes.

News Flash

May 9, 1934. At 8 p.m. today longshoremen struck in Bellingham, Seattle, Tacoma, Aberdeen, Portland, Astoria, Gray's Harbor, San Francisco, Oakland, Stockton, San Pedro, San Diego, and the smaller ports. About 2,000 miles of coastline were shut tight.

Brecher's recounting of the next steps shows how the strike drama then continued to unfold:

The lines of the conflict rapidly began to spread. The employers imported large numbers of strikebreakers—eventually 1,700, many of them recruited from the University of California—to unload the ships. The strikebreakers were housed in floating boarding houses (which were rapidly boycotted by union employees) and thus protected from pickets; those who sneaked ashore, however, were systematically brutalized by the strikers. Strikebreaking would have seriously threatened the strike, but within four days mass meetings of the Teamsters in San Francisco, Los Angeles, Oakland and Seattle decided overwhelmingly not to haul goods to and from the docks, thus making the strikebreakers' efforts fruitless . . . ; as much as seventy percent of the Teamsters' work was on the waterfront. [20]

That a very noticeable number of the strikebreakers were college students was responsible for a painful incident for me, despite the fact that I was vehemently opposed to their action and very much in support of the strike.

Story: Scab by Association

In the spring of 1941 I took classes at San Francisco J.C. to make up flunked high school courses so I could enroll at U.C. Berkeley in the fall of 1941. I managed to get a night job (11 p.m. to 7 a.m.) as a teamster. The job consisted of loading fifty-pound bundles of newspapers into trucks as they came off the presses. The paper was the *San Francisco Examiner*, the "flagship" of the Hearst empire, very conservative, and the largest paper in the city. The bundles had been automatically wrapped by thin wire as they left the presses. One lifted them with the indispensable "hook" of longshoremen and teamsters. I was a "college boy," had gotten the job with the help of my brother (who was head of the Transportation Department of the paper), and the teamsters had gotten the word before I arrived on the job the first night. Nobody had told me about the need for a hook, and it was too late to buy one. Many or all of my coworkers had an extra hook hanging visibly from their rear pockets but wouldn't lend one to me. I worked all that first night without a hook. Before three or four hours had passed, my hands resembled hamburger. I couldn't report back to work for three days. It would have been useless for me to have told them, "hey look, I'm different . . . ," nor did I try. To this day, informed workers in the Bay Area are hostile to college students, if also now for additional reasons.

The strike that began as a longshore strike on May 9 soon became a teamsters' strike as well by late May and then also a maritime strike, with ten unions involved (sailors, marine firemen, cooks, stewards, etc.). By late June, "San Francisco's economy was reeling and the business community decided the time had come to break the strike." (Brecher, p. 152) With thousands of strikers and still more sympathizers picketing, that was not a simple thing to do; nor could violence be avoided.

By July 3, hundreds of policemen using tear gas and riot guns cordoned off the docks with freight cars, and the battle of the docks began. That day, twenty-five were hospitalized, divided equally between strikers and police. But that was only the beginning. On July 5—"Bloody Thursday"—two strikers and a bystander were killed and 115 sent to the hospital, after a battle involving 2,000 strikers and the casual use of guns by the police. The battle had raged all day; by nightfall Governor Merriam had ordered almost 2,000 National Guardsmen to take control of the Embarcadero, using barbed wire, machine gun nests, and armored cars. With guardsmen ordered to shoot to kill and armored cars accompanying strikebreakers,

Bridges announced: "We cannot stand up against police, machine guns, and National Guard bayonets." Truce.

The city was awash in fear and hate and sorrow. On the following Tuesday there was a funeral procession for the dead strikers:

> In solid ranks, eight to ten abreast, thousands of strike sympathizers, with bared heads, accompanied the trucks bearing the coffins up Market Street to an undertaking establishment in the Mission two miles distant. [21]

Watching that procession was the first of the major jolts of that year to any political complacency I may have had snoozing within me, and more were on their way. By July 12, one week after Bloody Thursday and with all attempts at negotiation foundering, a general strike was in preparation; by Monday the 16th it was a full-scale reality in Oakland, Alameda, and Berkeley, as well as in San Francisco. Except for those ordered by the strike committee to continue to work (medical and hospital services, milk wagon drivers, etc.) and the nonunion department stores, hotels, and offices, virtually everything else was shut down, even theaters, bars, and night clubs: 130,000 workers joined the strike.

After a few days the general strike had ended, too grand and too strange a process to endure for much longer than that, despite widespread popular support. The issue that set the whole process in motion had been the demand for abolition of the shape-up. By October, that had been accomplished, its place taken by a union hiring hall: "a smashing victory for Bridges, his union, and his men." (Bernstein, p. 297) For years afterward, and still today, the union hiring hall, which spread to other areas and effectively means the "closed shop," has remained a thorn in the flesh of business.

The circumstances that provoked turbulence and militancy in San Francisco existed in equal measure throughout the nation, with diverse but often equally dramatic responses. Take, for example, Akron, Ohio and Flint, Michigan.

vi.

Sitdown!

In the 1930s, Akron was to the rubber tire industry what Detroit was for autos: the Big Three—Goodyear, Firestone, and Goodrich, plus smaller rubber companies—had their factories there, hiring over 40,000 workers. Half of the workers in Akron were out of work by 1933; and, as in San Francisco, unemployment plus hopes inspired by Section 7(a) led to an upsurge in union enrollment. In 1933, close to 50,000 rubberworkers signed up for the union—the company union.

In 1934, rubberworkers walked out when Goodyear instituted a speed-up. Despite promises and endless meetings in ensuing months, the union failed to support the workers' efforts to improve conditions. And then, in the spring of 1935, the rubberworkers, completely disillusioned and angry with "their" union, invented a new tactic—without at first knowing they were doing so. As Brecher describes it:

> a dispute developed between a dozen workers and a supervisor in a rubber factory. The workers were on the verge of giving in when the supervisor insulted them and one of them said, "Aw, to hell with 'im, let's sit down." Within a few minutes the carefully organized flow of production through the plant began to jam up as department after department ground to a halt. Thousands of workers sat down, some because they wanted to, more because everything was stopping anyway. (Brecher, p. 181)

It was the start of something big; by 1936 the sitdown strike had become common in the tire industry—common and successful. By 1937 it had spread to the automobile industry.

GM is still one of the two or three largest manufacturing companies in the world; in the mid-1930s it was unquestionably not only *the* largest, it was also one of the two or three most profitable—and among the very most intransigent opponents of unionism. The investigations of the Senate's La Follette Committee, which called the labor espionage activities of GM a "far-flung Industrial Cheka," showed that GM paid detective agencies $999,855.68 for spying alone, between January 1934 and July 1936. [22]

The greatest concentration of GM plants was in Flint, Michigan—for bodies, engines, spark plugs, almost everything; and the key plant among all of those was Fisher One, *the* body plant. The events now to be noted took place in late 1936, more than a year after the National Labor Relations Act (NLRA, the Wagner Act) had been legislated, and whose central provision was the "guaranteeing" of labor's right to have "unions of their own choosing"—this time backed up by enforcement and protective provisions and a National Labor Relations Board (NLRB) to see to them. Nonetheless the overwhelming issue for both workers and GM in the Flint strike was union recognition—in this case, the United Auto Workers-CIO.

The conflict became vivid one day in November 1936 when a unit of four body workers was reduced to three, to do the same work. The three stopped working, but the assembly line continued to run on, with incomplete bodies. The next day the three men were fired, which led to a spontaneous strike, a sit-down.

> The bosses ran about like mad.
> "Whatsamatter? Whatsamatter? Get to work!" they shouted.
> But the men acted as though they never heard them. One or two of them couldn't stand the tension. Habit was deep in them and it was like physical agony for them to see the bodies pass untouched. [23]

The dispute was settled within forty-eight hours, and the firings withdrawn, the decisions made pretty much at the shop level. The UAW (not yet a recognized union) saw its membership increase tenfold within two weeks. Strikes were rampant in the industry in those weeks; the key incident bringing on *the* Flint strike that began December 30 was brought on by a speed-up at Fisher One, combined with the revelation that GM was moving key operations from that plant to another and "safer" plant away from Flint: a tactic GM had employed more than once before. The workers were furious, called a lunchtime meeting to protest, and, when an organizer asked what they wanted to do, they shouted: "Shut her down! Shut the goddam plant!" And, having returned to the plant, a few moments later the shout went up: "She's ours!" (Brecher, p. 194)

There were thousands of workers holding the plant. There was little or no chance of GM seeking to take the plant by assault under circumstances that would have been problematic for a trained infantry assault battalion.

There was no violence for about two weeks. When it erupted, it was at a smaller plant nearby, Fisher Two, where there were only about one hundred strikers. GM made its choice to clear out the strikers there, it is believed, "deliberately seeking violence in order to force Governor Murphy to send in the National Guard to break the strike." (Bernstein, p. 529) GM got some violence: fourteen strikers were wounded and many others gassed, and several policemen were also injured (in part because the wind changed and blew their gas back at them). That violence was supplied by the local police: the larger strategic violence that would involve the National Guard was not forthcoming. Governor Murphy had to make the decision whether or not to send in the National Guard. His father had been imprisoned and his grandfather hanged by the British as Irish revolutionaries, giving him some reason to hesitate before opening the door to the probable slaughter of hundreds or even thousands of unarmed Michigan citizens.

The whole story of Murphy's actions and GM's failure is too complicated to be recounted here. [24] Suffice it to say that after more supporting strikes in and out of Flint, much finagling in and out of courtrooms and smoke-filled rooms, GM—one has to believe, much to its shock and most others' amazement—heard its chief William S. Knudsen say: "Let us have peace and make cars"—having just signed an agreement that effectively gave the UAW sole right to bargaining for GM's workers. After "the greatest labor dispute of the thirties . . . , the UAW had decisively breached the wall of antiunionism in the automotive industry." (Bernstein, pp. 532 and 551)

That this victory was neither the end of difficult labor disputes in autos [25] nor in the rest of industry is a matter of subsequent and bloody history. Its most violent moment took place in Chicago, on Memorial Day, May 30, 1937.

vii.

Massacre

From the turn of the century until the 1970s the steel industry was dominated by United States Steel (USS), the largest steel producer in the world and the first billion dollar company. USS was called "Big Steel." *All* the other companies—Bethlehem, Republic, National, Jones & Laughlin, etc.—were called "Little Steel." I ought to know: I worked for USS, after getting out of S.F.J.C. in 1938, using the shorthand skills I had picked up there. It just wasn't my kind of place, but there I was for over a year.

Story: Misfit

I happened to be a whiz at shorthand. The week I started looking for a job I had just won the state championship, at the ripe old age of eighteen. I wasn't exactly cocky, but I wasn't inclined to kiss anyone's patootie, either. The first thing I did was to go to an employment company. They sent me to a wholesale grocery firm, which offered me $65 a month for a forty-hour week. I said I wouldn't work for that, and they told me to get lost. Then I wandered from one office building to another in the financial district, knocking on company doors. Nothing, until one day I happened to knock on the door of the V.P. of Columbia Steel Company (a subsidiary of USS), J.B. duPrau (not knowing I should have gone through the secretary first). He asked what I wanted, I told him, he asked what I could do, I told him. He called in his secretary, Ione, asked her to find out what I could do. After that, we returned to his office and he said they would give me a job, at $75 a month. I won't work for that little money, sez I. Consternation. "What would you work for?" asked Ione. $150, sez I. That's a lot, they both said at once, and then huddled. "Suppose we start you at $90 for three months and then put it up to $130 if you work out?" asked the V.P. OK, sez I.

After a year or so, Jim called me in and said: "Doug, I wish to tell you two things: 1. You do excellent work and I like you. 2. You should quit before I have to fire you." I wondered aloud about the contradiction between the two points, and asked "How come?" So Jim explained that often, when there were other V.P.s (or even worse, a P.) in his office and I would stick my head in and say "Jim . . . ?" some other V.P. would say "Who in hell is that kid who calls you 'Jim'? And why isn't he wearing a necktie?" (Everyone wore ties in those days.) Etc. So I quit and went to work as a court reporter for the U.S. Bureau of Marine Inspection and Navigation (investigator of shipwrecks); but that's another story. Postscript: One day in 1951, when I was teaching at Berkeley and also doing a program for KPFA (the first no-ads station in the U.S.A.), I bumped into Ione, the first time I had seen her since quitting. Embraces, smiles, good feelings. Then she said a funny thing had happened. She had recently encountered Jim (who had also left USS, out of boredom), and he said something odd had occurred just the previous night. Jim was a steady listener to KPFA for its good music and, after the music had finished, he had left the radio on for a while. Then he realized he was listening to an economist from UC who began to talk about something that held his attention. And then it struck him that the speaker's name was "the same as that screwy kid who used to work for us at USS: Doug Dowd." Ione said she told Jim "It was *our* Doug." "No, no, no," said Jim," "it couldn't have been, this guy was a professor, not some screwy kid." "Shows how little he knows about professors," said Ione, who had gone to Stanford.

What has gone down in history as the Memorial Day Massacre took place on Republic Steel's grounds at its South Chicago Mill, the dirty work done by the Chicago police. To general surprise, Big Steel had come to terms with the Steelworkers' Organizing Committee (SWOC—which evolved into the United Steelworkers of America-CIO) in March of 1937; and in April the Supreme Court had upheld the constitutionality of the Wagner Act—in effect, of independent unionism. That there might be much difficulty with Little Steel after that seemed implausible: Little Steel had always followed faithfully (if not happily) in the footsteps of USS. But this was different, not just a matter of profits, but also of ideology. The result was a senseless tragedy.[26]

The president of Republic Steel in 1937 was Tom Girdler, known to be fanatically antiunion. He had been head of Republic for half a dozen years—the Rambo of the steel industry—before the events now to be described. John L. Lewis called him "a heavily armed monomaniac, with murderous tendencies, who has gone berserk." Rather than deal with a union, Girdler once said, he would shut down "and raise apples and potatoes." (Bernstein, p. 481) It would have saved at least ten lives and hundreds of injuries if he had just done that, before May 30, 1937.

On May 26, workers began to walk out on strike from the South Chicago plant. On that day and those following, amidst great confusion and uncertainty, there was episodic but serious conflict between police and strikers involving many injuries and arrests.

But on Saturday, May 29, Republic Steel granted strikers "restricted picketing" at the gate of the plant. With about half the workforce on strike by that time, it was vital to have enough pickets to restrain strikebreaking by the other half. That required something more than "restricted" picketing.

On Memorial Day a crowd of 2,000 or more workers and their families gathered near the plant to meet and discuss the picketing problem. As the meeting closed, a motion to establish a mass picket line at the plant gate was moved and carried. The totally unarmed crowd began to move across the field toward the plant; soon they were met by several hundred police. Someone threw a tree branch into the air. Before it had fallen to the ground, police shots began to ring out—ultimately, over 200 shots, according to a reporter. More firing, tear gas, and complete bedlam:

> Those marchers who were not dead or seriously wounded broke into full flight across the field. The police advanced, continuing to fire their guns and beating the fallen, now lying in tangled masses, with billies and hatchet handles. . . . The police seem to have become crazed with passion. Not only did they brutally

attack the fallen; they dragged seriously wounded, unconscious men over the ground; they not only refused first aid themselves but interfered with (a doctor); they piled severely wounded injured people atop one another in patrol wagons. . . . "Wounded prisoners of war," the La Follette Committee observed, "might have expected and received greater solicitude." Ten marchers were fatally shot. Seven received bullets in the back, three in the side. Thirty others, including one woman and three minors, were wounded by gunshot, nine of them, apparently, permanently disabled. . . . Only three policemen were hospitalized.[27]

So. The high hopes of workers after 1933 were justified in some cases, but not in others. It was not until the economic demands and possibilities of World War II that the trade union movement in the United States came to anything like a reasonable level of strength, considering that this was the leading and largest industrial society in the world. Meanwhile, in a multitude of other industries many more than the steelworkers had to suffer the costs of being part of a "free market" labor force. Enough of the conflict and the sorrow; at least for a while. There were also developments in the 1930s that were unsullied by blood and tears. Let us look now at the sunnier side of the Thirties.

viii.

Dancing on the Edge

It was a very musical decade. The 1920s had all that jazz, and, as well, Dixieland and blues. That kept up and grew through the 1930s, but with something else added: "swing"—complex "hot" jazz arrangements generously accompanied by improvisation. The acknowledged "King of Swing" was Benny Goodman, one of the great improvisers (with his big band as well as in his trio or quartet). Whether in the big band or the combos, Benny always had one or more black musicians—the first to do so, to my knowledge.

Whether it was because Prohibition was ended in 1933, or because there was no way to hold down the bounciness of (at least a large part of) the people with all that great music in the air, the Thirties were great for dancers and dances: "doing the big apple," "jitterbugging," or just plain "stompin'." It didn't hurt that among the most popular films of those years were many, many musical comedies, with the likes of Fred Astaire and

Ginger Rogers, and, a bit later, Gene Kelly and Cyd Charisse (among others). The films were often absurd in content, but the music, the dancing, and the "feel" were just fine—especially in what was otherwise a pretty depressing period, literally and figuratively.

Also vivid in my memory as an ongoing morale booster in San Francisco was the building of the two great bridges. One spanned the Golden Gate—an extraordinarily beautiful chunk of nature, made even more so by the bridge—and the other crossed the waters between "the City" and the East Bay (Berkeley, Oakland, etc.). Although it is hard to pin down the reasons why, it is indisputable that having those bridges going up, watching it happen over a period of six years, was a restorative experience—despite the countless accidents and many deaths of bridge workers. And when in 1937 the Golden Gate Bridge opened, that was a *sensational* day. The bay's skies at their bluest, with over 200,000 pedestrians (no cars the first day) walking and marveling: there can be few views as breathtaking as that from the middle of the bridge. (I sold peanuts for ten hours on the bridge that Sunday, and cleared all of $4.00.)

When the Bay Bridge was fully completed in 1939, and an artificial island built in the middle of the several spans (adjoining a real island, Yerba Buena), we had the San Francisco World's Fair on Treasure Island. At the fair there was a musical comedy and swimming show—"Billy Rose's Aquacade"—with Esther Williams, Johnny Weissmuller, and Morton Downey Sr. (even more vulgar than Jr., if that can be believed), and, for a fleeting, luminescent moment, yours truly.

Story: Show Biz

While I was being a thoroughly bored court reporter for the shipwreck gang I was also studying acting at a good school (with a scholarship, yet). My most noted performance, assuredly also absurd, was as the lead in O'Neill's "Emperor Jones," after which I was offered and haughtily turned down a Hollywood screen test: *I* was going to be on the New York stage. At the time I was living in a not very grand hotel into which poured, one week in 1939, the entire cast of the Aquacade (less the stars): dozens of dancers and swimmers and a baker's dozen or more of what were called "showgirls,"—very tall women with very large frontal properties. I became friends with a few of the cast, but in particular with the dancer Berk (a veteran of many years in New York and Hollywood) and his "companion" Sara, a "showgirl." Berk convinced me the only way I'd ever get on the stage in New York was to begin as a chorus boy, and he would teach me to dance. So I bought a marble slab the size of a dining table, got it up to the roof of the hotel, and practiced every day after work. The time came in 1940 when one of the dancers in the show got a spot elsewhere, and it was arranged that I take his place. Much to Muh's horror, I quit my secure job with the Feds, went on stage every day and night on a bicycle built for two and, as the music played, got off the bike with my comely partner, did a couple of shuffles off to Buffalo and, by design, fell in the pool. Neither the high point of the show nor of my life. Thus did my professional career begin, and thus did it end. When the show closed soon after, Berk and Sara invited me to go along with them to New York; but some inner voice—I was, after all, already well into being a Leftie and into books and the like and being tugged by myself to study! study! study!—whispered no. Perhaps as important for the decision I've never regretted was that when I asked Muh what she thought I should do, she—doubtless with much Yiddisher momma inner trembling—said it was entirely up to me. So I went back to S.F.J.C., thence to Berkeley. Muh's and academia's small gain was, a few admirers of my work in the Aquacade have told me, the theater's great loss. Let history be the judge.

As I recline on this couch of history it seems that in those years of song and dance most of us knew in our guts that we were on the brink of a widespread war—and with good reason. In 1931, Japan invaded Manchuria, by 1932 had established a puppet government and renamed it Manchukuo, and continued to invade Chinese territory throughout the 1930s. In 1935, Italy, marching from its colonies in Eritrea and Somalia sought to conquer Ethiopia for the second time (having failed to do so in 1896), and, in 1936, succeeded. In that same year, the armed forces of Spain based in Spanish Morocco rebelled against the legally elected republican ("Loyalist") government. My passions concerning what became the Spanish Civil War—and, even more, its importance as the opening act of World War II—lead me to discuss it further.

ix.

For Whom the Bell Tolls [28]

The leader of the insurgent forces was General Francisco Franco, who first gained fame by his brutal suppression of a strike by the coal miners of the Asturias (1934). As fervently anti-democratic as he was militaristic, a consummate fascist in his bones, Franco was declared "Generalissimo" and Head of State by the military junta of what it called "Nationalist Spain." Almost overnight that "State" was recognized by Germany and Italy—Germany providing some infantry but mostly air power (and perfecting its dive-bombing techniques used so effectively when they swept over northern Europe in 1939), and Italy providing over 50,000 ground troops to the Falange (fascist) forces.

While the war was still going on, Britain and France recognized Franco and his government; so did the United States, four days after the war ended on April l, 1939. Although the bulk of the Spanish people supported the Republic, the Loyalist forces were short of weaponry and supplies from the beginning, embargoed by the three major capitalist democracies just noted, notably, so far as I was concerned, by the United States—which, while indirectly supplying Franco (through Italy), by an executive order of FDR prevented a Spanish government's ship (the *Mar Cantabrico)* from leaving New York harbor with its load of weaponry. The only external source of supplies for the Loyalist forces was the Soviet Union, which provided light weapons—and all too much advice: in return for paying the piper, the USSR also called at least some of the tunes. [29] In San Francisco at that time there was considerable controversy over the Spanish war; the *Mar Cantabrico* episode pushed me over the brink from protest to find a deeper commitment.

Story: Sgt. Jack

I was still working for USS at the time, had been "dittoing" (there were no Xerox copiers 'way back then) political leaflets on their machines, paper, and time; going to meetings, and the like. I decided to join the Abraham Lincoln Brigade, the U.S. unit of the (Communist-dominated) International Brigade, fighting alongside the Loyalist forces. One of my political friends set up an appointment for me to meet with Sgt. Jack ____, a recruiter for the Brigade. We met in a seedy bar on lower Market Street. Jack had fought in China against

Chiang Kai-shek in 1927, and had already put in almost two years in Spain. He was the most hard-bitten man I had or have ever met. We talked for more than two hours and—I was not yet nineteen—even the conversation was for me close to terrifying. What he had endured had, I suppose, left him pitiless, dedicated to defeating the fascists at whatever cost—and who could say him nay? Had I gone through the ten years or so of violence and fury Jack had, perhaps I would have come out the same way. But for me, then and there, I couldn't square my idealism with his realism: I didn't sign up—which may say more about me than about Jack. I have known more than a few of those who did join up and who—despite the political and physical adversities they experienced—do not regret their service in Spain.

Fading in memory now, the Spanish Civil War and the controversy it provoked in (among other places) the United States, foreshadowed emotions aroused by the war in Vietnam: in the 1930s, as in the 1960s, the United States was on the wrong side. The great difference was that we stayed out of a civil war in Spain (formally) when we should have been supporting the Loyalist side; and we plunged into civil wars in Korea and Vietnam when we should have stayed out (of which, much more in chapters 3 and 4).

Meanwhile, the point of no return had been passed in Germany. Its rearmament program, taking hold from almost the beginning of Hitler's rule, had by 1938 made Germany into the best and most fully-armed nation in the world; with a militarized society supporting means and ends. The "western democracies"—most importantly, Britain, France, and the United States—were far from full-blooded opponents of fascism, and did little to stop and some things to assist the fascist nations in the 1930s. Despite the obviousness of the Holocaust already by the late 1930s, the best that can be said of the great democracies (and of the Catholic Church and the Pope) is that they never openly supported the slaughter. The worst that can be said, however, is that opportunities to help (accepting boats from Germany filled with Jewish refugees, for example) were rebuffed. Having grown up in a Jewish family (at least in part), I was very much aware of what Nazism meant in that respect—even though, with the name Douglas Fitzgerald Dowd, I was rarely targeted as a Jew. Which brings back one especially abrasive memory.

Story: Jew Boy

Soon after I joined the Cornell econ faculty in 1953, a small lunch was held for me, a sort of welcome. There were six or seven there. The lunch was mediocre, the conversation worse: after perhaps thirty minutes of conversational dullsville, the talk became lively—and also completely anti-semitic. Like my mother, I had never been a religious Jew; but I had observed how frequently and vehemently she (also with the name Dowd, through marriage) would lay into anyone making derogatory cracks about Jews (or others, for that matter). So, like mother, like son. I laid into my new colleagues, saying I wouldn't sit still for that kind of poisonous talk, and not only because my mother was a Jew. Surprise. Silence. And then: "Ah," said the Chair, "but you're different, Doug." The sweet irony behind that Story, sweet for me at least, is that they didn't know *how* different; as I later found out, one reason I was hired by Cornell was that the "short list" had gotten down to me and a very talented Jew from Yale. I was chosen over the latter after one of the profs pointed out, "We've already got too many Jews in the Department." There was only one; to avoid getting another, they knowingly chose a radical—I had been so (and unethically) described in the U.C. departmental letter of recommendation to Cornell—and got a Red Jew for their pains. Tee hee. (By 1960 only one esteemed colleague in the department—the one who told me about the choice process—was speaking to me. Great loss.)

Anti-fascism in the United States was confined to the few, and all too many who took that stand in the 1930s were officially classified as "prematurely anti-fascist": must one laugh or weep? For the Europeans and many in Asia, the 1930s ended with a deadly bang. Things were beginning to change in that direction in the United States: we adopted the draft again, with the Selective Service Act of 1940, and in March 1941 there was the Lend-Lease Act, which enabled the United States, though still a neutral, to "lend or lease" arms, warships, and other military supplies to any nation "whose defense is deemed vital to the defense of the United States"—which then meant Great Britain and China and, after the Soviet Union was invaded by Germany in June of 1941, to the USSR.

But that takes us squarely into the 1940s.

WAR!

We thought we were liberating Europe and fending off the imperialism of feudal Japan, but we turned up after the war occupying or controlling foreign countries all over America, Europe, Asia and the Middle East. . . .

—Edmund Wilson, *The American Earthquake* [30]

The 1940s fall into two sharply contrasting halves: the first half a crescendo of war and destruction, the second a combination made up of reconstruction and the mounting Cold War. But within each of those periods there were vast qualitative and quantitative differences, of course.

It was noted earlier, for example, that about sixty million people died in Europe alone between 1939 and 1945. The United States suffered (in effect) no civilian casualties, but about 400,000 in our armed forces were killed and another one million were wounded. [31] By comparison, Paul Kennedy estimates that there were 13.6 million German casualties and prisoners lost, and that "20-25 million Soviet citizens died premature deaths between 1941 and 1945." [32]

Not for the first, but perhaps for the last time, the thousands of miles of ocean separating the United States from the continents at war added to our other and numerous natural and historical advantages to make war something more like a large (if mixed) blessing rather than an unmitigated disaster. By comparison with other societies and except for our Civil War, we have been spared the worst and enduring ravages of war—and "we have not learned to hate war enough," as a friend of mine once remarked.

As 1940 began German tanks and infantry continued to roll over northern Europe and the Japanese to push ever more deeply into China in the invasion that had begun eight years earlier. In the United States, meanwhile, a sense of improved material well-being was taking hold, as the economy slowly but surely became more buoyant in response to expanding exports and rising military production. Just as surely, however—at least for some—a sense of foreboding grew, as Nazi and Japanese triumphs nibbled and gnawed away at the always diminishing possibilities that the United States could—or should—stay out of the European and Asian wars. By the summer of 1940, the Lend-Lease program had been legislated and signed; by fall, the military draft of World War I had been reinstituted.

The draft was singularly unpopular. Indeed by mid-1941 a protest movement against the draft was going strong: its slogan was OHIO ("Over the hill in October"). When, shortly after, the legislation of 1940 came up for renewal, it passed in the House by only one vote. In order to avoid the draft—and the dreaded infantry—I signed up for pilot training on December 5, 1941, and became a very incompetent one. (And, as a later Story will show, spent some rough time with the infantry anyhow.)

Story: Tallest Japanese Ace

I managed to destroy five U.S. planes while in training, and one or two later on, thus qualifying for ace-hood on the enemy side. That such dazzling incompetence was rewarded with a pair of silver wings was due to fortuitous circumstance: a young, pregnant, and hemorrhaging woman with whom I shared a rare blood type needed a blood transfusion in the wee hours of the morning I was to take a "wash ride"—that is, a flying test meant formally to confirm one's ineptitude. I was asked and consented to give the transfusion in nearby Fresno, CA. A few hours later the wash ride began with, sitting in the other open cockpit (these were WWI-type biplanes, we all wore scarves, goggles, and thought of ourselves as Buddy Rogers) the Commandant himself. It seemed like an odd persecution to me, but off we went into the wild blue yonder. (You might not know this, but in an open cockpit a few thousand feet up, you can smell the orange trees if there are any below, as there were, then and there.) When we finally landed after a typical performance by me, the colonel said he had two comments: "First: Dowd, you are the worst pilot I have ever flown with. Second: you pass—and thank you for saving my wife's life last night." He was trying to do me a big favor, of course, and I was most pleased; but in the years to follow, his kindness almost killed me (and some others, both over there and over here—as in Oklahoma City, when I was learning to fly the A-20s to which I had been assigned and, with an engine on fire, just barely missed the Biltmore Hotel, then the tallest building in all of Oklahoma).

Of course immediately after Pearl Harbor was attacked on December 7, enlistments rose astronomically, and the draft lost almost all of its unpopularity. But before that attack, there was a majority indifference to the wars in Europe and Asia, and preparations for U.S. participation were a result of direction from above—principally by FDR. As one eminent historian has put it,

> Had any pollster been looking for one idea on which the vast majority of the American people agreed . . . , it would have been that if Europe were so wicked or stupid as to start another war, America would resolutely stay out. [33]

Had there *not* been the Japanese attack on Pearl Harbor [34] one is left to wonder when—perhaps even if—the United States would have entered World War II. [35]

Not that the Europeans had been eager to oppose Hitler or Mussolini. In the summer of 1938 a conference representing the major steel producers of the world—the United States, Britain, France, and Germany—was convened at Duisberg for the purpose of arranging an international steel cartel. But more was to come.

News Flash

Munich, September 29, 1938: A settlement was reached today by the heads of government of Germany, Britain, France, and Italy (Hitler, Chamberlain, Daladier, and Mussolini), transferring the Sudetenland of Czechoslovakia to Germany. The conference, with no representative of Czechoslovakia present, was held under threat of war by Germany. At its conclusion, Prime Minister Chamberlain announced that the agreement ensures "peace in our time."

On September 1, 1939, the Germans marched into Poland. [36] For many months the war became a "*Sitzkrieg,*" a "phony war." But in April the Germans, doubtless encouraged by the passivity of Britain and France (and, probably, that of the United States), invaded Denmark and Norway, and in May began their new kind of warfare, a "*blitzkrieg*" of *panzer* tanks and Stuka dive-bombers, supported by highly mobile artillery, all this allowing the infantry to cut through Holland, Belgium and into France like a warm knife through butter. As May ended and June began, the British Expeditionary Force found itself pushed back on to the beaches of Dunkirk, and had to mount an evacuation over the Channel of 340,000 soldiers (about one-third of them French), in some large and some very small boats. Having succeeded at that massive rescue effort by a whisker, a month or so later they found themselves under intense bombing attacks which they barely survived—able to do so only through the heroism of some few hundreds of badly-outgunned fighter pilots.

Having failed to bring Britain to its knees, Hitler made his critical strategic error when in the summer of 1941 he opened the second front to the East, as the Wehrmacht invaded the Soviet Union. What at first looked like more butter for Hitler's knife turned out to be very hard rock. But the Japanese, encouraged by the first few months of easy victories of Germany in Russia, and goaded diplomatically by the United States, attacked Pearl Harbor, thus bringing us into the war. We had begun to send matériel to the USSR by the fall of 1941. After Pearl Harbor, those supplies (and also those to Britain) were much increased—and, beginning in 1942, the planes and weaponry were joined by U.S. fighting forces. [37]

When, in the fall of 1942 the German military offensive was finally broken at Stalingrad the Third Reich's days were numbered. It took the tenacity and courage of the British and the Soviet peoples to hold off the German onslaught; but it may be believed that the Germans would have been equally tenacious had they been attacked and invaded. What made the difference, finally, was, as one U.S. general put it, "Who had the most shit to dump on the other outfit"—or, more politely, in Kennedy's words,

> Once again, in a protracted and full-scale coalition war, the countries with the deepest purse had prevailed. . . . [38]

Favorably impressed by fascism's fervid anti-communism, the Western democracies paid too little attention to fascism's ruthless lust for power. And that indifference to the criminality of rightwing dictatorships expanded in the decades of the Cold War—dictatorships often supported and armed, even created by our government, with continuing high costs for the peoples whose "freedom" we were protecting, as well as still uncounted costs for our own society. Of that and related matters, much more will be said in later pages. Now we focus in on the political economy of the United States throughout the 1940s.

i.

Economic Blood Transfusion

Economic revival in the United States dated from the outbreak of war in Europe in September 1939. Progress, except for a brief lapse, was accelerating. Every force of degeneration gave way to concerted effort; dejection was jolted into alertness, which became purpose and system. Fatigue was replaced by high national morale. . . . It was like watching blood drain back into the blanched face of a person who had fainted.

—Broadus Mitchell, *Depression Decade* [39]

The changes in the U.S. economy precipitated by the war took hold in the fall of 1939 and were dizzying already by the new year: employment in manufacturing up by 10 percent and payrolls by 16 percent; and the index of industrial production rose by a fantastic 25 percent in the same period. Those were unprecedented changes, both in nature and rate; but the best was yet to come. For the last three years of the war (1943-1945) unemployment averaged well under 2 percent, despite the fact that the number of women in the labor force had risen by about six million during the war. Such data represent what has been seen as the "rosy" side of the picture. But as Mitchell wisely observes,

Actually, in the crucial respect of waste of economic resources, human and physical, the war was, particularly for the United States, a deepening of the depression. If the nation had ten million unemployed when the war began, a few years later, when it was well into the conflict, it had three times as many not productively employed. Count eleven million in the armed forces, twenty million in war production, plus others, not so conveniently separable, who were supplying the demands of battle, and it is clear that "full employment" was a flattering unction. [40]

Understandably, the conclusions about a war economy drawn by the business community, politicians, and the general public were such as to encourage or acquiesce in the creation and evolution of the subsequent cold war economy—on which the United States spent $8.7 trillion from 1947 to 1991—while along the way doing various kinds of often irreparable damage to others and to ourselves. All that will be examined more fully in subsequent chapters. [41]

As had been true for World War I, it became essential for the State to become an always more active participant in the economic process, providing centralized direction and control going well beyond anything the "free market" could or should handle on two related matters: production and prices.

The requisite cooperation was in fact under way by 1942, and a major accomplishment by 1943. The principal means to that end were the carrots of large sales and profits for business, and good wages and union security for labor. Farmers wanted and received high levels of production at good prices.

The State wanted to meet its extraordinary military needs. In the event, all got pretty much all they sought: the carrots were abundant, and the sticks of coercion were rarely needed.

The problem of rising prices was a reality even before Pearl Harbor. Personal income had begun to rise at a 6 percent annual rate in the six months following September 1939. That rate doubled in the rest of 1940 and doubled again (to a 24 percent annual rate) by December 1941. In 1939 and 1940, this made for little strain: the depression had meant much idle capacity. But between late 1939 and late 1941, for example, the production of steel ingots rose from 61 percent to 99 percent of capacity—as was the case (or more so) in virtually all of industry. Already by the summer of 1941, as Mitchell notes, "the defense economy was facing an inflation problem of wartime proportions."[42]

There had been inadequate attempts at controlling prices throughout the foregoing period; but on January 30, 1942, the Office of Price Administration (OPA) was given the necessary powers to regulate prices and rents, and to punish violators. Soon thereafter, another institution was put into place: rationing.

Inflation was very moderate during the war; there was, in fact, some kind of economic miracle: despite price and wage controls and rationing and half of GNP going to the war, the average citizen's level of material well-being rose significantly, while prices rose only a few percentage points from 1942 through 1945.[43]

One lesson of current relevance to be drawn from the wartime economic experience is that the people of the United States showed themselves able to rise to levels of cooperation and even selflessness that today seem incredible as, increasingly since the 1970s, there has been a downhill slide from that approximation to social solidarity. Nowadays, to have a decent concern for something or someone outside one's own backyard risks being taken as a suspicious character—and "NIMBY" an all too widely-understood acronym.[44] Doubtless there has never been a saintly society; it would not have survived, if ever it had existed. But to understand that is not the same as seeing the consuming selfishness of today as fitting a historical norm—or as being suited for our own survival. But of all that, much more, much later.

The sequence of depression and war prosperity—extreme though both instances here discussed may have been—well underscores just how much waste normally goes on in our economy. The measure of waste of the depression is illuminated by the fact that real production more than doubled between the late 1930s and the mid-1940s—even with the cream of the labor force (sixteen million young, healthy, and potentially productive people) off some place at war. And in addition to that quite extraordinary waste of human talent and energy as measured by all the unemployment of the 1930s, there was also at least as much underused productive capacity of the land, the factories, the mines, etc.—setting aside the substantial waste in what *was* produced.

The prosperity of the World War II economy in the United States was not a mysterious process. What ensued economically *after* the war, in the simultaneous context of worldwide reconstruction and cold war, is considerably more complicated, dependent upon and affecting the whole social mix: economic, psychological, political, military, and cultural. But there remain a few matters worthy of discussion concerning the war itself, though on something less than a grand scale.

ii.

From Here to Absurdity

What follows will not be a military history of the war, the big battles, the strategic victories and defeats of the various combatants, or the like. Of such military histories there is no shortage. It is generally in works of fiction that one learns of the meaning of the military in human terms: Remarque's *All Quiet on the Western Front* for World War I has its World War II counterparts in books such as Norman Mailer's *The Naked and the Dead*, Heller's *Catch-22*, and James Jones' *From Here to Eternity* (concerned with the peacetime army) and *The Thin Red Line*. I recount now some non-fictional Stories representative of both the authoritarian nonsense portrayed in *The Good Soldier* (Schweik) and the savagery and terror (and as always in the military, not a few matchless idiocies) found in Heller, Mailer, and Jones; with Story #8 involving some combination of fear, pathos, comradeship, empathy—and the usual element of foolishness.

First some points of background information. Combat almost always involves casualties due to "friendly fire." The fighting in New Guinea and environs was worse than the average in this respect, because it was jungle fighting, with battle lines uneven and invisible. My outfit, often engaged in low-level infantry support, was both making and taking friendly fire.

So they put a pilot—me—along with eight radiomen on a small landing. Between staging, fighting, and departing, I was with the landing force over a period of three months, my job to minimize U.S. casualties by U.S. forces. Much later, in the last year of the war, I was in charge of airsea rescue for my bomb group. Whatever else I experienced in those two very different activities, I learned that wartime savagery was not confined to our enemies. I'll begin with that, first concerning the ground fighting, then the war from the air. And it all began with one of General Douglas MacArthur's innumerable ego trips.

War Story #1: Dugout Doug

The "small landing" I became part of had no more than 3,000 men. We were to land at Arawe, on the southern coast of New Britain (a large island perpendicular to New Guinea), in what was meant to be a diversionary assault to draw Japanese troops, navy, and aircraft away from a major landing three months thence, about 200 miles to the west. Some were to get there on the big LST's and debark right off the coast; most of us, myself included, were to spend more than twenty-four hours in the open sea in tiny LCVP's—only big enough to hold about twenty men, with some guy to steer it and handle a machine gun. Before long we were awash in seawater and vomit. We had departed from the eastern tip of New Guinea just after dawn; but just before that, who shows up but Himself—surrounded, as always, by his many aides-de-camp and publicity flacks. An LCVP was promptly pulled up to shore, Dugout Doug and a few others got on, it backed out into the sea for perhaps twenty yards and began to chuff back—all of us watching dubiously while—cameras whirling—our fearless general got off looking fierce and like someone making a landing. I was so terrified by the very idea of my imminent arrival among enemies who would try to shoot me that I didn't think much of what Mr. Big Shot was up to at the time. However, about six months later an old copy of *Life* found its way to New Guinea, and by gum and by golly, there on the front cover was a photo of MacArthur making a brave landing—the very photo of our magical morning together. Sheeei!

War Story #2

The assault outfit I was loaned to was the 112th Cavalry, one of whose riflemen was—get this—Norman Mailer (!) whose *Naked and the Dead*, though concerned with the later and greater Biak landing (in Dutch New Guinea), opens with our teentsy operation. My job was to stay in radio contact with the guys from my outfit, talk them toward the difficult to identify and locate target, and see that it was well outlined with smoke, etc. We were doing badly there (as planned; indeed we were ultimately pushed back out to the sea), and everyone was very scared—and for some the fear became hate and murder. At one point, three Japanese soldiers were captured and placed in a primitive barbed wire stockade. Soon after, I saw two GIs open the gate of the stockade, prod the Japanese to "escape," and shoot them down in the process. Score three for our side. Everyone does it, even the flyboys:

War Story #3: Blue-eyed Bully Boy

A year or so later, my bomb group was in the Philippines, and I was in charge of airsea rescue. Our B-25s were bombing Formosa (now Taiwan) regularly. The rescue procedure was to accompany the bombers up to a point which became the post-bombing rendezvous area. My plane would circle—always in radio contact with our planes and with naval craft, anti-Japanese guerrillas on the ground, etc., for pickups, when necessary and possible—until all the planes had regrouped. And then we would accompany the "limping" planes back to base. One day, an early arriving B-25, its pilot evidently bored, began to circle a Formosan farmer and his bullock in an area close to the shore. It is only partially irrelevant to this Story that the farmer was one of several in Formosa who, at great danger to themselves, worked with us on rescues. When it suddenly became clear that the pilot was preparing to make a pass at the farmer, I began to yell at him over the air to cut it out; but too late: with his twelve .50-calibre nose-mounted machine guns, our handsome Dartmouth graduate caused both farmer and bullock to explode in a red blur. The sport of kings.

War Story #4

Most of the guerrillas with whom I worked helped us to bring out aircrews downed behind the Japanese lines in the Philippines. The man I came to know best was Rufino Gonzales. He had been a farmer. He was very brave on many occasions; and he was a member of the Hukbalahap (the anti-Japanese guerrilla force). Rufino occasionally brought his fifteen-year-old brother to the airbase with him. On one such day I noticed a white fluid oozing from his eyes and took him to see our flight surgeon. After commenting that the boy could lose his sight, he took care of him until he was cured. Both before and after that, Rufino invited me several times to meet and eat with his (very poor) family out in the countryside, which I happily did—until I realized the occasions had as a main purpose that I might marry Rufino's young sister (already married though

I was, as Rufino knew)—with whom I was led to take almost entirely silent walks, always accompanied by two elderly aunts. Through it all I became very fond of Rufino and admiring of the Huks (as they were called). When the war ended, I was sent to Clark Field (our largest airbase in Asia until recently), en route to the States. Very late one night I was awakened by widespread gunfire. The guns were being fired at Huks by members of the "Constabulary," the official police force of the Philippine government before, during, and after the war, which had collaborated with the Japanese for years. The Huks had worked with us, the Constabulary against us during the war. Details, details: the Cold War had already begun.

War Story #5: Necessity, the Mother of Invention

Mention of the flight surgeon reminded me of flight nurses, and a not so grim Story. One of many innovations of that war was the use of flight nurses. They were used to accompany wounded GIs on flights home, of course; more daringly, they went with the C-45s (cargo planes) to land in combat zones to evacuate badly-wounded GIs pretty much at the battle site—where they were often shot down, whether on arrival or departure. They were very gutsy women. I came to know one of them very well. Her name was Vicki, she was small and tough, was from New Jersey, and sounded very much like it. And she was responsible for another wartime innovation. On one of her missions to a combat zone, with a new pilot, the plane got lost and the pilot mistakenly sought to land at an airstrip on a Japanese-held island. When the guns began to blaze at them, the pilot realized his error, banked away and was hit, but was able to keep flying for a hundred miles or so before ditching in the sea. Nobody was hurt. The two pilots and the two nurses survived in a rubber raft for two days. The nurses wore what aircrews (that is, men) wore: a one-piece, zipper-down-the-front, mechanics' coverall sort of thing. To go to the john, Vicki and the other woman had to unzip and undress, on a six-foot and unstable raft. When Vicki got back to dry land—helped by me, with pleasant consequences for all as time went on—she really raised hell with the authorities, who more or less promptly had a new outfit designed that could be used in such circumstances with greater, though not great, ease.

War Story #6

Back to the landing. The eight radiomen with me were from a small communications outfit, commanded by Major D. (who got his rank in the National Guard). The major's responsibilities included keeping in touch with me about his men. He never did so. During the operation, one of the eight was killed, one lost a leg, and another lost his mind. When I finally got back to New Guinea after the debacle, my first act was to drive a jeep to Major D.'s outfit, some miles over the hills from my airstrip. D. was in his tent when I arrived. My intention was to remind him, calmly but firmly, that he had not taken adequate care of his men. There was more firm than calm, we became angry and came to the point of blows. At some point, exasperated with him, I said: "Aaah, fuck you!" Major D. responded by saying "Lieutenant (I was then a 2nd Lt.), when you speak to a superior officer, you say 'Sir!'" "You mean," I replied, "you want me to say Fuck you, sir!?" And D. repeated his order. And I repeated mine, without, of course, the "Sir!" The major shouted that he was going to have me court-martialed, ran to his jeep, and took off. I did likewise, and we raced each other to HQ Fifth Army Air Force, where I arrived first. I informed the colonel guarding Commanding General Kenney's door as quickly and graphically as possible the nature of the major's mission (who was right behind me, fuming). The colonel said "wait a minute, kid," went in to the general, shortly reappeared, and sent me in. Kenney listened, told me to tell the major to come in, and to wait outside. A few minutes later a very pale Major D. exited, I re-entered, and exited again with a ten-day leave to Sydney. (That was only one of four attempted court martials against me, all for insubordination of one sort or another; all failed.)

War Story #7

During that ten-day leave I soon became good friends with one of the most respected painters in Australia, Carl Plate. He was a philosophical anarchist, and among other things I learned from him one was about bureaucracy. At the end of my official ten days, we took a taxi to the docks for the old coastal boat in which I had arrived and was to return (there were limited air facilities at that time of the war). En route, Carl asked, "If we were to have a broken axle, and you were to miss the boat, would anyone up there notice your absence?" I thought for a minute or so and replied that I wasn't sure, but I doubted it. "Turn around," Carl said to the driver. I stayed for another four weeks; and when I returned, nobody had noticed my absence. (Had they, I would have been court-martialed for something more than insubordination, and it would have stuck. And Major D. would have been vindicated.)

War Story #8: Self-defense

It was noted earlier that I was in air-sea rescue for my bomb group. By the summer of 1945, I was in charge of it. As such, I attended staff meetings. In early July we had an evening meeting at which we were informed that our group had been chosen to be the first bomb group to be established in Japan, and that staff was to accompany the invasion to set up the facilities, etc. The next morning when I awoke I was almost entirely paralyzed, unable to get up. I was taken to the nearby hospital (at Lingayen Gulf, in northern Luzon), and given every conceivable kind of examination. At the end of two weeks or so of this, the Doc said, "Captain Dowd, you have what we can call 'hysterical paralysis.' After two-and-a-half years your body has decided you've been over here too long; it wants to go home." But General MacArthur had given an order in 1942 that *nobody* would go home until we had won the war (except those with a missing arm or leg). So the Doc said I'd just have to sweat it out. Also in the hospital was a school friend of mine from San Francisco, Roy N., a night fighter pilot recovering from a wound. He used to visit me in my ward. One morning— it was August 6, 1945—Roy dropped by to say that some of his buddies were coming over from the outfit that night with their saved-up booze ration (one got a shot of whiskey after each mission, which was usually left undrunk until it amounted to something), and having a little party. I said thanks, but as he knew, I couldn't move. Just wanted you to know you're welcome, he told me. Thanks, I replied. Perhaps twelve hours later, a great shouting and banging took hold in the hospital area. Roy came over, half-drunk, shouting "the fuckin' war's over!" (It wasn't, until August 15.) And excitedly Roy told me that some great mysterious bomb had been dropped somewhere in Japan, said to have the power of tens of thousands of tons of TNT (our usual maximum was one ton), and that the Japanese had surrendered. I don't remember just how I went from paralysis to movement, but shortly I found myself in a jeep Roy had commandeered, speeding over the sands of Lingayen beach, shouting ecstatically, "the fuckin' war's over!" Soon we came upon two figures making love on the beach. The male of the duo was my c.o. and good friend, Larry T., who just that morning had come to say goodbye to me as he prepared to depart the next day for the Japanese landing's staging area. And there I was, fully unparalyzed and shaking him, so to speak, *in flagrante delicto,* to inform him of good news, and never has anyone been as enraged with me as Larry was at that moment. He took off the next morning, and I never saw him again—to explain, to apologize, whatever.

After two and a half years in New Guinea and the Philippines, and except for two incidents yet to be noted, that's how it ended—and the Cold War began.

The Cold War was much more than a decades-long quasi-military confrontation between the USA and the USSR (and, after 1949, China and many Third World countries). It was the trunk from which our economic, political, and social history—virtually *all* of our history—grew and changed: until this decade. Now, in the 1990s, the swift disappearance of the Cold War has another imposing significance: we don't know what to do without it; and again, all dimensions of our existence are in the thrall of a disappearing Cold War.

That vast set of changes after 1945 requires prolonged examination of the origins, the nature, and the consequences of the Cold War, and of the manner in which the process served as the basis for U.S. dominance: for U.S. hegemony. Suffice here the horrific observation by the British Nobel Laureate in physics, P.M.S. Blackett, that "the dropping of the atomic bombs [on Hiroshima and Nagasaki] was not so much the last military act of the second World War, as the first major operation of the cold diplomatic war with Russia."[45]

But what happened *after* 1945 of course had its beginnings before the end of the war, as I was able to see for myself in two unsettling incidents, just about the time of that already noted, concerning the Hukbalahap. The first pointed to what was slated to happen in Vietnam; the other virtually announced the Cold War between the United States and the Soviet Union—military allies at the time.

Story: How to Win Friends

FDR had died and Harry Truman had become President in April 1945. By November I was floating loose between Clark Field and Manila, waiting to go home; and those floating around Truman had already begun to turn FDR's policies around, neither first nor last in Vietnam. It had of course been under French rule from 1860 and up to its occupation by Japan during the war. The Japanese allowed the French Vichy (pro-fascist) government to continue to administer Vietnam. But in early 1945, as Vichy rule in France was itself finally being displaced by anti-Nazi Gaullist forces, the Japanese interned the French administrators and troops, and took over themselves. Meanwhile, the guerrilla forces of Ho Chi Minh and the Vietminh were fighting against the Japanese, while also working with the U.S. Office of Strategic Services (which became the

CIA in 1947) and, among others, the airsea rescue services of the area (of which I was a part). There was considerable mutual admiration between Ho Chi Minh and his forces on the one hand, and FDR and the relevant U.S. armed forces in the area on the other. More to the point, the expectation was general that at the end of the war the United States would see to it that Vietnam would be free of foreign domination. Instead the new President was persuaded to arm and equip Dutch and British troops (newly-liberated from Japanese prison camps throughout Southeast Asia) and transport them to Hanoi and Saigon, to hold the fort—literally—until French troops could arrive. In November of 1945, while in Manila, I witnessed the loading of such equipment and troops and learned of their destination—from them. And shuddered.

Story: War to End All Wars, Once Again

I finally arrived back in the States by ship, at Long Beach, CA, in December 1945. As we disembarked, Red Cross women gave us coffee and doughnuts and that day's copy of the *Los Angeles Examiner* (the Hearst paper). On the front page there appeared a prominent editorial with a very prominent headline: "THE TIME TO STRIKE SOVIET RUSSIA IS NOW!" In the next week, along with 2 to 3,000 other pilots, I was detained at the base for meetings in which we were encouraged to join the air force reserve. At the end of this, I was called in by the colonel in charge. He informed me that I was the *only* man not to join up, and that unless I did so I would face the possibility of being drafted in the next war. "I've had my war," I said, "and thought everyone had." He dismissed me with a steely glare, and I left him shining his buttons.

Within a year, along with many other students—most of them vets—I was protesting the Truman Doctrine and the Cold War of which it was, up to then, the centerpiece. In the upcoming chapter, we take a long look at the larger structure.

PART II

TODAY SHALT THOU BE WITH ME IN PARADISE: THE SECOND COMING OF CAPITALISM

3 CREATING A COLD WAR AND A GLOBAL ECONOMY: 1945-1960

TURNING THE EARTH, PLANTING THE SEEDS

---

i.

Introducing Uncle Hegemon

Almost all who read these pages will have spent almost all their lives within the economic, military, social, and cultural universe of the Cold War. The now rising tide of critiques of the Cold War that portray it as some combination of sham and global tragedy are seen by most as wrongheaded or, worse, as done by those consumed by hatred of "America." [1] Except for here and there, now and then, a raffish (perhaps disloyal?) person or two, haven't the assumptions, presumptions, arguments, and policies of the Cold War been accepted, even praised, by all the respected voices in society—politicians, professors, journalists, entertainers, *tutti?* Certainly. But, like the addiction to cigarettes that locked in and held in the Twenties, that didn't happen right away, it had to be "sold."

Hard to believe, now; but in late 1945 and in 1946 it was even harder to believe that the United States should see itself as obliged (or entitled) to dominate the world economically, politically, and militarily. That is what the Cold War meant, and was meant to mean by its key players as it evolved: by Acheson, by Forrestal, by the Dulles brothers, and among others, by Harry Truman. As we shall see.

Substantial opposition was short-lived; ineffectual opposition (such as my own) continued throughout. The extraordinary and exuberant demonstrations all over the country on August 14-15, 1945, were cheering not the beginning of "the American Century"—so much longed for and encouraged by some—but the end of war: now and forever, finally.

From almost the moment Japan surrendered, the public began to receive its lessons about a Soviet threat—of the sort I had been given with that cup of coffee and the *Los Angeles Examiner* as I disembarked from the Pacific war in December 1945.

There was, of course, a major crisis in all of Europe and much of Asia. Virtually all nations—excluding the Swiss, the Swedes, the Canadians, and ourselves—were terribly weak, their people on or over the edge of malnutrition, even starving; all their economies were flattened, their usual political leadership vulnerable at best, and with not a few utterly disgraced. Pre-World War II conditions were gone forever; Europe was in a shambles.

The most influential voices in the new Truman Administration (plus those from the wobbly higher circles in Western Europe) interpreted all this to mean that if the United States did not take a strong hand, the Soviet Union would run rampant over Europe. Many changes in Europe were thus slated to emerge, many of them veering to the Left. That the Soviet Union would be the prime cause and the prime beneficiary of those changes unless the United States constructed a defensive perimeter to hold the Soviets back was the message assiduously and increasingly put forth from Washington—a message given a dramatic underscoring in 1946.

News Flash

Fulton, Missouri, March 5. Standing alongside President Truman, former British Prime Minister Winston Churchill said that the United States "stands at this time at the pinnacle of world power.... Opportunity is here now, clear and shining, for both our countries...; America should not ignore or fritter it away..., for it faces a peril to Christian civilization." From the Baltic to the Adriatic, Churchill said, "an iron curtain has descended across the [European] continent."

But even as Churchill was speaking the Soviet Union was petitioning for famine relief from the United States, and lacked the strength to construct either a literal or figurative curtain of cloth a few miles long, let alone one of iron "from the Baltic to the Adriatic." [2]

In examining the emergence of the Cold War it is necessary to look at the most relevant facts while trying to see matters from the presumed adversary's, as well as one's own, position. In this case, let us look at postwar USSR and USA as objectively as we can, and ask which was threatening—*could* threaten—the other?

It should need no reminding that as the war ended, the United States had the strongest economy in the world—we possessed *over half* of the entire world's industrial capacity in 1946—relatively and absolutely, indeed, ours was the strongest in the world's history; and much the same was also true militarily, politically, and socially. In short, the United States had everything going for it: wealth, strength, prestige, and popularity. And the Soviet Union?

> During the war, German occupation forces had killed an estimated 15 million to 20 million Russians and had completely or partially demolished 15 large cities, 1,710 towns, and 70,000 villages in the Soviet Union . . . destroyed 31,850 industrial concerns, 65,000 kilometers of railroad track, 90,000 bridges, 10,000 power stations, [and] 98,000 collective farms. . . . As a result Soviet industrial ouput in 1945 was but 58 percent of the 1940 level.
>
> "Economically, the Soviet Union is exhausted," reported U.S. Naval Intelligence in January 1946. "The U.S.S.R. is not expected to take any action during the next five years which might develop into hostilities with Anglo-Americans." In January 1947, State Department consultant John Foster Dulles contended that war was "one thing which Soviet leadership does not want and would not consciously risk."[3]

With such an enormous imbalance in the relative economic and military strengths of ourselves and the Soviet Union, if either nation should have circled its wagons in preparation for being attacked, the Soviet Union would seem to have been the more likely of the two—especially with its memories of having U.S. troops within its borders (along with many more British, French, Japanese, and Czechs) working with the Russian "White Army" as it sought to overthrow the revolution after 1917.

Following well-tested principles of propaganda, and given the implausibility of Soviet military aggression, all the more reason, therefore, to posit and exaggerate a Soviet threat to Western Europe and to build a broad variety of policies around that fear with repeated and resounding warnings—until what had once been dubious came to be seen as the gospel truth.

Nor was the gospel weakened when a fearsome internal menace in the United States was trumped up.[4] The Cold War and the various ramifications of McCarthyism were blood brothers that made domestic dissent both a lost cause and a risky process for those who opposed either, let alone both (as will be discussed shortly); and the damage done to our individual and social character in the process was and remains inordinate.

By the end of the 1940s, the foundations of U.S. global hegemony were visibly in place, and further construction was proceeding apace. For those overseeing that development, however, the year after the war ended—roughly from the fall of 1945 until the end of 1946—was not easy. A Gallup poll in late 1945 showed that a solid majority of our people believed Russia could be trusted to cooperate with the United States: come to think of it, they had been our major ally in the European war; were, in fact, *still* our ally.

But by early 1947 opposition to the expansion and uses of our power had become muted and useless. From that year forward, the battalions of the Cold War and associated U.S. global hegemony strode on stage in a mighty parade. Their defining institution was the "National Security Act," passed in July 1947, whose core creation was the "National Military Establishment"—its actual name—which incorporated the preexisting Department of the Navy with the new Department of the Air Force and Department of the Army, under the Department of Defense. (The latter had been called the War Department, from 1789 until 1947.) Also created were the CIA and the National Security Council (NSC). The latter—its members all appointed by the President—swiftly became the pivotal center of policy-making, with a concomitant hemorrhage of the powers of Congress and of the citizenry: a decisive step in the evolution of "the imperial presidency."

The critical set of events providing both the drama and the pretext for developing and expanding the powers of the National Security Act had Greece and Turkey at their center, and had begun to unfold even before World War II ended. By March 1947 the U.S. response to the Eastern Mediterranean situation had become the Truman (Greece-Turkey) Doctrine, and it constituted our first major strategic initiative of the Cold War era. A closer look is appropriate.

The conditions provoking U.S. involvement in Turkey and Greece were quite dissimilar. The deceitful manner in which the U.S. public was informed about the troublesome circumstances in the two areas was, however, very much the same, and it provided the springboard for launching the infamous "domino theory," a paranoid's basis for foreign policy: if Greece topples, Turkey will be next (or vice versa).

As for the realities, we begin with Greece. It had been ruled by a British-dominated dictatorial monarchy before World War II; it fell under Nazi occupation during the war. Wartime resistance to the Germans was led by the Communist-dominated National Liberation Front (EAM), also the single most popular political group in Greece after the war.

Truman's presentation to Congress ignored all that when he asked for $400 million in economic and military aid to Greece and Turkey, in March 1947. Also ignored was the fact that the Soviet Union strictly *withheld* assistance from the EAM forces throughout the entire period—in accordance with agreements made between Churchill and Stalin in 1944. [5]

Those agreements gave Britain the "right" to reinstitute its control over Greece as the Germans were being pushed out in 1944, and the United States flew in two British divisions. Still, by 1946, with the EAM holding perhaps two-thirds of Greece, Britain, too weak to maintain its power there, asked the United States—in the phrase of the day—"to fill the vacuum." One of the most respected of U.S. print and radio (and, later, TV) journalists of the time, Howard K. Smith (a long-time Anglophile), had this to say of the events:

> One would prefer to be generous to the British and say that they attempted to bolster what middle-way and democratic forces there were in order to create compromise and a basis for democracy. Unfortunately, there seems little evidence to support this, and one is forced to conclude that the British were determined to break the EAM and install in power the discredited monarchy and its blindly vengeful rightist supporters. [6]

I was then at Berkeley, and among those who started up a group called the Independent Students Political Action Committee (ISPAC). ISPAC worked on domestic issues entirely until the Truman Doctrine reared its ugly head. Our attempts to counter it included one event the mere memory of which warms the cockles of my heart.

Story: Lena and the Kid

There had been a presumably free election in Greece in 1947, the results of which placed the U.S.-favored bloc in power. The election was supervised by a UN committee, one member of which was a noted professor of statistics at U.C., and he concluded that the election was fraudulent. ISPAC organized a public meeting with this professor as the main speaker, and it turned out to be a great success—not, however, because of the good professor, at least not mostly. Other than him, our only other scheduled speaker was my radio commentator pal Sid Roger (of a later Story), and we decided that wasn't enough.

I had noticed that Lena Horne was giving a string of performances at the Paramount Theater in Oakland, and thought it a good idea to ask her to participate, on the hunch that she might be sympathetic to our cause. Having delegated myself to ask her (without a prior telephone call), I went to the theater, naively knocked on her dressing room door and, the naive occasionally having good luck, was admitted by her dresser (Lena was on stage).

When Lena arrived in the nicely-crowded room, more impressive (and tougher) by far in person than on stage or screen, she asked "What in hell are you doing in here, kid?" (Nobody calls me "kid" anymore, alas.) I told her about the program and said we'd like her to help out. Why *her?* she demanded: to sing? to dance? to speak? I was naive, but not totally stupid, and quickly (and with less than full honesty) replied "to speak." She accepted.

The meeting was well-publicized, and packed full, and Lena made a great speech against racism. Without taking a vote on it, I decided that I should be the one to pick her up from and take her back to the theater (in my ratty old '34 Plymouth) and, as the saying goes, from then on she owned me—not that she showed any interest in doing so.

In 1946, Turkey had also begun to warm up as did, for that matter, the entire Middle East—Egypt, Persia (Iran), Palestine, etc. That the United States would intervene to settle the area's issues as much as possible on its own terms was inevitable, given the strategic location and enormous oil resources of the region, mixed in with the effort to create Israel. As in Eastern Europe, Stalin was preoccupied with strategic considerations regarding the Soviet Union's bordering nations—among them Turkey.[7]

> Tensions, therefore, were high when the Soviet government [in 1946] asked Turkey to alter the rules governing ship movements through the Dardanelles. The Russians maintained that the existing regulations had not protected their interests during World War II. They wanted to get together with the other Black Sea powers, formulate a new set of rules, and establish a joint defense of the straits. The Soviet diplomatic note . . . triggered a whirlwind of action at the highest levels of the Truman administration.[8]

As so often throughout the Cold War, the White House and its NSC interpreted the diplomatic move on the part of the Soviet Union as being thinly disguised aggression, merely

> a ploy to secure bases in Turkey, take it over, and then gain control of Greece, the Middle East, and the Eastern Mediterranean. Once having sealed off these areas from the Western world, the Soviets would maneuver to achieve their goals in China and India.[9]

U.S. policymakers, in keeping with our own history of being free from any military threat by virtue of thousands of miles of oceans to our east and west and weak nations to our north and south, seem to have been unable even to imagine the fears of countries that have been invaded by or through their neighbors more than once—as with Russia.

Whatever the truth or falsity of the U.S. position regarding the Soviet Union, its consequence was to nourish the conditions in which the United States emerged as the post-World War II hegemon. To that end, and following the creation of the national security apparatus in 1947, additional momentous policies were institutionalized:

> At a commencement address at Harvard in June 1947, General George Marshall (then Secretary of State) proposed what became in 1948 the European Recovery Program. In its four years of operation, the program gave $13 billion to eighteen European nations (including Greece and Turkey) for a broad variety of investment projects. Over 70 percent of the aid was spent for U.S. goods and sold to Congress on those practical grounds, as well as a means of "rolling back the tide of Communism." [10]

> In the same year, the Organization of American States (OAS) was created; its purpose, to protect the hemisphere from "the interventionist and aggressive designs of international communism." In 1949 the North Atlantic Treaty Organization (NATO) was created, the military obverse of the Marshall Plan.

> Very much against President Truman's strongly-stated wishes, partial demobilization of the armed forces had taken place as the war had ended, in response to many GI and public demonstrations to that end. Despite the cutbacks achieved, and after what Truman called the "disintegration" of our armed forces, there remained 2.2 million in the military in the summer of 1946—more than seven times the number in 1939, with a military budget in 1947 more than ten times that of 1940 and more than twice that of the Soviet Union. Finally, the Selective Service Act of 1948 built the draft into our postwar history. (The United States had had a military draft only during the Civil War, World War I, and World War II.)

Story: Only #2

In 1948, I was simultaneously managing the campaign for a candidate for the State Legislature, and that in Berkeley for Henry Wallace, presidential candidate of the Independent Progressive Party (IPP, "the" third party of this half of the century). There was a popular radio newsman named Sid Roger who was a neighbor, a good friend, and a political pal. Once in a while I babysat for his family. And once in a while Sid would boost either or both of "my" candidates on his show. Then, the most popular columnist in the Bay Area was Herb

Caen. The one time I made his column was when he noted that my campaigns were probably the only ones in history that depended upon babysitting for financing their publicity. A somewhat more earth-shaking subsequent development was the booklet of the State of California's Un-American Activities Committee that listed and ranked those whom its chair—State Senator Jack Tenney, California's troglodytic preview of Joe McCarthy—deemed to be the leading Communists in the state. Sid was #1, I, ever an also-ran, #2. Sid's radio news show on one of the major stations in the Bay Area was sponsored by the CIO. It was canceled in 1950, on the same day the station refused to allow Harry Bridges to appear as a guest on the show. Subsequently Sid went on to be editor of the ILWU newspaper. To my sorrow, he passed away just recently.

Saying this leads me to explain something that might have come to your minds. Was I or was I not, am I now or have I ever been—shhhh!—a member of the Communist Party? Before I go on, I interject that until the Sixties, people like myself would refuse to answer or even discuss such a question, because to do so would pour kerosene over the blaze. My answer is perhaps a peculiar one, in two parts: 1) almost everyone thought I was, not just Jack Tenney and the FBI (which will be explained in a later Story), but also some friends who were and were not members; and 2) I was never asked to be. I believe I was never asked to be a member because of the way I conducted the meetings of a fairly effective left student group at Berkeley. This was in 1946-49 and there were, of course, many political factions attending our meetings. Frequently, someone from this or that group, including the local Communist Party, would make a stab at taking over the organization. I always sought to stifle such attempts at the very beginning with an open discussion about it before it could take hold, and the group stayed what it was called: the Independent Students' Political Action Committee. Insofar as we tended to move in something like harmony with the Party, I believe—I don't know— they thought I was doing no harm and might well be doing some good (for them, also), and would be best left alone. In any case, I was never approached.

The 1950s produced a large handful of other cold war institutions with names such as The Subversive Activities Control Board, mostly concerned with some form of control mechanism at home and abroad. Of which, more as we go along.

Standing behind these and related developments and giving them momentum and muscle was the successful development of the atomic bomb.[11] There can be no underestimating what that signified. According to Stewart Udall, Secretary of the Interior under JFK and LBJ:

> The atomic weapons race and the secrecy surrounding it crushed American democracy. It induced us to conduct Government according to lies. It distorted justice. It undermined American morality. Until the cold war, our country stood for something. . . , for moral leadership in the world. [12]

ii.

What Dead Sheep?[13]

Earlier it was noted that for several months before August 6, 1945 (the day the bomb was dropped), it was obvious that Japan had become too weak to continue the war in an effective manner. That observation was based on my own experience with the military effort against Japan, comparing 1945 with the preceding couple of years. But, one could say, how much could one lowly GI know? But what about the following trio? If they didn't have the big picture, who did? This is what they said:

> It would be a mistake to suppose that the fate of Japan was settled by the atomic bomb. Her defeat was certain before the first bomb fell.
>
> (Winston Churchill)

> It is my opinion that the use of this barbarous weapon at Hiroshima and Nagasaki was of no material assistance in our war against Japan. The Japanese were already defeated and were ready to surrender because of the effective sea blockade and the successful bombing with conventional weapons. . . . My own feeling is that in being the first to use it, we had adopted an ethical standard common to the barbarians of the dark ages.
>
> (Admiral William Leahy, CINCPAC—
> Commander in Chief, Pacific Naval Forces)

> I told him [Secretary of War Stimson] I was against it on two counts. First, the Japanese were ready to surrender and it wasn't necessary to hit them with that awful thing. Second, I hated to see our country be the first to use such a weapon.
>
> (General Dwight D. Eisenhower) [14]

News Flash

Hiroshima, August 6, 1945. At exactly fifteen minutes past eight in the morning, Japanese time . . . , a tremendous flash of light cut across the sky. It travelled from east to west, from the city toward the hills. It seemed a sheet of sun. Such clouds of dust had risen that there was a sort of twilight around. Under what seemed to be a local dust cloud, the day grew darker and darker . . . . A hundred thousand people were killed by the atomic bomb.[15]

And then, three days later, another atomic bomb, on Nagasaki: 35,000 to 50,000 people killed. Why? And why *two* bombs? To save lives, we are told. However:

> By mid-1945, Germany had formally surrendered, and Japan was clearly defeated. American warplanes flew round-the-clock bombing missions virtually unopposed. The fire-bombings of Tokyo in March resulted in 84,000 casualties. American and British ships shelled Japanese coasts at will and enforced a rigid blockade. Inside Japan, fuel and industrial productivity almost disappeared. Through the auspices of the Soviet Union, still technically a nonbelligerent [in the Pacific war], Japanese leaders frantically tried to negotiate a surrender, contingent only on the retention of the Emperor. In May, [Harry] Hopkins cabled Truman from Moscow: "Japan is doomed and the Japanese know it. Peace feelers are being put out by certain elements in Japan and we should therefore . . . act in concert about the surrender."[16]

As noted earlier, bombs dropped on Hiroshima and Nagasaki were not so much the last engagement of World War II as they were the first shot of the Cold War. For example, there is general agreement that the United States did not wish to have the Soviet Union enter the war against Japan: Soviet involvement certainly would have meant Soviet troops in North China and probably elsewhere in the Far East—with who knows what unwanted complications?

> The origins of the cold war can be seen, like a photograph beginning to develop, in the 800 pages of intercepted communications from 1945 released to a historian [Gar Alperovitz] as a result of a lawsuit filed against the National Security Agency . . . .
> For example, American intelligence officers read the private communications of the French leader, Gen. Charles de Gaulle. They came to understand France's fury at President Roosevelt's refusal to support its wish to rule Indochina. After Roosevelt died, the United States gave its blessing to France's return to Indochina, in large part to win French solidarity against the Soviet Union.

The documents also show that the United States had information suggesting that top members of the Japanese Army were willing to surrender *more than three months* before the United States dropped their atomic bombs on Hiroshima and Nagasaki 48 years ago. [17]

And there is an additional explanation: the military had an extraordinary new weapon in its possession and wanted to use it, if only to test it out. Even more depressingly, scientists did not prove themselves to be ethically more noble than the rest of us. One of the Los Alamos physicists, my friend Phil Morrison, who flew with the plane that bombed Nagasaki (in those early days a physicist had to go along to arm the bomb), told me that when the bomb was dropped and he saw it explode, he felt a sense of exhilaration like nothing before or since. Not long thereafter, he became a key founder of the Federation of Atomic Scientists, which saw its main task as preventing nuclear war. Which reminds me of a nuke story.

Nuke Story

At Cornell, in the late 1950s, a panel was arranged to debate the matter of nuclear testing. On it were two Cornell physicists, Phil Morrison and Hans Bethe, a historian, and myself. Phil and I were against testing, Bethe and Professor F. were for it. Bethe also happened to be President Eisenhower's science advisor (and important in the making of the H-bomb). It is relevant to what follows to note that Phil is seen by all who know him as a truly great teacher: after an hour or so of impassioned debate, with Phil doing much more talking than I, Bethe—a distinguished and normally sedate man—suddenly stood up and exclaimed: "You've changed my mind!" (But F. didn't change his mind.)

I have suggested in foregoing pages that the advent of Harry Truman to the presidency in 1945 was not an unmitigated blessing for the United States or the rest of the world. Yet, Truman's name has taken on always rosier hue as the years have passed, both despite and because of his contradictory personal and presidential characteristics, which deserve a brief glance.

Snapshot: Yankee Doodle Dandy

Until he took FDR's place in 1945, it seems that Truman's most satisfying career had been as an artillery captain in World War I. As President, he turned easily to military solutions for problems such as strikes (as when he unconstitutionally seized the steel mills in 1952) or political conflicts (as in Greece). But it was also in his administration that the first decisive steps were taken to halt—or at least very much to reduce—racism in the military, and he vetoed the antilabor Taft-Hartley Act of 1947 (which the very conservative and GOP-dominated Congress promptly overrode).

Truman was virtually unknown outside of Missouri when he was selected to be FDR's running mate in the 1944 election, a move generally seen as a means of dumping then Vice President Henry Wallace who, especially in foreign policy, was much closer to FDR than was Truman. If Wallace was too liberal in his international outlook to continue as V.P., the other principal contender, James Byrnes, was too conservative in his domestic positions to fill the bill. Truman fitted nicely in between.

Truman never spoke of "the American Century," and probably didn't believe in it, but he made or supported all the relevant policies. The result came to be called "cold war liberalism" in the 1960s—a combination of a muscular foreign policy with a "Fair Deal" domestic policy, both of them lubricated by a vigorous anticommunism. Truman was tenacious about both sets of policies; he was tenacious about everything: "Give 'em hell, Harry!" was the advice he liked and naturally took.

Certainly among the most momentous of his decisions were those having to do with U.S. policy in Germany and Japan. Both nations were occupied by our troops for many years and effectively controlled to the degree that cold war policies were ruling—with numberless and crucial economic and political consequences for all parties concerned.[18]

Truman confronted the problems in Central Europe and the Far East—most especially in Korea, China, and Vietnam—much as though he were the sheriff in "High Noon": facing down both the Asian enemies and the swaggering General MacArthur (as will be seen shortly).[19]

But he used none of his moxie to slow down what became the juggernaut of McCarthyism. Indeed, as will soon be shown, both the beginnings and the successes of McCarthyism are owed first and foremost to the arguments and policies of the Truman Doctrine enunciated after 1946: "The practices of McCarthyism were Truman's practices in cruder hands, just as the language of McCarthyism was Truman's language, in less well-meaning voices."[20]

What then do Truman's admirers see as his virtues and accomplishments? The virtues fall mainly into the "down home" quality he always manifested: "nothing fancy about Harry." That included his chip on the shoulder manner of dealing with almost any problem and almost anybody, from unsympathetic reporters to General MacArthur to Stalin (if not to Joe McCarthy or J. Edgar Hoover). Those in the political center, such as Bill Clinton, see Truman's Fair Deal domestic policies as his prime virtue; for those further to the right, the followers of Bush and Reagan, his prime virtue was his ardent support of the Cold War and the U.S. hegemony that was—and that provided—its bread and butter. We now examine the latter a bit more, with further looks in later chapters.

iii.

Brave New World Economy

As the world economy moved from weakness to implosion in the 1920s, and then found a worse fate in the 1930s—world trade dropped by two-thirds between 1929 and 1933—the economics profession and the western world's politicians looked back nostalgically to the nineteenth century, as a golden age.

The term is more than a metaphor, insofar as those nostalgic for that past also saw the international gold standard (which reigned for more than half a century before 1914) as being the prime cause of that "peaceful" and expanding era, and they believed that by holding on to it (or bringing it back) the good times would once again roll. In fact the effort to so, and what it precluded in the way of other (fiscal and structural) policies, made a bad situation considerably worse.

The rule of that standard then was the *de facto* rule by Great Britain or, more narrowly, of its (privately-owned and controlled) Bank of England. Britain was the world's hegemon in that period, and its economy increasingly dominated by finance more than production. "Economics" was simply and solely neoclassical economics, obsessed with the fantasies of "perfect competition" and the "free market" (as the age of monopoly rushed into existence), its policies confined to "monetarism"—exercised then, as now, through the central bank: The Bank of England then, the Fed (and, in Europe, the Bundesbank) now.

Such economics and such policies, dominant in the late nineteenth century, have ominously come to be so once more in our own time—inspired here and now by Milton Friedman. That the monetarists have so often held sway over public policy is a measure more of the power of the financial world over the State—as witness "even" Clinton's obeisance to Wall Street—than of the strength of their analytic position. It was precisely that kind of analysis and policy (and their disastrous shortcomings for the crisis of the Twenties and Thirties) that Keynes sought to displace with his *General Theory of Employment, Interest, and Money* in 1936.

In its nineteenth century heyday, the healthy world economy had depended upon strong waves of expansion induced by spreading industrialization, with interacting effects on domestic capital accumulation and world trade. Done in by its own successes—excess productive capacities when measured against limited purchasing power—and by the limited vacant economic space on the world's surface, the world economy and its national economies hurtled toward economic and military catastrophe.

But with the passage of the chaotic and bloody decades after 1914, the Cold War—not gold or monetarism or free markets—created a new and, by the 1950s, an always more rapidly and pervasively expanding world economy. All the major steps in that direction were led by the United States. The first and most critical among them had begun before Truman took office in 1945 and were accomplished by the time he left in 1952: the International Monetary Fund (IMF) and the International Bank for Reconstruction and Development (the World Bank) were created (at Bretton Woods, NH) in 1944, and the General Agreement on Tariffs and Trade (GATT) in 1947 (at Havana). Taken together, these three creations sought to do for the United States through conscious institutionalization what had come about for Britain, along with its vast empire "in a fit of absent-mindedness," in the very different world of a century earlier.

The world empire of the United States was umbilically dependent upon the Cold War, and may be seen as a sphere with two halves, both at home and abroad: 1) a militarized foreign policy combined with ample subsidies (especially for Germany and Japan) and movements toward the freeing up of world trade, and 2) a domestic policy combining social liberalism with political repression.

It should come as no surprise that when Truman left the White House his place was taken by a general, albeit an amiable one: "Uncle Ike." But the most powerful man in the United States for an agonizing two years or so was not President Eisenhower but Senator Joe McCarthy—the thuggish *capo* of anti-communism, U.S.-style.

Having said that, I cannot but remember that the 1940s ended with an event of rather different meaning, the birth of my son Jeff. That in turn prompts me to return to an area discussed for the Twenties but set aside until now and that could be seen as having at least some bearing on what follows.

iv.

Family Matters

It may be recalled that the family that produced me was a rickety construct, even by the rapidly disintegrating standards of the 1920s. The little cluster of which I became in some sense the *paterfamilias* in the 1940s was a refracted portrait of that early history: like my mother, I was divorced only once; like my father, I was married three times. My first wife was descended from Russian Jews, my second from Irish Catholics, and my third and present wife from Italian Catholics: or lapsed Catholics, and non-observant Jews.

Zirel, my first wife, was my dear cousin Marilyn's closest friend. She was thirteen when I met her at Marilyn's thirteenth birthday party. Of the perhaps dozen or so young people present, I alone was over fourteen: I was very tall, not ugly, and, because I was then seventeen, a very glamorous person for Zirel. For some years after that first meeting, I think it is neither inaccurate nor immodest to say that I was pursued by her. Zirel was attractive, bright, and funny, moving in the same political directions as I, and she was determined that I would be hers. We started to "date" once in a while when I was nineteen or twenty.

We had good reasons to be friends (and still are), but I doubt that we would have gone much beyond intermittent dating had it not been for Ada. Her husband, a prominent doctor, had died when Zirel was four; and Ada rightly perceived that—half-*goy* and already a bit shady—I was not on my way toward becoming the "nice Jewish doctor," of her dream and insistence for her daughter. So, Ada uttered a fateful injunction: "You must not see Douglas again." Zirel and I of course drew ever closer together. About two years later we were married—the day I finished army flying school at Williams Field, in Arizona.

I mentioned earlier that Zirel was a person of some determination: now hear this.

Story: True Grit

The day after we were married, I, along with my fellow shiny new pilots, received papers sending us by troop train to Salt Lake City, Utah, to await further orders. I said *troop* train. Zirel accompanied the pack of us to the train station and there, while *we* were all milling around, *she* managed to persuade the "conductor" to allow her to join me for the trip—and, what's more, to give us a compartment for ourselves. War, honeymoon, all that. We were periodically shunted off to a sidetrack, and the trip took several days. While Zirel and I stayed in our compartment; the dozens of young men (average age: twenty), bursting with good health, high spirits, and uncontained adolescent lust and envy, drummed on the door, and livened our days and nights with extraordinarily amusing japes. War is hell.

Soon after, off I went to my fate in the Pacific, not to return for another two-and-a-half years. The marriage, not made of sturdy stuff from the beginning, had become flimsier by our separation: Zirel had her distractions at the university and I my own variety in the Pacific for that long period. I may say that I remember the shocked look on her face when we first met upon my return—I was down to 140 lbs., my skin colored a sickly yellow by atabrine (an antimalarial drug), and all in all far from fit for the responsibilities of an adult emotional relationship. Nor, perhaps, was Zirel: both our childhoods had been devoid of the kind of parental love that allows emotions to develop healthily.

Be that as it may, I'll not forget the conversation we had in 1948. Zirel: "This is a shitty marriage; let's get a divorce." Doug: "Why not?" Zirel (who, like me, didn't know when to stop talking): "Or, we could have a kid?" Doug: "Whatever you want." I still can't believe it. But that's how Jeff and (because of the prevalent belief that one should not have only one child) Jenny came into the world. And we got the divorce a dozen or so years after that conversation.

The last time I saw Ada, many years after the divorce, it was as a kindness to give her a needed lift to Berkeley. As we were riding along, discussing the then status of "the family," I reminded her of her having forbidden Zirel to see me, lo! those many years ago. She fixed me with a hard look and said, grimly: "I was right."

But enough of this lovemaking; let's get back to business.

CRY "HAVOC!" AND LET SLIP THE DOGS OF WAR: McCARTHYISM, KOREA, AND OTHER NIGHTMARES

I saw the best minds of my generation destroyed by madness, starving hysterical naked,
dragging themselves through the negro streets at dawn looking for an angry fix,
angelheaded hipsters burning for the ancient heavenly connection to the starry dynamo in the machinery of night. . . .

—Allen Ginsberg, "Howl"

The college students of the 1950s were characterized—and reproached—as "the silent generation." There was, to be sure, a certain kind of silence; but, as one who was teaching during those years either in California or New York, I remember it as mysterious, the quasi-silence of a simmering pot.

There was substantial reason for students (among others) to simmer and smoke: the decade of the 1950s was rife with enormous changes demanding discussion and protest, but they were also years in which discussion and protest were punished in punishing ways. They were the years par excellence of McCarthyism and the simultaneous escalation of the Cold War, at home and abroad.

The years from 1945 through 1952, the Truman era, were those in which it seemed that through a mad magician's sleight of hand a victorious, immeasurably strong and free nation found itself ensnared by an Attorney General's List of Subversive Organizations, a Presidential Loyalty Review Board, purges of "reds" in the entertainment industry, the renewed military draft, a war as bloody in its effects as it was mystified in its origins and name (a "United Nations Police Action") in Korea, and, neither last nor least, loyalty oaths in unions and universities.

Story: You Can Run, But You Can't Hide

A national wave of loyalty oaths for universities began with that ordered by the Regents (trustees) of the several campuses of the University of California, in 1950. I was then a Lecturer at Berkeley, where the faculty opposition was initially formidable. Along with other Lecturers, Instructors, and Teaching and Research Assistants, I had helped to organize the Non-Senate Academic Employees Association to oppose the oath, and the Senate allowed us one delegate to attend their meetings. I was that one.

At the first, largest, and most fiery meeting, Robert A. Brady (who had chaired my Ph.D. committee and, as noted earlier, had written a major study of the rise of German fascism) proposed that the hundreds of faculty members at the meeting pledge to go on strike until the revocation of the oath requirement. A vote was taken and it passed with virtual unanimity. Brady then proposed that all who had voted "yes" sign a statement to that effect, and the statement was written up, and was passed around for signatures. As that was happening, another economics professor (who had been brought from Germany through Brady's assistance), after stating that he didn't know what he was signing, moved that a committee be appointed to study the situation, and . . . That was the end of that. The committee came up with its solution: all those sign the oath who will, all others appear before the Committee on Academic Tenure where they would explain why they hadn't signed—in effect, that is, a verbal signing. Subsequently, the California Supreme Court found the oath unconstitutional, the state legislature passed a bill requiring an oath for *all* state employees and churches and charitable institutions seeking tax exemptions (vetoed by then Governor Earl Warren), an initiative amending the Constitution was placed on the ballot, and the electorate passed it two-to-one. I signed, made up my mind to get the hell out of there as soon as I could, and I accepted an offer from Cornell University, which had no oath. But while I was on my way there, the New York legislature instituted its own oath. The welcoming committee at Cornell apologized, handed me the oath, and I signed it.

The Regents were responding to the swelling wave of repression in putting forth their oath; but they had shown a certain precocity some years earlier—1947, as I recall—when they sought to set a precedent not only for professors, but also for entertainers. A few years later the whole entertainment industry had caved in. But at Berkeley, one man on one night made the Regents look like damned fools.

Story: Don't Tread on Me

Paul Robeson was a giant of a man and a great man, in every way. He was a good six-and-a-half feet tall, a serious thinker, an electrifying actor and singer with a voice as deep as the ocean; very black, very handsome, very much admired over the world. He was often (mistakenly) thought to be a member of the Communist Party, U.S.A.—up to then one of the very few (largely white) political groups working for racial equality in the United States—in part because he made no attempt to hide his support for their efforts.

A concert with Robeson as the sole performer was scheduled for the campus. The Regents promptly stated that Robeson could appear *only* if he confined himself to singing: no speeches. After much kerfuffle (as they say in upstate New York), the concert was allowed, on those terms.

The prolonged controversy caused the main auditorium to be sold out and, to accommodate the overflow, a sound connection was made to the second largest hall on the campus.

As the evening began, the large stage was empty except for Robeson's piano accompanist. Robeson slowly walked on the stage before a stone-silent audience and, in a voice so low it seemed there was "space" between each vibration, Robeson began to speak. I remember what he said, word for word: "I have been forbidden to speak tonight, and I shall comply with that order—after explaining to you why it has happened. It is because I have shown support for what is seen as the devilish Communist Party, and have expressed my friendship for the Soviet Union. And why would I have done such things? Because I am a black man. Because I have traveled the length and the breadth of the United States as a singer and actor, and wherever I have gone I have taken the time to ask this question of the people I have met: 'How long do you think it will be before there will be full equality for black people in the United States—economic, political, and social equality?' Please believe me when I say that the most optimistic answer I have received is 1,000 years. My son can't wait that long; nor can I."

And then he delivered Othello's magnificent last monologue ("I have done the state some service, and they know't. . . ."); and then he began to sing. (As I am typing these words, I have shivered, as I and surely almost everyone in the audience that night did.)

i.

Growing in Office

Also chilling—but more in the reptilian vein than the Shakespearean—was Truman's explanation for his own actions and character. Truman recounts his personal history as that of a man possessed by honesty and high purpose. But his was a political career which from its very beginnings until he entered the White House was indebted to one of the very most corrupt of U.S. political "machines"—an honor for which there has been no little competition. And, while seeing himself as a man of peace and goodwill, Truman was ever quick with the forceful solution, always prone to characterize his political foes as "sons of bitches."

After all, this was the man of peace who repeatedly, unsuccessfully, tried to establish "Universal Military Training" for young people as the "ideal disciplinary approach for getting along with one another." In the 1950s, the patent absurdity of the concept defeated it.

As World War II ended there was of course a deep global crisis, socioeconomic and political. From the standpoint of the United States, its most important location was in the leading industrial capitalist nations of Europe and their dependencies—beset by shattered national economies and no global economy, colonies soon to be lost, and governments defeated or discredited over the course of the war.

But there was no *military* crisis as World War II ended. Because the Cold War produced a culture of militarization as it evolved, it has been easy to overlook that military conflict was an outcome, not a cause of the Cold War between the United States and the Soviet Union—the latter, as noted earlier, the country most severely damaged by the war in all ways.

In the United States there was a crisis of a different sort, a new and utterly inexperienced Democratic president facing a Congress solidly under the control of the Republican Party, aided and abetted by a large bloc of conservative Democrats, mostly from the South. [21] Had Truman and his principal advisors sought to gain from that Congress a program of economic aid and reconstruction for Europe only on economic grounds, there is no doubt it would have failed. But, as with the dropping of the atomic bomb for political rather than any justifiable military reasons, Truman went along (enthusiastically, one must note) with the use of dangerously inflammatory rhetoric, painting the Soviet Union as poised to invade one or another part of Europe. That the Soviet Union was not capable of such steps was clear—not least of all to those well-informed advisors.

It may be added here that both with respect to the economic crisis in Greece and the subsequent efforts to fund the Marshall Plan, initial attempts to justify the programs on humanitarian grounds were abandoned when it became clear they would fail. There was no single basis for finding majority support for the Plan; but putting together "humanitarian" with economic with strategic arguments turned the trick. The controversy was in part represented between my brother and myself. A Story.

Story: Brothers (Under the Skin)

In 1948, after the Marshall Plan had been passed by Congress, my brother and I were having a moonlit walk at Lake Tahoe and—as only rarely occurred—discussing politics, and he was upset about the Plan. "Why can't those goddamn Europeans take care of themselves, like us?" he demanded. Even though I also objected to the Plan, it was not on those grounds, and I did my best to try to convince Merv that the plight of the Europeans was not an outcome of laziness and stupidity; and failed. A few years later, I failed again, when I sought to argue against McCarthyism by, among other arguments, saying "Don't you realize that McCarthy would put your own brother in prison if he could?" "For Christ's sake, Doug" my brother replied, "now what have you done?" We began to come closer together on such matters during the Vietnam war: for my birthday dinner in 1973 he presented me with a life-sized bust of Nixon which was in fact a candle; we had our dinner and spent the evening as Nixon's head slowly melted away.

If humanitarian and plain economic arguments would not persuade Congress to legislate what became the Truman Doctrine, other arguments had to be found. And they were. By the time Truman presented his program to Congress (in March of 1947) his position had been militarized. It combined the stance of Undersecretary of State Acheson regarding Soviet "pressure" on the Straits of Dardanelles, in Greece and in Iran, with Assistant Secretary of State Clayton's conviction that the people of the United States must be "shocked into taking world leadership," and that of Senator Vandenberg that the President would have to "scare the hell out of the country" to get the aid for Greece and Turkey. In addition to the fact that Stalin had resolutely *refused* aid to the Greek guerrillas, the crisis in Greece, which had been portrayed as requiring U.S. aid within two months (from March) if collapse was not to ensue, received *no* aid until eight months later, by which time the crisis had subsided. Thus, as Freeland states,

> it is difficult not to conclude that the crisis of March 1947 had its origins in American politics rather than in Greece. [22]

The content of the Truman Doctrine had consequences in the United States going well beyond those in Greece; most vividly in providing both an institutional and rhetorical foundation for McCarthyism. However, you would never know it, listening to Harry Truman on the subject:

I cussed out old McCarthy every chance I got. He was nothing but a damn coward, and he was afraid of me. . . . And when Eisenhower let McCarthy get away with calling General Marshall a traitor. Why that was one of the most shocking things in the history of this country. The trouble with Eisenhower . . . he's just a coward. He hasn't got any backbone at all, and he ought to be ashamed for what he did, but I don't think there's any shame in him. (pp. 133-134)

Et tu, Mr. President? And then there is the question of J. Edgar Hoover, diligent hunter of civil rights activists (most especially Martin Luther King), of homosexuals and "reds" in government, universities, wherever; but not so diligent in pursuing those in organized crime. "Mr. President," asked Merle Miller, "what did you think of J. Edgar Hoover?"

To tell you the truth, I never gave him all that much thought. . . . As long as he did his job, I didn't pay too much attention to him. One time they brought me a lot of stuff about his personal life, and I told them I didn't give a damn about that. That wasn't my business. It was what he did while he was at work that was my business. [23]

So. Harry Truman departed Washington confident that his had been a presidency of grand accomplishments, at home and abroad. There were of course positive accomplishments. But much of what seemed to be accomplishment in his day and for a generation or so afterward has latterly revealed itself as a basis for present or future disaster—in the socioeconomic basket cases of Eastern Europe, the no longer subsidized neocolonial (of one or another cold war patron) societies, and in the "downsizing" and fragile Group of Seven economies: neither most nor least, that of the United States.

Now it is appropriate to examine the various elements and meanings of the Cold War for the economies of the United States, Western Europe, and Japan, as well as for the new and, for a while, dazzling world economy. After that, our attention will turn to the Korean war and some of the other unsettling developments of the 1950s.

ii.

Brother, Can You Spare a Tank?

Writing in 1963, the author of what remains the definitive economic history of the 1950s, after asserting that "'the poor are always with us' became a dated proposition in the 1950s," goes on to explain that it was in the 1950s

> that the United States truly became the affluent society. . . . Real per capita consumption (1960 prices) rose from $1,350 in the last year of the war to . . . $1,824 in 1960. Had capacity been more completely utilized and had the large military budgets of the decade been absent or even substantially reduced, the full-capacity peacetime consumption potential of the American economy would have been even greater. [24]

Such observations were reasonably common at the time they were assembled; still, one is led to ask why the capacity that *could* have been more completely utilized was not, and wonder how much less it was likely to have been utilized if the military budgets of the decade *had* been absent. Also, one must add that by 1963 the poor, far from having disappeared because of the presumed affluence of the 1950s, were instead becoming a national scandal. [25]

The ensuing "war on poverty" of the 1960s reduced national poverty significantly, but in the past fifteen years or so poverty levels have risen once more: at an accelerating rate and, strikingly, with the poor becoming poorer while—and, in important respects, because—the rich became much richer. [26] But let us now examine the the reasons for and the degree to which "affluence" emerged in the decade.

In addition to and preceding the decisive economic impact of the Cold War in the 1950s, were the kinds and amounts of "pent-up demand" for consumer and investment goods in the United States as World War II ended.

There had been "overfull employment" in the U.S. economy from 1942 through 1945; but inflation was kept to a remarkable minimum. Thus, high and sustained wages in the context of severe shortages of almost everything were not dissipated in price inflation and consumer savings, not least through bond sales, were at an all-time high. In addition, more than 16 million people were in the armed forces throughout the war, and something over 10 million at the time the war ended. Almost all of them saved money, and many of us received bonuses, accumulated "wages," and other forms of payments as we shed our uniforms—most especially, yours truly.

Story: The Mixed Blessings of War

In my case, I am pleased to report there was over $5,000 in cash, a small fortune in 1945 dollars, in large part due to the bonus for signing up for pilot training *before* the war—which I had done to avoid the draft and the infantry, two days before my birthday, two days before Pearl Harbor—signing up also for five years in the reserve, with a $500 bonus for each year of active service (= $2,000 for me). (In addition to the bonus, I had accumulated a lot of unused R&R time = $3,000+.) By late 1946, I had been in the reserve for my allotted five years. So: from an earlier Story it may be remembered I had not fallen under the spell of the colonel in 1945 who tried to persuade all of us to join the postwar reserve for another hitch. One day the telephone rang: "Captain Dowd?" "You must have the wrong number." "Is this Douglas F. Dowd?" "Yes, but I am not a captain, I am a mister." "This is Major L., Captain Dowd. You are in the reserve, and subject to call-up." "I am not in any reserve, I am not a captain of anything, and that's that." "Captain Dowd, you are due for your physical examination next Tuesday at 1500 hours at [some address]. If you do not appear, your name will be turned over to Selective Service and you will be drafted." I hung up. About a week later I received a letter from HQ Fourth Army Air Force, Hamilton Field, CA., in which there occurred this memorable military-ese sentence: "You have not answered the several letters addressed to you in your capacity as a reservist. A reservist who does not reply to the letters of HQ Fourth Army Air Force is of no use to HQ Fourth Army Air Force. If you do not answer this letter within ten days, your name will be turned over to your Selective Service Board for immediate induction into the U.S. Army as a private." After muttering a few oaths under my breath, I filed the letter in the garbage and never heard from them again, by phone or by mail. But some of my former buddies did, and found themselves in Korea.

The direct consequence of the pent-up war—connected demand was a scrambling for all kinds of consumer goods for several years after 1945: autos, furniture and appliances, dry goods and clothing, and a higher level of food consumption—for what seemed a very long time after the war one had to have a friend in the butcher shop to get a steak; and butter and other niceties were hard to find. To say nothing of housing: because of the mountain of purchasing power—plus many new families, and also because of the substantial rural to urban migration that accompanies and follows a war—there was an enduring shortage of apartments and houses in all cities.

The war had also meant the neglect of maintenance for the largest part of agriculture and industry and public transportation. Rundown equipment had to be replaced, often with technologically more advanced techniques. Countless war plants were to be converted to non-military production—from tanks to trucks, machine guns to typewriters, and so on. Rundown public utilities (water, gas and electricity, telephones) similarly needed replacement and modernization—something like the deterioration of our "infrastructure" that accompanied the Cold War years.

To all of which may be added the spending by cities, states, and the federal government: on roads, schools, bridges, and the like, not just because of wartime neglect, but because of expanding cities, expanding schools and colleges (the latter most especially, at first, because of the GI Bill which made university education feasible for millions, myself included)—and later, because of governmentally financed research and educational programs.

And then there were the direct and indirect economic consequences of the Cold War: the military spending that rose rapidly as the 1950s began (especially, but not only, for the Korean war); along with the rise in agricultural and industrial exports produced by U.S. aid programs and resurrecting economies abroad, all of them (including exports) having what economists call the "multiplier effect" (that is, two to three times private dollars of income and spending as a result of those public—and net export—dollars of spending).

Thus: all things considered, it would have been astounding if the period from 1945 through the 1950s had *not* been economically buoyant. What does deserve comment is that there was significant market slack from time to time, that there were no shortages of *any*thing, and no inflation (except as a blip at the onset of Korea).

There were no shortages of anything during the 1950s—or, for that matter, from 1948 to the present—despite extraordinary increases in consumption, real business investment, and many trillions of dollars of military and other forms of governmental spending. Indeed, the 1950s, though buoyant, did offer periods of concern, and were also seen as not providing rapid enough economic growth or enough jobs. *That's* what has to be explained about the economy of the 1950s, that even the momentum from World War II, plus the Cold War and the Korean War, and an expanding world economy, still left some slack in the U.S. economy. Why?

The years of economic expansion after 1945 have had numerous and diverse bases. The war-induced pent-up demands of individuals, businesses, and governments at all levels were petering out by the end of the Forties; indeed the recession that took hold in 1948 may be explained almost entirely by the dwindling down of that demand. The end of the 1940s was also the end of pre-Keynesian governmental policy; from the 1950s on, no recession until that of 1990 was ever allowed to show its head above the trenches without a burst of stimulative fiscal and monetary policies. It was what accurately came to be called "military Keynesianism." [27] The mix of policies was not, however, what Keynes would have proposed or accepted.

The recession of the late Forties was almost over before the Korean war erupted in June of 1950. As will be noted shortly, that war was an outgrowth, a cause, and an accompaniment of the accelerating Cold War, as in 1949 and 1950 the Communist revolution succeeded in China and the Soviets developed their own atomic bomb. All that, taken together with linked business and consumer expectations, transformed what in 1950 might have been a modest cyclical uptick into, instead, a strong expansion. As Gordon summarizes it:

> It was during this period, after the end of 1950, that the big rise in military expenditures occurred and a substantial budgetary surplus was converted into a sizable deficit. Federal expenditures on new goods and services more than doubled . . . between the fourth quarters of 1950 and 1951 [and] continued to rise, though more slowly, to [their] peak . . . in the second quarter of 1953.

As noted earlier, there was a brief inflationary surge as the Korean war began, and as both consumers and businesses were spurred by war memories to hoard (the business version of which is to add to inventories). Soon after price and wage controls were introduced (early in 1951) inflationary pressures subsided—to the point where there was "some recession in private buying" as both consumers and businesses found themselves overstocked. [27a]

The expansion was over by the summer of 1953: unemployment dropped to 2.5 percent in July. In the decades since then, the rate has never been that low again—nor, as matters now stand, does it seem likely ever again to be. The recession that began in 1953 was mild and had ended before the end of 1954—followed by another mild recession in 1957-58, mostly due to a decline in durable-goods investment. In both cases, the mildness of recession was assured by the new role of the State and the way in which "automatic stabilizers" came into play: government payments rose while receipts fell slightly. Consumption was well maintained. . . .[28]

The role of institutionalized State intervention in the economy was finally taking hold in the United States. After World War I, it will be recalled, the role of State was sharply diminished, and the ideology of "laissez-faire" capitalism enshrined. When that development was reborn in the Reagan era—and called "the free market economy"—it was accompanied by the highest levels and wildest types of deficit-financed State spending, acting as a support—indeed a life-support system—for private capitalism.

Saying this, it is time to turn attention once more to the political framework within which the 1950s developed, its principal "actors" being McCarthyism, the Korean war, and Dwight Eisenhower as President.

iii.
Nothing Lost, Save Honor

The loyalty review boards and Attorney General's subversive lists of the late 1940s were but the first chapter of what became a very long book. What was evidently unclear to Democratic policymakers is that the weapons of political repression they deemed useful to implement the Truman Doctrine could also be turned against them—and used for almost anything that might come to mind in what was becoming an increasingly mindless society.

The principal gunslinger of that unpleasant surprise was, of course, Joe McCarthy, junior Senator from Wisconsin (Rep.), elected first in 1946.[29] Whatever else the effects of McCarthy were, and they were many, there can be no doubt that the presidential election of 1952—the year in which McCarthy was at his most powerful (and easily re-elected)—would not have been the flop it was for the Democrats without McCarthyism. And, in one of history's many ironies, McCarthyism is unlikely to have existed without the Truman Administration's orchestration of the Cold War. The main truth about Joe McCarthy is, and was, the transparent humbug of his accusations and of his general position. He was, more than anything else, a sharpie in the familiar tradition of the snake-oil salesman.

Snapshot: Tail Gunner Joe [30]

During "twenty years of treason," as Senator McCarthy put it, the Democrats, led by Roosevelt and Truman, had "conspired" to deliver America to the Reds. F.D.R. got into World War II mainly to help Russia, and gave away everything to Stalin at Yalta; Harry presented China to the Reds and recalled General MacArthur because he was about to beat them; Alger Hisses were concealed in every government office, college, and corporation, ready to take over when Stalin pushed the button.[31] A drunk, a cynic, and an incompetent, McCarthy searched in 1950 for some means of gaining support for his re-election in 1952. His equally cynical advisers gave him that issue: Communists in the Truman Administration. At a public meeting in West Virginia he announced "I have here in my hand a list of 205 [employees] that were made known to the Secretary of State [Dean Acheson] as being members of the Communist Party and who nevertheless are still working and shaping policy...." It mattered not then, and evidently it matters not still, that no person on that "list" was ever in fact *named* let alone shown to be "guilty." What does matter a great deal is that our society was altering in such a fashion that an irresponsible brute such as McCarthy could gain enormous and intimidating power, achieved by climbing a ladder constructed of innuendo, lies, and threats. When he was finally brought to earth it was not because of the damage he was doing to the social process, but because his basic stupidity led him to accuse the U.S. Army of harboring Communists at high levels. Its spine temporarily stiffened by an enraged Pentagon, the U.S. Senate in 1954 voted to criticize McCarthy for bringing "dishonor and disrepute" to that presumably august body. Even that mildest of affronts was voted against by twenty-two of our distinguished senators. After that, McCarthy dithered into oblivion and in 1957 died of cirrhosis of the liver—still a United States Senator.

But when Joe died, McCarthyism did not. As its poison spread through the nation, it ruined numberless people while becoming the central issue of U.S. politics. It was relatively easy (and predictable) for anti-communism to mutate by the 1980s (and earlier) into anti-liberalism. In McCarthy's day, the "accused liberal" was portrayed as a secret Communist or, at least as effectively, as a "communist dupe"; more recently, the sin is one of being a liberal *per se*. Is it impossible to imagine that the brush could one day become so broad as to touch moderate conservatives *per se*?

The career of Richard Nixon exemplifies the development. His elections as U.S. Representative, then U.S. Senator, then Vice President, and finally, twice, as President, all had their foundations cemented in his mastery of anticommunism. Nixon was among the very first to scent political power for himself in that practice, when in 1946 he won a congressional seat on the basis of characterizing moderately liberal Representative Jerry Voorhis as a deep-dyed Red, went on to fame in the House Un-American Activities Committee interrogations of Alger Hiss in 1948, and won a senate seat in 1950 by portraying Helen Gahagan Douglas (a liberal) as a flaming radical. By 1952, Nixon was running neck-and-neck with McCarthy as the Big Chief of anticommunism. Running for Vice President and serving as Ike's bully boy, Nixon's ripe style was fully-displayed in his attacks on Ike's opponent, the conservative Cold Warrior Adlai Stevenson: "Adlai the appeaser . . . , a Ph.D. graduate of Dean Acheson's Cowardly College of Communist Containment." (Acheson, among the *illuminati* of Wall Street, was, of course, one of the Cold War's principal and most aggressive architects. But neither Joltin' Joe nor Tricky Dick ever let such details disturb his analysis.)

iv.

Into the Valley of Death

The seemingly endless horror of the war in Vietnam—the longest ever, and the most clearcut defeat for the United States—has allowed the much briefer but even more murderous Korean war to slip from popular memory, [32] as regards its origins, its nature, and its consequences. Yet it may be asserted that had it not been for the Korean war, and the McCarthyism and agitation over the Chinese revolution that accompanied and intensified it, the war in Indochina (and much else) would have been a lot less likely. [33]

Korea was the first hot war of the Cold War, and it was very hot indeed: its death toll remains by far the largest of the period, it took the world closer to nuclear conflagration than ever since (even including the 1962 Cuban missile crisis), and its ramifications seem to be endless.

The formal war lasted three years, from June 1950 into July 1953. Like the war in Vietnam, it was a civil war; and both wars required a massive involvement of U.S. troops and weaponry if the civil war was not to be quickly won by "the other side." [34]

Let us look first at the devastation the war caused in Korea, and then ask how and why it began, and why it was so ferocious. Jon Halliday and Bruce Cumings write,

The total number of people killed was almost certainly well over 3 million—possibly more like 4 million—in a nation whose population was some 30 million when the war started. Although these figures may seem high, if one takes into account the almost unbelievable intensity of the bombing, the shortage of medical facilities, the lack of food and the extreme cold and lack of shelter in the context of a scorched-earth policy and the systematic destruction of livestock, they are not implausible. By far the largest number died in North Korea. . . . Our estimate is that over 2 million North Korean civilians died and about 500,000 North Korean soldiers. In addition, some 1 million Chinese soldiers probably died (although one first-hand Chinese source has put the figure at 3 million). South Korean civilian deaths were about 1 million; Southern battle-related deaths were some 47,000; non-battle-related military deaths were probably higher. US deaths are put at 54,246, of whom 33,629 were "battle deaths." The total number of battle deaths among other forces came to 3,194. . . .[35]

From the beginning, General Douglas MacArthur was in charge of the U.S. (or, as it was called the "U.N.") effort.[36] He was removed by President Truman in April of 1951 for his headstrong interpretation of his powers (and refusal to see Truman as Commander-in-Chief), and his clear intent to carry the war into and over the skies of China by any means possible.[37] There were still two years of intensive ground fighting, conventional and napalm bombing, and naval shelling to be endured when MacArthur observed (in 1951, before Congress):

The war in Korea has almost destroyed that nation. I have never seen such devastation. I have seen, I guess, as much blood and disaster as any living man, and it just curdled my stomach the last time I was there. After I looked at that wreckage and those thousands of women and children and everything, I vomited.[37]

MacArthur had only seen the South. The North was bombed and burned much worse, and much worse was on its way. *Item:* up to the last days of the war, the U.S. Navy shelled the northern coastal city of Wonsan twenty-four hours a day uninterruptedly for 861 days. (During most of the period, peace negotiations were going on.) *Item:* Pyongyang, the capital of North Korea, was reduced to something less than rubble; photographs of it in 1953 seem to be of Hiroshima. *Item:* in the last year of the war, the main hydroelectric dams providing most of the North's electric power were blasted to uselessness. *Item:* napalm, much of it manufactured in Japan, was being dropped ceaselessly on villages throughout the North for three years, leaving nothing of life behind.[38]

What motivated such seemingly mindless destructiveness?

More: what was it that led MacArthur—and also Truman and Acheson—to propose and prepare for the use of atomic bombs in Korea and China?[39]

How and why did Korea take on such proportions? As the war was coming to a close, this is what Churchill said:

> Korea does not really matter now. I'd never heard of the bloody place until I was seventy-four. Its importance lies in the fact that it has led to the re-arming of America. [40]

Not quite as eloquent as some of Churchill's other pronouncements, but close to the bones of truth: as for so many other countries that have become graveyards, Korea's tragedy was a means to the larger ends of the Superpowers. Was it at least an end that can be dignified in words? It seems not. What did bring war to Korea?

The general and lasting impression about the origins of the Korean war, especially in the United States, is simple, too simple: North Korea invaded South Korea. Indeed there was such an invasion. But that fact, when examined in its historical context, raises more questions than it answers.

Japan established a "protectorate" over Korea in 1905, annexed it a few years later, used it and abused it in ways customary to colonial powers and, during the war, went beyond the established boundaries of even those cruelties and indecencies. [41] And then in 1945,

> Japanese armies, according to Soviet-American agreement, were disarmed north of the 38th parallel by Russia and south of the line by the United States. Lengthy conferences failed to unify the nation, for neither the Soviets nor the Americans wanted to chance the possibility that a unified Korea would move into the opposing camp. [42]

From the moment of its establishment as a dividing line, the 38th parallel took on a life of its own, and became a looming Frankenstein monster. The "line that was found . . . cut across natural areas of geographic, cultural, and climatic continuity." [43] How and why was the dividing line established? The answer to that question well represents the deadly mix of accident and design, strategy and hysteria, that underlay U.S. foreign policy as the 1950s began.

The Soviet Union had promised the United States it would declare war on Japan no more than three months after the end of the European war. In the event, that meant early August 1945; and it also implied the probability of Soviet troops in Manchuria and Korea. The importance of this probability and, among other matters, its role in creating the 38th parallel deserve sustained attention:

> If the Soviet Union dominated Korea, it could undermine Chiang Kai-Shek's position in China and place the security of Japan in jeopardy. Truman began to

search for a way to occupy Korea unilaterally, thereby removing any chance for Sovietization. His decision to use the atomic bomb against Japan was in part aimed at forcing Tokyo to surrender quickly and thereby preempting Soviet entry into the Pacific war. The gamble failed. [The atom bomb was dropped first on August 6.] On August 8 Stalin acted to ensure that he would play a role in reconstructing East Asia after World War II, declaring war on Japan prior to its surrender and sending the Red Army into Korea. Two days later, the State-War-Navy Coordinating Committee instructed Colonels C.H. Bonesteel and Dean Rusk [later JFK's and LBJ's Secretary of State] to find a line in Korea that would harmonize the political desire to have U.S. forces receive the surrender [of Japan] as far north as possible with the inability of the closest U.S. troops on Okinawa to reach the area before the Soviets occupied the entire peninsula. . . . Many American leaders doubted if Stalin would accept the proposal, but the Soviet leader agreed, probably in hopes of receiving a voice in the reconstruction of Japan. Truman's refusal to grant Stalin an equal role in determining Japan's future meant that Korea's reunification was unlikely from the start.[44]

Neither the Soviet Union nor the United States ever consulted with the Korean people at any level as to their wishes in this matter—naturally. As even the then conservative (usually GOP) *Herald Tribune* noted in its November 24, 1945, editorial, "There has never been a reasonable excuse for [splitting Korea in two parts], which divides a homogenous people. It is creating new political problems. The Koreans are being indoctrinated with Communistic ideas in the north and with theories of Western democracies in the south."[45] For the Koreans, when the Japanese occupation ended, two more began, followed shortly by perhaps the most ferocious war in history, in which a minimum of ten percent of Korea's population was killed, as some multiple of that was wounded, displaced and, in one way or another, damaged in who knows what ways, and for how long?

We need not dwell on the details of that civil war except to note the intermittent and serious fighting in both the North and South, but especially in the region surrounding the 38th parallel, between the main elements of the Korean civil struggle, always increasing toward 1949 and 1950.

The basic issues over which the war in 1950 was fought were apparent immediately after liberation [1945], within a three-month period, and led to open fighting that eventually claimed more than one hundred thousand lives in peasant rebellion, labor strife, guerrilla warfare, and open fighting along the thirty-eighth parallel—all this before the ostensible Korean War began. In other words, the conflict was civil and revolutionary in character, beginning just after 1945. . . .[46]

Both sides sought reunification, led by Syngman Rhee in the South and Kim Il Sung in the North. Both had followers on both sides of the parallel.

Both had to be constrained by their external supporters, and both were. When the North invaded the South in the early morning of June 25, 1950, it was after serious attacks within the preceding forty-eight hours from the South, and months of bloody exchanges, large and small.

It is likely that Korea was going to be dominated by the Soviet Union or China, although it is generally agreed that Kim Il Sung in the decade or so following World War II sought to distance himself from the two (ultimately conflicting) giants, and that he was skillful in doing so. Two things may be said with certainty: nothing could have been more disastrous for the Korean people than the three-year war that began in 1950, and none of the powerful nations ever had the interests of the Korean people in mind. Indeed, one reason for the remorseless ferocity of the war was that all Koreans, on both sides of the parallel, were generally referred to as "gooks." [47] And what that war and its permutations have meant for the rest of the world's people, ourselves included, has that yet to be taken as a matter for serious analysis—in, for example, high school history courses?

v.

I (Didn't) Like Ike

Without the parenthesized word, that was the slogan of the Eisenhower campaign of 1952. The fighting stopped in July of 1953, with an armistice. Ike probably won the election of 1952 with his promise: "I shall go to Korea." He went. It is generally agreed that only a Republican—perhaps only a Republican general—could find a way out of that war for the United States (as would happen again, if in a rather more bizarre political setting, when the Vietnam war ended).

Truman, who had begun the Cold War and laid the foundations for McCarthyism, could hardly have been entertained when he was accused of having given China away, and of having followed that up by placing us in an unwinnable war. One would like to have been there to hear Harry at that moment in 1952 when he was informed that McCarthy was calling for his impeachment as a traitor.

That the Cold War and a belligerent foreign policy were coming to substitute for a decent concern for the society at home is suggested by the fact that even though the economy and society were moving in waves of economic well-being in his two administrations, the Truman Democrats were easily shoved out of office in the 1950s. Also, even though under Eisenhower the economy was never strongly buoyant and ended the 1950s in weakness, and his favors to big business and cronies came to be the stuff of folklore—"The New Dealers have all left Washington to make way for the car dealers," quipped Adlai in 1956—Ike's popularity never stopped growing. There is no doubt he could have been elected to a third term, had it not by then become unconstitutional.

Eisenhower had a big grin (very important for a president), tended to speak in the endearing and stumbling ways that prefigured Reagan, was seen as having won the Big War and ended the Nasty War, liked Westerns and golf, and, like Truman—like the people of the United States, it seems—favored quick and military solutions.

Perhaps because he was an experienced soldier, Ike was not as incautious as some of our presidents have been, but he never burned the night oil searching out the complicated ways of peaceful solutions. Thus, while pushing for an armistice in Korea, he was also "unleashing" Chiang Kai-shek (by then, with U.S. permission, ruling over Taiwan—ex-Japanese-ruled Formosa), taking the chance of a full-scale war with China—and who knows who else and what else.

And it was after all "on his watch," as presidents seem to be saying these years, that we—mostly meaning the CIA—overturned the democratically elected governments of Iran and of Guatemala (1953 and 1954, respectively), if it was also his administration that broke the back of the Anglo-French-Israeli attack on Egypt in 1956.[48] In doing that, Ike not only punctured the balloon of further imperialist designs by Britain and France—vain, in any case—but also increased the relative strength *and* the "responsibilities" of the United States.

Already in 1957 Ike was induced by his mentor John Foster Dulles to proclaim the "Eisenhower Doctrine"—which, after giving aid to King Hussein of Jordan against a left threat, and landing 10,000 U.S. marines in Beirut against a rumored military threat from Iraq, was permitted to disappear from our language in 1959—a change, finally, for the better.

vi.

Enough Already

We need linger no longer on the details of the Fifties; nor can I bear to do so, except, in order to give a sense of one more of its awful qualities, with this:

Story: Information Booth

I joined the faculty at Cornell University in 1953. In that year, as for always before and another two decades or so after, abortion was illegal in the United States. In 1955, a woman student came to explain why she had missed an exam: she had instead had an abortion. And she wanted to inform me that it was with a "real doctor" in Pennsylvania, led to perform safe and inexpensive abortions because his own daughter had died from an illegal and botched attempt. The student gave me the name and telephone number of the doctor for the use of other women over time, and said she would let it be known that I had the information. Over the next fifteen years or so I was at Cornell, other women did likewise; and by the time I departed the university in 1971 I may well have become the best-informed source for safe abortions in the states east of the Mississippi. Which may have been the most useful thing I did there; but I hope not.

When the Sixties began, and the young Kennedy spoke of his New Frontiers, it was not generally expected that those frontiers would be at the Bay of Pigs (1961), would bring the world to the edge of World War III in the Cuban missile crisis (1962), and would take us to Indochina and the longest war in our history.

Kennedy was himself a product and a beneficiary of the Cold War and—anything but a critic of Joe McCarthy—an enthusiastic anti-communist. It was he who made the most significant early escalation of our military involvement in Vietnam, where there were 22,000 GIs by 1962. The folks of "Camelot"—those who came to be called "the best and the brightest"—were neither good enough nor smart enough even to seek to find their way through and out of the poisonous vines that were strangling the possibilities of decency and good sense for this country—and for much of the rest of the world.

It is not the Nixons and the Reagans who represent the full meaning of the cold war-shaped consciousness and character of the United States in the past several decades—it is those for whom we have had at least some respect or, if not that, then some affection: for Truman, for Ike, for Kennedy, even (perhaps especially?) for LBJ. Many people wept when they died; but the tragedy was in their lives more than in their deaths; was in the deadly and soul-killing policies they all supported and helped to create—policies the support for which, after all, made it possible for them to become Presidents of the United States.

And there is something else to be said. In laying out its cold war battalions abroad, the United States was not only militarizing its own economy, its own politics, its own culture (and to an important extent those of its allies), it was also requiring the non-capitalist countries of the world to become militarized, and even more so. Indeed, it has now been "confessed" (boasted, might be the more accurate word) by the CIA that this was our intent all along, for in the process we were crippling the possibilities of those countries moving toward realization of both their economic and political ideals. In those countries, leadership could endure only insofar as it was a militarily-inclined and fear-propelled leadership.[49]

And who can now say how much damage has been done thereby to the future possibilities of our species? *HOWL!*

4   THE SIXTIES:
FASTEN YOUR SEATBELTS

i.

The Worst-laid Plans of Mice and Men

> And it's one, two, three, what are we
> Fighting for?
> Don't ask me, I don't give a damn
> Next stop is Vietnam!
>
> —Country Joe and the Fish,
> "Feel-Like-I'm-Fixin'-To-Die Rag"

The Sixties was the decade whose deeply and often violently conflicting patterns of attitude and behavior probed and questioned matters once viewed as beyond serious dispute among "reputable" people. By the end of Sixties, indeed, to be seen as "reputable" could be taken as an insult as much as a compliment: the authorities had themselves become "disreputable."

When it is recognized that the Sixties were also the years in which our long and long-secret involvement in Vietnam (as far back as 1946, we shall see) could no longer be kept from public view it becomes easier to understand the contrasts between what were, in fact, organically interdependent processes. A nation cannot be as prosperous as the United States by the Sixties and continue to hide its tens of millions of poor from itself, or its riches from those who are poor; nor can it plausibly claim to be fighting for freedom 10,000 miles from home while many millions of its people are oppressed, largely unable to vote, and subject still—if only rarely by the 1960s—to being lynched. Etc.

From its earliest years the United States had been a nation of—and benefitting from—sharp differences among its people, but the always swirling river of our history nevertheless made us the most successful of industrial capitalist societies. In the Sixties, however, significant numbers of us, mostly but by no means entirely "under thirty," came to view that achievement as seriously flawed, and the river that carried us there as poisoned.

To us it was clear that the burden of guilt for the inequitable society and the dirty war lay on those in power who deviously concocted and continued that war: "the best and the brightest."

Pop culture and official discourse rapidly reflected the reality. The "F-word" and its many four-letter siblings were folded into our official history when the late and not sufficiently unlamented President Nixon uttered it and most of the others on the Watergate tapes that undid him—as when in the midst of the currency crisis of the early 1970s, a conversation between Nixon and his right-hand man H.R. Haldeman went this way: "Mr. President, the press is asking for a comment on the lira." "I don't give a shit about the lira," said our puritanical President.

It seems relevant (and, I trust, not merely vain) to repeat a paragraph from an essay of mine written from Italy in early 1967 when I was teaching there and feeling frustrated by my distance from the tumult and the shouting at home. The essay was entitled "An End to Alibis: America Fouls its Dream" and it concluded by commenting on what had come to be called a "credibility gap":

> A credibility gap there is, between the Administration's words and the facts. The more important credibility gap, however, is between the image that Americans like to have of their society, and what Americans work for and do, what their society is. This is not to say that, in terms of what is done, America is worse than other societies, Americans worse than other peoples; our evil consists of believing that we are better than others—and it consists as well of our being able to be so much better than we are, of our being able in fact to take our image towards reality. The gap between what Americans are in practice, and what with our ideals and our resources we should be, is as a Grand Canyon that separates actuality from possibility. President Johnson indeed represents us; like us, he cannot face—perhaps cannot comprehend—the truth. But Johnson's Gap is a line scratched in the sand; we the people have allowed the earth to open. It is this gap, this chasm between reality and ideal, that defines the American crisis. It is this gap into which "America" slides. (*The Nation*, February 1967)

Throughout that raging decade there was the crack of rifles and the stench of gas both at home and abroad, and smoke rose from the ghettoes here as it did (much more, of course) from the villages in Vietnam.

The climax was reached in 1968, here and there: the assassinations of Martin Luther King and of Bobby Kennedy, the withdrawal of LBJ from the election race, and the Chicago convention upheaval, here; the crushing blow of the Tet offensive in Vietnam, the "events" in France and Italy and Germany and the Czech uprising, one after or joining the others in a bewildering and frightening parade, there. In Chicago we carried huge banners proclaiming "Prague West."

Here now, a very long News Flash, a quick glimpse of only some of what was whirling through the minds and feelings and lives of the people of the decade:[1]

1960

- Black students begin the first "sitdowns" at store counters in Greensboro, N.C., a major stimulus for the unfolding civil rights movement;

- Kennedy/Johnson narrowly defeat Nixon/Lodge in the presidential election;

1961

- Ike departs from the White House with a surprising warning about "the military-industrial complex," just after the United States had broken off diplomatic relations with Cuba;

- January 20, the inauguration of JFK;

- April 15, the failed Bay of Pigs (Cuba) invasion begins, with air strikes by CIA-trained and equipped Cuban pilots, and ground invasion by other refugee Cubans (CIA-trained and equipped in Guatemala);

- August, the construction of the Berlin Wall begins;

- December, JFK (for the first time openly) sends several hundred U.S. troops ("Green Beret advisers") to Vietnam;

1962

- Students for a Democratic Society (SDS), with its "Port Huron Statement" of principles, is formed;

- James Baldwin's essay "The Fire Next Time," an eloquent and prophetic warning of the nature and depth of the racial crisis, is published in *The New Yorker*;

- October 22, beginnings of the Cuban missile crisis. It is much forgotten now, but that crisis—occasioned by the approach of Soviet ships to Cuba carrying nuclear missiles—was like watching a horror film unfold. The world was carried to the edge of a second nuclear war—not for the first or last but the scariest time of the Cold War years.

In a book published in 1992, the general public is finally allowed to know just how close we came to mutual annihilation in 1962, and just how recklessly all three parties—Cuba, the Soviet Union, and the United States—behaved. Beginning as the Cold War was ending, there were five meetings bringing together representatives from all three powers who had been part of the decision-making process—in our case, Robert McNamara, who had been Secretary of Defense in 1962. And this is what he now says:

> by the conclusion of the third meeting, in January 1989, it had become clear that the decisions of each of the three nations immediately before and during the crisis had been distorted by misinformation, miscalculation, and misunderstanding...." [2]

1963

- The feminist movement is energized by the publication of Betty Friedan's *The Feminine Mystique;*

- Martin Luther King leads a march in Birmingham, attacked by police dogs directed by Sheriff Bull Connor; June, civil rights worker Medgar Evers is murdered in Mississippi; August, King delivers the "I Have a Dream" speech at "The March on Washington"; September, four black girls die in a church bombing in Birmingham;

- June, a Buddhist monk immolates himself in protest in Vietnam (with many others to follow); November 2, President Ngo Dinh Diem and his brother are murdered (an act generally understood to have had at least the acquiescence of President Kennedy);

- November 22, President Kennedy is assassinated, and Johnson assumes office; November 24, the U.S. military presence in Vietnam is "escalated";

1964

- The bodies of three civil rights workers in Mississippi who had been missing for forty-four days—James Chaney, Andrew Goodman, and Michael Schwerner—are discovered. Subsequently the murderers are found to have included and been led by the Sheriff's department, and are sentenced to ten years for having violated the civil rights of those they murdered. [3] Chaney was a local young black man; Schwerner was a student at Cornell, and Goodman's parents were Cornell alumni. In that same period, working nearby on the Mississippi/Tennessee border, was a group of about fifty Cornell students and a few faculty who, like the Southern Non-Violent Coordinating Committee (SNCC, of which the three victims were a part), were working mostly on voter registration— for which one could be beaten (or murdered) with impunity in those days. There will be a *Story* or two about the Cornell group a bit later, one involving the FBI.

- August 10, with only two negative votes, the Senate passes LBJ's Gulf of Tonkin Resolution, which "legalizes" our invasion of Vietnam;

1965

- February 7, the bombing of North Vietnam begins;
- February 21, Malcolm X assassinated in New York;
- Civil rights march from Selma to Montgomery, Alabama (under protection of the National Guard); three days later, Viola Luzzo (a marcher from Michigan) is murdered in nearby Lowndes County;
- Watts riots erupt in Los Angeles;

1966

- January 21-22, first "hippie" conclave, San Francisco;
- April, United States begins to bomb Hanoi and Haiphong for first time; U.S. troops now outnumber those of the South Vietnamese army;

1967

- April 15, Martin Luther King speech against the Vietnam war; draft card burning in New York City;
- July riots in Detroit and Newark leave sixty-nine dead; H. Rap Brown says "violence is as American as cherry pie";
- "Summer of Love" in San Francisco;
- October 21-22, "March on the Pentagon";

1968

- January Tet offensive of the National Liberation Front of Vietnam (NLF)— now seen as the turning point of the war—stuns U.S. military and the home front;
- March 31, LBJ announces withdrawal from election race;

- April 4, Martin Luther King assassinated;

- June 6, Bobby Kennedy assassinated;

- Week of August 25, Democratic Convention upheaval in Chicago;

- Nixon/Agnew defeat Humphrey/Muskie in November;

- Black and white students at Cornell continue a series of protests against university investments in the Union of South Africa, culminating in the occupation of the School of Business and Public Administration (BPA).

And thereby hangs a Story:

The several demonstrations, although gaining support over time, were not seen as having sufficient momentum. Those who had served in the civil rights movement a few years earlier decided to apply a popular maxim from that movement: "the best way to get a mule's attention is to swat him on the nose." Translated for our purposes then this came to mean: occupy the BPA building, with the demand that the Trustees divest the university of its South African investments. Some thought to break into the building during the night; others, myself included, saw another way as superior: a friend in the University Administration was happy to provide us with a key to the building. When the SDS and black students and their supporters arrived at the door late at night, key in (my) hand, the door suddenly swung open, first to our consternation, then to our amazement: beckoning us to enter, alight with wicked smiles were my son Jeff and a Cornell student named Huey Lewis—subsequently better known by his songs and his band, Huey Lewis and the News.

1969

- Black students exit occupied Student Union at Cornell, carrying guns obtained after armed white students had sought to attack them;

- Nixon announces troop withdrawals from Vietnam ("Vietnamization") and increases bombing;

- August 15-17, Woodstock;

- September, Chicago Eight "conspiracy" trial;

- October 15/November 15, Vietnam Moratorium/Mobilization in D.C. and many other cities, the largest demonstration against the war;

- Lt. William Calley charged with multiple murders at Song My ("My Lai massacre");

- December 6, black man with gun stabbed to death by Hell's Angels at Rolling Stones concert in California: an emblematic end to the decade.

That long list leaves out many other awful happenings; as it also left out most of the wondrous dazzle of those years—the songs; the great films (most influentially, "Easy Rider," "Bonnie & Clyde," and "The Graduate"); the grand, if not great writers, such as Mailer, Heller, Vonnegut; and lots more, at least some of which will get its turn in due time below.

And it must be noted that the paper on which that list was being written (so to speak) was the larger socioeconomic process of the time, a process whose combination of militarism and spreading consumerism made it easy for a normally passive population to be convinced it should be very angry indeed with us upstarts and what we were for and against—angry enough, for example, to assault us as we marched.

ii.

A Nation Dividing Against Itself

The "silent majority" was only one of many successful ploys developed by the public relations experts who, in greasing Nixon's path to power, were simultaneously transforming U.S. politics into a media game played for the few against the many—including, not least, that motley group which, in accepting its classification as a "silent majority," also saw itself—almost enthusiastically—as aggrieved. They became the foot soldiers of what Garry Wills has called "the politics of resentment," in an army commanded by Nixon, for whom, it seems clear, resentment was the prime emotion, the warp and woof of his life.

Those dubbed the silent majority were normally opposed to anything that might threaten the comforts of their material or mental condition. And even though many who fell within the category of that "majority" were bothered by or opposed to the war in Vietnam, they were even more bothered and opposed to the movement against it (and the movement against racism and poverty).

For example, Reagan was elected Governor of California in 1966 (against the only recently very popular Pat Brown) and Nixon elected President in 1968, unquestionably in part because of the anger and fears raised by what *we* saw as our efforts to cause the United States to act in keeping with its stated principles. In addition to the "fear and loathing" of "the movement," as will be discussed later, the triumph of harsh conservatism was a natural accompaniment of the accelerating decline in the Sixties of an always scarce social decency—brought near the vanishing point by the end of the Eighties.

The political economy of those years was central to the decade's tangle of developments: it both had to and could be vital because it was interacting with and critically dependent upon the "noneconomic" processes of the time. Thus we begin with that process: economic expansion at home and in the world economy; what made it possible, and what it made possible.

iii.
The Political Economy of Global Monopoly Capitalism[4]

To comprehend the welter of changes in the 1960s, it is necessary to be less abstract in showing the connections of economic with "noneconomic" processes; more abstract in moving briefly to a relatively high level of generalization. We begin with the latter.

Two social developments of the Sixties normally seen as economic—technological change and economic growth—can be described in superlatives: 1) technology changed immensely and swiftly, both quantitatively and qualitatively; and 2) the rapidity, spread, and duration of economic growth and development were unprecedented. But understanding the spectacular behavior of these, separately or together, requires an analysis of their dependence upon 3) the complex set of processes and institutions that matured in the Sixties, here given the name "global monopoly capitalism."

Just as one needs a machete to make way through a jungle, it is necessary to have a sharp analytical tool to move toward any understanding of modern capitalism and, in using that tool, to understand also the many and vast differences between today's and Adam Smith's and (almost a century later) Karl Marx's capitalism. The crucial contribution in that respect was made by Baran and Sweezy in their analysis of "the generation and absorption of the surplus under conditions of monopoly capitalism."[5]

Those familiar with Marx's *Capital* will know that his theory concentrated on the *generation* of the economic surplus, through labor exploitation; in his time there was no need to find ways to *absorb* it. That was accomplished in the nineteenth century through the voracious capital accumulation of the booming industrialization processes.

Marx anticipated that capital would find it impossible to continue that process profitably by the early twentieth century—and he expected socialist revolution to be the outcome of the slowdown of capital accumulation and the resistance of the ever more militant working class he saw as growing organically from industrial capitalist development.

Veblen thought otherwise. Although he did not use the term "economic surplus," his analysis was similar. He was most especially concerned with the large and growing share of waste in and because of the surplus. Veblen expected that always more ingenious ways would be found to *waste*— through advertising and sales promotion, trivial product changes and, among other forms, the biggest waste all, through what he called "a strenuous foreign policy" and war.[6]

By economic "waste" one means the opposite of humanly and socially useful goods and services, as distinct from what might be profitable for businesses and/or keep a particular system from sinking. As will be discussed at greater length in a later chapter, a careful examination shows that at least *half* of our gross domestic product may be classified as a waste of goods and services. Thus, production in the world today, and most of all in the United States, uses ever more efficient production techniques in the *plant,* but because so much of *what* is produced and sold so efficiently is itself wasteful, the result is a string of cruelly wasteful *economies*—as hundreds of millions of people through no fault of their own live on or over the edge of material disaster.

What evolved in the late nineteenth century, and has been called "the second industrial revolution," was the technology and business organization that would bring about mass production: through cheap metals, cheap ocean and rail transportation, cheap fuels, cheap machinery, cheap raw materials, and cheap food.

What *had* to go along with all that if it was to be both profitable and peaceful—as a necessary but not a sufficient condition—was mass *consumption,* which soon was to mean the mass consumption of expensive durable consumer goods. The first appearances of that essential development (as was noted in our discussion of the Twenties) were in the United States.

But it was not until after World War II and the era of global monopoly capitalism that the appropriate kinds and levels of consumption became generalized even in the United States, to say nothing of elsewhere. It was in the Sixties that mass durable goods consumption was thoroughly—but still insufficiently—achieved in Western Europe, North America, and Japan.

The phrase "mass durable goods consumption" has a deceptively simple ring to it. Such consumption was far from a "natural" ingredient of the industrial capitalist process. Had it been so, it may be asserted that the two world wars, the intervening global depression, and the chaos and convulsion of the first half of this century might well not have occurred. When such mass consumption did evolve, it had been made possible by the political economy of the Cold War—the creation, the nature, and the consequences of the Cold War. Earlier, the political/military origins and consequences of the Cold War were examined; now it is necessary to examine the workings of what came to be called "corporate liberalism."

iv.

What Price Affluence?

Military Pyramids

The history of wars is pretty much co-equal with history itself. What has made for virtually countless wars? However that question might be answered, it would be foolish to believe that they have been an outcome *only* of economic conflict, unless one were to define "economic" so broadly as to exclude any other possibility. In the industrial capitalist era, however, it must be said that wars—beginning with our own Civil War—complex though they remain in their origins, have had a core of political economy at their center both as cause and consequence.

That leaves much room for distinctions, however—not least the distinction, in this century, between the two world wars, and between both of them and the Cold War (and its numerous hot wars). In an important sense, the two world wars may be telescoped into one, with a long pause—the twenty-year "armistice"—separating them. The frenzied combination and intertwining conflicts of nationalism, capitalism, and colonialism that by 1900 had been brought to the explosive point by the ravenous appetites of industrialism, far from being resolved by the war they created, exacerbated all of those conflicts within and between the industrial capitalist nations. The ensuing global economic disasters of the Twenties, reaching previously unimaginable depths in the Thirties, assured kinds and degrees of political upheaval that carried the world to its most destructive war ever.

The emergence of the United States from that war was accompanied by a paradox unique to history: almost all the rest of the world had suffered such physical and social destruction that the United States, standing far above all others in both economic and military strength, could rule without significant resistance—could rule even popularly. However, to become the most undisputed and indisputable "hegemon" of all time, but to preside over an economic wasteland, was at best a mixed blessing for a potent capitalist power: from whence the nourishment of abundant and expanding markets in a world economy flattened by the physical destruction of war, and both paralyzed and polarized by its political catastrophes and debacles? Our creation of the Cold War became the crucial answer to that question.

In an earlier discussion I sought to show why the word "create" is appropriate in this connection. For readers who rightly demand more than I have put forth in support of a critical position, I refer to the recent study of H.W. Brands, *The Devil We Knew: Americans and the Cold War.*

From the standpoint of the leading industrial capitalist countries one immense advantage of the Cold War was its exportation of war to the periphery while, at the same time, expanding their own access to the easily exploitable labor in those same areas—and, until recently, to find ways profitably to absorb the economic surplus at home: through some combination of an extraordinary increase in levels of average real income (money wages supplemented by "the social wage"), mixed in with and dependent upon equally extraordinary levels of waste of capital, labor, and resources.

The new set of social ways and means here called global monopoly capitalism came more casually to be called "cold war liberalism" by many of its opponents, "corporate liberalism" by its proponents. Call it what one will, it was not the capitalism of old; and, although it had the virtue of immense material benefits for perhaps a fifth of the world's people, the defects of that virtue were even more substantial: worsened economic conditions for the already badly-off other four-fifths, political and social and much military ruination for Third World countries, and the militarization and brutalization of our society—among others. A high price to pay for lots more cars and TV sets and other goodies for a small minority of the world's peoples, but the price was either paid by the weakest or unnoticed as it was being paid by the strongest: us.

v.

Cold War Cornucopia

World War II, like earlier wars, was very stimulative of technological change: think only of electronics, jets, nuclear power. And then think about the connections among and between them and other innovations and a broad range of saleable products and services (useful or not), and between all of that and social existence, etc., etc., etc.

But war does not by itself construct the platform on which its potentially useful products will be further produced and consumed. In the case of World War II, in fact, the social—even more than the physical—destruction came very close to doing something like the opposite.

There was a hiatus of about ten years after 1945 before economic growth and development could be seen as having taken hold in North America, Western Europe, and Japan. As that happened, technological possibilities long known were put to use and further inventions facilitated, and each new technological improvement paved the way for many more, as always. In our time, there have been so many, and so many of them so fundamental, that the technological process has threatened to get out of hand—if it has not already done so. [7]

This seems an apt place to recall that what happens in the realm of technological development and use is never pre-ordained; that it is *always* socially determined, both in origin and consequence. Depending upon the social context, technological change can have positive and/or negative results.

Thus, whether a technique of product is developed, and if developed whether and how it will be used, are *of course* determined by human beings in a particular social context. I am not alone in believing that the three most powerful and destructive technological developments of the past century have been the automobile, television, and nuclear power. In a sane society we would use the auto only sparingly, the other two not at all. (Take a moment to imagine what our lives would be like if we had an adequate public transportation system, and used the private auto largely for recreation; if our consumption and our politics were much less rather than always more dominated by TV; if there had never been an atomic weapon, a Three-Mile Island or Chernobyl disaster. Though far from ideal, we might at least have had less infantilized and far safer lives.)

The years in which the United States consciously and deliberately took steps to reconstruct a global economy were of course the very years in which the Cold War was under construction, the years in which, after the United States, Germany, and Japan were becoming the key nations of the world economy—as measured by their strength, their dynamism, and the stimuli they provided to others. Also, Germany and Japan were critical for our economic and strategic/military needs in the Cold War, and not only because Germany was heavy with 350,000 U.S. troops while Japan served as our "aircraft carrier" for Korea, Vietnam and, should the occasion have arisen or needed to be created, China and the Soviet Union.

It is more than an aside to note—in these days of rousing cheers for the free market—that both Germany and Japan, the most powerful economies after our own in this century, had histories of economic development that owed less to the free market than to what might now be called "managed" capitalism—where the management was by a very tight interlocking of private and State interests. In Germany the lead was taken by the Prussians, the militaristic Junker agricultural interests, and the highly cartelized industrial and financial sectors. Something of the same results were achieved in Japan (which consciously copied Germany in organization and function) through the very small group of overlapping industrial, financial, agricultural, and trading conglomerates—the Zaibatsu—and its intimate relationships with the militaristic State.

But until the Cold War era, neither Germany nor Japan was by itself or part of a monopoly capitalist *system,* as the term is used here. Monopoly was the norm, and both were capitalist; but neither had the strength to create and rule a *global* system—try as both might before and during World War II—nor the inclination to build a domestic political economy that would gain the consenting support of, among others, the working class (which, rather, they both brutally suppressed). For such a global system, at least two conditions had to be met: great and unchallengeable economic and military strength and the absolute and relative weakness of all others.

What was needed for a new global economy, in short, was a replay of Britain's pre-eminence of the nineteenth century—but in broader and deeper as well as different ways, to accord with both the needs and the possibilities of the last half of this century.

In addition to the many differences between the needs and possibilities of the different eras there were deep differences between the two nations. One critical distinction in their rise to hegemony was that Britain did so as one by one other nations began to industrialize, whereas the United States strode onto a stage not so much empty as littered with the wreckage of all the other once-strong nations. Among the other important differences, two are most pertinent here: 1) just as Britain is said to have accrued its great empire "in a fit of absentmindedness," so it also became the leading commercial, financial, industrial, and military power in the world's history without, one may say, having to concern itself much about ways and means; and 2) Britain had neither the advantages nor the disadvantages of fashioning its rule within the framework of a Cold War.

Thus, if the years after World War II were to fit the needs of the United States and capitalist nations in general, a new and complex world system had to be created. Much of that new system's framework and the main processes working within it were well on their way to completion as the Fifties ended; but it may be said that neither President Eisenhower nor his principal advisors were sufficiently aware of the necessary economic content of the new global system if it was to function smoothly and in high gear. It was in that respect that the Kennedy Administration and its "new economics" constituted a crucial development, as reflected both in trade policy and in domestic economic policy and behavior. What had been close to a hit and miss set of policies were thus transformed into mutually supportive elements of a guided global system.

It may be useful to add that although JFK was then and still is viewed as pretty much of a New Deal liberal, the economic policies of his administration belong to the conservative wing of Keynesianism: a substantial tax cut to encourage business investment (tax credits and accelerated depreciation allowances) and a NAFTA or GATT-like "trade expansion act" in 1962, along with rising military expenditures (which served to support—and be supported by—rising military involvement abroad, most notably, but not only, in Vietnam).

The trade legislation occupied more of Kennedy's political energy than any other single piece of legislation, and was the source of his substantial compromises on what might otherwise have been (or, according to some insiders, might *not* have been) a more liberal administration. Kennedy was caught in a very tight corner: U.S. markets had to be opened up to imports from the leading capitalist powers if the latter's economies were to grow adequately and their politics accommodate to ours. However, U.S. agriculture, business and organized labor (then, unlike now, relatively influential) had their own felt needs: agriculture to make its way more easily into European markets, business and labor to keep out European imports. The key to resolving this conflict was seen by JFK's advisors in bringing about an expanding *world* economy, in which U.S. exports *and* imports could rise, making everyone happy. For a while everyone *was* happy among the big economies.

This was not because the Trade Expansion Act of 1962 was passed (which it was). The cornucopia began to pour forth its goodies rather because a recovery was already under way by the time JFK took office in early 1961, and because the burgeoning military Keynesianism—stimulating Germany and Japan as well as the United States—along with other lesser "discretionary" stimuli were able by 1965 to foster an expanding world economy and, at home, to provide for what by then had come to be called full employment: an unemployment rate of 4 percent.

Having mentioned it more than once, it is time overdue to take a look at Keynes and to see what "Keynesianism" is.

Snapshot: Keynes

He was born in England in 1883 (the year Marx died), the son of a famous economist, whose fame he would surpass. By the 1920s, he was the leading English-speaking mainstream economist, especially famous for his three-volume *Treatise on Money*—a distinctly *non*-Keynesian analysis compared with his later work. Keynes, though he (like almost all economists) probably never read Marx, (like almost all economists), scorned his ideas; and, although he saw capitalism as vulgar and wasteful—"a congeries of possessors and pursuers"— thought it the least bad of all possibilities.

Britain, the leading industrial capitalist country up to World War I, was trapped in economic stagnation throughout the 1920s, to be joined in an even deeper depression by the rest of the capitalist world by 1930. Contemplating all that, the economics profession, guided by the ludicrously outdated ideas of J.B. Say (a French follower of Smith, writing in the 1830s), believed that the depression and its high unemployment were due to workers' insistence on excessively high wages: a real laugher, considering that millions of workers were seeking soup lines to avoid starvation, and that many of them did not find them, and starved.

In his very abstract *General Theory of Employment, Interest and Money* (1936), Keynes showed that the problem was what he called "inadequate effective demand" (which could also be seen as "underconsumption" because of inadequate purchasing power set against "oversavings" and excess productive capacity). For Keynes the solution was to increase purchasing power and use the excess capacity through governmental fiscal policy: more specifically, government expenditures ("social consumption and investment"—on subsidized public housing and infrastructure, for example) financed by federal deficits and by taxes on the best-off 10 percent, to reduce unproductive savings. The alternative, Keynes argued, was permanent depression and the end of capitalism—that is, he was a conservative in the deep sense of the term; an "enlightened" conservative. (Despite which, the first introductory textbook incorporating his ideas in the United States, Paul Samuelson's *Economics* (1947), was banned in some states for being "communistic.")

In one form and to one degree or another, Keynesian policies were put into practice in Western Europe and the United States before and especially during the Sixties, although in the United States the great emphasis on and role played by military expenditures gave us "military Keynesianism." Keynes had anticipated that such social insanity could keep the economy going, noting that "one could of course build dreadnoughts [that is, battleships] and take them out in the Atlantic and sink them; one could, as the Egyptians did, build pyramids; one could hire ten men to dig a deep hole and another ten to fill it again; one could. . . ." make a wastebasket of one's society. And we have gone far along that path.

It is a mark of how matters have changed since Keynes died, in 1946, that his own position has now come to be called "Left Keynesianism."[8]

While those developments were going on in the early 1960s, and as the Cold War was becoming an integral part of global existence, many vital organizational changes were transforming economic life within and between the major industrial capitalist nations, and between all of them and the nonindustrial (or newly-industrial) countries of Africa, Latin America, and Asia. They were years of much technological excitement: computers and jet flights and plastics and container ships and electronic newspapers and a whole range of other products and services becoming familiar to all as facts of life. And in the business world, just as exciting—and very much dependent upon the speeded-up processes of transportation and comunication and the galloping new world economy—was the looming dominance of the enormous multinational/transnational/supranational corporation.

vi.

Superhoods

In the seventeenth century, Hobbes characterized the then increasingly powerful British State as "Leviathan." In this century, the German political economist Franz Neumann characterized Hitler's Germany as "Behemoth." But neither of those terms, suggestive though they may be of surging and ominous strength, suffice to convey the giantism of our institutions and the tidal strength of our social processes—giantism and strength that, whatever benefits they may bestow, tend to leave us feeling impotent, induce us to become (or remain) passive.

Outstanding among the key elements of global monopoly capitalism have been the following, of which the first and the second—the supercorporation and the superstate—may be thought of as its heart and brain:

1. A vast increase in both the absolute and the relative economic and political power of what are no longer giant but have become supercorporations—within and between industries, sectors, and nations. The average person, even though well-informed on most matters, can be excused for not having more than a vague idea of what is meant by "supercorporations"—until recently "giant" having sufficed as the adjective. Thus and herewith a few details and an easy source through which to find many more as time goes on. All the following data are taken from *Fortune* (April 29 and August 5 1996), which every year compiles many pages of data for the 500 largest industrial corporations in the United States and the 500 largest in the world. Some highlights:

The top 500 U.S. corporations in 1995 had revenues of $4.7 trillion, up 9.9 percent from 1994; assets were $10.5 trillion, an increase of 9.7 percent; profits were $244 billion, up 13.4 percent; employees rose only by 0.2 percent.

The top ten of those 500 were GM, Ford, Exxon, Wal-Mart, AT&T, IBM, GE, Mobil, Chrysler, and Phillip Morris.

The top 500 global corporations (of which 153 are from the United States) had revenues of $11.4 trillion (compare with U.S. GDP of $6 trillion, 1995), up 11.1 percent; assets were $32 trillion, up 4.2 percent; profits were $323 billion, up 14.7 percent, and employees were 35 million—up only 1.8 percent.

The top ten global corporations included seven Japanese, three U.S., and one British/Dutch company. Though fourth in revenues, GM's profits—

$6.9 billion—were just twenty times those of the number one company (Mitsubishi), with $346 million. Phillip Morris, though ranked twenty-eighth in the world, ranked fifth in profits ($5.5 billion)—although, interestingly, those profits were 15.3 percent greater than 1994, while revenues declined by 1.2 percent.

In 1970, there were about 7,000 multinational corporations (MNCs, now called transnationals, or TNCs), more than half of them based in the U.S.A. and the U.K.; by the 1990s there were 35,000 TNCs, fewer than half based in the United States, Japan, Germany, and Switzerland. The world's productive assets are estimated at about $20 trillion; 300 TNCs control $5 trillion: that is, 300 companies, effectively controlled by a few thousand executives at most, directly preside over a fifth of the world economy and indirectly considerably more than that.[9]

Another way of gaining a sense of the enormousness of these companies is by comparing their "numbers" with those of the most powerful national economies. In 1995 the global top ten's sales added up to around $1.5 trillion, just about equal to the gross domestic product of Germany, considerably more than Italy's, and one-quarter of the U.S. GDP.

Further perspective is gained when it is noted that the top 500 U.S. corporations constitute a small fraction of all U.S. corporations, that incorporated businesses are not even a tenth of all businesses, that the top 500 take in about two-thirds of *all* profits, and that the top ten account for 30 percent of the 500's profits.

Had enough of the supercorporation? Then onward and upward with the other main elements of Monocap.

2. An equally striking increase in both the quantitative and qualitative roles of the superstate at all functional and geographic levels.

3. The strengthening and spread of "consumerism" in the United States and its replication in all the leading and most of the lesser capitalist and noncapitalist economies.

4. The reconstruction and strengthening of a global capitalist economy/empire under the leadership of the United States.[10]

5. The concomitant growth of a "military-industrial complex" in the United States, with lesser variations elsewhere.[11]

6. An extraordinary accumulation of debt by persons, businesses, and governments.

7. Required and facilitated by all the above developments, the extension and refinement of mass communications techniques for commercial and political exhortation and manipulation: what may be thought of as the lubricant of global monopoly capitalism.

vii.
The (Almost) Seamless Web

Taken together, the defining characteristics of that system provide an appearance of invulnerability. Indeed, Baran and Sweezy, whose 1966 Monthly Review Press book *Monopoly Capital* gave the matter its first coherent analysis, seemed to see it *as* invulnerable, except for upheavals emanating on its periphery—in Africa, Latin America, Asia. Despite some serious problems for the smooth functioning of the system in, for example, the war in Indochina, the Third World on balance did more to strengthen than to weaken global monopoly capitalism. The critical processes that made for its now long-term crisis came rather from relationships in the core.

The seven elements enumerated above had functioned together to produce a new and powerful social and economic system; but, as with earlier systems, what was once functional (to use the sociological term), evolved and interacted so as to become dysfunctional. As the Seventies wore on, those same seven elements interacted to bring one trouble after another, not least important the historically novel economic phenomenon of "stagflation"—prolonged recession combined with prolonged inflation (to be discussed in chapter 5).

Later we shall see how the intractability of stagflation, its resistance to being overcome by "normal" fiscal and monetary policies, led (most particularly in the United States in the Reagan years) to extreme measures whose side effects have made the years of stagflation seem something to look back upon with nostalgia.

And then, the most telling and disastrous development of all for the postwar system: the end of the Cold War. It cannot be stressed too much that without the numerous and interdependent developments of the Cold

War, the global monopoly capitalist system neither could nor would have been born, nor could it—in its terms—have flourished. The ongoing attenuation of the Cold War has been accompanied by a process of socioeconomic bewilderment, a sense that the keys to economic and social stability have been misplaced, or lost. In time, one may hope, the end of the Cold War will be seen as the beginning of possibilities for a sane society. As yet, it has produced little but grotesque attempts to maintain military spending and to continue to pass—that is, to sell—the ammunition, to anyone, anywhere. And, like Scarlett O'Hara in *Gone With the Wind,* we'll think about the consequences, if at all, tomorrow.

For those who wish to think about them today, just pick up the day's news, as you consider 1) that "In the United States, from 1947 to 1991, the sum of military budgets (in dollars of 1982 value) amounted to $8.7 trillion . . . [compared] to the total value of U.S. industry and infrastructure . . . of $7.3 trillion"; and 2) that in recent years about $1 *trillion* have been spent on the military every year in the world; and 3) that until recently about a third of that was spent—or received—by Third World (that is, mostly poor) countries which, now that the Cold War is declining are taking up the slack in military expenditures from the rich countries. [12]

That the Cold War was an unnecessary as well as a prolonged disaster has been asserted more than once in preceding pages (and will be again later). That "we won the Cold War" has now become a popular rationale for having created and supported it. But now that it is becoming always more difficult for any State to maintain the secrecy of that period—one of its subtler but also very important crimes and dangers—it is also becoming feasible for studies such as the one now to be recommended— *We All Lost the Cold War*—to be written and published. [13] This one, using only recently released documents, reveals not only the fundamental idiocies creating and driving all who became parties to the Cold War and the conflicts it produced or exacerbated, but how much of current strife must be viewed as lingering effects of that presumably defunct social disease.

All the foregoing generalizations need additional support, and will get some in later pages. Right now it is time to switch back into focus some of the tumultuous sociopolitical events of the Sixties, as they played themselves out against the political economy, the warfare, and the many internal clashes of that wild decade. In doing so, we shall see that there is no reason for nostalgia, none at all—except for the camaraderie that existed among those trying to survive and to overcome the madness and the cruelties of military and social brutality.

viii.

The Crack in the Mirror: Rebellion On and Off the Campus

When some hundreds and ultimately some hundreds of thousands of university students (and not a few professors) undertook to protest and to demonstrate during the Sixties, it was not only what they saw as the ills and evils of the larger society that they attacked; before long the target also became the university itself: the aims and means of higher education.

As most readers will know, many of the battles now to be discussed were swiftly or slowly lost; but some notable ones were won and have had lasting and significant beneficial effects on and off campuses: improvements which those who develop hysteria over what they castigate as "political correctness" are busying themselves to eradicate.

During all but five years of the Fifties and Sixties, I was teaching at Cornell University (in the others I was at Berkeley or in Bologna, Italy). Cornell already had a reputation as an unusually political university in the 1930s, and it swiftly became attuned to developing a politics of resistance in the Sixties.

During the 1950s there were always small left of center groups "stirring up trouble." And already by 1960 there were substantial organized activities against nuclear testing leading to, by 1962, a Congressional "peace candidate" (a law professor, whose manager I was)—among the very first of what became a small but growing species.

From 1963 through 1966, there was a Cornell group working in the civil rights struggles in the South. In the spring of 1965 a sit-in against the war in Vietnam took place, by which time the student-initiated, -owned, and -operated "Glad Day Press" had been in place for several years, and had become a center for reproducing and printing essays, pamphlets, posters, etc. for civil rights and antimilitary matters on a large scale, selling them at (or below) its very low costs throughout the nation.

One of our main printers was Mike Rotkin, who subsequently went on to do graduate work at U.C. Santa Cruz, serving as the city's (first) socialist mayor for some years; he now sits on the faculty there. Another printer was Bruce Dancis (soon to be in a Snapshot), who also went to U.C.S.C. and then on to graduate studies in history at Stanford, after spending almost two years in a federal prison in West Virginia for his activities as principal organizer of the draft resistance in the East. (He is now Arts &

Entertainment Editor for a good urban newspaper.) Throughout the Sixties, the Glad Day was an effective training school for people who became "movement printers" all around the nation.

From 1965 on, Cornell was one of the most important centers for the struggle against the draft and the Indochina War and, insistently, against apartheid in South Africa. And, among other such matters, at the end of the decade there was the extraordinary episode of black students occupying the Student Union, being attacked by white students with guns, and getting guns themselves. In short, Cornell was considerably more involved, and for much longer, than almost any other university in those years.

The events now to be described occurred and were effected mostly, though (as will be seen) not entirely, at Cornell by its students and (many fewer) faculty. I begin with a long Snapshot centered on two of the most influential figures at the university in the Sixties.

Dan and Bruce

Dan Berrigan is a Jesuit priest (now seventy-five) and a fine poet and a lover of life in all its dimensions—and a very funny guy. Bruce Dancis (now in his early forties) comes from a Jewish socialist family in New York, graduated from the Bronx High School of Science, received a New York Regents' scholarship for Cornell, where he was a cross-country runner—and is also a very funny guy. (It is almost incidental to this tale that in 1965, Bruce's first and last academic year at Cornell, he took introductory econ with me.) As the Sixties ended, both Dan and Bruce were headed for prison. Some of the doings earning them that unwelcome honor now follow.

Soon after his ordination, Dan found himself in France as part of a group coming to be known as "the worker priests." The Church thought that unseemly for Father B. and sent him off to Latin America "to work with the natives." That he did, along with other Jesuits, together with whom he helped to further the emerging "liberation theology." So the Church yanked him back to the States and made him a university chaplain—at Cornell, in the year of our Lord 1967, where Dan was like kerosene arriving at a fire. Teach-ins against the war (of which more below) were already going on, the draft resistance, Bruce as its leader, was well underway, SDS was gaining considerable momentum, the war in Vietnam was escalating furiously, and the air was filled with protest and songs. Bruce, lead singer in a local rock group called Titanic, had as one political "weapon" the organization of block dances (one with the irresistible name of "Sink the Draft with Titanic")— which could make being against the war an enjoyable activity for a few hours.

Sub-Snapshot: Abbie Hoffman

Bruce is his own person, but he was spiritually honed by Abbie. Abbie was one of the founders of the Yippies, anarchist in outlook and breezily contemptuous of the status quo. By themselves the Yippies couldn't have accomplished much (who can?); but having them along for the ride was always helpful and once in a while decisively so. (Many of them thought me pretty stuffy.) Bruce and Abbie worked together on a famous and effective—and still my favorite—piece of political theatre when the Yippies entered the New York Stock Exchange, went up to the balcony, threw dollar bills in the air, and caused a temporary breakdown of the exchange—while also revealing something basic about that place and the people who make money that way. Abbie wrote several books, the most widely-read probably the one with the inviting title *Steal This Book*. He was one of the Chicago Seven, the presiding judge for which was Julius Hoffman, not only no relation but the very opposite of Abbie's clone. In consequence, the trial was intermittently uproariously funny, whatever else that it wasn't. Abbie was (probably unjustly) accused of selling cocaine, knew that a trial would send him to prison, and chose instead to go underground. For many years he lived a normal (and married) life in northern New York, though a fugitive, and, changing his name and appearance only slightly, never ceased his political activity. Along with almost all who knew him, I loved Abbie; we all mourned when—as one who had been clinically depressed most of his life—he went gently into the night by his own hand.

As an instance of the twining of spirits of Abbie and Bruce I submit the bare details of another lovely event:

Button, Button, Who's Got the Button?

Early in November 1966, the Glad Day Press made two buttons, one about six inches in diameter, the other less than half that size. Their lettering were identical in color—dark blue—but with different words and background colors. The larger pink one proclaimed "I am not yet convinced that the Proctor is a horse's ass." The smaller baby blue button (meant to be worn by a different person) said: "I am convinced." The Proctor of the University was in effect the campus M.P., with, as time went on, increasingly political functions. (Appropriate for the then Proctor, who had been in the FBI and had a photo of pal J. Edgar on his office wall.) Students who were "movement-oriented" began to wear the buttons. On November 17, Bruce, wearing the larger button, found himself in a scuffle on the steps of the Student Union, initiated by the Assistant Proctor, who had finally and completely lost his cool. A very large man, he grabbed and hauled Bruce, tore the button from his jacket, and in general, if I may put it this way, showed that he too was a horse's ass. The scuffle (as it was always called) made the student paper several times as editorials, professorial proclamations, administration releases, all inveighed against the button's horrendous insult to the Proctor, who was unswervingly described as a man of the highest this that and the other. A key moment in the fast-breaking development (as I think journalists would put it) was that two days after the first scuffle, an earlier scheduled meeting of Vice President Muller with students protesting student cafeteria and other policies was abruptly cancelled because there were students present wearing "the button." Let it be said simply that the whole matter turned into a large step ahead for the Left of the Cornell political spectrum, because if there was anything that just didn't sell by 1966, it was stuffiness.

Back to Dan and Bruce. As time went by, we become a trio, tootling around New York and surrounding areas in my old wreck of a car, speaking against the war. Dan would begin, mesmerizing the audience with his eloquence, humor, and wisdom; I would follow, with a somewhat professorial analysis of what we were doing in Vietnam and why we should get the hell out of there; and Bruce would end up with an organizing pitch— Tinker to Evers to Chance (the great double-play combo of the great 1906 Chicago Cubs, for the information of you young geezers).

Dan, along with eight others (including his brother, Father Philip Berrigan), rose to national prominence when, at the Selective Service Office in Catonsville, MD, they lifted several hundred 1-A draft files, carried them to the parking lot, burned them with homemade napalm (reporters and photographers present by invitation), joined hands to recite the Lord's Prayer, and became "the Catonsville Nine." The initial reaction of antiwar people to that action was largely negative, for the Nine had deliberately provoked their own arrest. But in months and years to come, it was shown to have been a galvanizing act for—most especially—many hundreds of nuns and priests.

Something under a year after the act, the Nine went to trial. During the trial, in Baltimore, we had a block-long picket line going around the Courthouse, which also holds the Post Office. None of us was allowed to enter the building, but normal Baltimoreans using the P.O. were. One event nicely revealed the stereotype held of us picketers: I was dressed for the occasion in a grey flannel Brooks Brothers suit, neat as a pin. As I was passing the entrance as part of the line, a distinctly messy man exited the P.O., looked me straight in my very clean face and shouted "Why don't you take a bath??!!"

A good 1972 collection of essays about the Berrigan brothers, *Witness of the Berrigans* was put together by Stephen Halpert and Tom Murray. I provided one of the essays in which, loving and admiring both the brothers very much indeed, I went on to point out that the brothers (not by their intention) had themselves become heroes, performing deeds over and over again that ordinary people could not contemplate doing themselves. (The most recent one [December 1993], involving the damaging of a fighter aircraft on a base in North Carolina, has placed Phil back in prison again in 1994. Dan had been too ill to participate.) My argument was and is that the politics we need is one that must seem possible for ordinary people to construct and join.

Bruce was tough as nails, and his politics were clear, sensible, and well-argued. He was very much trusted by those who knew him—much more so than any other political "leader" I have known, and a leader he was, of the draft resistance. But Bruce also made the critical contribution that gave Cornell the largest single SDS group, and also one containing a considerable group of draft resisters (my son Jeff included).

Those times now being so distant, it may be necessary to state what a "resister" was.[14] There were many honorable ways to refuse to serve in the war in Vietnam: as a conscientious objector on ethical/religious grounds, by leaving the country, by finding ways to be exempted. But the resisters as the term is used here fought against the draft publicly and ran the risk of imprisonment quite simply because they declined to take other honorable ways out. I remember especially one Cornell student, Chip Marshall, who as a college boxer had permanently injured his shoulder. The draft authorities had been informed of this injury and *wanted* to give him a physical exemption (if only to keep him *out* of the army), but at his physical, Chip denied the injury and underwent considerable physical pain as the medics manipulated his shoulder to test him. (Subsequently he shared a prison cell with my son, for reasons to be discussed in a later Story. Jeff taunted the draft board by dropping in now and then to place radical writings of one sort or another in his file, taking the simple position that he wouldn't fight in their shitty war, and they finally just left him alone, probably deciding the war in Vietnam was difficult enough without having him over there.)

SDS and the draft resisters were usually in conflict—competition is a more accurate word—on campuses throughout the nation, as is often and self-defeatingly so of the various fragments of the U.S. Left. As noted above, that was not so at Cornell, largely because of Bruce's political efforts and skills; as it was also true that when in late 1969, as SDS was splitting in two by the formation of the "action faction" (which became the "ultra" wing of SDS, and self-destructed within a year or so), Bruce's last act before going to prison for his draft resistance efforts was to persuade the Cornell SDS group not to succumb to any temptations it might feel to march off in that direction. (In that very large and tempestuous meeting of about 500 members, Jeff was on the "action faction" side and I on the other—both us very vocal, to the vast amusement of all but ourselves).

That year, 1969, was a very tough year, and always getting tougher, as resistance to State policies mounted and the crackdown of the Nixon gang became always harsher. Whatever other reasons there may have been for some protest groups to become more prone to violent tactics, one was certainly a growing feeling of hopelessness and, for some, desperation—especially after Chicago of 1968.

This was played out in my own family, as Jeff and I came increasingly to quarrel over what radical protest should mean, and my daughter Jenny had her heart broken. Jenny, who turned fifteen in the summer of 1969, was the "mascot" of Cornell Draft Resistance/SDS. Whenever there was a march, Jenny would be at the head of it, proudly carying the flag (with its "omega" symbol, the sign for resistance in physics)—this while she was thirteen and fourteen. It may be said that she loved the small group of resisters with whom Jeff was closest and with whom he ultimately went to prison: Chip and Joe and Michael. Jenny went to Woodstock with the the Unholy Four in August 1969 and stayed the course in a battered old truck (not without much worrying on my part).

In September 1969, though Jeff and his pals were not Weathermen, they participated in the "Days of Rage" in Chicago. When they returned to Ithaca, and were sitting around our house talking about Chicago in a macho fashion—how they threw rocks at this car or that window, etc.—the whole afternoon became unpleasant. As they left, Jenny began to weep, saying, "Daddy, they've lost their humanity." She was almost right—but they hadn't lost it, only misplaced it for a while.

Back to Dan. The Catonsville Nine were convicted and sentenced, but some, including Dan, went underground to escape imprisonment.

Dan and Phil and the others of the Nine who were nabbed at one time or another finally got out of prison; but the rehabilitation program hadn't worked very well. Subsequently they went on to do other naughty things (as recently as 1993, as noted above), one of them leading to their being accused of planning to kidnap Henry Kissinger and to blow up the Pentagon. But that's another

Story

It's a long one, and I might as well put it in here, even though it happened in the Seventies. In the summer of 1970 a friend who had earlier done graduate work with me at Cornell telephoned me from London, where he was by then teaching. He was very active in the efforts to increase European resistance to the war in Vietnam, and he asked if I could go to Sweden for a week or so to do some lecturing and radio work, my way to be paid. I said sure, and would it be OK to take Kay along (at my cost) and to stop off in our beloved Italy en route. OK. Before leaving, I attended a previously scheduled meeting in Manhattan with two nuns about a Dan Berrigan hideout question, and asked if they wouldn't like to have a couple of weeks respite at our nice place on Lake Cayuga, upstate, where they could also take care of our cat, the garbage, etc. They said fine, and we agreed to meet at Kennedy Airport on the day of departure so I could give them the keys and instructions about the cat, etc. One of the nuns, Sister Elizabeth McAlister, was then the companion and is now the wife of Father Philip Berrigan (with three children), then an inmate in Lewisburg Federal Penitentiary. A few weeks after returning from Europe, I was invited to give an economics talk at Bucknell University, near Phil's prison. Just before I left Ithaca for the talk, a man named Boyd Douglas telephoned and said he was a Lewisburg inmate with privileges to leave the prison to take classes at Bucknell, was a friend of Phil's, had seen a notice about my talk, and would like to speak to me about something important. I said OK, we met at a fraternity house on the day of my talk, and he told me how Phil had convinced him that violent revolution was necessary (which I said I doubted because I knew Phil did not hold such a position). And, he went on, there were some things he himself thought had to be done, and what did I think, as he proceeded to propose one violent act after another. I told him we were having enough trouble trying to organize a demo now and then without also trying to overthrow a very large nation violently which, in any case, I disagreed with on several grounds. We parted, I gave my talk, and went back to Ithaca.

Months passed. In early 1971, I was living in San Francisco, while teaching as a visiting prof at Berkeley. One morning as I left the house to go to work two men jumped at me from an auto, both brandishing guns, identified themselves as FBI, and served me with a subpoena (which only federal marshals have the right to do) to appear as a *prosecution* witness at the trial of the Harrisburg Seven (which included both the Berrigans and Sister Liz), accused of seeking to kidnap Henry the K., before, during, or after executing their plan to blow up the Pentagon. That very evening, I was scheduled to give an antiwar talk at the University of San Francisco, along with Sister Liz and (of all people) Jane Fonda. Before the event began, Liz told me she had some bad news. She was accompanied by one of the attorneys for the Seven. He showed me a magazine article (*Saturday Evening Post*) concerning the Seven in which was reproduced a letter from Liz to Phil (in prison, written after my Manhattan meeting with Liz), wherein she, evidently trying to perk up Phil's spirits, said she had met with Doug about his mission to Sweden to get $8 million from the Swedish government for the U.S. antiwar movement (!!!), and that she and Sister Mary were going that day to meet me at Kennedy "for instructions." She didn't specify that the instructions were about a cat and garbage. It seems that this Boyd Douglas, who was a stoolie working for, among others, the FBI, had gotten the letter from Liz to hand to Phil but gave it first to the feds, and they in turn had the CIA follow me all around Europe. And now my time had come to be a witness for the government and name names and all that jazz.

How do I know about the CIA? Briefly, the man who arranged the Swedish trip told me that his brother had informed him that I had been trailed through Italy and Sweden, and when my friend asked his brother how he would know that, the latter was forced to tell my friend that he was secretly in the CIA (his cover was in a publishing house). Nice world, all told, nezpa? He quit the CIA shortly after that, and wrote a book about them.

Anyhow: the attorney with Liz said the defense also wanted me to testify, in order to show that Boyd baby—the principal witness against the Seven—was an agent provocateur. When the news came out that I was going to have to appear, a sizeable group of Cornell students announced their plan to march to Harrisburg (seat of the trial) to protest. When the government heard about this, they decided not to call me, probably because up to that point protesting students had not been involved. And then the defense decided not to call any witnesses, and I was off that particular hook. And the Seven were declared innocent. And went on to other obstreperousnesses. God's in His heaven, and all's right with the world, and this Story has finally ended. (Except for this, just remembered: when that news first made the U.C. paper, *The Daily Cal,* the headline was "UC Prof Nabbed by FBI." As it happens the faculty at that very moment was considering asking me to rejoin them on a permanent basis; but I never heard from them again—except from one prof who disliked me and who, some weeks later when we met in an elevator, said "Dowd? I thought you were in prison!" "You didn't pray hard enough," I replied.)

ix.

One Nation, Indivisible; Land of the Free, Home of the Brave

If a chaplain and a student at Cornell could keep the pot boiling that much, it is easy to imagine what would happen if lots of others independently and cooperatively moved along similar paths; as indeed a lot of others did, in those days.

One such path began to be cut out in the fall of 1963 as a graduate student in physics, Charlie Haynie, arrived back in Ithaca after having spent the summer in Fayette County, Tennessee, where a desperate and failing voter registration effort that had begun four years earlier was still being waged and lost, and waged again.

The effort had begun when a young black man was tried for a misdemeanor (having nothing to do with civil rights) and, there being no white lawyer who would defend him in the county, had found a black lawyer in Memphis. The latter, a Mr. Estes, informed the court of the injustice of a situation where a defendant, unable to vote, was to be tried before an all-white jury. One of the officials present said "Why, we ain't got nothin' against niggers voting; all you gotta do is go down to the courthouse and register." So the blacks began to do just that, only to be punished economically and/or physically for doing so.

Their struggle had slowly but surely gained attention outside the area, and Charlie Haynie was one of those who had gone there to help out in the registration effort. Fayette County, which borders on Mississippi, was then the fourth poorest county in the United States: no doctors, no dentists, no real schools for black children, no services of any kind for blacks (who outnumbered whites three to one in the county)—except in black churches, also the only place where blacks could meet safely for any purpose. It was cotton country, ex-slave plantation country, the land still almost entirely held in large chunks by, of course, whites. The black people of Fayette suffered the same kinds of economic and social misery as their counterparts immediately south of them in Mississippi; and Haywood County, Tenn., just to their north (about which, more in a minute), was the regional center of the KKK.

Charlie got together with two or three of us to tell us what was going on down there—this in the same period in which SNCC's organizing activities were on the rise—and at Cornell we decided to try to get a group together that would spend three months in the summer of 1964 to help with voter registration. The effort required a lot of prior money raising to support what ultimately became about fifty volunteers for that summer in the county—and, before long, it created what was up until then the most intense political experience in Cornell's history.

What triggered the latter was a vote by the Student Council to donate $1,000 to the Fayette County Fund (our group). The minority of the student board that had opposed immediately called a referendum, to be held just three weeks thence. The intervening period was marked by continuous debates, speeches and, on occasion, fights; and the student paper was filled with it every day. (In the event, Dick D., the editor, who had been aloof the way professional journalists are supposed to be, became one of the volunteers; and later he became Editor of "The Week in Review" of the *New York Times*, which he may still be.) When the arguments began, we were way behind; at the vote, we won two to one. And then came the summer.

Story: We Shall Overcome (Some Day)

It was that very hot summer, the weather for everybody, another kind of heat for those working for justice in the South (already noted above, the deaths of Chaney, Goodman, and Schwerner in Mississippi). Our group suffered no deaths, but not for the lack of "them"—which always included the Sheriff's gang—trying.

One bad day was in Haywood County, when Danny B., a volunteer (who also became an editor, of the ILWU paper *The Dispatcher,* in San Francisco), entered a diner with a couple of local black men and sat down. Without a moment's hesitation, the proprietor picked up a large skillet and roundhoused Danny in the head, breaking his jaw. We then planned a parade and demonstration in the town to protest, on a Saturday about ten days later.

I flew to Washington to seek protection for what we expected might well become a disaster. Bobby Kennedy was Attorney General and LBJ was President. I had sent a wire asking to meet with RFK at a certain date and time, while also having our volunteers call their parents to have *them* call their people in Congress for some pressure, and to meet me in D.C., which about sixty did. I hadn't expected RFK to see me, and he didn't; but the man in charge of civil rights, John Doar, did. I brought in all the parents with me, and Doar, in his *very* crowded office, patiently explained why under the law it was impossible to provide protection before a crime had occurred. The parents raised hell, many of them hysterically, and as we exited Doar asked me to stay. He said he hoped I understood about the law; and he added that there might nevertheless be something he could do but that couldn't be talked about just then.

On the day of the demonstration, some hundreds of us marched through the town. Quite visibly here and there along the route and at the town's center were men—about a dozen, all told—in dark suits holding walkie-talkies. Nobody in Haywood County except the preacher and the undertaker ever owned a dark suit, let alone a walkie-talkie. [15] No matter, one local white lost his cool and assaulted one of the dark suits. A few weeks later the assailant was tried by one of those local juries and—surprise!—declared innocent. But we had been effectively protected, and thank you John Doar.

But that was the only occasion on which we were protected. I well remember another occasion when a would-be white attacker, thinking he had everything going for him, almost took me out. Our meetings were always held in churches at night, for almost all the local people worked long days. Though scheduled for 8 p.m., the meetings usually began toward 10 p.m., at what we called Fayette County time, and ended past midnight. One very dark night, I was driving five men to their homes in my topdown 1955 white Chevy, and we were taking the short way by driving along a very narrow one-lane dirt road— no way for one car to pass another—just below the Mississippi border. Suddenly a pickup truck curved into view from the opposite direction, with one white man in it. He stopped and got out, carrying a shovel, and I knew what he wanted to do with it. Not only was the night very dark, however, so were my companions. Until we all piled out of the car, our white adversary thought it was him versus some white college punk from the North. By the time he had charged a few yards, however, he realized that he had made a very bad mistake, raced back to his truck, and deftly backed up all the way until he was completely out of sight.

And then there was the FBI. Some weeks before the above incident, I had gone to the Federal Building in Memphis to ask the FBI to arrange some protection against what was being done to our group and to the local black people as the voter registration effort was going on. I got no cooperation at all;

in fact I was made to understand that we all were the lawbreakers. As I exited their office and walked out in the hall, my attention was drawn to an official bulletin board on which there was a poster with a photo of then Supreme Court Chief Justice Earl Warren, attached to the usual notice of "The Ten Most Wanted Men." The Warren poster called for his impeachment.

x.

Public Education

In that same year, the "teach-in" against the war was invented. It started spontaneously at the University of Michigan in 1964, but was soon energized into a national movement, principally by a very vigorous and rugged sociology prof at Case Western Reserve University (Cleveland), Sid Peck.

From the first teach-in to the last (the "last" because they were superseded by the Mobe and its and others' demonstrations, to be discussed soon), the guiding idea was that the government's policies in Vietnam could not survive the light of day: every teach-in had at least two speakers, supporting or opposing the war. The government sent people from the State Department, the Pentagon, from the Congress, even someone from the CIA—and I don't know of one meeting where the government "won." It wasn't that we were such great debaters; it was that they didn't have a case, and the more they talked the worse they looked.

Of course the audiences were largely made up of students and faculty; but it must be remembered that when the teach-ins began, the general attitude toward the war—also that held by most on campuses—was one of indifference or support. And McCarthyism, though not under that name, still contaminated the world of political opinion—still does—and those who went against U.S. foreign policy were accused of everything ranging from cowardice to duplicity to subversion to stupidity—or something else execrable.

As by now you might expect, I was one of those who went around speaking at the teach-ins, and was in a good spot to note the changes taking place with increasing rapidity between the spring of 1965 and that of 1966. By the latter time—the war having become considerably more costly, obvious, and violent, not least on the nightly TV news—audiences were becoming so supportive of the antiwar position that it became difficult to get a government speaker to participate. After many occasions when we had to leave an empty chair on the stage for the bashful warriors, we began to reduce the teach-ins while increasing protests of one sort or another. But one of the last teach-ins I still remember; a memory of a "victory" tinged by sorrow.

Story: The Goddamn Man

I was asked to be the antiwar speaker at Ball State University, which is in Muncie, Ind. (the town used by Helen and Robert Lynd for their justly famous "Middletown" studies; also, as is little-known, where this century's Klu Klux Klan was founded). It was a packed auditorium, and not as friendly as most were by that time. My opponent had been the U.S. Consul in Saigon for the preceding two or three years. As the argument went on, he climbed up an analytical ladder that began by arguing we were there to protect and enhance the freedom of the South Vietnamese, and when that didn't sell he climbed up one step after another until he finally almost yelled that OK we were there to keep China from conquering all of Southeast Asia. I won't bore you with what I was arguing in response, except to say that the other guy had completely lost the audience by the time his argument had climbed up into China.

When it was all over, and this is the point of the Story, a very tough-looking man (he was a U.S. Marine, it turned out) came up to me, bristling, and this is what he said: "Goddamn you, Dowd; when you started out I knew you were wrong; now I know my government's a goddamned liar. I'm home on leave after two hitches in 'Nam, and tomorrow I go back for my third. Goddamn you!" He turned around and left the hall, and left me not knowing what to think or feel; but I still remember feeling lousy.

But something had to be done, especially if one remembered that the folks at home had done close to *nothing* to halt the slaughter in Korea (with which peace had—and has—yet to be signed). Lots else *was* being done in the way of marches and protests of one sort or another; but it needed pulling together. The people who had built the teach-ins were part of what became a naturally coalescing group called The Mobilization Against the War in Vietnam: "The Mobe." Like the teach-in outfit, the Mobe was born in Cleveland, again with the energetic prodding of Sid Peck. [16]

A key influence in this whole development was A.J. Muste, a bone marrow pacifist of long standing (he had first gone to prison for his efforts in 1919). All did not agree with his pacifism, but he was probably more respected than any other person in the rapidly expanding antiwar movement. Most productive was his insistence from the beginning of our efforts that the Mobe coalition be "non-exclusionary": any march, any protest, any demonstration must be open to all, with no need to provide credentials or take a position on anything but opposition to the war in Vietnam. In practice this meant that the Mobe would ask no "organizational" questions and that its Steering Committee (of which I was a member from the start) would be formed in accord with that principle. The consequent process often seemed a weakness of the Mobe to some; in my judgment it was a main source of whatever strength we had.

Story: Orders from Above

Not that non-exclusion didn't cause problems, of all sorts and almost all the time. One major set of problems had to do with the seemingly endless wrangles over means and ends—some petty, some not at all so; some had to do with organizational competition within the coalition, and most time-consuming of all of those were those prompted by the small but aggressive Trotskyist element on the steering committee. For example, there was that day in Cleveland in 1969 when one committee member—representing a presumably independent organization that was in fact one of several fronts for the SWP—was patiently and destructively holding up our ability to make decisions. Exasperated, I finally yelled across the table: "Jerry, if you don't shut your fucking mouth I'm going to come across the table and strangle you!" Jerry went right on with his obstructions, and I in fact began to climb over the table at him when Fred H., the head of the SWP, said very quietly: "Shut up, Jerry." And like a naughty little boy, Jerry shut up.

The substantive questions dividing us from start to finish had to do with pacifism, tactics, black power, imperialism, and, among other matters and more than most, the conflict between the Communist Party and other socialist groups, most especially the Trotskyists. At the original meeting whose aim was the creation of the Mobe, we were all asked to identify ourselves organizationally; and I was amazed to hear, for the first time, someone publicly identifying himself as representing "Communist Party, U.S.A." The only sound heard for a moment or two was that of Joe McCarthy exploding in his grave.

The Mobe began with about twenty separate groups involved—SNCC, some church groups, SANE (an antinuclear group), SDS, CORE, Women

Strike for Peace, the teach-in outfit, CPUSA, the Socialist Workers Party (Trotskyist), and many others. By its subsequent transformation in 1969, "the New Mobe" had more than twice as many groups in the coalition, and, by 1971, more than another doubling, and another new group: "People's Coalition for Peace and Justice."

The quantitative increase of groups did not ultimately represent a proportionate increase in strength, for at least two reasons: 1) the Sixties had stirred things up in such a fashion that what was wrong with the United States became displayed always more for examination and criticism, with each "issue" developing its own group; while, 2) at the same time our always limited sense of human solidarity led to a process in which the coalition had increasing difficulties in focusing squarely on *any*thing, and was instead tending to run off in different directions all at once. The result, of course, was a serious loss of possible gain on either the broad or the narrow objectives. (As co-chair of the People's Coalition for Peace and Justice as the disintegrative process became plain to all, I know whereof I speak.)

Did the three coalitions just noted (and other groups) accomplish much? or anything? As we look at our society in the 1990s—and at its growing poverty and deepening racism—it is not easy to find a clearcut answer, except on one matter: we *did* get out of Vietnam.

Perhaps the antiwar movement had little or nothing to do with that? Perhaps the explanation is simply Watergate, the removal of a "strong" president (Nixon), ready to nuke the Vietnamese as a last resort, and his replacement by a wobbly one (Ford)? Because the antiwar movement continues to be maligned today, and deprecated even by some who once supported it but see the effort as having been worthless, a pause to seek an answer seems worth the paper and ink it will take.

Watergate was a crucial moment, to be sure. But it must be noted that Nixon did not accidentally stroll into Watergate: he lurched into it. As may now have been forgotten (or never known about) by most, Nixon was intermittently driven into a mental corner by the always larger demonstrations against the war. And when the so-called Pentagon Papers were made public, that gave him an extra and decisive push into extreme defensive action.

The Pentagon Papers

Of the many who worked in the government in those years—in his case, high up on the National Security Council—one was Daniel Ellsberg. Ellsberg had been a gung-ho Marine Captain in Vietnam before becoming a strategy expert for the NSC. While serving in Vietnam, he met and fell in love with a visiting pacifist (whom he later married). From that point on he began to pay more attention to what was happening; by 1971 he came to believe it proper to steal and, with the help of his children (from a former marriage) to copy the 7,000 pages of the "Pentagon Papers"—a top secret detailing of U.S. involvement in Southeast Asia from World War II to 1968. Ellsberg gave copies to Senator Mansfield (Foreign Relations Committee) and to the *New York Times* and the latter published extensive excerpts from them. These revealed the step by step penetration of the United States into all of Indochina, and the innumerable lies (as well as the stupidity) accompanying the process. The materials were memos and the like of the NSC over the years (principally in the Kennedy and Johnson administrations).

When the news first broke (June 13, 1971), Nixon was not at first displeased, for the dirt belonged largely to the Democrats and was proof of criminal irresponsibility on the part of his old enemy, the press. Soon thereafter, however, his paranoia about ongoing leaks from his *own* inner circle combined with the aim of showing Ellsberg—rapidly becoming a hero to the antiwar movement—to be a traitor, to push Nixon to take the extraordinary step of having some of the "Watergate" burglars break into the office of Ellsberg's psychiatrist in the hope of finding materials that would cast doubt on Ellsberg's character. Ellsberg, instead of being found guilty of treason, escaped that fate: the judge threw the case out of court because of that break-in.

In numerous writings and speeches, Ellsberg has credited the strength of the antiwar movement for having provoked such crudities on the part of Nixon, on the one hand and, on the other, for having caused the Nixon Administration to withhold from ever employing its trump card in Vietnam: nuclear weapons.[17] To which I may add that in the several meetings I had with Vietnamese spokespeople from both the southern National Liberation Front (NLF) and from North Vietnam, it was always their position that they knew they could force the United States out of Indochina if only we could be restrained from using nuclear weapons against them—and they believed the antiwar movement was the principal force for preventing that from happening.

Ultimately the antiwar movement could number literally hundreds of demonstrations and millions of participants—a phenomenon whose magnitude none expected when it all began in the early Sixties. (And something to keep in mind in these days of gloom.) Of all the efforts with which I was closely concerned, two massive demonstrations stand out—one in the fall of 1967,[18] the other in the fall of 1969. And between them was the unforgettable upheaval of Chicago in the summer of 1968, more of a police riot—as Walter Cronkite called it—than a demonstration. We look at all three.

Story: The Armies of the Night [19]

In the early fall of 1966, the Mobe had been formed. In the next few months, many small and a few large demonstrations were emerging, like the crocuses at winter's end; at the same time, moves toward a cessation of the fighting between the United States and Vietnam were underway. And then, for reasons *never* explained, the United States began to bomb Hanoi, including nearby hospitals. The Vietnamese understandably refused to go on with peace efforts under such circumstances. And the antiwar movement accelerated. That included the first organized burning of draft cards, in Sheep Meadow of Central Park in Manhattan, in April, when 175 cards were burned. Bruce Dancis was the main organizer; for which efforts he ultimately was incarcerated in a medium security prison for almost two years. Soon after, the Spring Mobilization of 1967 brought forth large demonstrations in Washington and San Francisco, and many smaller ones around the country.

Something like the opposite of cause and effect, more and more troops were sent to Vietnam. By the end of 1967, the number of U.S. troops in Vietnam was approaching its peak: 550,000 at any one time. Over the course of the open war, 1964-1974, over 3.5 million U.S. troops served in Indochina. And, as the death and destruction mounted, and the nature of it began to dominate the evening news, the Mobe planned its biggest ever demonstration: "March on the Pentagon," October 21-22. It is pertinent to note that immediately preceding that date (and independently organized) was a very large "turn-in" of draft cards by the Draft Resistance and a week-long "Stop the Draft Week" in the San Francisco/Berkeley area. The latter began calmly enough but soon became confrontational—no doubt encouraged by Governor Reagan's expressed wish that it was time for "a little blood to flow."

The Mobe's plan was to assemble around noon on October 21 at the Reflecting Pool (where the great 1963 civil rights demonstration had been held), have speeches—including my own, as money raiser—and then, a peaceful march to the Pentagon. We had gained a permit for the march and the right to be in the area for forty-eight hours.

It soon became a very young and very "American" occasion, for better and for worse. Instead of a peaceful march to the Pentagon after the speeches, a few of the university groups more or less spontaneously began a race to see which group—each displaying its banner—could reach the steps of the Pentagon first: Harvard, Cornell, Columbia, etc.—not, however, by the officially approved route.

To shorten what could easily become a much longer story, chaos became king. By midnight the chaos had settled down to a long and very cold stay, leaving a few hundred of us sitting on the ground, arms locked, facing federal marshals and troops of the 82nd Airborne—us determinedly peaceful, them with bayonetted rifles. A level playing field, so to speak.

My son sat next to me as the night went on and on, as all the while our arms were locked. Jeff is a very big guy, and just as courageous. But that night—he was not yet eighteen—he seemed to me to be as scared as I. Which was plenty scared. The front rank of us sat facing a line, having been told it was illegal to cross it. (We were sitting perhaps twenty yards from the front of the Pentagon itself, which the permit allowed.) So we sat. And froze. And intermittently, the soldiers would push their feet under our feet, or legs, or asses, causing us, naturally, to move a bit; and then they would push more, and then begin to beat us and arrest us for moving over the line—that they had just moved *toward* us.

All that was bad enough; but there was more on its way. Because it was so cold, we had built little fires behind our group, where one could move back to warm up a bit. During one of the moments when we were being pushed and the usual hell broke loose, one of our people began to egg us on to go to it, while himself—from well back—throwing burning pieces of wood toward the soldiers: stupid enough in itself, worse in that the fiery pieces were of course falling on us even more than on the soldiers. It was Jerry Rubin who started that. He had never been one of the people I had admired in the movement; from that moment on, I changed from not being his admirer to being his opponent—as a later Story will confirm.

Many were arrested that night, and many were injured. The next day and night—we still had a permit—our people were back again, and another 700 were arrested and many more hurt. Inevitably, some of our people did some stupid things, but (apart from throwing burning wood) they were not dangerous to life or limb. That night—unbeknownst to us then, of course, a precursor to 1968 Chicago, Kent State, Jackson State, etc.—shocked many of us deeply. When we returned to Cornell, and at the suggestion of Dan Berrigan, many of us spent a week fasting and talking together, wondering, not least, what kind of government is it that treats people the way we had been, that night? Not the worst government in the world, by far; but not the government of "the American Dream." We were not the only ones to have such wonders.

The Pentagon and simultaneous San Francisco demonstrations gave a big boost to the antiwar movement, both in its antidraft and "Out of Vietnam" aspects. And as the demonstrations multiplied and began to include always larger numbers of "respectable" non-students, the politics of the whole nation began to be affected. Even those of my conservative brother Merv.

He wrote me from San Francisco, telling me that he had been in the march there, the first such experience of his life—his two sons were eligible for the draft. He thought the march was important, but he thought it unfortunate that so many were dressed sloppily, and that many of the placards were vulgar. Still, he thought it was great; and it was not his last time in the streets.

xi.

Mash!

As 1968 began, so did the extraordinary Tet offensive in Vietnam. The Vietnamese suffered horrendous casualties, considerably more than the United States; but those of the United States were our highest of the war. Taken together with the endless flow of statements from the White House that we were "winning the war," "boys home by Christmas," "light at the end of the tunnel," and the like, to have the Vietnamese launch *the* major assault of the war—after so many years of *our* imminent victory—broke the back of domestic support for the war. To say nothing of what was going on in Vietnam itself: U.S. enlisted men were "fragging" their officers (that is, among other things, lobbing grenades into the latters' quarters). By early 1968, scarcely a TV story on the war would be without at least one picture of a GI with a peace symbol on his helmet.

LBJ withdrew from the presidential race in an address to the nation on March 31; Eugene McCarthy and Bobby Kennedy had entered it by then. And by April it began to look very much as though one or the other, or both together, were going to get the nomination. (A reminder: Martin Luther King was assassinated on April 4, and Bobby Kennedy on June 5, 1968.)

In January and February of 1968, not knowing of course what was to happen with the Democrats, the Mobe began to make plans to be at

Chicago for the summer convention—expecting to place LBJ and his running mate Hubert Humphrey at the center of our protest.

Throughout the fall and winter of 1967 the various elements of the antiwar movement had been struggling with the question of what to do about the Democratic convention in the following August. Some groups (SDS, for example) took the position that the best thing was to ignore it, for the costs of doing otherwise would be high: Carl Oglesby, one-time leader of SDS, went so far as to predict that Chicago would be "death city." Oglesby was by no means the first or only voice to note that the United States had entered a new and increasingly violent period in its political history. It was after all the same year that the black people of both Detroit and Newark suffered heavily from police violence and destructive fires.

The argument for a substantial Mobe presence at the Chicago convention was made from the beginning by Tom Hayden (one of the founders of SDS in 1962, a member of the steering committee of the Mobe by 1967). He and Rennie Davis argued in a detailed fashion for a week-long demonstration, no matter what the possible costs, for we were in a "revolutionary situation." The argument was presented in the form of a thirty-page "position paper" to the steering committee of the Mobe at a January meeting in one member's apartment in Manhattan.

As summer began and the time came to get ready for Chicago, I spoke vigorously against it to the SDS group at Cornell, and helped to persuade them *not* to join us (a rare experience for me); but I felt I had to be there, as a steering committee member.

Earlier, in April, a plenary meeting of representatives of all the members of the Mobe coalition was called, to meet in an isolated camp called Lake Villa, on the western shore of Lake Michigan (in Wisconsin). I was only one of many of the participants who spoke against the entire plan. As Hayden spoke in response to me and others, his remarks about me, both in tone and content were such as to be unforgettable: by the time he was through, many of the hundreds present could have been forgiven if they had concluded I was an undercover agent for the feds. (There were in fact several present, we later discovered, one of them on the steering committee itself.)

So. August in Chicago was a terrible confrontation of our thousands against Mayor Daley's police and the National Guard. It may be that such a disaster couldn't have been avoided, that we *had* to be there, but I still doubt it. The people who were drawn to participate were not told to expect what they got; they expected a demonstration that would be as peaceful as we could keep it. It wasn't: we didn't initiate the violence or behave with brutality; but some of our people made it easier for the authorities to do so.

The Chicago police and Mayor Daley (as well as, probably, much of the Democratic establishment) wanted to beat the hell out of us. Of the tumultuous five days and nights I spent in the streets of Chicago during the Democratic Convention, Wednesday stands as the worst. I had left bloody and gas-filled Michigan Boulevard for a few minutes of respite, gone to the next street and turned the corner so I was paralleling Michigan, walked the block, and was preparing to return whence I had come when three police buses pulled up and stopped. Descending from each of them were thirty or more "blue meanies." They were ordered into platoon formation and sent marching at a military half-trot. As they trotted, they chanted loudly and in unison: "Kill! Kill! Kill!" had a literal sound. As suggested above, some of *our* people believed that a harsh confrontation was not only unavoidable but, for that reason, desirable: sooner now than later. To argue that confrontation was avoidable, as I did, was to say that we were politically ill-equipped to come out of it stronger, in the short or the long run, neither least nor only because of how we would be (and were) treated by the media: we had much more work to do.

The media treatment of Chicago let the blame for the violence fall squarely and unfairly on us, and heightened the hatred of those who already hated us. Meanwhile, on our side the shock of Chicago certainly caused an unknown but significant percentage of our people to pull back in fear and passivity. Perhaps the Nixons and Reagans were slated for triumph anyway, though I doubt the inevitability of that. Chicago made it easier for them and harder for us, from that point on.

As that shocking and exhausting week ended, I took a train back to New York. I remember still the sight of my fellow passengers, none of whom I knew: many bandaged, almost all with drawn faces and glazed eyes, many of them having been totally mystified bystanders to the days of chaos and violence.

It was, of course, an election year. Bobby was dead; Gene McCarthy was shoved around both physically and politically in Chicago, all the pros playing hardball: not his game. Humphrey had served LBJ on bended knee; to make matters worse, although it was known that Humphrey was against the war, it was also clear that he wasn't against the war as much as he was *for* being our next President. He had a reputation for representing New Deal social decency at its best: if so, the best had come to be not good enough, not for us.

Having a different principle for every occasion may not have set Humphrey apart by more than a sliver from other presidential aspirants, past and present; but in the spirit (ours, at least) of the Sixties it meant that for some unknown but clearly high number of antiwar people, it was heartbreakingly impossible to make oneself work for Humphrey—even knowing that Nixon was the sole realistic alternative. The blame was on Humphrey, not those of us who refused to hold our noses and become part of such dirty business.

Consider the following instance of how LBJ spoke of and treated Humphrey, in public. On a day when Humphrey was in the news for having taken a (good) position on educational policy, but without having cleared it first with LBJ, the latter in a press conference announced: "Boys, I've just reminded Hubert that I've got his balls in my pocket." This, along with other recorded examples of Humphrey's obsequiousness (and LBJ's brutal ways) unfortunately abound. [20]

Unable to believe that either major party held promise for stopping the war or starting the United States on a better path, other—very small—political groups involved themselves in the elections. One of them had begun early in 1968 in California: the Peace and Freedom Party. It was significantly strong in the San Francisco and Los Angeles areas (and much less elsewhere). It had brought together strong antiwar sentiment with also strong efforts to eliminate racism and poverty; and it effectively—one may say uniquely—succeeded in developing a black/white coalition. Its principal leaders were Eldridge Cleaver, Bobby Seale, and Huey Newton.

Snapshot: Soul on Ice

That was the title of Cleaver's book, published in early 1968. It was the true story of a long-time con, thief, rapist, and who knows what else—all recounted grippingly by Cleaver: the man himself. Cleaver was (perhaps still is) a large and very muscular man, one of those who used his nine years in prison to get into or stay in shape. He is articulate and persuasive and intimidating. If Bobby Seale was the most practically effective of the Panthers' leading figures, Eldridge and Huey were the most eloquent, and the most lustful for power.

P&F was doing a very effective job of spreading the politics of peace and freedom when in the spring of 1968 the leadership decided to join the presidential election race in California, with Cleaver as candidate for President. I was at Cornell at the time and, along with a fairly sizeable group throughout New

York, we decided to form our own branch of P&F—the second, after California's. We saw ourselves as an educational and protest, not electoral, group—at first. I was among those adamantly opposed to involving ourselves in electoral politics, and not merely because we had started late and were little known in the state.

But by the summer, and in the developing chaos of that time, the majority in the New York party decided to go electoral. I figured the hell with it, and stayed out of the effort. However, one fall weekend when I was in Manhattan to visit with my mother as she stopped off between planes, I realized that P&F was having its "convention" at a hotel in the city, and decided to drop in for a look before driving north and home to Ithaca.

As I entered, a group of my friends approached me to inform me that I *had* to let myself be nominated as Cleaver's running mate—this, although they all knew I saw the electoral thing as foolish and as damaging to our long-term political efforts in the state. We argued back and forth and I continued to refuse totally—until they told me that the only alternative to me was his California running mate, Jerry Rubin (they knowing my attitude toward him, which they shared). We were having enough difficulties in New York without having the likes of Jerry speaking for us.

So, after much huffing and puffing, I gave in, Cleaver agreed (preferring, I believe, Rubin), and I became candidate for Vice President of our fair land.

Cleaver had many passions; the one ranking highest when I knew him was his determination never again to let "them" get him back in prison. Before the November election, he skipped the country, believing—probably correctly—that he was going to be tried and convicted on some charge or another. But before his departure we had shared a platform or two—a memorable experience.

There was an evening at Syracuse University, for example, when the large university crowd was encircled by at least twenty of Cleaver's men—standing in the outer aisles, all noticeably armed.

As the least important speaker of the evening, I gave my speech first to the fitful and uneasy audience—not caring much about my speech, and certainly not expecting what they were soon to hear from Eldridge. On the brink of leaving secretly for Algiers, he was both angry and tense. My years in the army had accustomed me to the F-word; but I had never heard so many of them in a rat-a-tat-tat such as Cleaver's that evening. Because I sat on the stage, I could observe the faces of the audience: whether faculty or students, they seemed to be in a state of semi-shock. To paraphrase Saddam Hussein, it was the motherfucker of all political speeches.

Cleaver went underground and overseas; shortly thereafter, bureaucratic wheels moving as slowly—and as absurdly—as they are wont to do, I received a note from the N.Y. Secretary of State informing me that my presidential running mate was disqualified because he was too young (!).

Cleaver returned to the country after many years in Algeria. It is widely believed (also by me) that Cleaver came back to the States in a deal with the feds: he would stay out of prison if he would also stay out of politics, electoral, street, or otherwise. In any case he became a professed fundamentalist in Christianity and a dispenser of capitalist ideology for a few years, even for a while selling men's leather pants with an outstanding codpiece as a selling-point. I don't follow his doings these days, but the above has reminded me of another Story.

A Midsummer Night's Dream

One night in August of 1970, I received a telephone call at about 2 a.m. from Tom Hayden, from L.A. (I was in Manhattan for a weekend meeting of Mobe people.) Tom said there was a ticket waiting for me at Kennedy to take me later that morning to Paris and then to Algiers. Could I go? What for, I asked. Can't say, said Tom. The hell with it then, I said. You gotta, said Tom. I don't, said I. Please, he said. Oh, then, OK, I said. (By now are you wondering why you are reading a book by such a fool?) So, weak with exhaustion, I hurried out to the airport at about 8 a.m. As I was picking up my ticket, I saw some political heavies from the Hayden "family" gathered around a telephone and asked them what's up? They were on the phone to Algiers, not by chance, and I demanded to be put on. I found myself speaking to Bob S. (now a respectable reporter) who insisted I should drop *tutto* and get my ass to Algiers. Why Algiers? Why me? Because Eldridge is planning to have a press conference to announce his new theories of world political development, and he wants you here to give the whole thing an air of—how to put it?—dignity. Who: me? Fuck it, I said, hung up, and tumbled in my car and drove home to Ithaca. The next day, press conference day, it turns out, was the one in which the TWA plane was hijacked while sitting on the ground in Israel, all of it covered minute-by-minute—and nobody would have showed up for Cleaver's press conference, no matter how much dignity I might have given it. (And it was cancelled, anyway.)

In the preceding year too many serious things had been going on for such fun and games, at the university and throughout the nation—among them, an extremely dangerous face-off at Cornell and the gas-drenched Mobilization of November 1969 in D.C.

News Flash: Black Students with Guns at Cornell

Ithaca, N.Y., April 19: After days of rising tension, with the Cornell campus surrounded by 400 armed police from sheriffs' departments around the state, a group of black students exited Willard Straight Hall (the Student Union) carrying guns. They were accompanied by Vice President for Student Affairs Stephen Muller, with whom they had negotiated an agreement—yet to be ratified by the Cornell faculty, most of whom are said to be opposed to its provisions.

What could have induced a group of black students at an Ivy League university—to which, only a few years before, few if any of them could have gone—to occupy a building and *arm* themselves? In 1962, there were but four black faces in the student body (of about 15,000) at Cornell. In 1963, a new university president introduced a new program—the Committee on Special Educational Projects (COSEP)—to find, and where necessary to fund, a group of black students to study at Cornell. By 1968, there were a few hundred black students there. Except now and again, they were by no means made to feel anywhere near as welcome as other students. I recount two illustrative happenings of early 1968:

1) On the night of the day in April when Martin Luther King was assassinated, it was the white students who freaked out: they proceeded in significant numbers, for example, to throw shit on the doors, and to burn crosses in front of the living quarters of black students. Among other matters. Just boys, playin' around. Yup.

2) Earlier that year, a couple of dozen black students asked to meet with a dozen or so faculty on a once a week basis for several weeks to discuss the possibility of some courses meeting their interests but that were not offered at the university—for example, a course discussing and analyzing black literature; the history of black people in the United States; the economic conditions of black people compared with others in the United States; *anything* that might help black students understand their own culture and history better, by studying it—the way, for example, that the white folks do (in fact, *must* do).

The informal committee was made up of faculty from the humanities and the social sciences, including me. After many careful and positive discussions, the group came up with a genuinely modest proposal for just two courses: Black Literature in the United States, and the Political Economy of the Black Ghetto in the United States. The first was proposed to be given by Professor Dan McCall of the English Department, who had written a well-received study of Richard Wright, and the other by myself. (I was then teaching Urban Economics.)

It is the normally sensible custom in universities not to allow a new course without first making sure it doesn't duplicate existing courses. For these two courses, there could be no problem of duplication: that was indeed why our small faculty-student group had been meeting, but the proposals had to be presented before the relevant Arts College Committee. After the chair of English proposed the Black Lit course, I did so for the econ course.

There were then some minutes of desultory discussion, and then Professor K. of the History Department began to poke away at my proposal—or, more accurately, at me.

After a long and what became a heated argument between us—the other professors listening with delight, there being so few lively moments in such meetings—K. said, "Well, Dowd, the difference between you and me is that *I* don't think I know everything." "I see no difference there, K.," I said, "*I* don't think you know everything, either." After a moment of heavy breathing and muffled silence, the Dean called for a vote: seven for, one against. Now and then, you win, especially if there's a horse's patootie on the other side.

K. was one of several professors who left Cornell the following year, as did the late Allan Bloom, whose discussion of the events at Cornell—in his *Closing of the American Mind*—is a pastiche of untruths and fantasies. Unsurprisingly to me, both were among the earliest and most active of the windmills energizing what is attacked as "political corrrectness"—about which, a note here, and some further comments later on.

In the good old days, any anti-poor, anti-black, anti-woman, anti-gay, anti-democratic, anti-you-name-it person could just let go with snide, insulting, and vicious remarks about the members of the foregoing list. Since the Sixties, however, such an academic molester now and then has found her/himself having to *defend* indecent "ideas." But those with the habit of unchallenged rule are not without resourcefulness: nowadays, as Calvin Trillin has put it so nicely, the academic barons can say the same old crappy things and seem to be virtuous by introducing their remarks "with the proud phrase, 'Well, this may not be politically correct, but. . .'" And then let go with the same old poisonous hate, scorn, or degradation. [21] Never give an inch.

Back to those armed black students at Cornell. Despairing of achieving a full curriculum, let alone agreeable and safe living conditions in anything but the very long run, they decided after five or six years of hopeful patience to speed things up by a demonstration. Justified or not, their choice of time and place were astute: the time, "Homecoming Weekend," when the campus is inundated by parents; the place, the student union, which also served as a hotel—for many of those same parents.

Remarkably, although students had marched and demonstrated and all that, up to that point, no building had been occupied (though more would be in that year, including one noted earlier in the Story concerning South Africa). So, from the beginning it caused quite a stir—especially among white students, and most especially in their fraternities.

Pretty much all of SDS and the draft resisters and a fair number of faculty ringed the student union (not an easy thing to do, for it is a very large building sitting on a fairly steep hill). A crowd of frat boys remained outside, booing and cursing. And got a few back.

Inside, the black students had good reason to fear that the worst might yet be on its way. The tension in there, in what was something like a bunker, must have been almost unbearable; it certainly was on the outside. And it rose in the building when the students heard of armed white students and arranged then to have guns smuggled into the building. (To this day I have never known by whom or how.)

To make matters worse, something like anarchy was developing on the campus. At one point, for example, a committee of the faculty reluctantly asked me (because of my relationship with the black students up to that point) to act as a go-between between the black students and the university president. I sought out the president, only to learn that he was then—and for the remainder of the crisis—hiding out, unable to be found for several days. We interrupt this bulletin for a bit of background:

Story: A Man for Some Season

In 1968, students had begun to protest against the university's substantial investments in South Africa. In early 1969, seeking to calm the waters, the Administration organized a symposium of speakers entirely chosen by itself. The only two I can remember now are Allard Lowenstein and University President James Perkins. Lowenstein was thought to be a calming influence because he had worked in the civil rights movement and had been aligned with Eugene

McCarthy in 1968. But by 1969, as tensions rose, he was moving toward the middle; and, rather than calming the waters, his talk agitated them.

And then the President took the stage. Before coming to Cornell he had been with the Carnegie Foundation, when he became—and remained on that day—a board member of Chase Manhattan Bank, a major investor in South Africa. As he took the stage and began to speak in vague and soothing ways, Bruce interrupted to bring the subject to university complicity in South African repression. Not much after that, a black student walked on the stage from the wings, placed his hand on the President's shoulder, and the President hurriedly left the stage—choosing to run and fight another day, perhaps; not, however, on the day I sought him out at the faculty's request. Or the day after that. (The trustees asked for his resignation shortly after the Student Union occupation.)

Meanwhile, while I was trying to find the President, those 400 armed sheriffs had surrounded the campus, with ideas of their own, in addition to those being fed to them from official and unofficial sources—not a few of them involving the use of *their* guns.

As the tension rose, and there was no President to be found, VP Muller had the courage and good sense to enter the building to try to work something out. What he accomplished was an agreement to take before the Trustees and the faculty, meant to persuade them that a Black Studies Program, with the normal accompanying elements of such programs (some faculty, major requirements, etc.) would be created in a reasonably expedient fashion. The faculty meeting on the issue was boisterous and angry, and Muller a very unpopular man, with very few publicly supporting his position—among them, of course, myself. That did nothing to raise the very low level of my popularity with the faculty.

It was finally accepted, even though it meant the Trustees had to shove it down a majority of the faculty's throats, amidst alarms about the end of learning, barbarism, you name it. About five years later, I was invited back to Cornell to give a talk by some offbeat students, by which time a few things were evident: 1) the demands of the black students had been institutionalized and were functional; 2) except in those respects, the place seemed to me to be the same university it had been twenty years earlier: good students and faculty, excellent library, beautiful view, and weather alternating between too hot and too cold, with a few intermissions of incredibly beautiful spring and fall.

Nor can I overstate how pleased—tickled—I was to see in the *New York Times*, April 7, 1993, that the new President and Chief Operating Officer of TIAA/CREF (the largest pension fund in the world, and the one used by private universities, Cornell—and my pension—included) was (and still is) Mr. Tom Jones, who is also by now, I understand, a Trustee of Cornell University. Tom was one of the leaders of the black students' occupation, and he can be seen in one of those unforgettable photographs of black students leaving the Student Union with guns in their hands— Tom at their head, gun in hand.

Tom Jones was also part of the efforts of 1968 and 1969 to get Cornell to divest itself of South African investments. So it comes as no small pleasure to report that in the glossy TIAA/CREF 1994 Report to its members, there was a picture of a smiling Tom—and I don't mean *Uncle Tom*—including this statement from him: "The CREF Social Choice and Money Market Accounts continued to do well. The major event of the year for Social Choice was the decision by the Trustees to remove the South African screen. This action came as a result of improving prospects in that troubled country." Right on!

xii.

Give Peace a Chance

By the fall of 1969, the opposition to the Vietnam war was set to move to its peak with two events, linked to one degree or another: the October 15 "Moratorium," throughout the nation, and the November 15 "Mobilization" in Washington and in San Francisco.

The Moratorium was the creation of a small group of young people who had worked closely with Eugene McCarthy's campaign in 1968. They represented a position that saw an enormous number of people who were increasingly against the war, but who were also nervous about the composition and tactics of the Mobe coalition. Most influential in the Moratorium leadership were David Hawk, Marge Sklencar, Sam Brown, and David Mixner. (Hawk had been a student at Cornell, where we had known each other.)

Just as many Moratorium people thought the Mobe "too radical," much of the Mobe had the reverse attitude by seeing them as insufficiently so. Of course there was substantial overlap on important issues.

As time went on, and midst much suspicion, argument, rumors of betrayal, and the like, it nevertheless worked out that on October 15 the Moratorium would have demonstrations all across the country, large and small, with all kinds of statements, positions, etc., all wanting the United States out of Vietnam. And the attempt was ongoing to try to have cooperation between them and the November demonstration in D.C. One manifestation of that attempt was that David Hawk and I went around to many meetings in the East where the two of us spoke, each endorsing the plans of the other.

The Moratorium was an enormous success. It was fairly estimated that on October 15 a good twenty *million* people stood somewhere—in a street, a field, a campus, a town square, somewhere—clearly showing opposition to the war. Even divided by two, that's a lot of opposition: nothing like it, anywhere, any time.

Meanwhile, the plans for the Mobe's November 15 were troubled all along the way, efforts to coalesce with the Moratorium the least of those troubles. From September on, there was trouble with the Weathermen, trouble that surfaced violently in the "Days of Rage" in Chicago in September, that erupted again at Dupont Circle in D.C. on November 14, and once more on November 15—with lots of incidents coming from other directions, including the White House.

In what came to be called its Dirty Tricks Department, the White House enjoyed sending forged letters from one protest group to another (preferably from a black to a non-black group), demanding money, or threatening this or that—all, of course, to divide the coalition. [22] We did what we could to minimize such divisions through timely communication—as, for example, in September of 1969 in Chicago, during the "conspiracy trial" of seven of our steering committee members (along with, at first, Bobby Seale—later dropped from the case). The Mobe was meeting to plan the November mobilization in D.C. and, as well, to have a support demonstration in Chicago for the Seven—at the same time that the Weather faction of SDS was organizing for its "Days of Rage": same time, same place, same issue, and a masterpiece of what not to do to support those on trial for conspiring to break the peace.

Chicago of September 1969 was a disaster, but a minor one. November 15 loomed ahead, and support for it mushroomed. It began to seem as though there would be—as indeed there were—several hundreds of thousands in D.C., and another 150,000 in San Francisco. Given the continuing disputes and divisions within and around the Mobe, the belief grew that the main task of the leadership would be to keep the whole thing from blowing up in our faces, from whatever source—groups in the coalition or the White House.

At the instigation of the Moratorium people, a few of whom had White House connections, an agreement was worked out whose aim was the prevention, or at least the minimization of violence from any quarter. The three parties to the agreement were the Moratorium, the Mobe, and the White House: all taking a stand against a violence—though, as will be seen momentarily, the White House was at the same time planning one more dirty (and violent) trick.

A communications center was set up in a federal building, at which representatives of all three groups would be present from 7 a.m. until the day's events were completed. I was the Mobe's representative. There was constant telephone and walkie-talkie contact with our marshals throughout the crowd and on all the routes leading into and away from the demonstration. At any sign of trouble, the information went to the proper location and our marshals gathered to quiet things down. And it worked; but only for most of the day.

I was keeping a moment-by-moment journal, to chart what was happening. By mid-afternoon, I had begun to feel foolish, for everything seemed to be working out well and by cooperative design. Then, about 3 p.m., some of our marshals radioed in to say that on the roof of the Justice Department there were troops with rifles clearly visible—something which it had been agreed would not be allowed to occur, the troops' very visibility being, as we knew from experience, a provocative act in itself.

I immediately informed the White House rep (who was Ehrlichman most of the day, but not just then), and demanded that the troops be placed out of sight from the street. But the marshals continued to report their visibility and the consequent and growing agitation on the line of the departing march. Suddenly, without any change of activity on the part of the marchers, troops poured out through the doors of the building and into the streets—and that was the beginning of many hours of nightmare in Washington, D.C.

Before dusk, downtown Washington was awash in tear gas, including police headquarters (as well as our own monitoring office); hundreds had been beaten and arrested; and the streets had become a horror. The struggle to get out of town had become chaotic and dangerous; thousands simply hid in churches.

We held a press conference the next morning, hoping we could prove—from my journal, among other sources—that the day's violence was due to some combination of carelessness and stupidity on the part of the White House, at best; at worst, a consequence of intent. The reporters were there, but our information showing the sequence of cause and effect was allowed by the media to be effectively obscured by stories of crude dramatics and excitement. [23]

October and November constituted the peak of antiwar demonstrations, as the growing divisions within the movement wasted its strength—while at the same time Nixon's strategy of "Vietnamization" was introduced: a steady reduction of our ground forces in Vietnam, while we increased our bombing from the air. The latter meant both a dramatic drop in U.S. casualties and in the bad news every night at dinner, and allowed the dependence on the draft to be replaced by a volunteer army. Insofar as a vital source of the strength of the antiwar movement lay in the opposition of potential draftees and their families, "Vietnamization" constituted a crucial turning point: not for "winning the war," which we could not do without using nuclear weapons, but for weakening the antiwar movement.

If "Vietnamization" meant reducing U.S. casualties, it was of course at the expense of the people of Indochina: in the ten years from 1964 until the end of the war in 1974, the United States dropped more bombs on Vietnam, Laos, and Cambodia than had been dropped in the entirety of World War II in *all* its theatres. And of course the territory comprised by those tiny countries is as a tiny handkerchief compared to the large carpet of European and Asian territory bombed in World War II.

It is unfortunately more than symbolic that the Sixties ended with the nation's capitol choking in tear gas; and that being so, the Sixties constitute a tragedy for which a desirable resolution was placed and remains still beyond reach.

The tragic nature of that outcome is underscored when it is realized that until 1969 both the White House and the Congress were under the control of the Democratic Party, and more by its liberal than its conservative wing. That set of political realities if combined with the expansiveness of the economy in those same years *could* have moved us several large steps closer to a safe and sane and decent society. Some progress was made; but because the liberalism making for that progress was "cold war liberalism" it was unavoidable that in the same process the seeds of domestic dissent and conflict and despair were being planted. Their bitter harvest was to be reaped in the next generation.

xiii.
Requiem for a Heavyweight [24]

Sometimes a Great Nation [25]

All our presidents have of course represented something characteristic of our society. In helping to change the society for the better, the very greatest of them—a Lincoln, an FDR—have often brought out the best in us: the definition of their greatness.

It was almost painful to observe Lyndon Baines Johnson as he sought to be one of our rare *great* presidents: he often, explicitly, and loudly proclaimed that he and, with less emphasis, we were going to build a "Great Society."

Perhaps, given what our history had produced in attitudes and institutions, that couldn't be done; perhaps (and I believe this), it could. But Vietnam put finish to that dream, just as much as it did to the lives of tens of thousands of U.S. soldiers and those of three to four million Vietnamese (not counting Laotians and the million or more Cambodians whose slaughter must be laid at our door).

LBJ, whatever his larger-than-life faults (among his larger-than-life everythings), had unquestionably pledged himself to bringing about changes that a large percentage of the population needed and that many were clamoring for; and it was his way—and very much "the American way"— to want to bring those changes rapidly and in one BIG package.

So the agenda was established; the Great Society would offer something to almost everyone: Medicare for the old, educational assistance for the young, tax rebates for business, a higher minimum wage for labor, subsidies for farmers, vocational training for the unskilled, food for the hungry, housing for the homeless, poverty grants for the poor, clean highways for commuters, legal protection for the blacks, improved schooling for the Indians, rehabilitation for the lame, higher benefits for the unemployed, reduced quotas for the immigrants, auto safety for drivers, pensions for the retired, fair labeling for consumers, conservation for the hikers and the campers, and more and more and more. [26]

Had all that been accomplished—and some of it was—it would have amounted to a substantial improvement in the quality of life here, and would also have served well as a platform for further needed changes: universal health care, comprehensive environmental programs, etc.

Johnson was probably the most astute politician of the post-World War II era. As he took over the presidency in November 1963 the times were ripe for what he almost immediately began to propose; that, it may be said, is a large reason for his having proposed it, and for our ability to judge him as "astute." But there were other and less pragmatic reasons. LBJ saw himself (with less than accuracy regarding poverty) as having arisen from a socioeconomic background rife with the defects he sought to eliminate in his social proposals.

In the decades to come, however, LBJ will not be remembered as the president who created a great society, but as he who plunged us irrevocably into the quagmire of Vietnam. [27] One can blame LBJ's advisors, one can blame JFK and *his* predecessors—most especially Truman—for having presented Johnson with a fait accompli; but one can also say that when Johnson took office there was still sufficient "space" to begin to pull the United States out of Vietnam, decently and honorably. It may indeed be argued that there is always sufficient space to behave decently and honorably (however belatedly), rather than to lurch on with murderous activities.

But like so many others before him and around him and after him, Johnson from the beginning was more concerned with his own honor and pride than the nation's; and like the others, he also lacked any reasonable understanding of the nature of the conflict in Vietnam, let alone of the North and the South.

Because of my involvement in the antiwar movement, I came to know many Vietnamese—in their own country, in meetings in Europe and, subsequently, as students in my classes in the States. Of the many tragedies associated with the war against them, worst were the permanent losses they and their families, their society, and their beautiful land have suffered. Here let me say simply that the cultural differences between the Vietnamese and ourselves, their view of the meaning of life and of family, their long historical achievement (until invaded by the French in 1860) of what was essentially a decentralized village democracy, the human achievement and good sense of their traditional economic system—all this and more redound to their favor by comparison with *our* accomplishments.

But the war imposed our politics, our culture, our ferocity on them—as though we are a people insensate and by nature violent. When I was in

Laos and North Vietnam in the spring of 1970, it is not an exaggeration to say that both lands, pockmarked by a seemingly infinite number of bombs, looked like the surface of the moon. In Vientiane, my companions and I visited Laotian refugee camps, where in a space that might have been comfortable for ten people (at most), there were several hundred, sleeping like logs next to each other on several tiers of "shelves." They had been bombed out from their regions on the principle of "denying water to the fish"—the water being the sustenance of the land, the fish being the guerrillas, the Pathet Lao.

My companions Noam Chomsky and Richard Fernandez and I managed to get an appointment with the then Prime Minister of Laos, Prince Souvanna Phouma (in an elegant and air-conditioned villa built for him by the U.S. Rural Development staff there—the subsequently admitted cover for the CIA in Laos). When I asked the Prime Minister how he, working with the still covert U.S. forces, could permit his country and his people to be destroyed, he blithely answered that it was for their own good. [28]

LBJ's contempt for and ignorance of the people in Indochina we were killing and so many were dying for is all too well revealed in an episode of 1964 noted by David Halberstam in his celebrated 1972 book, *The Best and the Brightest.* The United States had for some time been engaged in covert activities (largely by the so-called "Green Berets"), a process accompanied by the accelerating collapse of the Saigon government. LBJ's reaction to this deterioration was to investigate the possibilities of bombing the North (which we began to do later, in February 1965)—it being his mistaken assumption that the (southern) NLF's strength was entirely a creation of North Vietnam, rather than an assertion of the long and continuing attempt to achieve independence. So: punish North Vietnam. But Johnson, hoping that such punishment would cause the North Vietnamese to give in—and thus quickly take the whole problem out of his hands—also wanted to know as much as possible what their reaction to such bombing would be. When the CIA's answers proved to be uninformative, Johnson exploded:

> Wasn't there someone working in the interior of their government who would slip out with a stolen paper saying what they [Hanoi] were going to do? I thought you guys [CIA] had people everywhere, that you knew everything, and now you don't even have anything about a raggedy-ass little fourth-rate country. All you have to do is get some Chinese coolies from a San Francisco laundry shop and drop them over there and use them. Get them to drop their answers in a bottle and put the bottle in the Pacific. . . . [29]

After assuming the last two sentences to be a despairing joke, we are left with the attitudes of a liberal President of the United States that leave one wondering about, for example, what Reagan's might have been. Of course we needn't depend only on wonder. When he was Governor of California, Reagan, much exasperated with opponents of the war, not least of all those at Berkeley (concerning whom he thought it might be time "to spill a little blood"), offered his agreement with General LeMay that we should "bomb Vietnam back into the Stone Age," adding that "we could then pave it over and use it as a parking lot."

Fatally joined to his misunderstanding and underestimating of the Vietnamese determination to get foreigners out of their country, was Johnson's belief that he could move toward his Great Society and victory in Vietnam at one and the same time: guns *and* butter. That belief was grounded on an analysis—the military's as well as his own—that were the United States to escalate the war by bombing and (if that didn't work swiftly) the insertion of a sufficient number of ground troops, the war would be over in a trice. He therefore believed that neither the fiscal nor the human costs of the war would become politically significant. In all those respects, he was no worse than those who preceded and followed him. It was during Johnson's years that Senator William Fulbright—one of the few establishment critics of the war—came to speak of "the arrogance of power."

As the definition of a "sufficient number of troops" or of bombs rose from the tens of thousands to the hundreds of thousands, the money costs and the casualties soon constituted an imposing political (and ultimately military) disaster. LBJ's way to avoid all that was to escalate militarily to end the war, and to keep its money costs secret—even from his own budget chief. He lied to the latter by hiding $10 billion (!!!) in some accounting cubby hole (enabling us to wonder how much else has been and is being hidden in such cubbyholes). In doing so, he was also making it impossible for that expenditure (multiplied by three or more times for its aggregative effects) to be made without a substantial inflationary impact—felt and paid for in various ways in the United States and in Western Europe from the late Sixties on. One consequence was that the German Bundesbank (their Fed) began to place pressure on us to end the Vietnam war in 1968.

All the while, the pressures were rising on Johnson as a person and as President. He began to take an always more, almost fanatic interest in the war, and to be obsessed with its details, which he sought to manage more and more. Naturally both he and his presidency (and the war) paid for such distorting behavior.

The consuming tragedy for LBJ's presidency—setting aside here the costs for so many others—was that as he went from 1964 to 1968 his relatively great strength as a politician came to be, had to be, transformed from gaining conservative support for his liberal domestic programs to holding liberal support for his aggressive military program. In the summer of 1967, the *New York Times* made this comment (in an uncharacteristic stream-of-consciousness style):

> the program for the cities [is] gutted and aid for the poor at home and abroad shredded, open housing [is] dead and the tax bills shelved and gun-control and the wiretap ban lobbied out of sight and some cost-free consumer protection on the ropes and political campaign financing and reforms already canned for winter storage. . . . With much luck and hard work [LBJ] will wind up the first session with a military draft bill that wasn't his, antipoverty and foreign aid bills that barely resembled his, and a reworked education act, and a thinned-out air-pollution program, and a crime bill aimed more at rioters and Supreme Court Justices than crime, and. . .[30]

As Doris Kearns makes clear in *Lyndon Johnson and the American Dream*, drawing from numerous conversations with Johnson regarding his history as a boy and young man, he had a bottomless need for approval, matched by an equally strong need for power—the latter to be used to gain his will when approval was lacking. His inclination to humiliate when necessary (or, sometimes, just for the hell of it), is the stuff of innumerable stories, whether recounted by Kearns, Halberstam, Sherrill, or others. Try this one on for size (remembering, boys and girls, that it is the President of the United States of America of whom we learn):

> When he had to go to the bathroom in the middle of a conversation, it was not unusual for him to move the discussion there. Johnson seemed delighted as he told me of "one of the delicate Kennedyites [all of whom he despised, envied, feared] who came into the bathroom with me and then found it utterly impossible to look at me while I sat there on the toilet. You'd think he'd never seen those parts of the body before. For there he was, standing as far away from me as he possibly could. . . ."[31]

Johnson was a large man, almost a caricature of a Texan: ambitious, proud, "hongry." He had big ideas and bigger plans, but he fell flat on his face trying to keep from being the first U.S. President to lose a war, instead he lost everything: his one-time popularity, his power, and his presidency; and he made an appalling contribution to ruining the Vietnamese and, on a lesser scale, the U.S. military and the U.S. economy.

He stepped out of the election race in March of 1968. Subsequently, and probably out of a sense of abdicating not just his office but the war itself, he consented for the United States to enter into peace talks with the North Vietnamese and the Saigon government, in Paris. It was an infinitely difficult matter on which to make *any* kind of progress: many weeks were spent just trying to decide what the *shape* of the table would be, in order not to grant or seem to grant to any of the three a particular pride of place, or power—or something. Finally, some genius proposed a *round* table, and that was accepted. As summer approached, the talks were underway, and so was I, to Paris and this Story:

Not Your Everyday True-False Exam

Along with four other profs—George McT. Kahin of Cornell, Jonathan Mirsky of Dartmouth, Marilyn Blatt Young of Michigan, and Howard Zinn of Boston U.—all of us known to be active against the war and thought to be reasonably well-informed, I was invited to meet with the North Vietnamese Peace Delegation in Paris. We did so for a week. We were picked up at our hotel by the Vietnamese every morning at 8 a.m., and taken back at midnight. We spent all those hours answering questions by one or another member of the Hanoi delegation.

The question asked recurringly, and in effect the *only* question asked, was this: *If* Johnson were to sign an agreement to cease bombing the North, 1) *would* he keep it? and 2) *could* he keep it? The first question had to do with Johnson, the second with how power works in the United States. We argued in front of the Vietnamese for all the long days and evenings of that week; and whatever they did or did not learn, we five, disagreeing among ourselves to one serious degree or another, all learned something in that tight little seminar. And afterwards.

Averill Harriman was LBJ's ambassador to the meetings. Before we left Paris, we arranged an appointment with him, in which we spoke at great length about what seemed to us to be the sincerity and flexibility of the Vietnamese. We might just as well have been talking to an empty chair. When we returned to the States, we expected to meet with the press, with whom a conference had been arranged. *Nobody* came. Large coincidence, that *nobody* came? (Johnson did sign the agreement not to bomb the North; and it was soon broken.)

So now we've finished with almost all of the Sixties, which will seem to have been good times rolling, compared with what's careening around the corner: "the New Nixon." *Oy vey.*

It was Nixon, or, more accurately, his P.R. gunsels who thought of calling him "new"—meaning broader in interests, perhaps even inching toward decency, instead of continuing as the snake who had risen to prominence entirely by his work with the House Un-American Activities Committee.

The *first* "new Nixon" was proclaimed when he ran for president in 1960; from then on, there has been a series of them, continuing fungus-like to grow to the present day—even after he went (I hope!) to his just reward.

My mother, 1920s.

*Number one dad: My father finishing first at a Stanford/Cal track meet, 1908.
Earl Warren, who was on the same team, is in the distance, coming in third.*

With my brother Mervyn, Alameda, CA, 1927.

Alameda, 1918. Muh and Dad are the couple in the center, and Grandma Dowd stands second to right.

A day of genuine celebration: the Golden Gate Bridge on opening day morning, 1937. San Francisco was hard hit by the depression, but as a relatively high income town, the descent was not to the absolute depths of the rest of the nation. The building of the bridges provided many jobs, directly and indirectly; it also did something noticeable—even at the time—for morale. (Reprinted courtesy of the California Historical Society, San Francisco. FN-19702.)

With Lt. Hugh Bowden, a navigator in my outfit, New Guinea.
The bananas didn't really taste that good.

With Zirel, waiting overseas orders, North Carolina, 1942.

Primary flight training, Tulare, CA, 1942.

With Jeff, 1949.

Peace!: Marching with Kay on San Francisco's Market Street, 1964. I was teaching at Berkeley's summer session; shortly thereafter I went South to Freedom Summer.

*Haywood County, TN, summer 1964: I'm with Danny B. (far right)
and two other volunteers.*

With "Square" Morman, one of the best organizers, and his family, that summer.

Cornell's first anti-Vietnam war sit-in, Barton Hall, April 1965. ROTC supporters verged on violence when troops could not parade around the gymnasium. (From the 1967 Cornellian, *Division of Rare and Manuscript Collections, Cornell University Library.)*

The Resistance organizing the first mass draft card turn-in (October 16, 1967). Left to right: Felix Kramer, Lewis Zipin, and smoking his non-filtered Lucky Strikes, Bruce Dancis. Willard Straight Hall, fall 1967. (From the 1969 Cornellian, *Division of Rare and Manuscript Collections, Cornell University Library.)*

Jenny, early '60s.

Spring Mobe, 1967. More than 1,200 Cornell students and faculty marched from the UN to Central Park. 125,000 people were on hand to listen to speeches by Martin Luther King, Stokely Carmichael, and Dr. Benjamin Spock. (From the Cornell Daily Sun, Kramer New Left Collection, *Division of Rare and Manuscript Collections, Cornell University Library.*

Cornell at the Pentagon—or rather, on the Pentagon—in October 1967. (From the 1969 Cornellian, *Division of Rare and Manuscript Collections, Cornell University Library.)*

I WANT YOU TO BUY

First issue of the Cornell SDS magazine for which I wrote, 1968. First Issue *reflected the New Left's countercultural stance, including reviews of the Rolling Stones and Country Joe and the Fish alongside articles on the war, apartheid, and women's liberation. The editors picked Jeff Grossman for the cover for his scruffiest-man-on-campus look.*

No. 1 · · · · · The First Issue · · · · · Jan. 29, 1968 · · · · · 15¢ (if you have it)

Marching to the Ithaca, NY, draft board, December 3, 1967. Chip Marshall (second from left), who almost never wore such clothes, wore a coat and tie that day to mark the solemn occasion of turning in his draft card. The others from left to right: Lisa Johnson, Chris Carroll, unidentified student, Jeff, Bruce Dancis, Mike Rotkin, Jim Murray, and English professor Jonathan Bishop. (From the 1969 Cornellian, *Division of Rare and Manuscript Collections, Cornell University Library.)*

Moratorium Day at Cornell, November 1969. (From the 1970 Cornellian, *Division of Rare and Manuscript Collections, Cornell University Library.)*

Baltimore, May 17, 1968: Frs. Philip Berrigan (left) and Daniel Berrigan (right) watch as two baskets of draft board records, removed from the Catonsville, MD, draft board office, burn. (Credit: UPI/Corbis-Bettmann.)

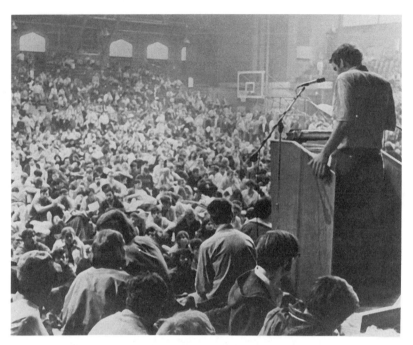

Jim Murray addresses the crowd at a mass SDS meeting in the Cornell Armory, April 19, 1969. Students met in support of the Willard Straight Hall takeover by black students. (From the 1969 Cornellian, *Division of Rare and Manuscript Collections, Cornell University Library.)*

With Mike Rotkin (right) and an unidentified student. (From the 1969 Cornellian, Division of Rare and Manuscript Collections, Cornell University Library.)

April 20, 1969, 4:10 PM: Tom Jones and Larry Dickson exit Willard Straight Hall, following the famous one-and-a-half-day armed occupation by 120 students. (From the Ithaca Journal *[April 21, 1969], Kramer New Left Collection, Division of Rare and Manuscript Collections, Cornell University Library.)*

Right-wing graffiti, May 1969, during the SDS-led anti-ROTC demonstrations at Cornell. These signs are aimed at prominent members of the "action faction"—David Burak, Chip Marshall, and Jeff—and at me. (From the 1970 Cornellian, Division of Rare and Manuscript Collections, Cornell University Library.)

Heartbreak House: A Cornell SDS meeting just before the "action faction" break, spring 1969. Jeff (far right) is sitting on the far side of me, in more ways than one.

*At Jeff's wedding, Venice, CA, 1989. Left to right: Jenny, me,
Zirel, Jeff, Jane (my new daughter-in-law), and Anna.*

*With Veblen,
our bichon frisé.*

PART III
PARADISE LOST

5   PRESIDENT QUEEG[1] AND HIS MERRY MEN; AND THE REMAINS OF THE DECADE: 1970-1980

> Now all things melt and shift in the moon's light.
> The walls before you alter. The landscape
> Alters. Familiar things
> Take unfamiliar shape.
> The building you knew at noon of such a height
> Will shrink by dusk. The very street
> That led you to your house begins to change,
> And as you walk the thing within your mind
> Takes form before the echo of your feet.
>
> —Archibald Fleming, "The Destroyers"

i.

Control Freak

Nixon was among the most powerful politicians in our history, but his weaknesses—mostly centering on his need for always more power—splotched him like measles. He was elected to the House, to the Senate, and twice to the Presidency, but was there anyone (other than Tricia) who ever *liked* him? He always cultivated the appearance of decorum and his idea of the well-dressed man—while also and always wearing the rictus smile of a bowing undertaker. And oh, those shifty eyes.

How he must have envied (and probably hated) Reagan! However vast Reagan's crimes, he was nailed on none of them; however dishonest, trusted by (almost) all. Nixon could never get away with anything (or did he?); and a reading of *The Haldeman Diaries* shows that he was distrusted even by his closest associates, the gang that couldn't shoot straight, nor did he ever trust them.[2] Users all. Small comfort to us that they deserved each other.

But Reagan: promising to balance the budget, he quadrupled the national debt while trashing the idea of decent social policy and crushing its always scant realities; he pulled off Iran-Contra and the S&L giveaways and Iraqgate (with the ongoing and subsequent help of Bush), plus who knows how much else. And although almost everyone assumes, believes, or knows that Reagan did all those things, could he *ever* have been impeached? Are you kidding? Were Reagan able to run again he would win hands down.

Our wretched Tricky Dick resigned because he knew he would be impeached—though as he saw things he had done no wrong. As Nixon used to say, however, let me make one thing perfectly clear: the difference between RN and RR was not one merely—or mostly—of personality and style. The main tendencies of our nation and of the global economy were changing drastically as Nixon took up the presidency, without which he would not have gained his narrow victory in 1968 and his landslide reelection in 1972. And it is unlikely that Reagan could have swept into office in a society sitting on solid foundations.

In his often clumsy ways, Nixon spurred on the many sorry changes already underway as the 1970s began. He was undone not by his conservatism or even by his petty and great crimes so much as by the very ways and means that had brought him to power.

As the Sixties ended and the Seventies began, Nixon stood as Colossus, one leg in each decade, dominating—the self-made and principal beneficiary of his imaginative and vital role in fostering and strengthening the essential and virulent anti-communism at the heart of the evolving Cold War.

His fame grew like weeds after his opening congressional campaign in 1946, against the mildly liberal Representative Jerry Voorhis (D., CA), which placed Nixon in Congress. From then on he became the Houdini of political dirty tricks—neither first nor last with his tenacious campaign against Alger Hiss, neither least nor most important (except to me) in the dirty trick which, in 1970, put my son in the slammer (as noted later), neither most nor least criminal the series of petty crimes and major lies that knocked him out of the presidency.

Nixon could have survived, perhaps flourished, even with his personality and temperament, except for the three major problems that had him scurrying for solutions in his years as President: the always more imposing political and military crises in and about Vietnam, deepening troubles in the world economy, and the onset of domestic and global stagflation.

Nixon had not set the stage for any of those, nor did or could he resolve them satisfactorily; he did not function much worse than those preceding or following him. Nixon didn't invent the misuse of presidential power, nor was it he who initiated the "imperial presidency." The first honor doubtless must be shared among all of our presidents (if also in unequal degree); the second, the imperial presidency, a mere twinkle in Teddy Roosevelt's eye, was a bouncing boy when Wilson left office and nourished by FDR; it was ready for its crown by the time Truman went home to Missouri, and JFK died wearing it.

To the degree that Nixon might be seen as directly responsible for deepening and spreading disaster, the focus would belong on Indochina, rather in the area of political economy. We turn to those first things first: Nixon (and Kissinger's) policies on Vietnam, Cambodia, and Laos, and the associated and increased disruptions at home.

Here first a memory from the home scene that reveals something of the tenor of the times on campus as 1970 began.

Story: Peace Feeler

In 1969, after his failure to behave with even minimal competence in the face of upheaval both during and after the black students' occupation of the Student Union, the President of Cornell was asked by the Trustees to depart. As noted earlier, there was considerable opposition among the faculty to ratifying the agreement the black students sought; even more considerable was the support from the student body: the gymnasium was occupied by 8,000 students (more than half of the student body) for several days, the president finally and reluctantly attended, made an empty speech, and the gym stayed occupied. Finally the Trustees saw to it that a mutually acceptable agreement was made. A new president was appointed to take us into the 1970s, a relatively calm and non-ideological scientist, acquainted with the stubbornness of facts.

As tension continued, the new president thought it wise to try to understand it and, among his many efforts to do so, he asked me to participate in a meeting of all the top brass of the university. As I entered the Board Room, filled with all those heavies, I remarked—pleasantly enough, in intent: "My, this must be a very important meeting." "If you're here, Dowd," snapped one of the VP's, "it *can't* be important." (Not bad, I thought. However:) "That mouth of yours will get you in trouble someday," I snapped back. And it was all uphill from there, a yapfest of mutual "dissing" (as they say these days), little in common among us but the source of our paychecks. When I left Cornell at the end of the year, not to return, sorrow was measured.

Already in 1968, when running against Humphrey, Nixon knew that either losing or winning the war had become politically impossible: a way had to be found to get out of there in a process that would maintain our dignity as the world's most powerful society. "We cannot allow the world to see us," Nixon insisted, "as a pitiful, helpless giant." Just as Ike had promised to get us out of Korea, Nixon promised to get us out of Vietnam.

Nixon's ends and means on the war in Indochina were of a piece with all his other policies: he was unprincipled or, as one wag put it, he had a different principle for every occasion. He needed to rule, and he needed to win—or, at worst, not to lose. Nixon didn't care how we got out of Vietnam, so long as it seemed we had won. So, in his first year or so in charge, he and his incredible sidekick and national security chief Kissinger embraced and clawed while praising and scorning each other, and put into effect a terrible stew of policies.

The most systematic and publicized of the latter was "Vietnamization": pulling U.S. ground troops out of Vietnam while increasing the U.S. air war— "increasing the number and changing the uniform of the corpses," its accurate if unofficial description. The most covert of their policies was the stepped-up air war over Laos and Cambodia, and their invasion by U.S. troops—and, as a direct consequence, the killing of at least one million Cambodians in the 1970s. The conclusion by William Shawcross, author of *Sideshow*, the best book on Cambodia is succinct and exact: "Cambodia was not a mistake; it was a crime." [3]

ii.

Bully Boys

"Vietnamization": a clever, coherent set of interdependent and relentlessly coldblooded policies. First, beginning slowly but accelerating, get the U.S. ground troops out of Vietnam while, secondly, increasing the U.S. air war over North Vietnam and over any parts of Cambodia thought to be used as supply and troop reinforcement routes for the North Vietnamese, simultaneously escalating the already heavy bombing of Laos to further weaken the Pathet Lao (the Laotian counterpart of the Vietnamese independence movement), and, to top it all off, substitute an effectively volunteer U.S. army for the draft, in order to eliminate the critical antidraft muscle of the antiwar movement.

Aside from any qualms left over from your Quaker background, good thinking, Mr. President. Also a combination of great haste and revolting means and ends, when one learns from Haldeman and from Shawcross that the plans to bomb Cambodia were put in place almost before Nixon and Kissinger had learned where the bathroom was in the Oval Office. Their murderous plans for Cambodia had the overall name of "Menu," with the progression of targets named "Breakfast," "Lunch," "Snack," "Dinner," "Dessert," and "Supper." And then throw up.

The bombing of Cambodia (a neutral nation) began on March 17, 1969;[4] by the time it ended, fourteen months later, 3,630 raids—carried out by flights of fifty or so eight-engined B-52s (flying mostly from distant Guam or Okinawa), each carrying many dozens of 750-lb. bombs—had occurred. And, as will be seen, all this was done in a pattern of unprecedented secrecy[5]—from the aircrews and their superior officers, from relevant congressional committees and cabinet members, et al.—as well it had to be: it was all illegal in U.S. and world law, for Cambodia was a neutral power.

As these horrors were unrolling, the antiwar movement was responding with rising numbers and outrage. For me the process brought about a trip to Hanoi and a confrontation with Ross Perot in Laos (that wake you up?), part of a long set of memories of experiences in and around Vietnam—beginning in World War II, thence to Berkeley, to Cornell, the teach-ins, the Mobe, and then, in 1970, back to Indochina—and, as 1970 drew to its end, a related foray into (as they say, of all places) Carbondale, Illinois.

iii.

Backdrop: From Southeast Asia to Academia and Return

In the last year of World War II, I was doing air-sea rescue work in the Philippines and in the waters of the South China Sea between there and Indochina, assisted on land by local guerrilla forces. While waiting to go home after the war ended, I was made aware one day in Manila of U.S. participation in helping the French get back into Vietnam. All that led me to incorporate studies of Southeast Asia into my education, and when I began as a Lecturer at Berkeley in 1950, my main course was "Economic Development in Southeast Asia." Thus I stayed attuned to the ongoing realities of, first, the French war in Indochina and, next, the taking over of that war by the United States when the French gave up in 1954. And in 1953, when I began to teach at Cornell, I was in the presence (but not a member) of the leading Southeast Studies Program in the United States (whose director, George Kahin, fifteen years later, was one of those with whom I went to Paris to meet with the North Vietnamese Peace Delegation).

As the man said, one thing leads to another. My first major political involvement with the war in Indochina was when the teach-ins began. I soon became their executive head, and that in turn led to my becoming part of the evolution and the steering committee of the Mobe. A key person in the Mobe was one of the leading pacifists in the United States, Dave Dellinger; also the most trusted of all of us by the Vietnamese—both the southern (NLF) and northern revolutionaries (Viet Minh). It was Dave who suggested me and my four companions to the Vietnamese for the Paris meeting; and it was Dave who suggested me and my two companions, Noam Chomsky and Richard Fernandez[6] for the March 1970 trip to Laos and North Vietnam.

Story: Shhhh! Spooks at Work

I found out that I was going to Indochina in what has to be seen as a mighty peculiar fashion. One afternoon at my Cornell office the phone rang, and this was the gist of the conversation: "Professor Dowd, this is Mr. X at the Department of State. We understand you are going to North Vietnam soon...." "I am?! Nobody has told me." Confusion on the other end. "Anyhow, Professor Dowd, we wanted...." "What do you mean, 'anyhow,' what the hell are you talking about?" "Professor Dowd, I can't tell you how, but we have come to understand that you will be invited to go to Hanoi, and the Department of State would like you to carry certain requests for us concerning the U.S. prisoners held in the North." After a heated interchange I informed X that I too was much concerned with the U.S. prisoners, and that ending the war and getting out of Vietnam was the one best thing we could do for them; and as for the Department of State, it could kiss my patootie. It was not until the following day that I received a call from Dave asking me if I could go to Hanoi. And a footnote: When I got my FBI files a few years later, I also asked for any CIA files, which they sent—all 200 pages. The CIA had followed me at the request of both the FBI and the Department of State; in those files was a word-for-word copy of an impromptu speech on U.S. antiwar sentiment I gave before about 400 Vietnamese in Hanoi: impromptu, unduly long (even without family stories), cheered by them but not, I suppose, by the CIA.

iv.

Cry, the Beloved Country [7]

En Route: Noam and Dick and I had schedules that didn't allow us to leave the States together. I was to meet Noam in Paris (where I had a meeting), and we were to meet Dick in Copenhagen and go together to Thailand, then Laos, and then to Hanoi. My meeting in Paris was with Maria Jolas, and is worth an internal Story.

Maria could be described as the Mother Courage for the U.S. draft evaders/ resisters in France. She was from Louisville, KY, wore flowered housedresses, was by no means slender, and was about as down-home as you can get. Her late husband Ernest and she had been at *the* center of the *literati* in Paris in the interwar period, something like a French Bloomsbury Group. Maria never spoke a word of French in my presence (other than to French people), but she had translated Joyce's *Ulysses* into French (a book difficult enough to work with in English for the rest of us). Anyhow, when we met she said she had arranged a small dinner for the evening, with Wilfred Burchett and Mary McCarthy. The latter was more glamorous than the former but while she mostly gossiped that evening, Burchett was very helpful for my oncoming visit. An Australian communist, he was one of the best-informed journalists on Vietnam. Of all journalists, he was the most trusted by the North Vietnamese; he had been covering the war over the years, and he had a lot to say. The food at the neighborhood *bistro* was splendid, I paid for all of us with a modest flourish, and the trip was off to a great start.

The next day I met Noam, and spent the next three weeks in a frequently interrupted but—at least for me—wonderful dialogue. He had become the most influential linguist in the world, while at the same time he was carrying on a running battle against U.S. foreign policy (in articles and books and demonstrations) that continues to this day. Dick joined us (carrying a basketball!), we stayed overnight in Bangkok, and then flew into Laos, where we had to stay for a week.

Laos: We had to stay for a week in Vientiane, the main city of Laos, because the only way one could get to Hanoi was on the International Control Commission (ICC) plane, which only went there once a week. The three members of the ICC were Poland, Canada, and India, and it had a rotating chair. India—hostile to North Vietnam because of the latter's presumed friendship with China (of which more in a minute)—was in charge during our stay, the head man disapproved of our visit and, although he couldn't stop us, he could make us wait. A week. It was worth it for us, however.

During that week we were able to confront the Lao refugee disaster that our bombing had created, and also to interview the Lao Prime Minister. We were also able to learn something about U.S. reporting from Laos, and to tangle with our latter-day saviour, Ross Himself. But first this:

All the News . . . : After we had met with and interviewed the Lao refugees, and had seen the horrifying way they were living and learned of the bombings that made them into refugees, we returned to our hotel (one of two in Vientiane, a town of perhaps 10,000 people), and went to the bar where, as usual, was sitting David, the only U.S. journalist filing from Laos (for the AP). We had chatted slightly on an earlier occasion, in a friendly fashion. That day, still reeling from the refugees' stories, I asked him whether he had interviewed, filed any stories on them. No and yes, in that order, he said. Why not yes to both? Unnecessary, David said; he got all the information he needed from the U.S. "redevelopment" (!) agency—the local CIA front. When I began to assert the irresponsibility of getting his information that way he replied in a memorable fashion: "Look, Dowd. I'm not writing for the fancy people who read the *New York Times;* I'm writing for the folks in Dubuque." "And you're the only source they have there in Dubuque, whose only basis for understanding the Laotian war is therefore contaminated—by you," I replied. Half-drunk already, as usual, he proceeded then to finish the job. (And, some time in the 1980s, I noted without pleasure that David had become a foreign correspondent for—of all papers!—the *New York Times.*)

Enter Santa Claus (without the snow): The next day, when we returned to the hotel from our previously-described meeting with Souvanna Phouma, there in the lobby was Perot, along with a gaggle of over fifty reporters, nurses, and gofers, just arrived in Perot's chartered Braniff DC-8. Mission: Hanoi. This was March, but it turns out that Perot was still trying to get to Hanoi on his failed Christmas visit to the POWs, and the Braniff was loaded with Christmas presents. Anyhow, Perot had heard about us from David, and that we were soon to go to Hanoi, and that we were in contact with the North Vietnamese Consul (whose consulate was just outside of Vientiane, despite the warring relationship between the two countries.)

This is 1970, remember: Perot very rich from his software capers, looking just as he always did in the news—dark blue suit, white shirt, uptight necktie— strutting around and, in all that heat, dry as a bone. So he comes up to the three of us, and "Ah hear that y'all are going to Hanoi," and "How'd y'all like to use y'alls' influence (!) with that Vietnam consul fella to persuade him to let mah Braniff fly into Hanoi, meet with the prisoners, have the nurses examine and attend to them, drop off their Christmas presents, and then *de*part?"

After the talk with the likes of Phouma we were in no mood to screw around with the likes of Perot. I tend to lose my normal easygoing ways in such circumstances; but by comparison with Noam, I was like a sleepy cat. He was eloquently angry and Perot, unused to being spoken to except by supplicants, was flustered, blustered, purpled up, and almost began to sweat.

We had previously met with the consul in order to arrange for a visa, and were scheduled to visit him once more on the following morning at 8 a.m. Before leaving the hotel, we had learned that Perot and his bunch, taking a leaf from the Sixties, had planned a protest demonstration outside the consulate that same morning—I know all this is hard to believe, but we're talking Perot— and to keep it up until they too got a visa.

Mind you: Hanoi and the rest of North Vietnam were being bombed regularly and heavily (including while we were there), all denials by the United States to the contrary notwithstanding. NO planes, including the ICC plane, could land during the day, and at night one flew into a dark field and then, when the plane was perhaps 200 feet off the ground, a few runway lights blipped on and, as soon as the wheels slowed, off again, and the plane was surrounded and boarded by soldiers. And Perot could not dig why *he* and his large group couldn't just fly in with their big U.S. plane, do their thing, and leave gracefully.

So, while we were visiting with the consul, he asked us what did *we* think he should do about the demo that was already shuffling around outside. We agreed it would be good to let them stay out there in the hot sun a few hours, when they might finally get the idea about how foolish they were. About noon, we exited the consulate (an old country house) into the heat and the dust—

and the no water, and the no toilets—to walk through a *very* angry bunch, not a few of them from Texas, including one unreasonably large reporter who went after me physically, calling me a fuckin' traitor (which, by his and Nixon's and at least half of the citizens of the U.S.A.'s definition, I was), and all that. Perot was still dry as a bone; and still the dumbest billionaire in the world. Or maybe not.

North Vietnam: finally. What a muchness! Only some of it can be communicated here, and that with terrible brevity. China has been mentioned before: remember that teach-in when our Saigon consul said we were fighting the Vietnamese because they were a surrogate for the Chinese? He may even have believed that. Well, the very first thing we did on our very first morning was to visit the National Museum in Hanoi, where the most striking exhibit occupies the walls of an entire room with paintings that portray the war between the Chinese and the Vietnamese—that began a thousand years ago and that, as the Vietnamese see it, will never end. (And that continues today.)

Children: Every morning at about 4:30 in Hanoi, one was awakened by loudspeakers giving exercise directions, and people were exercising out in the street. And thousands of bicycles. So I would get up, and wander around Hanoi. Believe it or not, nobody led me, nobody followed. And that created a problem for a while, because Vietnamese street signs were undecipherable to me. I thought of unrolling a ball of string as I walked, honestly. I just took care, walking the way a cat does in new surroundings: a short distance out, and then back; and so on. And while taking care, the very first morning, I was passed by a dozen or so Vietnamese children, ages roughly six to twelve I think, all of them with red scarves around their necks, all of them talking, laughing, arm in arm—all of them, when they saw very tall and blue-eyed me, clustering around me as though I were a quarterback in a huddle. I almost wept (as now, I almost weep): the joy of it, the sorrow of it.

Scholars: On another morning, Noam was to be taken to the university, where he would give a seminar on linguistics (Hanoi, 1970!), eagerly awaited by the relevant faculty. As just noted, days started early in Hanoi, and at 6 a.m. Noam's host arrived to whisk him away. Noam was suffering from diarrhea; and I informed his host of that as they were leaving. When he returned from the university, Noam told me that in the midst of his seminar a man entered and, without a word, handed him a roll of toilet paper—a rarity not seen in North Vietnam by us—and life went on.

It is worth adding that on our journey from Paris, Noam had made it clear to me that he had antipathetic feelings toward the North Vietnamese: he had much admired the NLF of the South, a fiercely independent, essentially anarchistic group—very much in harmony with the pre-French village democracy of Vietnam. [8] But, as the U.S. military presence in the South expanded, the NLF's survival came always more to rely upon arms from the North; and, as happened in the Spanish Civil War, to have to conform always more to the disciplined communism of the North. However, even before our time in North Vietnam had ended, Noam had changed his mind: he had come to admire the North Vietnamese too, to believe that their "disciplined communism" was different in kind and spirit and origin from its distant cousin Stalinism, that Ho Chi Minh—always called "Uncle Ho"—was an extraordinarily gifted political leader, that the ways and means of the Viet Minh were their response to always worsening Western transgression, not natural to their own culture, or their own aims.

I would add that the aims of both the NLF and the Viet Minh were to build a Vietnam that would be communitarian and solidaristic—as it had been in its free past. However, it was Ho's genius (and of those with whom he worked for so many decades) to understand that in this century there was no way to recapture Vietnamese village democracy except through some approximation to democratic socialism, which could not possibly occur unless combined with a nationalism that would banish the foreigners from their country—and that the long and bloody struggle needed to accomplish that required larger aims consistent with the Vietnamese past. You can argue with all that if you wish; you would be less inclined to do so, were you to study out their history.

POWs: While Noam was giving his seminar, Dick and I were taken to interview three U.S. POWs, all naval pilots. It was very difficult to go through that experience, for more than one reason: the evident misery of the three men, the setting in which the interview took place—controlled, staged, tense, problematic in every sense of the word, not least in that we must have seemed to the pilots to be allies of their captors. It is still difficult, to think about, to write about. I feel obliged. We asked what we could do in terms of communication with families, etc., on our return, and that worked out o.k. Then, each of them made a statement; and you knew the statement was not going to be pro-war; as you also knew that POWs—at least some of them—would have good reason to be against war. My own impression was that two of the statements had been written by someone else (or might as well have been); but that one of them was at least partially the pilot's own: it was against that war and the way it was being waged. Neither Dick nor I accepted anything we saw or heard without skepticism. That "third" pilot returned to the States, he was attacked for having allowed his views to become public (not through us, however); and he defended himself, and reaffirmed that part of his statement to us that I have just noted. After the war. There is no doubt that POWs in North Vietnam were treated badly, up to and including various forms of torture. Their worst treatment was often that given to them by civilians on the spot where they crashed: under-standably. POWs are never treated well; and they are usually treated badly—as are prisoners always and everywhere.

Little Old Ladies: but not in tennis shoes. Little old ladies smaller than my 5'1" mother, and thinner, and always dressed in black, and almost always running—we would say *jogging*—running and carrying, with a six- or eight-foot pole on the shoulder, carrying a box or a can on each end—running slowly, but running, steadily, in Hanoi, on the country roads, little old ladies, running and carrying. At one time, I was able to test the weight of one of their loads: big and healthy though I was, it was very hard for me to get it off the ground. Jesus, I thought.

Their Big Shots: We sometimes ate alone in the hotel; more often we had dinner with the editor of *Nham Dan,* the principal—maybe the only—news-paper in Hanoi. He was a man in his sixties. He was very neat, he always wore the same suit, the same shirt and tie, the same shoes—I looked. Always clean, the clothes so worn they were almost diaphanous: the clothes of the editor-equivalent of the *New York Times.* He had gone to prison first when he was seventeen, had spent thirty years of his life in political prison. We always had a translator present, even though the editor and Noam both spoke French well (but Dick and I did not). So the conversations were in Vietnamese, translated. One evening, while the editor was discussing something political, our waitress expostulated with him, more than briefly. The difference seemed sharp, and seemed to be carried on between equals. One can't be sure, of course, without knowing the language, but there is body language, too, and I've never seen that body language between a big shot and a waitress any place else.

And then there was our meeting with Prime Minister Pham Van Dong, the principal reason for our being there (although the conversations with the editor covered much the same ground). He lived in a simple house on the edge of Hanoi. Also in his sixties, at least. Calm, gracious, handsome, dressed well (also in old clothes). He brought us up short when he asked the big question—which we took to be hypothetical—this in mid-March 1970: "If it were known that the U.S. army had invaded Cambodia, what would be the effect in your country?" We argued back and forth in his presence for a long time. I said that all hell would break loose in the United States; Dick thought something less than that; Noam said, perhaps, but it wouldn't make any difference. Then Pham Van Dong said the invasion had in fact been going on for weeks, had begun slowly, was speeding up. That was in mid-March. On April 30, Nixon announced that U.S. and South Vietnamese troops had undertaken an "incursion" over the border into Cambodia. ("Incursion": sounds like fun, if you say it over and over.) All hell broke loose: Kent State University and Jackson State University, students wounded and killed; demonstrations, speeches, protests, all over, over, and over. As I had expected. But Noam was right: it didn't make any difference (except to those hurt and killed). Hell cooled down, froze over; the war went on, always more murderously. Nixon was re-elected in a landslide—despite or because of the invasion?

After our discussion, Pham Van Dong turned to casual, more personal matters. One of them involved him asking about my children, and what did they think about the war? When I told him about Jeff's politics and activities—and allowed that he was a bit wilder than I—the Prime Minister said "Tell your son I think he is on a good path." (At the time, I was afraid to encourage Jeff by telling him.)

And Their Beloved Country: We spent a few days traveling around south of Hanoi, along the famous Highway 1, some of it along the coast and the lovely sea, some of it inland. It is a beautiful country, lovely plains, stark hills and mountains, farms landscaped as though by a gardener; but innumerable bomb craters—thousands and thousands of bomb craters, always—made use of, some growing rice, some with ducks swimming in them (some with flowers); and we walked along the bombed-out dikes, bombed to cause floods, bombed to deny sustenance to the people ("What bombed-out dikes? We never bombed any dikes."); and we walked through tiny villages (I remember one early morning, when Noam and I were wandering around alone on a dike and some very small children came running up to us, amazed at seeing such strange creatures; and Noam took out his wallet and showed photographs of his children, and ..., again, the tears come to my eyes); and we came to the river with the bridge that had been bombed an infinite number of times, and that still stood, its girders crooked and bent, still in use; and we visited a cave, ill-lit, cramped, hardly high enough for me to stand up straight, in it a machine shop right out of the late nineteenth century for repairing axles and such things, in which perhaps fifty people had been working all through the very long war, and we had a tiny lunch with them, and they sang, and went back to work: Potemkin village, maybe. I think not.

They had been fighting for their independence against the Chinese and the French for what must have seemed forever. But the scale of the fighting enlarged as World War II ended. How could I forget the leaflet in the museum, a leaflet dropped by the French by the thousands in 1946, warning the people to cease their resistance, not to work with or for the Viet Minh. And the photograph on it was of the open door of a barnlike building, a door perhaps twenty feet high and wide. And out of the door were pouring human skulls, pouring out like melons, top to bottom, the door stuffed with skulls, the French leaflet—the French, in Indo-china, they had always said, were engaged in a *mission civilisatrice*—a leaflet bragging that there were 10,000 skulls pouring out of that door, skulls created in the devastation of 1946 (some of it by U.S. matériel). The leaflet was an incentive to some to cease resistance, perhaps; evidently not to most of the North Vietnamese who, by the time we lifted our helicopters off the Embassy roof in Saigon, had been fighting the French and us (and our subject forces) for *thirty years.*

Pham Van Dong told us that the U.S. antiwar movement made it certain that the Vietnamese would win their long war; that our movement prevented our government from using atomic weapons against the Vietnamese, and it was only those weapons that could defeat them.

We did our very best to destroy those people and their beautiful country using every other weapon; and most of our people do not yet and will not ever understand the nature or the scope of the war crimes we committed in doing that: carpet bombing (more bombs by us in Vietnam, than by all sides in World War II put together), and napalm, and the chemical destruction of their forests, their agriculture, their bodies, their children (and no small number of our own men); an air war with one side only having planes, GIs heavy with weaponry, and, by comparison with the Vietnamese, giants. We did just about everything that could be done to destroy their beloved country, and came all too close to succeeding; and, in adopting those ends and those means, we destroyed a very important part of our own country, made it harder to love.

And Home Again: We flew back over the Pacific, getting to Hong Kong, Hawaii, then San Francisco. While waiting for my New York flight I telephoned Ithaca and was told: Jeff had been arrested and indicted for conspiracy, etc., in Seattle; a big rally on campus had ended up in a riot, the underground fugitive Berrigan had been there on stage, and gotten away again. Hurry home. I did. And the rest of the year worked itself out, taking me to Sweden and much else, most of which has been discussed earlier—or at least as much as I intend to discuss—except for what happened at Carbondale, Illinois. Even for that year, that was a lulu.

Story: How Not to Buy a University

Throughout the entire Indochina War it was a source of constant mystery and irritation to the State Department and the CIA and the White House that any university that had any kind of Southeast Asia studies department also tended to be a center for antiwar information and efforts—even when, as was normal, there were some profs supporting the war. By 1970 the feds were exasperated with reality, and they decided to buy themselves a reliable center—

covertly, of course. They poked around here and there, east and west, north and south, and much to their surprise (and also to mine, be it said), they could find not one trustworthy place. They did find themselves a prof who, with a little imagination, could be seen as a Southeast Asian expert and would do almost anything to be a Director of something. He was from Germany, as it happens, a Prof. W., and he was all set to mount his throne when and where it was placed: and that place, finally located by the CIA, was Southern Illinois University, in lovely Carbondale, Illinois.

The plans were going ahead swimmingly, until one young assistant professor of philosophy learned of the big gift of money to Old SIU and what it was for, and began to disseminate that information and lo and behold, a large number of students and a small number of professors decided they had been insulted by their own university, and protests mounted and mounted and mounted—until to quell them, the university had to arrest many hundreds and, having no place to put them, had to build a temporary stockade for that purpose. Things had begun to get out of hand; and continued to do so, as the news spread beyond the environs of Carbondale, Illinois.

A scholarly organization—Committee of Concerned Asian Scholars—of the very sort that had prompted the feds to try so hard to get a place, so to speak, of their own—called a conference, to be held at Old SIU. A very large number of prestigious scholars was invited to deliver papers, mostly on Southeast Asia; and they all accepted. And the President of SIU, who had never seen or even dreamed of such a spread of scholars in his university, could scarcely turn down the request for the requisite facilities, etc. Indeed, he could scarcely not give a welcoming address on the opening day of the conference. He was, one might say, trapped.

The campus was jammed, the hall was jammed, the students were all out of their stockade, the number of faculty now in resistance was multiplying like rabbits, and the President made his welcoming address. And I was next on the program, not with a paper on Southeast Asia, but one entitled (a bit cruelly, all things considered, at that time and place): "What Must a University Be?" That my answer was very much in contrast with what the President had been up to was of course true; as it was also true that the P. (as Haldeman always called Nixon in his *Diaries*) squirmed as though with ants in the pants throughout my talk and those that followed. There were no further plans made for a Southeast Asia program for Southern Illinois University. Or any other such CIA program.[9] Sometimes you win one.

v.

Our Big Shots

And their "Vietnamization." It meant going halfway back toward our covert political warfare in South Vietnam, Laos, and Cambodia that created "friendly governments," first in Saigon in the 1950s and '60s (as well as in Laos along the way), and in Cambodia by the end of 1970; accompanied by continuous covert fighting on the ground and from the air in Vietnam and Laos. All this before our official entry into the war in 1965, all unbeknownst to virtually all our citizens and most of our government. Thus did institutionalized lying became as natural as breathing in and breathing out; and, as we contaminated and destroyed in Indochina, we could not help but do something of the same to ourselves.

Our military and political history in South Vietnam emerged from its shadows and became public as the war itself became public, in the Sixties. We learned of the Green Berets (and with the help of John Wayne—who, like Reagan, never heard a shot fired in anger—made heroes of them), of the creation of eight Saigon governments, each more artificial and more repressive of its own people than its predecessors (the prizewinner perhaps being that of General Ky—with his movie-style uniforms, his public admiration of Hitler, and much else hard to square with the multitudes dying for "freedom"). Much less familiar even now is what we did to Laos and Cambodia (which, with variations on the theme, we repeated in Central America, later), which "Laotianized" and "Cambodianized" their wars—that is, our wars in their countries. We saw a lot of Vietnam in print and on TV; here we make up for the silence (except for the lies) on Laos and Cambodia.

Both of these countries are tiny, with populations of two to three million in Laos, six to seven million in Cambodia—before our embrace. Neither country was a paradise, but both were reasonably stable, traditional peasant societies, with an agricultural base good enough to allow comfort for all. No more.

When we flew into Laos on our trip to Hanoi, what we saw could have been the pocked landscape of the moon. At that particular moment, Cambodia was still more like its ancient past than its tortured present: its Prince Norodom Sihanouk had been able, until Nixon and Kissinger, to keep Cambodia distanced from the war, neutral. (Except that the Ho Chi

Minh resupply trail snaked in and around the border.) So what did we do to transform these two peaceful countries into hellholes?

First, Laos. The enemy of the United States in Laos was the Pathet Lao. As often happens in colonized and nonindustrial lands, this group, initially seeking to preserve cultural identity and to increase the freedom and well-being of their almost entirely agricultural population, was shaped by events into becoming a revolutionary force. (One of its "revolutionary" steps was to start rural schools in which the language of instruction was Lao—whereas all instruction theretofore had been in French.) After 1954 and Dienbienphu, the prospects for Laotian independence seemed bright indeed; had it not been for the Vietnam War. Like Cambodia, Laos shares its border with Vietnam—and the United States was determined to do everything in its power to isolate and squeeze North Vietnam.

In Laos, that meant "to deny the water to the fish," where the fish were the Pathet Lao, and their nourishing water the countryside: so bomb the countryside, pushing out the peasantry while destroying their lands; and at the same time, mount a mercenary army. Thus, the war in Laos was turned over to the CIA, which in turn handed the ground war over to a local warlord (that is, gangster), "General" Vang Pao—which also elevated him from being a petty to a mighty drug lord. And that's not all: Laos became the third leg of the "Golden Triangle" (the contiguous portions of Laos, Burma, and Thailand).

> During the Vietnam War, the most important source of America's heroin supplies became the Golden Triangle. . . . Then, in the early 1970s, came the fall of the French Connection. The U.S. and France broke up the trafficking drug rings, and Turkey suppressed opium production—much to the joy of the warlords of Southeast Asia, whose opium the CIA was merrily flying to market. . . . By that time the hundreds of thousands of American soldiers in Southeast Asia had created a rich hard-currency market for the local products.[10]

Laos was bombed, invaded, and thrown aside like a wornout toy by our leaders. It may find ways over the decades to recover itself (it is now ruled by the Pathet Lao); or, more likely, may not. Cambodia's recent history is very much different—and more hideous by far—and that history is the direct responsibility of the United States. [11]

Our "incursion" into Cambodia in March and April of 1970 subjected it to carpet bombing—although it was not carpets that were bombed in Cambodia, of course, it was people, and their lands—in the name of destroying "COSVN" (Central Office for South Vietnam) and matériel and weapons depots. COSVN probably existed only in the CIA/military mind; and if weapons depots were destroyed in any significant numbers in the fourteen-month heavy bombing of Cambodia, they didn't show up in the war that the United States was losing.

Carpet Bombing

It takes place from great altitudes, usually above 30,000 feet (that is, more than five miles up), beyond the reach of anti-aircraft artillery; and it is intrinsically indiscriminate. The nature of the "job," as seen by the aircrews (mostly based in Guam or Okinawa) was aptly described when one of them told a reporter "It was like taking the train in from the suburbs at nine and coming back at five, except the train is more interesting and you can see something out the window." There was a great revulsion in the United States when the My Lai massacre of 1968 came to light. That involved the deliberate and coldblooded gunning down of several hundred civilians, including mothers with their babies. The carpet bombing of Cambodia (and before, during, and after, of Laos and of North Vietnam) must have meant the killing of unknown thousands of civilians, including mothers with their babies. A friend of mine who was a bombardier in Europe in World War II tells of his experience, in what was as it happens, the first carpet bombing with napalm:

> At our altitudes—twenty-five or thirty thousand feet—we saw no people, heard no screams, saw no blood, no torn limbs. I remember only seeing the canisters light up like matches flaring one by one on the ground below. Up there in the sky, I was just "doing my job." [12]

As for the people at home, all they saw of the carpet bombing in Indochina was on TV, films of the giant B-52s, with their "sticks" of dozens of 750-lb. bombs falling gracefully away from the bomb bays, like the petals of flowers. Sort of pretty. Of course in those same years there were many pilots flying low level missions—in screaming F-104s and A-6s, helicopters and the like—strafing, bombing, napalming "hutches" (sounds better than "homes") and the "gooks" inside and outside them.

As all this military strife was escalating in 1969 and 1970, the stage was being set for Sihanouk to be deposed; that is, for the United States to have Cambodia as its ally. While Sihanouk was out of the country, a coup put Lon Nol in his place; he was recognized by the United States, our troops invaded, the bombing was stepped up (leaving almost a third of the population homeless), and, after a long string of related disasters, the Khmer Rouge came to power. The latter, whose numbers were barely in the hundreds in 1970, were entirely a product of the breakdown of traditional Cambodian society through the impact of the Vietnam war and Cambodia's forced involvement in it: all part of a side-show. Some excerpts from an interview with Sihanouk in New York in 1979:

> What separated me from Lon Nol in 1970 was that he wanted to make war against the Communists and invite the United States into Cambodia. I knew that if we did so we would be completely involved in the Vietnamese war, we would lose our peace, and everything in Cambodia would be destroyed. If the United States had refused to help Lon Nol after the coup he would have collapsed. [I] would have returned and stopped the war. It didn't happen because Nixon and Kissinger did not want Sihanouk back. Nixon called Cambodia his "best investment." Kissinger hated me. . . . There are only two men responsible for the tragedy in Cambodia today, Mr. Nixon and Dr. Kissinger. Lon Nol was nothing without them and the Khmer Rouge were nothing without Lon Nol. . . . By expanding the war into Cambodia, Nixon and Kissinger killed a lot of Americans and many other people, they spent enormous sums of money . . . and the results were the opposite of what they wanted. They demoralized America, they lost all of Indochina to the Communists, and they created the Khmer Rouge.[13]

In what is no way an amusing history, the cream of the jest is that when the United States supported the Khmer Rouge (as covertly as possible) throughout the years of its devastating rule over Cambodia, its principal ally in that regard was China, both seeing Vietnam as an enemy, as did the Khmer Rouge: the enemy of my enemy is my friend.

Once in power, the Khmer Rouge (who, among other matters, were anti-urban) deliberately relocated virtually the entire population of Phnom Penh (the major city) to the countryside, wrecked the city itself, and slaughtered at least a million of their fellow Cambodians. It is simply inconceivable that any of this would have happened had it not been for U.S. involvement in the affairs of Vietnam.

It is impossible to find any official statements from the United States during the Nixon years or subsequently that might constitute even the beginnings of an admission of what we did, let alone (not that it would help much) an apology—to say nothing of any attempt to find ways of undoing the vast harm we have done to those people who never did and never could do any harm to the United States.

As these words are written, horrors are unfolding daily in ex-Yugoslavia, in Somalia, in the Middle East, and elsewhere; but they also continue to unfold in Cambodia. As they do so, the United States continues to act as though the Cambodian horrors are the doings of others, and the United States continues to base the nature of its own limited involvement in UN efforts to bring peace to Cambodia on how that affects our policies toward Vietnam. And you will have to look long and hard before you will find the one percent or so of our people (at most) who know anything about the foregoing history or, among those who know some of it, more than a handful who care much. One way or another.

Once more: enough already. When Nixon resigned in disgrace, it opened the doors for us to leave Indochina. But the Vietnamese are astute students of our society, and they knew we wouldn't leave voluntarily; knew that Nixon's resignation would mean a period of indecision and weakness regarding the war in Vietnam; knew that we could not reintroduce ground troops, could not step up the conventional bombing; knew that we could not use The Bomb.

So the Vietnamese initiated large-scale ground attacks into the South and sliced easily into Saigon. And we helicoptered out, with as many Vietnamese as could hanging on to the 'copter skids—and falling off, many of them, to be among the last deaths of the war—and, somehow, awful symbols of that war. Things being what they are in this era, we watched that on the tube, also.

And as we did so, sneaking up behind us, as it had been doing for a few years, was big trouble for the economy.

vi.

Here We Go 'Round the Prickly Pear

Uniquely strong in 1945, the United States could not maintain its own strength unless the other major capitalist powers regained theirs; nor could the latter do so except, so to speak, by artificial respiration of the sort noted earlier: the creation of international financial and trade institutions (the IMF and World Bank and GATT); relief and rehabilitation efforts as the war ended; immense loans (especially to Britain); the Marshall Plan; carrots and sticks designed to move Europe toward a "common market"; and, among other stimuli, the always rising military expenditures (especially, but not only) in Germany and Japan, which did so much to stimulate and support their economies, as well as ours.

Alas! there is no failure like success. Nixon's brusque remark concerning the Italian lira (reported at the start of chapter 4), was occasioned by the monetary confusions taking hold in the early 1970s that were themselves the outcome of the robust world economy. These "confusions" were dramatically marked and exacerbated by actions of Nixon that violated the rules we had created at Bretton Woods. In 1968, even before Nixon took office, we had already refused to sell gold at the "guaranteed" price of $35/oz. to private purchasers; by 1971 Nixon felt impelled to "close the gold window" to all comers, private or public—and, going much further in violation of all understandings, had affixed a ten percent import "surcharge" (a polite term for a tax on imports, or a tariff).

The reason for tip-toeing around such doings was that the United States, like all (dare I use the word?) imperial powers, had to make it feasible for its member states to function effectively without using mostly force. As both the biggest exporter and importer in the world after World War II, it had to find ways to let the secondary powers (Japan and Western Europe) keep their economies healthy by exporting to us, as well as importing from us. What Nixon did—had to do—in 1971 was to make it harder for them (and us) to do either. Why?

The United States had begun to run a deficit in its international balance of payments no later than 1960.[14] The causes of what became an enlarging and transformed deficit were changing over time—those most important of them having to do with the growing strength of the European and Japanese economies, capital flows from and to the United States, shifting patterns of (rising) military expenditures at home and abroad, and their diverse consequences. It should be remarked that for the hegemonic power to run a deficit in its trade balance (that is, an excess of imports over exports of commodities) is "natural," an enrichment resulting from its combined productive, financial, and military power.

Britain, the hegemon of the nineteenth century, continuously ran a substantial trade deficit, as its per capita real income increased and its distribution became at least somewhat less unequal. But Britain's empire was accumulated in a very different world. The most crucial difference that had become also a critical problem for the United States by 1970 was the drain on our balance of payments due to extraordinary military expenditures abroad; and as will be seen, whatever the ongoing benefits in terms of profits and jobs, there were also important negative effects on the domestic economy. Britain was the military as well as the economic ruler for most of the nineteenth century, but "Britannia ruled the waves" for nickels and dimes, compared with the trillions we have paid out since 1946.

Among the important causes often cited for the deterioration in our balance of payments, high on the list has been the always rising volume of U.S. direct investment abroad (the ownership and control of mines, wells, plants, etc. in other countries). Such investment, because it entails purchases of all sorts in other countries, also requires purchases of their currencies. It is as though we are importing those goods and services; thus, other things being equal, such expenditures constitute a "drain" on our balance. Quite apart from reminding that Britain too had vast direct investments abroad, however, there is a most illuminating fact concerning our own: the return of profits from past and ongoing investments in the postwar decades has increasingly exceeded our capital outflow (including net payments to foreign investors in the United States)—most dramatically, the net inflow of capital from oil investments.

> The strength of the return flow of profits has been based largely on the enormous profits earned by the oil industry, particularly in its Middle Eastern operations. Between 1950 and 1964, direct investment by the petroleum companies in Asia, Africa, and Latin America totaled $3.1 billion. The return over the same period from those areas totaled $15.2 billion. . . . In the period from 1965 to 1971, of the total balance-of-payments gain from all direct investments . . . of $21.9 billion, $16.5 billion was accounted for by the Middle East and Latin America.[15]

The United States had a trade surplus for all but three years from 1950 through 1973, maintained through the ever-rising capital goods export surplus that offset the ever-rising consumer goods export deficit. Despite favorable balances in capital goods exports and direct investment, however, the U.S. payments position was done in by an also ever-rising government balance, almost entirely composed of military expenditures abroad: 70 percent of the payments deficit by 1974.

On August 15, 1971, Nixon made a major speech to the nation in which he announced his "NEP" ("New Economic Policy," probably not knowing that in 1923 Lenin had announced *his* NEP—New Economic Program— in the Soviet Union). It had several components, most important among them: stop gold sales entirely, raise tariffs, reduce capital outflows and— surprise—mandatory price and wage controls to curb inflation. The man appointed by Nixon to head up the price control system was the very judge who had presided over my son's trial: as we'll see, just the man for both jobs.

Story: Hizzoner

Jeff's trial was in the U.S. District Court in Seattle, where he and his pals were sentenced to a year in a maximum security prison. The Circuit Court of Appeals agreed to hear an appeal on the "riot" decision, and ordered Jeff's judge to release the seven on bail. Judge George Boldt refused the higher court's order. (Had that ever happened before?) The order was repeated, and evidently accompanied by a copy of how the rules of our judicial system are supposed to work, for the seven were let out: after six weeks, and just in time. A maximum security prison is dangerous for all prisoners, and most especially for young ones: not least, but not only, because of gang rape. Jeff was released exactly on the day he had been told that if he did not consent to sex, he would be gang raped. When I read of the Circuit Court decision in the San Francisco news I called Jeff to congratulate him. "Wake up, Doug," he growled; "they'll get us somehow." Shortly thereafter they were called back and found guilty by the same judge of contempt of his court, the alleged contemptuous act having occurred on the day they had been originally sentenced. One of the seven was a young woman, very small, and eight months pregnant. When her turn came to say something to the court, the judge called "time" on her, she continued to speak, and suddenly forty (that's 40) U.S. marshals rushed into the courtroom, and knocked her to the floor as Jeff and his friends tried to defend her. Judge Boldt was reported in 1992 to have had Alzheimer's disease at that time—and, as well, while he was controlling prices.

vii.

Stagflation: Between a Rock and a Hard Place

Had the economics profession been paying closer attention to the organic and structural changes of the twenty years or so after World War II instead of to its quantitative behavior, they might have seen that alternating waves of expansion and contraction had been, at best, suppressed; and that the various kinds and areas of suppression—as with suppressive drugs—were producing the collateral consequences of greater import that would become considerably more daunting than the normal business cycle: stagflation. And by 1974 the first signs of stagflation were already causing tremors—just about the time Nixon boarded that helicopter to fly off into the sunset.

The term "stagflation" was first used in the mid-1970s. It puts together two normally opposing economic tendencies: one, toward high and stubborn unemployment and underutilized productive capacity; the other, toward steadily rising prices. In prior economic history, there had been brief periods (a few months, but not as much as a year) when the economy began to contract into recession while prices still rose; but never had there been a period when both endured, in one serious degree or another, for an entire decade, as happened in the United States and in Western Europe in the 1970s. And by the time their continuing existence was recognized, something else ominous was being understood—to utilize accustomed fiscal and monetary policies to control one was to exacerbate the other. Stimulate the economy with spending and lower interest rates to increase profits and employment, and inflation is intensified; do the opposite to reduce inflation, and bring on a depression. Hard cheese.

Contemplate the representative data that follow, and shudder for those who had to make believe they were in charge—like Nixon.[16] In 1973, of the twenty-four nations that comprised the Organization for Economic Cooperation and Development (OECD), accounting for over 90 percent of world capitalist production, over half had double-digit inflation rates; in 1974, only two (West Germany and Switzerland) did not. In the dependent nations, annual inflation rates were running anywhere from 35 percent to ten times that. And in the same years, a worldwide recession took hold, bringing rising unemployment and shrinking world trade and production. A glance at the key figures for industrial capacity utilization and unemployment in the United States comparing the late Sixties with the Seventies illustrates the transformation:

	Industrial Capacity Utilization	Unemployment Rate (with and without Discouraged Workers)	
1966-68	88.5%	4.5%	3.6%
1972-74	85.2	6.4	5.4
1977-80	83.6	7.9	7.0
1985-87	80.2	7.7	6.8[17]

In short, the free and easy days were a thing of the past. As the early stages of emerging crisis came to be noted in 1973 and 1974, they were seen as aberrations, and both its recessionary and inflationary aspects as an outcome of the dramatic oil price increases imposed by the Organization of Petroleum Exporting Countries (OPEC).[18] There can be no doubt that OPEC policies caused economic trouble. But it is necessary to recall that world economic conditions, including those of the United States, had begun to deteriorate before the oil price increases of December 1973. Indeed, an important part of OPEC's actions was prompted by its members' need to obtain rising oil prices to meet the inflating prices of the commodities they imported. Still, in the context of already existing uncertainties and increasingly baffled leadership, OPEC's actions insured that an already bad situation would become much worse, and come close to getting out of hand by the end of the decade.

When the 1970s began, decay was already setting in. What had been "functional" had become "dysfunctional": the main elements that created global monopoly capitalism and that allowed it to function smoothly came to interact perversely. Here we can only summarize the argument underlying that flat assertion.

1. The era of the supercorporation and the superstate is perforce one of vast private and public bureaucracies. The costs, the misused power, the wastes, and the inefficiencies associated with the functioning and growth of these bureaucracies came to surpass whatever positive effects there may have been from the incomes generated in and by them—as, with the passage of time and altered circumstances, the essential functions of bureaucracy came to serve less for creating new bases of strength and more for seeking to hold on to what had been gained earlier.

2. The normal practices within and between (especially big) businesses, and between businesses and politicians and governments—classified as "corruption"—have, with the exfoliation of giant corporate and State entities and of their functions, deepened and spread to new and always more spectacular levels, producing financial and political quagmires for all concerned—to the cost of taxpayers, consumers and workers. We in the United States have enjoyed sniping at the recently revealed swamps of corruption in Italy and Japan without seeing as clearly as we might that we share with those countries degrees of corruption that are both as intransigent and as socially crippling as theirs.[19]

3. The creation by North American, European, and Japanese capital of productive capacities for durable consumer and capital goods along with

a rapidly advancing technology was, of course, a major stimulus in the long expansion. By the 1970s the resulting facilities had already become seriously duplicative, producing intense competition for critical raw materials and for markets, with consequent whipsaw effects—the competition for raw materials yielding upward pressures on costs, the competition for markets causing downward pressures on sales and profits. The growth of excess productive capacities from the 1970s on—in autos, appliances, metals, chemicals, electronics, etc.—has slowed but not stopped. Even in weak markets, given the normally anarchic organization of world production and investment, capacity has increased.

4. The stupefying increases in the levels of debt and the spread of always more casual financial practices from the 1960s on—involving consumers, businesses, and governments, nationally and globally—were intrinsic to the financing and support of the unprecedented expansion of those years. But already in the 1970s—with the worst yet to come—alarms were being sounded about precarious debt/revenue ratios for all concerned, ratios whose threat to financial stability can only be lessened through rapid economic expansion—in turn requiring accelerated indebtedness.

And debt did accelerate—but far more for consumption, military expenditure, financial speculation, and "take-overs" than for productive investments. The painful consequences of that economic infantilism have been all too evident in the past ten years or so. Although it cannot be said that there is an identifiable amount or ratio of debt beyond which certain disaster awaits, it is certain that the heedless expansion of debt in a structurally weak economy threatens a financial crack, while at the same time it also makes any movement toward recession more difficult to reverse. In addition, both problems—financial collapse and recession—are likely to be greater the longer they are suppressed by "more of the same."

5. Neocolonialism was vital in providing stimuli and support for the economic expansion of the major powers, and the military expenditures required, stimulated, and facilitated by that effort and by the Cold War of course did much to sustain economic expansion. However, the great increases in military expenditures since the 1950s taken together with the wars they have accompanied, while helping to hold off depression, have also provided a hard basis for inflation, and not only because they are economically speaking almost pure waste. Moreover, the technological

tendencies of military products over time, while they may or may not have provided "more bang for the buck" (as Eisenhower once put it), also came to mean "fewer jobs for the buck." Thus: if government expenditures were made on school construction or public housing, instead of on guided missiles and the like, for example, it has been calculated by academic, congressional, and union studies that 30 to 100 percent more jobs would result per dollar of that expenditure. [20]

6. The swift alteration of rural/urban/suburban and occupational patterns (from commodities to services), and, within the cities, of the pre-World War II political economies, was an integral and profitable ingredient of the postwar accumulation process. Investment and incomes boomed with the expansion of industrial and residential suburbs, shopping malls, and the much else that accompanied such developments.

But more recently attention has had to focus upon the loss of urban jobs and tax bases and the rising percentage of low-paying and insecure jobs. Those processes have to be seen as contributing to the need for always rising (especially) urban expenditures which instead of rising have faltered and declined, thereby increasing the need still more—whether for social decency or social stability. For some years now, all major cities have faced an enlarging set of seemingly intractable economic, political, and social problems, intensified greatly by the rising needs and justifiable demands of a variety of urban groups which, whether granted or—as is now almost always the case—refused, add to the cities' fiscal problems. Much of the fiscal crisis of the cities is attributable to the decades of high federal expenditures on the military, combined with increasing income deficiencies for the urban population as economic expansion has slackened—and as racism and poverty have deepened in a society whose consumeristic passions dominate all others.

7. The strong grip of consumerism on the people of the United States (and, increasingly, elsewhere) deserves a comment of its own. Unquestionably a major effect and cause of the long expansion and of the political stability associated with it, functioning consumerism necessarily depends upon the combination of rising incomes and the persuasive and mind-changing powers of the mass media over its universal audience to "teach people to want what they don't need, and not to want what they do."

Since World War II, the entire population, not just those of middle and high incomes, has been taught to accept, to want and, in an important sense therefore, to believe it needs, a level and composition of consumer goods that is quite simply beyond the present or potential income capacities of at least half of the population. What that means in the way of developing social frustration, easily breaking into anger—anger edging over into violence—goes beyond the economic and into the political and sociopsychological realms.

Our population—and not only ours—has been taught to neglect its individual and socially-shared needs, to see itself as "consumers," whose main social activity is "shop 'till you drop," whose social slogan is "More!" and whose ethic is "Why not?" Within processes such as those, it takes little prodding to stimulate volatile and irrational combinations of envy, fear, and hate; to excite always more what have always been dangerous racist attitudes and actions.

It has thereby become normal and natural for our politics to extend dangerously beyond what Garry Wills described as Nixon's, already in 1968: "the politics of resentment"[21]—for now we move toward encasing ourselves in a social ice age.

viii.

A Bump in the Night

Despite and because of all the stimuli of the Fifties and Sixties, there was a severe recession, 1974-75; and it was worked out in ways that helped to define what is meant by stagflation. First, the stage may be set with some figures that compare the recession of 1957-58 with that of 1974-75—both recessions in the era of monopoly capitalism, with the later one showing the first signs of arteriosclerosis:

	1957-58	1974-75
Duration in months	8	16
Decline in real GNP	3.5%	4.3%
Decline in industrial production	13.5%	14.8%

Peak unemployment rate	7.6%	9.1%
Manufacturing utilization rate	72.4%	69.0%
Change in Consumer Price Index	+2.3%	+13.5% [22]

Not only do those figures point to the worst recession since the 1930s, they also show the startling behavior of rising prices in the face of falling GNP, jobs, capacity utilization—almost everything. A telling example (from a telling sector) is that of GM: hit by a recession that collapsed the auto market, they laid off a third of their work force and raised prices by 10 percent—followed in short order by Ford and Chrysler.

But that, of course, is not the end of the stagflation story. Another part of it, as Kemp points out, is that

> Business confidence fell to a low ebb, as evidenced by the reduction of stocks of goods and the reluctance to embark on new investment, evident from 1973. When something like recovery began [in 1976], it was significant that the economy failed to attain its previous rates of growth, levels of investment or productivity gains . . . [and] ideas about what constituted full employment and the tolerable level of inflation were being revised upward. [23]

Connected with the foregoing developments, in some sense their other side, was what has been called the economy's "financialization," or, calling attention to some overlapping patterns, "the hollowing" and accompanying "deindustrialization" of the U.S. economy (to be discussed a bit later).

Putting all these notions together, the result is an evolution which, showing its first signs in the Sixties, had become pronounced in the Seventies and the basis for deep troubles and numerous business and political scandals by the Eighties. Behind all those unlovely changes stood a unifying source: an economic individualism that had always made a virtue of self-interest but that within the heady processes of cold war and monopoly capitalism had become transmogrified into an unabashed ethic of greed. By 1986 all this had gone far enough that it seemed perfectly natural for my alma mater the University of California at Berkeley to have as its commencement speaker Mr. Ivan Boesky (not much later to be carted off to prison, having been caught with his steam shovel in the bank vault), whose theme—I wish I were making this up—was "Greed is Good." [24]

That was a rapidly spreading development by then, representing a more forthright position than the business community had taken in the Sixties and Seventies—as I knew from some odd experiences.

Story: Big Crock

Paul M., who had been my teaching assistant at Cornell in the 1950s, and whose Ph.D. chair I had been, came to be ensconced comfortably in the Graduate School of Business of one of the Ivy League universities. Openly moderate himself, he found my relative immoderateness, so it seems, pleasing. (Also, when as a graduate student he thought he was outclassed, I thought not; and I had gotten him his comfy job.) He moved up easily at his university, and gained a certain amount of power. By then, the big corporation getting always bigger, there was much talk—believe it or not—of "the soulful corporation," and "corporate ethics," and other such oxymoronic phrases. Paul had come to be involved in setting up conferences on such matters—usually with several profs, some execs, perhaps a politician—and many times he placed me in them with, I thought, a wicked gleam in his eye. There was always a handsome fee ($500-$1,000 a day, all tax deductible for the corporate sponsor), and who was I to turn down a chance to take a well-paid whack at such folks. And pay off some bills.

In 1973, one of the conferences was held at the very large spread of Ray Kroc, east and over the hills from Santa Barbara (near Reagan's ranch). Kroc, of course, was the owner and honcho of McDonald's. There were sixty in the audience, all V.P.'s, either of McDonald's or of Coca-Cola, along with Kroc and the P. of C-C. Among the speakers were Ike's former chief economic advisor, and Milton Friedman, and, sticking out like a big red thumb, yours truly.

So: when my turn came to address this crowd of biggies, all sitting in Kroc's very svelte amphitheatre, deep leather seats, each with a console for this and that (all paid for with your taxes), I began by saying that the realm of ethics with which we should be concerned was not that of lifting currency from the cash register but, in various ways, the wronging of customers, of employees, of other societies, and of nature—getting something for nothing at the expense of others, and letting the devil take the hindmost. And went on from there. The audience stirred throughout. When I finished, Ray Kroc rose to ask the first question.

Which was not a question. "In my experience, *professor*," he said, coating the word with slime, "university people don't know what in hell they're talking about." "But you do, Mr. Kroc?" I asked. "I read recently that you gave one million dollars to CREEP [25] for the reelection of Nixon. Now in *my* experience, presidents—of universities, countries, businesses—don't usually know as much as many others in their work, because they are protected from information they don't want to hear. I know at least a dozen people who know more about Vietnam than Nixon does, for example; but as President he doesn't wish to know anything that might tell him he has been wrong about *anything.*" Before I could go on, from the back of the hall a C-C V.P. shouted "I'll buy that!" All eyes, including that of the C-C P., turned to look at him, as he cowered back in his seat, evidently realizing that he would soon have a different job, if any.

We had a very fancy lunch afterwards. I had the honor of sitting across from His Holiness Milton Friedman who, however, was so busy pocketing the silver he took no notice of me. (I had occasion to go to the bathroom at one point, and I swear that on the wall was an original Renoir—small, to be sure; but still. . . . Well, wotthehell, Ray worked real hard for all those hundreds of millions. Didn't he?)

Story: Down in Flames

I was involved in several such conferences before the Kroc, and a few after, but the one now to be told concerns what was to be my finale; and about time. (No space to tell of a couple of beauties in New York when I was still teaching back there, one involving the muckymucks of Western Electric, when a particularly incensed executive rose out of his chair at one end of the seminar table and ran across the top of the table to strangle me at the other end, where all I was trying to do was to explain why SDS made a lot of sense.) The one now to be told has to do with the Fluor Corporation.

Mr. Fluor had a small engineering/construction company which after World War II, while the U.S.A. was expanding all over the world, had also expanded to be right up there (just under Bechtel) by 1974, when I met with them. Their specialty was complicated mining construction projects, their biggest one then going on in another U.S.A.—the Union of South Africa. There were fifteen to twenty executives, all of whom had been with the company from its beginning, all very competent in their craft, but none of them—with the exception of Mr. Fluor—having developed the kind of outlook appropriate to a supercorporation dealing with global this and that. Mr. Fluor thought that had to change, and with Paul's help he had UCLA set up a conference, with me as the sole speaker for three days (at a fancy hotel in Irvine, CA—staging by Fellini), $950 a day, plus expenses.

After making out like *la dolce vita* for a while, we finally assembled, and I said my piece: it turned on the question of ethics and the work going on in South Africa. It wasn't a very warm day when I began, but after half an hour or so the conference room felt as though a volcano was erupting. Mr. Fluor asked me to leave the room for a bit. The bit stretched out for some time. Mr. Fluor came out with the UCLA public relations man who was the gofer for the meeting, and they explained to me that the execs in there refused to listen to me anymore, not one more word; and a couple of them, it seemed, wanted to beat me up, so I should leave by the back door. Anyhow, I was told sorry, and we'll pay you for the whole three days just so there won't be any problem, and don't call us, we'll call you. Paul wrote a while later, and said it was clear I had worn through my welcome in the business world. I agreed it was time for them to find their souls without my help, wept all the way to the bank, and that was that.

At the time all that corporate ethicking was going on, there was also a real world spinning around. And among others of its developments was an expansion and then an explosion of private lending from the big banks to the "developing" countries. The process had begun in the Sixties, and taken off in the Seventies.

Its beginnings had to do with the first stages of a decline in corporate profits and a slowdown in business fixed investment in the States at the end of the Sixties. That in turn led to the successful pressures of the big banks to have the government reduce its grants and low-interest loans, to be replaced by profitable private lending. This rising wind of lending took on something like hurricane force in the Seventies when the oil crisis 1) created tens of billions of "surplus petrodollars" for the OPEC countries, deposited principally in U.S. banks, making the latter itchy to find borrowers, and 2) the poorer (non-OPEC) countries, always in deep need for a variety of reasons and pushed in even more deeply by the fact that the price of oil is denominated in dollars, had to (or did) borrow more and more (and at the escalating interest rates of the 1970s). [26]

So the rich got richer. Although in the early Eighties it did seem for a while that all those very bad loans to dictators and roustabouts—whether in Zaire or Argentina or Mexico—were going to sink many big banks here, there, and elsewhere. To prevent that, very big deals were done that saved the banks—and had you and me help to pay for it as taxpayers (here), and the populations of the borrowing countries pay for it in "austerity programs" (there). [27]

But this rich country also got poorer, in the depletion of its ongoing and future productive strengths. [28] Our business wizards spent less and less of their time trying to produce commodities efficiently and more and more of it making money out of wheeling and dealing: hostile and friendly "takeovers," "leveraged buyouts," selling and buying and selling again the merrily-titled "junk bonds" (Milken's contribution to civilization), and, among other fancies and delights, whizzing up and down in the stock market, illegally facilitated by inside info whenever available. A main structural outcome of all this was the love match between "deindustriali-zation" and "financialization."

As if all this were not enough to hold back the re-entry of good times, there were two other continuing and closely-related developments to make matters more difficult: the internationalization of the U.S. (and the "Americanization" of the global) economy, and, within and driving that process, the growing strength and global dominance of the giant transna-tional corporations (TNCs, MNCs, supernationals). Joyce Kolko's com-ments in these regards are astute:

> The transnational corporations (TNCs), as we know them today [1988], emerged at the end of the 1960s. Their push toward the LDCs [less-developed countries], the periphery of Europe, and, to a lesser degree, the CPEs [non-capi-talist nations] was a result of the higher cost and, in Europe, of the growing militancy of labor and increasing competition in the industrial capitalist coun-tries. The technology of communication and remote control and new contain-erized developments in shipping made the establishment of component production in low-wage areas of the world both possible and profitable. One outcome was the partial dissolution of national boundaries, as trade was increas-ingly between branches of the same corporation. [Among other consequences] it allowed real prices, and hence profits, to hide from taxation, and a distorted picture of world trade, especially in commodities, emerged. [29]

And she goes on to say, regarding the mid-Seventies recession:

> Aggregate investment outlay for the OECD nations as a whole shifted from plus 7.1 percent in 1973 to minus 4.6 percent in 1974. [In addition, there was] a massive liquidation of inventories throughout the industrial capitalist states. . . . through 1975, accompanied by the cancellation of orders. The general collapse of demand directly influenced world trade, the leading industries, development in the Third World . . . , and the deepening recession. There was a domino effect across the interna-tional economy, shaping internal political activity and relations between states. An important dimension of the emerging crisis was the synchronization by 1973 of the business cycle in the industrial nations, the first since the Great Depression. Cycles before the 1930s had been less severe, in large part because they were not synchro-nized on a world scale. "An 'all-systems go' in many countries simultaneously was the most important mishap in recent economic policy history." [30]

The recession of 1974-75—both its occurrence and its stagflating char-acteristics—was, for those few inclined and able to hear it, a fire alarm ringing in the night.

ix.

Days of Reckoning

It is clear that the characteristic feature of modern industrial capitalist nations is that they are all concentrated in their economic structures and that a giant State has become central to their life processes. The critical element is the indispensable and contradictory role of the State, and its whys and wherefores. James O'Connor's 1973 *Fiscal Crisis of the State* can be very helpful in understanding what was happening.

O'Connor posits three main areas in the economy: the monopolistic, the competitive, and the State sectors. He assumes the economy to be marked by surplus capital and surplus labor—what have been discussed earlier as excessive productive capacities and substantial unemployment. It is the interaction of all the foregoing that gives the economy and the State their quality and their direction. The quality is that of a monopoly capitalist warfare/welfare State; the direction has combined imperialism, militarization, and the varieties of social oppression (racial, gender, etc.) that bring us to our present condition. The future (as seen by O'Connor in 1973) was problematic at best, and most likely a grim struggle:

> If monopoly capital's ideological and political hegemony is not effectively challenged, if a unified movement is not organized around opposition to monopoly capital's budgetary priorities, the fiscal crisis will continue to divide all those groups and strata that today fight in dismal isolation for a greater share of the budget or for a smaller share of the tax burden.[31]

The sour struggles whose probabilities O'Connor had foreseen while they were still in embryo have gone on in ever more dismal isolation, marked by the abrasive politics he thought would arise from the relationships between the three sectors of the economy. His explanation of how the seeds of plenty planted in the Fifties and Sixties would come to produce such bitter fruit warrants closer attention.

We may dispense with the two narrowly economic sectors briefly: 1) The monopolistic sector is the pride of the U.S. economy, where productivity, high profits, and the highest wages are (or were) found—where the greatest concentration of business (supercorporations) and labor (trade unions) exists, and where productive capacities are (except also for agriculture) most obviously in surplus. 2) The competitive sector is where most businesses and many more people than in the monopolistic sector function. Usually, productivity and profits are relatively low and technology nondynamic; wages do not allow a decent livelihood; and labor is in surplus. The sector is composed largely of small retailers and producers, businesses that often have substantial power on local issues but, except for limited influence through the two political parties, are bereft of national power.

The State sector (local, state, and federal) is responsible for State expenditures and activities. The nature and the importance of that set of responsibilities is clarified by O'Connor in ways that were provocative in 1973 and that are, if anything, more central for understanding today than earlier:

> State expenditures have a twofold character corresponding to the capitalist state's two basic functions [accumulation and legitimation]: social capital and social expenses. *Social capital* is expenditures required for profitable accumulation [—consisting] of projects and services that increase the productivity of a given amount of labor-power and projects and services that lower the reproduction costs of labor. The second category, *social expenses,* consists of projects and services which are required to maintain social harmony—to fulfill the state's "legitimization" function. They are not even indirectly productive. . . . The best example is the welfare system, which is designed chiefly to keep social peace among unemployed workers. (pp. 6-7)

In the process, the State indirectly generates as well as absorbs and redirects a growing part of the economic surplus. The State has been and remains the most rapidly growing of the three sectors—irrespective of who reigns in the White House. Although the State's function is to provide economic stimuli and social stability it has been both the source as well as the mitigator of the tensions accompanying the socioeconomic crisis that began to take hold in the Seventies. Its ways of doing both have deepened and contained the crisis.

Those are the ways of monopoly capitalism, often called "full capitalism" by O'Connor, the "warfare/welfare" state by others, the socio/military/industrial complex by a few. There has been more than welfare and military spending, of course (agriculture, highways, all that interest on the debt, etc.), but what falls under those two headings has had the most power behind it—concentrated business power behind "warfare," lots of votes (workers, old people, blacks, et al.) behind the "welfare" (a very small percentage of which is actually for welfare recipients). The reason is that both fit in well with the dynamic needs of monopoly capitalism:

> both welfare spending and warfare spending have a two-fold nature: the welfare system not only politically contains the surplus population but also expands demand and domestic markets. And the warfare system not only keeps foreign

rivals at bay and inhibits development of world revolution (thus keeping labor-power, raw materials, and markets in the capitalist orbit) but also helps to stave off economic stagnation at home. (pp. 150-51)

The State thus accomplishes many vital functions for maintaining U.S. capitalism: 1) the social capital provides facilities and skills that reduce the costs and increase the profits of business; 2) the social capital that takes the form of income maintenance enhances purchasing power; 3) military and paramilitary forces abroad and at home create and maintain a framework within which orderly business can be transacted; 4) the research and development associated with military production, an important part of social capital, enhances productivity in at least some areas and subsidizes investment in the monopoly sector; 5) jobs are provided both outside and within the State sector. Since the Sixties, something over 25 percent of the work force has owed its jobs directly or indirectly to State payrolls and contracts. [32]

What then and why then, if all this is so useful to the maintenance of the system, has there been and is there a worsening "fiscal crisis of the State"? It has been asserted time and again in earlier pages that the main culprit has been the faltering of the processes of economic expansion and thus the slowed increase of incomes, much exacerbated by accompanying and serious inflation. [33]

Thus it was in the 1970s that the domestic politics of the United States came to turn away from what had been the New Deal/Fair Deal/Great Society programs and toward the conservatism of the Ford and Carter administrations—and then into the maw of cruel Malthusianism of the dirty dozen years of Reagan/Bush.

Pleasurable—and often valid—though it may be to blame Reagan for our ills, it must be said that the emergence of new tendencies strengthening the political Right is not to be explained principally in terms of the presidential personalities involved. Rather, such personalities and such policies became acceptable, even enthusiastically so, to a population that time and circumstance had been tutoring in greed and fear, and that thus learned to be ever more careless and mindless of its own social needs, and heartless concerning the needs of others.

The system began to sputter and shake and its core began to disintegrate in the 1970s, for it had depended upon that rising taxation which in turn could be painless only so long as incomes were rising even faster. But the real income of four-fifths of the population had ceased to rise in 1973, and has not done so since—a whole generation. In that same period, as O'Connor warned would happen, there has been rising and politically-encouraged conflict between the "lesser peoples" of the competitive sector, as against those higher up on the scale. The encouragement of racism, militarism, and ideological simplicities by those who steered and lifted Reagan into power was lubricated by harsh economic realities. It became easier to teach that the inability any longer to buy as much as one wished—while also trying to pay for earlier purchases and higher taxes—could be blamed on "welfare cheats"; not, perish the thought, on decades of military expenditures and other forms of massive waste, or on unutilized productive capacities, or capital invested in cheap labor areas abroad, or factory closings or . . . no, no, no, none of that. The brutal message fell on receptive ears: let anger and greed be your guide.

Whatever else minds had become tuned to, they had come to find most beautiful the sounds of consumerism. However, like the other elements of the new capitalism that had been vital to the effective functioning of the system, it too had become a major problem to its parent system. [34]

So the first half of the 1970s were economically tormented. It cannot be known what their second half would have been like if RN had not been forced to leave D.C. in a hurry; what we do know is what we got with Ford and Carter. But before looking at that and them, let's kick old Nixon around just one more time, just for the hell of it.

x.

Arrivederci, Humpty-Dumpty

Nixon's desire to be reelected has perhaps been matched in our history, but it could not be exceeded; nor could his paranoia about the evil forces that might prevent it. Considering that by 1972 the Democratic Party was in full disarray, so much so that its presidential nominee would be George McGovern, there was no way that Nixon could lose. [35] But he believed that there was a way he could lose, the way he thought he lost in 1960 against Kennedy: dirty tricks from the opposition. So, get there fustest:

> The Watergate break-in, coming in a campaign year when Nixon led all rivals in the polls, seemed undermotivated and over-bungled. He was clumsy at everything else, why not at crime? . . . The anti-Establishment administration, still counter-insurgent in victory, staged a bloodless coup against itself, trying to steal votes in

an election it had already won. Richard Nixon, from his need to struggle, stole the White House from Richard Nixon.[36]

In some sense it was, as Nixon characterized it when Watergate first made the news, "nothing more than a third-rate burglary." But as the investigation of Watergate proceeded, at first as merely a job for the D.C. police, one culprit after another was identified and, in that process, one more "third-rate burglary" after another that had preceded Watergate came to the surface.[37] As that was happening, the Nixon administration became engaged in an ever more complex, broadening, and deepening cover-up. At some point, not just the hired burglars and Cuban refugees who had been doing the work, but those on the White House staff began to come before the police and grand juries and to tell tales and there at the bottom of the pile were the Watergate tapes. From his first days in the White House, Nixon had a secret taping system installed, to know what others were doing but—at least as importantly, one can believe—also to constitute an oral record that might become a written "monument" to his presidency. Pride, Humpty-Dumpty, goeth before a fall.

The Watergate break-in was in June 1972. Not much began to come to the surface until after the election; and then, like the unrolling of a very dirty rug, the truth began to be laid out—much aided and abetted by the information provided by "Deep Throat" to the Washington Post team of Woodward and Bernstein and, more wounding than anything else, what seemed to be the spontaneous revelation (before the House Judiciary Conmmittee) by a White House staffer of the taping system. After those tapes were listened to—or, as in the case of the famous "eighteen-minute gap," no longer intelligible—the die was cast. In late July, over a period of four days, the House Judiciary Committee approved Articles 1, 2, and 3 in the impeachment of Richard M. Nixon: for the cover-up, for contempt of Congress, and for abuses of power (including numberless wiretaps on his own staff and others).[38] On August 9, 1974, Nixon resigned the Presidency—and we all watched him on the tube as he got into the Presidential Helicopter and flew away.

And we got Gerry Ford. The less said of him the better. He saw himself as having one major foreign policy triumph, the incident surrounding the U.S. cargo ship Mayaguez, and the renewed bombing of Cambodia.[39] His major domestic triumph was his mighty campaign against inflation. His program, as befits one whose happiest days were in college, was entitled "Whip Inflation Now!"—and we were all asked to wear a lapel button stating "WIN!" The button didn't turn the trick, inflation soared alongside continuing recession, and Gerry became a full-time golfer. Out of the blue, in walked Jimmy Carter.

At the same time, the authorities at San Jose State were preparing, for the eighth and what they hoped would be the final time, to get rid of that pain in the neck, yr. obdt. servant. For the eighth time, things went awry—this time with a little help from a friend.

Story: Birds of a Feather

The Western Economic Association held its annual meetings in June of 1976 in San Francisco, and I gave a paper on stagflation. At the close of my talk and the discussion period, a pleasant man came up and introduced himself, saying "I'm Dan Ellsberg. And I wanted to tell you how much I enjoyed reading your book *The Twisted Dream;* and that it in fact changed my mind on a lot of things. Could we get together and have a chat?" Irresistible, all things considered.

We both lived in the city at that time, and we had many chats and became friends. Our paths crossed, but not regularly. And one day I was pleased to have him inform me that he had been asked by some faculty group at SJSU to give a talk, in the university's principal auditorium. When he arrived, I walked up and said hello, he asked how I was, I told him the eighth heave-ho attempt against me had just begun, and sat down to enjoy his talk. He started by saying that SJSU should count itself very fortunate to have someone as fine an economist and so on as DFD on its faculty, and ashamed of itself because the effort was being made to fire me—once more. And then he went on and on singing my praises—to my mixed embarrassment and pleasure. And finally got around to his scheduled talk. And the eighth attempt sank under its own weight, leaving me carefree. Until the next semester. When the P. tried again. And failed. And then the tenth. And failed. And then the P. called me in to say it was all a mistake, I was to have tenure, and welcome aboard, etc., and it was OK for me to teach on leave at UC Santa Cruz the next semester, because that had been arranged by me before (just in case). But the next semester, while I was at UCSC, I received another letter firing me again—number eleven—and after breaking into the Dean's Office with an AK-47, binding and gagging his wife and children, threatening to pull out the P.'s fingernails one by one and pee on his shoes, they all signed a piece of paper giving me academic citizenship. From 1972 to 1978 it went on. Every semester. Fugm.

xi.

Carter's (Very Brief) Age of Limits and Human Rights

By the normal standards of saintliness, Jimmy and Rosalynn Carter would not qualify; but nobody who has resided in the White House has come as close as they. They are both serious Christians, deep believers in the theology and practitioners of the ethics: relatively pacific and concerned with humanity both here and elsewhere. As a graduate of Annapolis and quondam nuclear sub commander, Jimmy would be ineligible for pacifist ranks; but both during and since his presidency, he has made more efforts for bringing about or keeping the peace than any of its other occupants since World War II. That alone makes him look pretty good; that alone helped to sink him—which the economy would have done anyhow. Carter was unusually—one may say suicidally—honest for a politician. Our history knows no other President who has informed the electorate that the time had come for material expectations at home to be lowered and power abroad to be shared—what could be more un-American than that? The problem was that (again, very unpresidentially), things worked out as he said they should, and his support went down the political tubes.

First, materially. In keeping with the processes noted earlier (increased foreign competition, disinvestment, and deindustrialization, etc.), the economy was losing its ability to provide enough jobs, and especially good jobs, with all that meant:

> The new unemployment counted formerly well-paid, unionized industrial workers among its principal victims. It was an unemployment that would, analysts said, be eliminated only when the service sector of the economy could absorb former production workers. Because fast-food chains pay substantially less than car manufacturers, the implications for the middle class were both clear and disturbing. In fact, wages for employees in the service sector fell much more rapidly than wages in mining and manufacturing. From 1975 to 1980, average weekly wages in manufacturing fell by 1.7 percent; they rose in mining. By contrast, workers in retail sales saw their wages fall 12 percent, and construction workers lost 15 percent of their 1975 income in five years. . . . Carter had nothing to offer in the way of halting or reversing these changes. The causes of America's problems, he said, were world history trends that American action could not hold back. . . . He argued that the new age of limits need not be intolerably painful; that with "honest and competent management" the American government and people could function on less.[40]

With jobs always harder to get, and good jobs almost impossibly so, with prices and taxes and interest rates rising more in the late than the early Seventies, it was not entirely irrational for the average person to be dismayed when their President said, in effect, relax and enjoy it. He had campaigned as one who would end inflation and waste, whether due—as he saw it—to unnecessary military spending or to social spending that served "special interests" more than human or social needs. In the last two years of his tenure, he was proposing increases in military spending of 5 percent per annum (identical with the realities of Reagan's first years), and social spending continued to serve special interests (much) more than human or social needs. Washington D.C., as they might say in rural Georgia, plays hob with gentle souls, and all the more so when times are tough:

> The age of limits proclaimed by Carter transformed the special interests from natural allies to natural enemies. Who was going to get that federal dollar—the farmer or the welfare client? Was it to be bridges or B-1s? It made the task of Democratic leadership in Congress and in the Executive Branch next to impossible. It set in motion a Darwinian process in which only the most efficient and powerful lobbies could protect the interests of their clients. The most powerful lobbies tend to be the best funded, and since corporations and industries are better funded than unions and populist causes, the influence of wealth and power in politics is always magnified in time of economic stagnation.[41]

All the more so, too, with that same (relatively) gentle soul's aims to reduce the militarism of U.S. foreign policy and gradually to use our power instead to increase democracy and human rights in LDC's. Most harmful to Carter's popular support was the combined economic and political whammy coming from the Middle East. And, as usual, the roots of the problem were soaked in oil. It will be recalled that in the early Fifties the United States took it upon itself to see that the democratically-elected and nationalist head of Iran's government, Mohammed Mossadegh, with abundant help from the CIA, was overthrown, and his powers usurped by the U.S. supported (and armed and enriched and lauded) Mohammed Pahlavi. Installed in 1953, the Shah-in-shah of Iran (king of kings), as he modestly had himself called, proceeded to modernize and militarize—and Americanize—the Persia out of what became instead: Iran.[42] When the Shah was overthrown by the forces of the Ayatollah Khomeini in 1979 and a fiercely fundamentalist Islamic Republic was proclaimed, the popular appeal of the Ayatollah was based squarely on the felt desire on the part of the largest part of the population to throw off just those the processes the Shah had, in his Americanizing years, introduced.

By 1979, the Shah was fatally ill, and Carter was persuaded by two cold warriors (Kissinger and Brzezinski) and an oil man and banker (David Rockefeller), all cold war/oil pals of the Shah, to hospitalize him in the United States. Mobs in Teheran broke into the U.S. Embassy and seized sixty-nine hostages. Carter had to choose between being quick and tough and start up who knows what processes, or move slowly and hope for the best: as an election was approaching.[43] The fact that Carter tried to deal with the crisis decently (up to a point) was, finally, held against him.

In his years in the White House, Carter was also pushing on South Africa to liberalize at home and to stop contributing to the slaughter or hard line against those trying to free up Zimbabwe and Namibia and Mozambique and Angola from the good old days of colonialism—going so far as to appoint the one-time disciple of Martin Luther King, Andrew Young, as our Ambassador to the United Nations, thus enraging many here at home as well as many abroad (and pleasing many in both areas). Meanwhile, and getting some additional enemies, he was leaning on various governments in Latin America to cease using the torture techniques learned in the United States against their political enemies (again through our dear CIA), and to loosen up a bit—with predictable reactions from hardnose types like General Pinochet, in Chile. Unsurprisingly, as Mead points out,

> while Carter policies in Latin America and Iran were sandbagged by nationalist, anti-American feeling there, his Africa policy was castrated by nationalist, right-wing feeling here. Young's statements about the constructive role of Cuban troops in Angola and his sympathy for the Palestinians were close to the minimum required of a United States that hoped to be taken seriously in the world as an ally of peoples aspiring to freedom and nationhood. Yet even these mild and tentative speeches by Young were savaged by the American press and the political leadership. Although Young's views are center-right by world standards, he was portrayed in this country as an extremist.[44]

I have tried to suggest that Jimmy Carter was a basically decent and well-informed human being, in the political center (if also less centrist in comparison with his fellow citizens and fellow politicians in his ethical stance). Because he is a conservative in political economy, he also limited himself to proposals and remedies which are essentially ways of cleaning up the status quo—something like taking a vacuum cleaner to the Augean stables.

As the presidential campaign of 1980 was burping its way through history, the inflation rate in one month reached 18 percent, unemployment had gone from 5.8 (in 1979) to over 7 percent, and short-term interest rates had risen to 21 percent. In desperation, Carter abandoned persuasion and tried a rescue mission in Iran—losing two helicopters, a transport, and eight soldiers.

Nobody gets reelected with such a clutter staring him and the electorate in the face; especially when grinning at them from the other side of the rostrum is the greatest con man in U.S. political history—complete with crooked smile, tinted hair, broad shoulders, and even broader distortions of truth and possibility: the American Dream Incarnate. Carter didn't have a prayer.[45]

That's the way the decade ended for Carter; the bitterness of the subsequent years had been injected into the bloodstream of San Francisco too, my sweet and funny and humane city—we all thought—some two years earlier, in an experience I'd like to forget, but cannot; an experience that prefigured the social brutalities of the onrushing Eighties.

Story: Depths Below Depths

When the United States made the Philippine Islands its colony at the turn of the century, like colonial powers we opened our gates to immigrants from the Islands: men only, however—farm workers, sailors, janitors, etc. (They were routinely castigated and beaten for associating with white women.) As time went on, a "Manilatown" developed—a lively ten-block neighborhood of dance halls, restaurants, and rooming houses, made up almost entirely of Filipino (and some Chinese) men, at the edge of Chinatown; and adjacent to the financial district. By the 1970s, the latter was expanding swiftly, and Manilatown had been gobbled up and made into highrise office buildings—except for its one last residence, the International Hotel.

The hotel's fifty or so residents were mostly pretty old and pretty poor men, just living out their lives. In the mid-1970s, the hotel was sold to a multinational conglomerate, and slated for quick demolition. When the news of that began to spread, a coalition of extraordinary breadth grew up to prevent it, to keep the Filipinos from becoming homeless. It was "extraordinary" in that it extended from pacifists to militants, ordinary decent mainstream people to liberals to radicals, vegetarians to revolutionaries; etc., and because it functioned over a period not of weeks or months but of years, not shrinking but growing, in both numbers and determination.

One of the "big names" who got involved was named Richard Hongisto. He had run a campaign for Sheriff and won, not unimportantly because his platform included some very "San Francisco" political positions, including support for the residents of "I-Hotel." In 1977, the people who had bought the place began to get itchy, began to increase the pressure on the city for eviction and demolition. Our response was to increase the duration and depth of our picket lines around the hotel.

One night in 1977, a night that followed many preceding nights of rising police pressure against the picketers, beginning early in the evening we found ourselves massed around the hotel, arms linked, as mounted cops drove their horses into our bodies, pushing us into the sides of the building. Something new; and really scary. (San Francisco is both a city and the entirety of the county; and when property is involved, both police and sheriff's deputies get into the act.) It was a nightmare that went on and on until, between one and two a.m., more and more cops with swinging batons and great muscular horses with sweaty flanks and flashing hooves moved in to crush us always more. And as that pressure reached its almost unendurable maximum who should appear, hatchet in hand, but Sheriff Hongisto (who had just announced his candidacy for Mayor in the upcoming election), surrounded by his deputies, making his way to the main door of the hotel, chopping away with his hatchet, breaking down the door, bulling into the building filled with terrified little old men. Victory in our time. At six a.m. that morning it was all over: all over for the residents of I-Hotel, all over for the mellow glory that had been San Francisco (for those who knew what had happened), all over too for Sheriff Hongisto's hopes—for the next political act of our coalition, which had supported him for Sheriff, was to fight bitterly to see to it that he would never win another election in that city. Nor has he.

The empty hotel stood for over a year, untouched. In 1979 it was entirely demolished. In 1997 the garish empty hole remains. Next time you're visiting the city go look for it: Kearny and Jackson Streets. It's not in the tourist guide, but you'll know it when you see it.

6   CLOUD CUCKOO LAND: REAGAN 1980-1988

> Was it for this our fathers kept the law?
> This crown shall crown their struggle and their ruth?
> Are we the eagle nation Milton saw
> Mewing its mighty youth,
> Soon to possess the mountain winds of truth,
> And be a swift familiar of the sun
> Where aye before God's face his trumpets run?
> Or have we but the talons and the maw,
> And for the abject likeness of our heart
> Shall some less lordly bird be set apart?
> Some gross-billed wader where the swamps are fat?
> Some gorger in the sun? Some prowler with the bat?
>
> —William Vaughn Moody, "An Ode in Time of Hesitation"

The 1980s are and will remain indelibly associated with Reagan. It was a decade which, when its processes and data are examined, must be viewed as taking our society toward economic frailty, bitter political strife, and social tragedies. In those same years, Reagan was the most powerful individual in the United States—perhaps in the world. Despite this, and except among a very small minority, he is given no responsibility for any of that, and his popularity has never shown a sign of faltering. From among the variety of sordid data to be presented in this chapter, perhaps the most revealing of Reagan's magic are those concerned with the distribution of income—remembering that we are people thought to be more closely tuned-in to our incomes than any other facet of existence:

[T]he combined net worth of the four hundred richest Americans had *trebled* from $92 billion in 1982 to $270 billion in 1989 (while the U.S. median family income barely stayed ahead of inflation) . . . [and] the top 1 percent of Americans had increased their share of national income from about 8 percent in the early 1980s to the 12 percent range by the end of the decade.[1]

In our present period of continuing economic weaknesses and rising social abrasiveness—rising along with serious efforts to revive Reaganism—it becomes important to understand how such a man came to be elected and overwhelmingly reelected both governor of the largest state in the union and president of the most powerful nation in the world's history. In 1950, nobody would have believed any of that could happen; but by the early Sixties, Reagan and what was rapidly becoming a potent circle of rich supporters were already aiming at a Reagan presidency. By the early Seventies it had come to seem only a matter of time until he would occupy the White House.

i.

A Man of the People

The key years shaping Reagan's political thought and career were not those of his youth as a New Dealer but 1952-1964, when he served as "the voice" of General Electric on its very popular weekly "General Electric Theater." GE, as noted earlier, was the most ideological of the major corporations, going back to the 1920s: antiunion, anticommunist, paternalistic, and against social legislation—at the same time that it was in the vanguard of price-fixing and "self-government in business," the U.S. variation on German cartelization processes.

Reagan became the effective political voice of GE not only on TV, but also on the "rubber chicken circuit" of Rotary Clubs and the like. He always gave what came to be called "The Speech": the reactionary political position of GE. It was a comfortable role for Reagan: he didn't so much learn his lines from GE as learn and recite as though by rote a more persuasive way to put what was becoming his own position—pro-big business, anti-independent unionism, anticommunist, anti-New Deal.

In his rhetoric and his attitudes, in his *style*, Reagan incarnated the illusions, ongoing disappointments, angers, and fears—most importantly, perhaps, the adolescent dreams—of the *voting* part of all segments of the social spectrum. What Nixon and Agnew had called the silent majority had become the voting majority by the Eighties—"the middle class," as that term is defined in the United States: neither the really poor nor the really rich; small proprietors, blue *and* white collar workers, farmers.[2]

But of critical importance for the rise of Reagan was that other and overlapping big business grouping, an unknown percentage of which is also open to racist appeals, religious fundamentalism, militarism, and assorted other dubious elements of the American Dream—a sociopolitical concoction whose potency and dangers, demonstrated too often already, are not likely to subside as they gain strength in the United States.

The most successful con men always take themselves at least as seriously as they hope others will, and Reagan had been plying that skill from the time he began calling baseball games on radio from a studio (pretending to be actually witnessing the games), and doing it very well.[3]

What could be more of a self-con—seemingly one taken as seriously by Reagan as he expected us to (and got away with it, as always)—than his comment during the Iran-Contra inquiry:

> I told the American people I did not trade arms for hostages. My heart and my best intention still tell me that is true, but the facts and the evidence tell me it is not.[4]

The Iran-Contra facts going against Reagan's "heart and best intention" not only constituted a violation of his own "heartfelt promise" *never* to trade arms for hostages, but, more importantly, he broke enough laws to warrant impeachment. Not a chance that would happen, and somehow we—Congress, Special Investigators, you, and I—all knew that: to impeach Ronnie, as George Bush might put it, would be like making doo-doo on the Statue of Liberty.

Reagan epitomized what increasing numbers in our country have become or are becoming: cold-hearted, substituting sentimentality for compassion; simultaneously scornful or hateful of social analysis, but confident experts on a long list of complex social problems; quick to support wars, but unwilling to endure our casualties (while being indifferent to others'); and, like Reagan, except as a filmgoer or maker, never having been in a tight spot.[5]

Like him, too, we tend to profess belief in the Puritan ethic of hard and honest work, while mostly looking for a quick deal, something for nothing, and the more the merrier. Of course Reagan differed in at least one very big way from the "middle class" whose hero he is: he came to be surrounded, financed, and guided by a group of experts at achieving those merry deals for him and themselves on the very highest level. For which, we—including most of his supporters—will be paying for a long time.

In what Reagan represents of us, then, partially or entirely, he and we are responding to the main and altering signals of a social system whose faults and virtues of, say, a century ago, have been magnified and diminished. But we are also responding to a well-oiled construct.

Reagan was a well-groomed facade. His grooming began as preparations were being made for Reagan to become Governor: he made several "goofs" about welfare (stating that three times as many people were receiving welfare than the easily-available facts showed, for example). His team soon hired BASICO (the Behavior Sciences Corporation in, of course, Southern California), which then "worked on the whole concept of the man."

> The BASICO team assembled simple answers for Reagan, framed in terms of his theme, and arranged them into eight books of five-by-eight cards that would focus his and the voters' minds. From that time on BASICO became the keepers of the candidate and his cards. . . . "We were with him every waking moment during the entire campaign. . . . You'd follow him into the rest room before he goes onstage, giving him a last-minute bit of advice."[6]

Although no fully satisfactory explanation of Reagan's enormous popularity is ever likely to be made, Veblen's notion of "emulation" would be one ingredient in what might become such an explanation. In his first book, *The Theory of the Leisure Class*, Veblen, taking issue with the Marxian view of class struggle (which saw the industrial working class led by its circumstances to organize itself to overthrow capitalism and create democratic socialism) argued that people are more inclined to seek to be *like* than to overthrow those "above" them; to "emulate" the rich and powerful.

> With the exception of the instinct of self-preservation, the propensity for emulation is probably the strongest and most alert and persistent of the economic motives proper. In an industrial [capitalist] community this propensity for emulation expresses itself in pecuniary emulation. . . . The abjectly poor, and all those persons whose energies are entirely absorbed by the struggle for daily sustenance, are conservative because they cannot afford the effort of taking thought for the day after tomorrow; just as the highly prosperous are conservative because they have small occasion to be discontented with the situation as it stands today.[7]

But because the show biz of politics is important not only in what *is* placed before us that makes us support someone or some policy (or buy some product)—most especially on TV—but also in what *isn't* seen or discussed, adequately, or at all, I think it useful to show just one of the ways in which the show is or is not made to go on, thus helping or hindering us as we make up our minds.

Story: Cut

In 1975, as many people and organizations of all sorts were preparing to celebrate our 200th birthday in 1976, I received a call from a TV producer's office (with ABC). They were planning a show for the big birthday, and I was one of several people they wished to interview as possible participants—all of us working in "Silicon Valley" (I at San Jose State University). Their program was to have three segments, one concerned with the first years of the nation, the second with the early years of this century, and the third with the post-World War II period. Each period would have a theme, and for the postwar period it was to be the nature and extent, and the meaning of and attitudes toward, the military-industrial complex—whose technological heart is located in Silicon Valley. In addition to whatever graphics and so on they planned, they wished to have voices speaking from contrasting positions: military, political, industrial, and antiwar. Along with several others from the area, I was to be tried out for the last (of course). We taped for about two hours, and modesty does not prevent me from saying that everyone—producer, director, cameraman, soundman, secretary—was enthusiastic. I was chosen, they worked on some finishing touches, and they said I might hear from them about any needed changes later.

About two months later the producer called from New York, with only one question: the tapes had been shown to the appropriate execs in New York, and they were very upset with what I had said about the dollar amount of military expenditures by the United States from 1946 to 1975—which was in the trillions of dollars, of course. They said they couldn't allow that "shit" (their word) on the air unless I had a good source for it. The producer was almost pleading with me to find a good source. I said I didn't have to look, it was common knowledge, it was in the annual *Economic Report of the President of the United States for 1975* (signed by Gerald Ford, President), gave him the page numbers, said I'd make copies and send them on, he said great, no problem now. I did what I said: and never heard from him again. The program was scheduled to appear on July 4, 1976, of course, and I looked in the TV guides, the newspaper, finally at the tube itself, and there it wasn't.

An ex-student and fan of mine (by that time an established medico in NYC, in his fifties) who had been awaiting the program, called and asked what had—*not*—happened. He took it upon himself to go to the ABC offices and inquire: my contribution had been nixed by the bosses, the producer threatened to resign, they told him to go ahead, and he did. And the whole show was nixed.

ii.

The Last of the Big-Time Spenders

Carter beat Ford in 1976, through no special virtues of his own—more likely, despite his special virtues. In 1980 Carter couldn't have beaten anyone: least of all Reagan.

As the economy continued to deteriorate in his tenure he was handed the blame for much he had tried to prevent and, by continually reminding the people they had to lower their expectations, he committed political suicide. Not that he had to; Reagan would have trounced him—or anyone else?—anyway. [8]

Never knowing what the economists (among others) were talking about, perhaps not even caring so long as it all felt good, Reagan was enthusiastic about his "team's" ideas—even as the "ideas" changed drastically from meeting to meeting as his experts shoved the U.S. economy toward a cliff.

The tragicomedy had begun to unroll in the election campaign; by the time Reagan reached the White House, the economic strategy had been fully worked out by David Stockman.

The United States came to be run for eight years by a gang mixing low comedy with high thievery, a Rogues' Gallery made up of old California pals of Reagan, like Ed Meese and Michael Deaver; [9] cloak and dagger fanatics like Ollie North and Bill Casey; a motley bunch of improbables such as Alexander Haig, Jeanne Kirkpatrick, Raymond Donovan, Don Regan, John Poindexter, Larry Speakes, Robert McFarlane, and (sigh!) George Bush.

Before examining the various dimensions of "Reaganomics" as they were put into place and functioned (or malfunctioned), it is useful to remind ourselves of the promises and the presumed whys and wherefores of its "supply-side economics." They are neatly and accurately summarized by Harrison and Bluestone:

Step 1: The personal tax cuts were to encourage work and personal savings, while corporate tax cuts and deregulation would presumably lead to a boom in short-term investments and innovation. Step 2: The additional work plus new investment were supposed to increase productivity and thereby boost the United States' global competitiveness. Step 3: The increased productivity and new-found competitiveness would permit an increase in exports, GNP, wages, profits, and family incomes. Finally, Step 4: Rising wages and increased profits would put the national economy on a trajectory of steady, inflation-free economic growth and enhanced economic security . . . [:] the temporal *order* of the recovery was to proceed from government-induced tax cuts and market deregulation to increased savings, investment, and innovation . . . [and] productivity, and then to renewed international competitivenss, and finally to rising wages and a higher standard of living.[10]

Although inflation was brought down, so, however, was the economy, in the recession of 1981-1983. GNP grew, but never approached the rates of the Sixties; the rate of savings, far from rising, dropped to the lowest level since 1939; those who received the benefits of individual tax cuts went on a spending spree and businesses "invested" in takeovers rather than real facilities; aggregate debt (households, nonfinancial businesses, and government) almost tripled in the decade between 1976 and 1987 and rose much more by the end of the Eighties; real interest rates remained high (given all the deficits and debt)—the highest of any decade in this century—causing the dollar to soar and our global economic position, deficits and debts to worsen, as also much of real investment at home was financed by foreign capital—while domestic capital went abroad.[11]

It's repetitive, but bears repeating: Reagan entered the governorship of California promising to reduce taxes and spending—after attacking those who had preceded him for not doing that—and then raised both taxes *and* spending to their highest levels. He also entered the White House having promised to lower taxes and spending and balance the budget. Well, he lowered the taxes of the best-off 20 percent and especially the richest 10 percent, raised payments for everyone else, increased spending, ran the highest deficits in history, and raised the national debt from 1 to 3 *trillion* dollars—more than had been accumulated throughout the whole of preceding U.S. history.

All this says nothing, just yet, about what happened to jobs, to unions, to infrastructure, to social programs, or enough of what happened to our position in the world economy. A closer look at tax and spending cuts first, and to their connections with the rest of the economy next.

iii.

Look Ma! No Hands!

At the heart of Reaganomics was not what can be thought of as "economics" at all (which is not to suggest that all would be well had it been): strongest were the ideological and political (and emotional) desires to increase military spending, to cut the taxes on high personal incomes and on corporations, and to cut spending on social programs. Setting aside the record-breaking military spending program, an examination of the other items reveals a heart throbbing return to the good old days of Ulysses S. Grant and Chester Arthur or, failing that, Cal Coolidge: back to the Gilded Age, back to the Roaring Twenties—and, as Phillips has argued, with a vengeance.

To attempt that in the 1980s was not like turning a clock back, it was like smashing it with a sledgehammer. Social force and violence had to be used to get rid of innumerable socio-governmental institutions that had been in the process of creation throughout the entire century—whether to keep the economy from its lemming-like tendencies to run wild in one direction or another, to provide safety nets for the otherwise (and politically dangerous) gaping holes in the always stretched fabric of modern industrial capitalist societies or, among other needs, to provide some kind of order in terms of resource use and depletion. [12]

That even (perhaps especially) a coherent application of such ideas to the leading global monopoly capitalist power would be a step toward social lunacy was beyond the ken or concern of Reagan and his claque. But when into that home brew Reagan mixed the dynamite of the most grandiose military Keynesianism, whiz-bang banking frolics, and other forms of largesse from an always fatter State cash cow, the *nouveau* econ was as economy-busting as it was mind-boggling.

It is impossible to know whether the tax cuts or the increased military spending was primary in the "program"—both were conscious attempts to enlarge the incomes and wealth of the already rich. Now read this:

> With the Democrats marching side by side with, and occasionally even ahead of, Reagan on the tax and military spending issues, the media 1) were even quieter about what an incredible windfall the 1981 tax cuts were for big corporations and the rich and 2) missed reporting altogether an astonishing Pentagon raid on the U.S. Treasury that eventually won the Defense Department untold hundreds of billions of dollars.

[This was not exposed] until David Stockman [Reagan's budget chief] published his memoirs in 1986 . . . [in which he says] Defense Secretary Caspar Weinberger and Frank Carlucci worked a bookkeeping trick on [Stockman] . . . at a January 30, 1981 meeting [where] they agreed to a compromise seven percent "real" increase in military spending. . . . The trick came when Carlucci suggested that the seven percent growth [proposed by Reagan] begin with the 1982 budget—which happened to be $80 billion higher than the 1980 budget of Carter [which itself involved a five percent annual increase after 1977]. [Thus was won] *an extra $80 billion per year* in spending authority above and beyond what even conservative hard-liners had said was needed to restore U.S. military prowess.[13]

iv.

How to Wreck an Economy Without Even Trying

The Reagan administration was able to get away with its particular brand of socioeconomic mayhem because of a set of intersecting and mutually strengthening processes that had been decades in the making, and that accelerated in the Seventies. Among the most relevant and important were these: 1) a population the largest part of which had found its purchasing power declining in the face of rising taxes and worsening (if any) job possibilities, as it had also allowed what political strength it may have possessed (specifically that located in its trade unions) to decline; 2) a business world always more dominated by a) the very largest corporations, b) companies under increasing pressure to "restructure"—locate production where the cheapest labor is and poorest people are, lay off workers and close plants, become always more heavily laden with debt as a result of either friendly or hostile "takeovers"[14]—at the same time that they became much more financial than producing firms; 3) an agricultural sector in which the family-sized farm continued and speeded up its trip toward extinction, aided and abetted by the highest level ever of debts; 4) a society in which social problems mounted and interacted—most especially in the cities—producing great anger and fear among those in the bottom third of the population and fear and hatred in much of the rest; and 5) importantly resulting from and fitting in with all the foregoing, legislatures on all levels—federal, state, and local—in which getting and staying in office meant moving with those tides, and, almost always, benefitting from them in diverse ways. In short, and hoping not to oversimplify, by 1980 the United States had become deeply corrupted at the top levels (business, government, education, health care, everything), and political demoralization spread like weeds.

By the early Sixties Reagan had begun to look very good to those who became his "Friends"; by 1980, he looked like Santa Claus to those already fat with wealth and power, and he came on as some combination of Daniel Boone and Rambo and Bob Hope and—no offense meant—the new Messiah, to all too many others. Whether he knew what he was doing or not—does it matter?—he pleased the high and mighty, who fueled him all along the way; and he snookered or intimidated an easy sufficiency of the rest. And won reelection without a sweat in 1984.

We'll return to the work of Reagan's wrecking crew in a few pages. Not only can I use some respite from shoveling around in the barn with those *dreckmeisters,* but the mere mention of the year 1984 tenses me up for some deeply personal (and more than socioeconomic) memories, from funny to very sad, the recounting of which is not mostly meant to illuminate the historical process. For those on the verge of becoming or being old geezers (or their female equivalent), some of it may be helpful for grappling with the always intricate personal problems of dealing with a loved one's death: while also remembering that the line between the political and the personal is often hard to find.

v.

Women and Life and Death

Kay. When I went to Cornell to teach in 1953, across the fence from us was the family of which Kay was wife and the mother of two boys. Like me, she had married someone who could have been a good friend but was not a good mate—not that either of us was thinking in that way as we became friends. Kay grew up in a poor farm family in upstate New York—much like Dan Berrigan, and with a face so much like Dan's—"the map of Ireland"—they could have been twins.

She graduated from the College of Home Economics at Cornell—one of the four "state schools" in that otherwise forbiddingly expensive Ivy League university—where her concentration was on child development.

Her first job was at a women's prison in Framingham, Mass., where she took care of the infant children of the inmates and, as much as she could, of the inmates themselves.

Her husband was an attorney, very much the conservative spokesman of Ithaca, N.Y., and its chief judge. Kay did not participate in politics of any sort, then. After her second child was born, she had her own nursery school, as a means principally of being with her child. Subsequently she became a research sociologist in child development at Cornell.

We began to become friends "over the fence," then at dinner parties, then playing golf together on Cornell's course—this was in the mid-1950s. At first Kay was amusedly tolerant of what she and her husband saw as my bizarre political position. As time went on, she discovered that her deep humanism, when applied to the political controversies of the time, meshed easily with my stands and activities; while through her I began to appreciate the need for those "on the Left" to attend to their own humanity.

After a couple of years, we were surprised, shocked, and terrified to find we were in love with each other: I remember vividly the day I knew—we were golfing and I was watching her as she addressed the ball and I thought, Christ! I love her! No such feelings had happened before for either of us. In retrospect, it is clear we were slowly and painfully growing up, and unconsciously (and without verbalization) serving as therapists for each other. Finally we knew we had to end our marriages, out of decency and to fill out our lives. After much pain and damage all around (especially for the children) we were married, in 1962; and continued to grow up, some pain always there, but giving way to an ever-deepening joy in life and each other.

Kay died in February 1984. Counting the time before and after our marriage we had been together for more than twenty-five years. I do not think of myself as having been a brute before knowing her; it was rather as though I was living in a very cold air-conditioned emotional room. Kay's warmth and *generosity*—to children, friends, animals, to me—was a living lesson for me, was like learning how to read: it was the opening of a new world. I can dare to say it: I felt so safe with her, so accepted, so loved; trusting and trusted and trustworthy; more alive.

Kay died of emphysema, from smoking.[15] It is a disease which, once identified, allows easy prediction: one, two, or three years to live. When we knew that she had only a year or so to live, I took early retirement from the university, which meant I was off half of every year. We went to our beloved Bologna for six months, almost all of which, however, she spent in intensive care; as was true in her last six months in San Francisco.

Emphysema is a disease of suffocation; drugs allow you to breathe enough to survive, but always more drugs, less life. Kay, who loved life so much, said she wished not to go on. We discussed it with our doctor and he consented, cutting back on the life-giving drugs, increasing morphine to minimize pain. Her last words to me were "I'm not afraid. I feel at peace."

Like anyone who loses a long-time beloved mate, I was lost and bewildered—still turning to her to remark on something lovely, or awful, or interesting. . . . My friends knew, and all tried to help—too much. As soon as the semester ended, I took my bike and fled to Europe, with the intention of biking around until autumn, thence to Italy and home again some time in December.

I was entirely alone for months: biking, eating, reading, sleeping; rarely a conversation. It was like standing under a freezing shower for a very long time, with the exception of one warming experience in Namur (Belgium) with another wonderful woman, Sister Marie Augusta Neal.

Story: Red Nun

In 1965, Sister Marie was one—the most vital—of our group of four profs at Cornell who gave what I still think of as the best class I've experienced. The course was entitled "Why Are There So Many Poor People in a Rich Society Like the United States?" There were sixty-five students, all admitted to a university, but this was their first university class—at a Cornell summer session. In the first lecture, I began by giving an economic-historical discussion of the distribution of income and wealth. Sister Marie, looking as nunnish as can be, rose to her feet as I finished to point out how inadequate my explanation was, neglecting (as it had) the sociological roots and setting of this and that and the other thing. Her analysis was more "radical" than mine, going as it did to the very roots of the matter. And so it went for the six weeks of the class—Sister Marie was not only the most startling of the four of us to the students, but the most searching. And the most effective, despite and because of her small voice and her great dignity.

After that we stayed in touch. She had me come to lecture in her sociology class at Emmanuel College in Boston (a Catholic "girls'" school); to the annual meeting of the Conference of (hundreds of) Mother Superiors of the United States, in Chicago in 1969, where my topic was "Poverty and Power," as all hell was breaking loose in the real world outside (and after which I was surrounded by dozens of interested sisters); and in Los Angeles to a group of several hundred nuns who, because of their teachings and connected activities, had been suspended or kicked out of their order (the Immaculate something or other, as I recall) and who, in their gymnasium, almost all wearing colorful dresses rather than habits, seemed a marvelously blossoming garden, and were a grandly enthusiastic audience.

Sister Marie took her Ph.D. in sociology at Harvard. When she sought to join the ceremonial procession (in her habit), a functionary sought to prevent her, she being the first sort of *that* kind of person ever to be in such a procession. She is an angelic hellraiser: about the structure of power in the Church and, a separate but connected matter, the role of women in the Church; and, regularly, about the various dimensions and causes of poverty. She has written many books, is always on the go.

She was in Namur to confer with some young sisters in her order, and I had known about it, telephoned and we agreed that I would bike over there and spend a few hours. When I arrived at the convent and asked for her—me looking rough, and large, and all—there was a certain consternation; but finally she appeared, we talked, and then we went out to dinner at a nearby small restaurant. There were two other nuns at a table not far distant—very interested, and always more so as Sister Marie, small and slender and anything but a drinker, consumed her share of a bottle of wine and, very possibly for the first time in her life, became noticeably, if not heavily, drunk. Like Kay, she came from a poor Irish family; she too had strong reservations about the Church, but chose to spend her life fighting its wrongs directly. Bless her and her works.

I went on with my isolated biking, into Holland, then Germany, to Denmark and Sweden and then Norway. At one point, in Oslo, I remember waking up and wanting just to give up, to die—but, apart from not wanting to do that to my kids, I didn't have the energy to kill myself. Unable to bear being alone anymore, I took the train, two days from Bergen to Bologna— where I had lived and taught and visited off and on since 1966; and where, in a real sense, my life began again.

Bologna. I didn't wish to look up friends there, I did wish for the city's—how to put it?—human warmth, its traditional solidity, its civility. I had been away from San Francisco for four months; I planned to stay another three months or so: just reading, and biking around that lovely human-sized museum of a city and its countryside.

Occasionally I patronized a fine bookstore on the *Strada Maggiore* which, but not the main reason I went there, was a women's bookstore, one of very few in Italy. On a morning just before I was preparing to visit the store, the phone rang and it was Jeff, from L.A., worried about me (although he didn't say so). He may have saved my life once before, this time he may have done again, in a different way.[16]

Story: Miracle on Strada Maggiore

Jeff had been with us in Bologna in 1966-67, and attended a *liceo* (in effect, for him, a high school). He didn't know Italian, but all classes were *in* Italian. So he had to have a tutor: Luca F., just graduated from the University. He was bright as could be, funny, and very Left; and he and Jeff got along famously, if also with some disputes. On the many occasions I returned to Bologna in subsequent years, Jeff would ask me to look for the always on the move Luca, say hello, etc. On this morning, he asked if I had located him. I said no, but I had inquired around, and that Anna Maria G., a good friend of Luca's, was returning from out of town in a day or so, and she would know where he might be. Jeff said, "there was another Anna who was friends with Luca and me, Anna H." I said hang on, looked in the phone book, found her home phone, said I'd call her. Then went to the bookstore, where I wished to buy some books for some children whose father had me to lunch every week to help his English. I asked the proprietor to select and wrap the books for me, and as she was doing so I asked—this being a woman's bookstore—if she knew a woman named Anna H. I told her I was trying to find Luca F., and this Anna H. might know his whereabouts. "Who *are* you?" she asked, clearly suspicious. "I'm Jeff Dowd's father," was the only thing I could think of to say. She came around the cash register, embraced me, and said that *she* was Anna H., and how well she remembered Jeff—who, with my money, had rented a small apartment *specifically* for pot parties with Luca and friends. That was in 1966, as the student movement was just beginning in Italy; Luca, Anna, and pals were very much a part of it.

By the early 1970s, the student movement had both stimulated and become part of something larger and more substantial in Italy: La Lotta Continua (loosely translated into Americanese, "Keep struggling"). Anna was instrumental in bringing the group into existence in Bologna, and vital to its activities. By the mid-1970s in Italy, as elsewhere, political frustrations for Left groups often led to the emergence of factionalism and tendencies toward violence. At that time, Anna, unwilling to follow that path and also unwilling to give up, began her women's bookshop, which soon became a social and cultural center for women from Bologna and elsewhere. Although I didn't know it until much later, I had come to be friends with a much-loved and widely-admired woman.

As the friendship began, I was not "looking for a woman"—if anything, I was in some kind of hiding; nor was Anna "looking for a man." That neither of us was doing so very probably made it possible for us to become friends, easily and comfortably; and that she was Italian and I from the States and she considerably younger than I made the friendship more interesting, rather than being the obstacles such differences might have constituted had we been circling around each other with something more complicated in mind. Which, without either of us seeking it, soon evolved.

I became aware of something like that happening first when, on December 7 (my birthday) I invited her and Anna Maria to dinner at my place. The next day I was to go to Amsterdam for about ten days and as the two Annas were leaving, it suddenly struck me that I didn't wish *not* to see her for that long. But immediately I recalled the famous disclaimer of Groucho Marx: "I wouldn't join any club that would have me"—and I thought, anyone that young, that *every* thing, who would have me would have to be unbalanced, and went off to Amsterdam saying to myself, forget it, pal, be grateful for her friendship.

When I returned to Bologna and first saw Anna our relationship took a sudden turn when she invited me to meet her that evening toward midnight at a large party given by some good friends of hers, whom I did not know; and I was led to understand that we would then go to her place.

Bologna is an elegant city in all ways, not least in the clothing of Anna's friends and family. My clothing was confined to what I had been able to pack around on my bicycle for some months: in short, I looked like a bum, especially in the winter. To make matters worse, I had a bone spur problem on one foot (for which I had a scheduled operation in San Francisco in just two weeks), so serious I could barely walk more than a few yards without pain, so I rode my bike everywhere, even for short distances.

When I arrived at the party, I was limping, messy, very upset, and very late: Anna had given me the right number (#5) but the wrong street. It is now past midnight, I have just turned sixty-five, I am walking/biking up and down narrow streets in the cold and wet ringing the bell on every #5 I could find, and making many friends. Finally I gave up, got the telephone book at a bar, and looked under Z . . . , all I could remember of the family name of the friend's house. I finally found a Z . . . . at a #5 on a nearby alley, went there, found a very crowded party up several flights of stairs, very, very late—and. . . . there was Anna, unperturbed that I was late, incredulous that she had given me the wrong address, admiring my Yankee ingenuity at finding her anyway, and hustling me out of there—whether out of shame at my appearance or the desire to be alone with me. Or both. Or neither.

By the time Anna took me to the plane about two weeks later, we *were* circling each other, neither of us knowing where either of us stood.

Within days of my return to San Francisco, we were exchanging telephone calls. In mid-January she said she could perhaps come to visit San Francisco for a bit in February. Did I want her to? Don't ask. She was to arrive about 8 p.m. That evening I learned the meaning of good karma. It was a beautiful, starry, and fresh, not cold, San Francisco night, I had gone to help celebrate the opening of a new Chinese restaurant owned by my dentist, and took with me to the airport a borrowed large red balloon on a string. So, as Anna toiled off the plane, there I was, big red balloon on a string, big grin, open arms, happy as a clam; and her smile would have lit up the other side of the moon. And we drove into the beautiful city on that starry night in my marvy black Peugeot convertible with its red leather seats—1966, but still a gem—where my house (now our house) sits on the very top of Russian Hill overlooking the bay with a garden as big as the Ritz, tall cypresses. . . . Fairy tale.

Early on, when I knew I loved her, I told Anna how pleased I would be if ever she wanted to marry me—but no pressure, I was so very happy just to be with her, I didn't have to be married. To which she said nothing. More than a year later, in 1986, we were in the hills above Berkeley one day, where she was ordering books from some small press, and the day was sunny and clear, and as we left the building and were crossing the street—I can see it still—she stopped, turned to me, and said "I want us to marry." It was done, soonest. Now I am with this woman most of the hours of every day—so beautiful, so knowing, so giving and receiving, so angry at those social cruelties and insanities that enrage me, so gentle and so tough: and every once in a while, she looks at me and says: *bellino*. Lucky Louie.

Jenny. Then there is my daughter. She has the same gentle beauty as Muh; and she too is a teacher. She has been teaching bilingually to second and third grade kids in the Salinas Valley for many years now. They are the kids of migratory workers, mostly Mexican—pickers of vegetables and fruits, underpaid, overworked, always poor and desperate, much alcoholism, child abuse, everything: the people of Cesar Chavez.

I have visited her classrooms over the years; have seen what she does for those children, how she loves them, her many photographs of them looking (at least for that moment) delighted; and have wondered what their lives will be like, but could have been like, if only. . . . I know how much time and money—her own time, her own money—she spends to warm those kids' lives with care and joy (including visits to their villages in Mexico). Luckily for those children—luckily for Jenny—she has found her vocation.

As I write this, the 1994 election returns have just come in. Now Jenny and others will have to confront the vicious law passed by the voters of California who think they are helping themselves by denying education and health care to the children of the desperate poor. She will do whatever she can; and it will be as much the right thing to do as can be done in this always crueler society.

But now we've got to get back to those plug uglies who helped us along that rotten path, back to those permanent adolescents who were looting the store in the Reagan years: multiplying the deficits, tripling the national debt, "hollowing" the economy, shouldering production aside in favor of finance, and, nor last nor least, criminalizing the savings and loan industry, to the special gain of themselves and other louts. Now a brief closer look at those messes, just close enough to sniff the stench, identify the origins, and then back away to something else with an unpleasant odor.

vi.

Greed and Glitz

In 1989 the S&L scandal raced across our consciousness like a streaker, only to disappear into the mists whence it came; like so much else of its kind. It took and takes a lot of cooperation among and between the Reagan, Bush, and now Clinton administrations, between Democrats and Republicans, financiers, crooks, and builders (and a certain acquiescence? indifference? connivance?—*some*thing hard to forgive on the part of the media) to accomplish and continue that dirty deal:

> the savings and loan disaster was actually a success story for the politicians. They managed the crisis year after year to protect their clients from loss, then they abruptly informed the voters of their obligation to pay—right after the 1988 election. Yet no one in government was made to answer for the enormous injury they inflicted on taxpayers. The same political officers continued in power—still managing things in much the same manner. [17]

In a capitalist society it is to be expected that the most powerful in the business world will wish and be able to design many of the laws within which they function, that their political power will be greatly disproportionate to their percentage of the population.

The 1920s showed how fickle capitalists can be regarding the rules of their own game. The 1980s showed something more: when the rules are changed or bent to legalize relatively excessive behavior, some significant number of people—in business and government, from the world of crime, and just plain greedy individuals who get a chance—will violate even the loosest of rules, run wild, and place the entire system in jeopardy.

A reminder that the trail that leads into the financial jungle of the Reagan years had its beginnings in the excess capacities that became evident in the late Sixties, and that were pervasive by the Eighties. Lots of investible funds rolling around loose from the heady years of expansion, but why put them into the increase or improvement of more productive capacities? Why not sell massive amounts of junk bonds to finance multibillion dollar takeovers, and make lots of moolah while also controlling the threats of competition from excess capacity?

Earlier it was shown that throughout the 1970s banks and the rich were searching for places to put their surplus cash, and found ready borrowers among households, takeover artists, our own and poorer countries' governments—meanwhile constructing an increasingly precarious financial structure.[18]

Bankers, once the most prudent of people, zipped over to the fast lane to prod homeowners to borrow for trips, motorboats, vacations abroad, and other luxuries on the equity in their still unpaid-for homes; and mostly financially dimwitted people, dipping their toes in the water first with money-market funds and CDs, are by now splashing around in the deep waters of derivatives—which *nobody* understands—and against whose potential and likely disasters there will be no lifeguards.

As if all that were not enough, the smallest and the largest corporations, most especially the transnational corporations, found it both possible and necessary to become speculators in foreign exchange and, along the way, created something like a new and omnivorous financial sector.

> Item: 1995 [from *Institutional Investor*]. The latest triennial survey reports the daily volume as $1.23 trillion a day. In reporting this, the *NYT* made the understandable error of saying "year" instead of "day."[19]

And the share of foreign exchange transactions used for *non*-speculative purposes is now down to less than 2 percent. But I was relieved to read (also in the *Institutional Investor*) that the "chief forex dealer for Barclays Bank," Doug Bate, has an enlightened outlook: "We tend to look at our business as a sausage machine. The more meat you put in, the more money you make." We're in good hands.[20]

Into this jangling scenario sauntered the "thrifts"—which the S&Ls used to be called and indeed were. They were organized in the Thirties, almost entirely as local banks, to finance home mortgages for "the middle class." They got their funds largely from the savings of the same groups of people to whom they loaned for the purchase of homes. And their rules placed a ceiling on what they could pay their depositors, as the interest cost of borrowing for a home was kept low.

The Garn-St. Germain bill (1981) for deregulating the thrifts was one of the first of Reagan's triumphs, which should have been seen as a warning shot across our bows. Instead, it served as an invitation to reckless financial practices for households and all financial institutions, among them and leading the pack, the S&Ls—whose ownership and control were increasingly taken over by sharpies, fools, and downright crooks. The S&Ls now got their capital in every which way (at always rising costs) and made loans and investments of every which kind, not least in junk bonds. [21]

Just how much the bailing-out of the S&Ls will ultimately cost can only be estimated: the lowest estimate I have seen is $200 billion, which has already been spent; the highest is $1 trillion, which takes into account the accumulation of costs and interest payments on the government borrowing necessary to accomplish the bailouts—bailouts of what and whom? First, it is worth mentioning that a significant but unknowable percentage of the costs incurred by the agency created for this purpose—the Resolution Trust Corporation—go to the lawyers ($600/hour!) and accountants involved; second, the bulk of costs of the deposits being covered are in the high range, not those of the traditional "little guy"; third, with rare exceptions, the criminality involved, widespread, substantial, and "genuinely criminal"—its players including one of Bush's sons—is lightly punished, or not at all. Like Michael Milken, the freebooters have made great sums of money from criminal activity, are exposed (some, by no means all of them), tried, perhaps punished—but not as much as if they had stolen $50 from a service station—and most end up rich.

Deeply involved in the corruption and failure of the S&Ls were and are all levels of government—the presidency, the bank regulators, Congress, the FBI, and the CIA, for example—and a generous representation from the highest levels of business and finance. The truths of how our financial system has become so rickety, and so riddled with criminality, are quite simply staggering, even to one who has long been a critic of the system. It is a system on a drunken spree. But those who will have the hangover, the ordinary citizen and taxpayer, were never invited to the party. Unfortunately, it is but one aspect of the corruption—of both business and government—that spreads over our society like an oil spill.

vii.

The Return of the Robber Barons

In discussing "oligarchic democracy" in an earlier chapter, what could be seen as a puzzle was noted: the political institutions of the United States are among the most democratic in the world; yet the policies of its government—local, state, and federal—have consistently and increasingly been bent to the interests of the few. The earlier discussion was focused on matters dividing owners and the rest of us "on the supply side," in matters concerned largely with production. That continues, as the weakening of organized labor and resistance to environmental controls are accomplished through the political power of business interests. "Oligarchic democracy" has to do with the "natural" influence that highly unequal economic power has on the sources and uses of political power—an influence that comes from and shows itself not only in the relatively narrow confines of business activities and interests, but in the larger socialization process in which the media dwell. [22]

Given the structure of power, that which then most energizes the overt conflicts between business and other social interests is the most basic of all the concerns of those who own and control the society's capital: the distribution of income and wealth. And, since the substantial expansion of governmental fiscal activities during and after the 1930s, that concern has come increasingly to focus upon the composition of expenditures and, to the present point, who pays for them: taxation.

Given that the members of the House and Senate usually owe their elections and re-elections to a relatively small handful of rich and powerful supporters who never cease to seek a lowering of their own tax burdens, saying nothing of themselves—well, whaddya expect? Already by 1988 it was noted that:

> If Congress had done nothing since 1977 to alter the U.S. tax code, passed no new legislation at all, nine out of ten American families would be paying less. That is, a smaller share of their incomes would be devoted to federal taxes. Yet,

paradoxically, the government would be collecting more revenue each year—almost $70 billion more—if none of those tax bills had been enacted. [23]

And the net consequence in broader terms was a beauty, if you were a rich individual or corporation:

> From 1980 to 1988, revenue from the Social Security payroll tax increased by 23 percent as a portion of total federal revenue, while the personal income tax declined by 6 percent and the corporate income tax by 23 percent. [24]

Well, at least there was a nice symmetry: taxes 23 percent up for ordinary folks, taxes 23 percent down for the corporations and their owners. And if that's too abstract for you, try this: the personal tax exemption in 1948 was $600. In 1990 dollars, that would equal $7,781. In 1990 the personal exemption was in fact $2,050. Ho ! Ho ! Santa Reagan made almost all of those who voted for him lose $5,731 in deductions—among other things. [25]

viii.
Them that Has, Gits

The Sixties became a period of income improvement for the bottom 40 percent of the population, increasing their *share* of the income pie as real income grew at its highest rate; but their betterment ended with the Sixties, and it's been bad news since. The top 5 percent had to settle for being plain wealthy until the Great Barbecue that flamed up in the Eighties and has become a bonfire.

The generalizations to follow [26] point to growing inequality of incomes, the slow growth of incomes for the bottom four-fifths of the population—most especially for young families (twenty-four to thirty-four years old)—and the good income growth for those in the top fifth and the spectacular, even obscene rate of increase of those in the top 5 and 1 percent:

- The economic recovery of the 1980s was unusual in that the vast majority of Americans were, in many ways, worse off at the end of the recovery in 1989 than they were at the end of the 1970s.

- Despite growth in both gross domestic product and employment between 1989 and 1994, median family income in 1994 was still $2,168 lower than it was in 1989, suggesting that overall growth does not, under current economic circumstances, lead to improved economic well-being for typical families. The 1980s' trends toward greater income inequality and a tighter squeeze on the middle class show clear signs of continuing in the 1990s.

- The slow or negative rate of income growth after 1979 did not affect all families equally. The incomes of the top 5 percent rose 45.3 percent 1979-89 and another 4.9 percent 1989-94; the incomes of families in the bottom *95 percent* fell 1989-94, those in the bottom 80 percent between 5.7 and 9.1 percent; the incomes of the top 1 percent rose a stunning 87.5 percent 1979-89.

- The income share of the top 5 percent in 1994 (20.1 percent) is more than a third greater than that of the bottom 40 percent (10.2 percent).

- The income of the typical American family grew slowly or declined after 1979, despite the fact that the number of families with multiple jobs rose in those same years to almost half, compared to less than a third in 1967.

- A major reason for the growth of those family incomes that have risen is that a greater share of our national income has been in the form of capital incomes . . . whose fast growth is primarily due to strong growth in interest payments . . . caused by high real interest rates. . . . (M/F, 29, 31) Two-thirds of the value of all stock—which has risen at record-breaking rates over the past decade—is owned by the wealthiest 10 percent; the capital incomes of the top 1 percent doubled, 1979-89. (M/B/S 5, 10) Such figures make it easier to understand the great pressure for the abolition of (the already much-lowered) capital gains tax.

- Unsurprisingly, then, inequality in 1989 was greater than in 1947; by 1989-94, it worsened further.

- Those already rich in 1977—with average incomes of $231,383—almost doubled their incomes between then and 1990, while the incomes of the bottom 50 million people fell by almost 10 percent, with terrible increases in poverty and homelessness; this is one of the more dramatic meanings of the policies carved out in the Reagan years.

If something other than unlimited greed and rapacity pushes the already very rich to become much richer, what would it be? Madness? [27]

And the dervish has yet to stop his whirling. Plus you ain't seen nothin' yet, if Gingrich and, sadly, Clinton have their way.

This recent redistribution of income *upwards,* increasing already great inequality, was the inexorable outcome of the slowed economy of the 1970s, on the one hand, with the high military spending, corporate rampages, and Malthusian social policies of the 1980s.

An examination of income *growth,* as above, brings into focus a generalization relating changes in the *level* of the national income with changes in its *distribution.* When economic expansion causes the national income to rise, the biggest *absolute* gainers are naturally those with the highest shares: 10 percent of a bigger pie is of course larger than 1 percent of that same larger pie. In addition to that simple arithmetic of change, those at the top, with their ability to expand their incomes through their income-earning assets, have their fortunes—and incomes—enhanced even more through the economy's successes: on top of all else, the rich grow richer because they are in a strategic position to take advantage of the increased opportunities of expansion.

Wealth measures the sale value of possessions and property. Almost everyone owns something of value, but the society's income-producing assets, the most vital of which is corporate stock, is owned by a very small percentage of the population. Moreover, the considerably greater inequality of wealth than of income distribution is directly connected to political power. These connections mean that the wealthy are strategically positioned to neutralize the apparent distributive income and wealth effects of governmental income, estate, and inheritance taxes.

Given the subsequent changes in our political economy that have favored the wealthy and those in the financial sector, the inequalities for "net financial assets" have of course risen substantially. The Stanford economist Paul Krugman commented on the process in the fall of 1995 as follows:

> It's not just that the top 20 percent have gotten richer compared with the rest. The top 5 percent have gotten richer compared with the next 15 percent; the top 1 percent have gotten richer compared with the next 4 percent, and there is pretty good evidence that the top 0.25 percent had gotten richer compared with the next 0.75 percent. [28]

Patience, bottom 99.75 percent, it'll trickle down, as the elephant said when he danced among the chickens.

Lawrence Mishel and David Frankel add information emphasizing and articulating the upward wealth redistribution of the Eighties:

In the 1980s, the financial assets owned primarily by the wealthy grew considerably, while tangible assets, which are spread out more evenly, increased only slightly. This caused the distribution of wealth to become yet more unequal . . . [the] average net worth of the richest 0.5 percent of families rose 6.7 percent between 1979 and 1989, while the average net worth of families in the bottom 90 percent actually fell by 8.8 percent. This means that the gap in overall financial security between the rich, on the one hand, and the middle class and the poor, on the other, has widened even further. In addition, there has been a striking increase in the wealth gap between older and younger families. [29]

Kevin Phillips provides a look at the same development, but using somewhat different measures—"millionaires, decamillionaires, centimillionaires, and billionaires"—when he informs us a) that in 1981 there were 600,000 millionaires and twice that many in 1987; b) that in 1985 there were 38,855 decamillionaires and almost triple that in 1988; c) that of centimillionaires there were 400 in 1982 but 1,200 by 1988; and d) that billionaires had increased from thirteen in 1982 to fifty-one by the time Reagan bowed out of office, exhausted by his labors for the nation.[30] He had succeeded at the task he set for himself, which was to make the United States "a place in which you can get rich."

Meanwhile the official poverty rate in 1973 was 11.1 percent and in 1979 it was 11.7 percent; then 12.8 percent in 1989 and 14.5 percent in 1994—and rising.

Some of the details are worth singling out: [31]

- Not only are there more poor, they are poorer. The dollar gap between actual incomes and the poverty line per family member rose 8.9 percent between 1973-79 and another 11.9 percent between 1979-89; and the percentage of the poor who have incomes below half of the poverty line, 32.9 percent in 1979, had risen to 38 percent in 1989. (M/F 168-69) In 1994 it was 40.5 percent.

- Within each race/ethnic group, children (under eighteen) are the age group most likely to be poor: 54.3 percent of all black children and 41.3 percent of Hispanic children. Child poverty increased from 14.2 percent in 1973 to 16.2 percent in 1979 and then to 19.6 percent in 1988. (M/F 168-69) In 1994 the rate was 21.8 percent.

- Poverty among whites rose from 9 to 10 percent between 1979 and 1989, while falling slightly for blacks and Hispanics.

- Poverty rates for the elderly (over 65) dropped from 19.7 percent in 1967 to 12.0 percent in 1988, due to transfer payments. Without such transfers, the rate would have been 52.0 percent in 1988. Many of the elderly are now just above the poverty line and therefore vulnerable to cuts in benefits.

- The increase in poverty in the 1980s was due partly to declining governmental aid to the poor. For example, government taxes and benefits removed 39.7 percent of persons in female-headed families with children from poverty in 1979, but only 22.8 percent in 1988.

- In 1989, 22.4 percent of poor working adults worked full-time, year round, while 34.1 percent worked at least fifty weeks and remained poor.

- Whites have consistently made up the majority of poor female-headed families, and between 1979-89, 59.1 percent of the increase of poor female-headed families was for whites.

- There are more married-couple families in poverty than female-headed families, 40.2 percent as against 37.8 percent. Of those married-couple families 64.3 percent are poor because of low hourly earnings, because they were made up of full-time, full-year workers.

- And largely unknown or not understood by those whom it principally affects, unemployment compensation and social security benefits became taxable after 1979 and even more after 1984. Thus,

> the lower classes have not been able to hold their own in the private economy; even the large increases in government transfer payments did not prevent an erosion of their income shares. [32]

Not quite the information one gets from the White House, Congress, and the media—or, for that matter, in most econ classes.

ix.

Après Nous le Déluge

It is time to conclude this dour look at the economy of the Eighties by bringing the focus back briefly to the larger economy within which incomes were changing: at what was happening to jobs, and to our national and international finances.

In all those respects, be reminded that the economy was in deep and growing trouble before Reagan took office—and that his election was in part facilitated by the grievances associated with those troubles. First, jobs.

In one of several probing essays by Emma Rothschild, she discusses the rapid growth of jobs in the 1970s—the most rapid of any industrial country—while pointing out that

> The new American jobs were concentrated, however, in two sectors of the private economy—services and retail trade—and, at least in the early 1970s, in one public sector, state and local government.

That pleasant picture provides one more instance of why, standing alone, quantitative data can be misleading about social processes. In the private sector, more than 40 percent of the jobs created between 1973 and 1980 were in "eating and drinking places," "health services," and "business services."[34] And note:

> the *increase* in employment in eating and drinking places since 1973 is greater than total employment in the automobile and steel industries combined. Total employment in the three [service] industries is greater than total employment in an entire range of basic productive industries: construction, all machinery, all electric and electronic equipment, motor vehicles, aircraft, ship building, all chemicals and products, and all scientific and other instruments.

After further exploration and detailing of what occurred to the occupational structure in the 1970s, Rothschild concludes that

> the United States is moving toward a structure of employment ever more dominated by jobs that are badly paid, unchanging, and unproductive. . . . The employment expansion of the 1970s, of the Carter years, was bizarre. . . . There may be far worse to come.[33]

Indeed there was, as the occupational structure continued to veer away from well-paying and protected manufacturing (and other blue collar) jobs, and toward bottom level service work.

And continued to do so in important part because the U.S. economy became increasingly unable to meet—or in some cases even to try to meet—the competition from abroad except by transporting our productive capital abroad, leaving downsized or empty factories at home.

As U.S. capital poured into Europe and cheap labor countries and our imports and borrowing rose, the United States accomplished a transformation in its balance payments from creditor to debtor which—either in its size or its rapidity—is unmatched in world history. In 1981, as Reagan entered the White House, the United States was owed $141 billion by the rest of the world, and as such we were the world's largest creditor; by 1988—hold on to your hats—the United States owed the rest of the world $525.5 billion, and had become history's largest debtor.[35]

The public debt went through a similar dramatic transformation. The figures for the accumulation of deficits in Carter's years compared with those of Reagan are, to say the least, astounding—the more so when one remembers that Reagan *always* ran for office promising to balance the budget. The last three years for which Carter was responsible were 1979-1981, and the deficits were $40, $74, and $79 billion, respectively. Reagan's lowest year on the other hand was 1982, his first: $128 billion. His highest was 1986: $221 billion. He ran up the national debt from $1 trillion to $3 trillion.[36]

But the official story isn't the whole story. The S&L ripoff was given its main push under Reagan, beginning in 1981 (with the Garn-St. Germain bill), and it was the cooperation of his administration with (both houses and parties of) Congress and the incoming Bush administration that created the successful muffling of a fiscal horror: something in the nature of an ongoing—perhaps endless—$50 billion annual cost of the bailout and associated costs.

That rather large amount is catalogued as "off budget," and is thus not counted as part of the annual deficit—although you and I pay interest on it and unless you and I pay it off some time we'll carry it for all time. And the same kind of machinations (as noted earlier) are accomplished with the annual borrowing from the Social Security Trust Fund. The estimates are that the amount—also "off budget" (wouldn't it be loverly to be able to count your rent and groceries as off budget?)—began with about $40 billion in 1986 and is at least twice that now and expected to rise to $200 billion in the next decade or so.

So, putting all that together—and rubber gloves are advised for the process—it is an understatement to say that the official budget deficits since the late Eighties need an additional $100 billion to make them less crooked. That means that Reagan's last fiscal year of accountability (1989) with its official $154 billion deficit in reality came closer to $250 billion (or as much as $350 billion, probably, but who cares, by now?), and that Bush's first year had a deficit between $450 billion and the moon.

Does it make a difference, after all? Like so much else in economic affairs, in life itself for that matter, what difference it makes depends upon how the origins, the nature, the analysis, and the possible ways of dealing with such a condition indicate that a given problem is intractable, difficult, or—believe it or not—as much a set of opportunities as threats. Rothschild notes:

> There is no reason at all that the deficit should not fall, while the level of government spending increases: this is what should happen, in fact, if what needs to be done in the U.S. should best be done by government.

You'd never know it from what has occurred since the Clinton administration took hold: it has seen the debt as something between intractable and super-difficult, and has let itself be stymied, not least because most of Clinton's economic advisors are from the middle to the right of the analytical road. Of which, more in the next chapter.

Meanwhile, a return to the realities bequeathed us by the Reaganites. In the summer of 1988, Rothschild summed up an important part of those realities:

> The Reagan administration has increased government spending, increased transfer payments, increased the Federal debt, and invented unprecedented disincentives to private saving; it has also presided over the most sustained fall in profits since the 1930s. [37]

When I was a schoolboy, we read about the ("Punic") wars of Rome against Carthage, the third and last of which (149-146 B.C.) ended when the Romans razed Carthage to the ground. Carthage, it is believed, was a beautiful construct; and though the general who destroyed it is not much remembered, the remark by Agricola about that triumph has lasted: "They make a desolation, which they call peace." The Reagan gang made a desolation of our economy, and Reagan called it "hitting the jackpot."

But that isn't all he and his colleagues did: there was foreign policy—including the bombing of Libya,[38] the invasion of Grenada, and, among other matters and worst of all, what was done in El Salvador and Nicaragua in our name, which was central in the Iran-Contra crimes, and where many died and at least two societies were ruined,[39] for what could be seen as whimsical purposes. Except there was nothing funny about any of it.

x.

Glory Be

Reagan entered the White House at a moment of great triumph in the foreign arena: the freeing of the hostages by Iran. His normal bellicosity had been helped along by the renewal of tough words and deeds in Carter's last year: expanding military expenditures, pulling the United States out of the Moscow Olympic Games because of the USSR's invasion of Afghanistan in December 1979, and after some see-sawing about both Nicaragua and El Salvador, a perhaps reluctant, but in any case strong support of the effectively fascist government of El Salvador, along with strong rhetorical justification.[40]

Other than continuing and extending Carter's policies in all the foregoing respects, Reagan left global conflicts to themselves, and concentrated on destroying the economy. Perhaps bored with playing that dismal game for a couple of years, and stimulated by additional tumult in the Middle East—notably, Lebanon—in late 1982 Reagan jumped into the bloody waters with both feet—much encouraged by his hawkish Secretary of State, George Schultz.

The new troubles in Lebanon were not initiated by the United States but by Israel when, in its ongoing conflict with Syria and the Palestinian Liberation Organization (PLO), it invaded Lebanon (1982) to destroy Syrian missiles and PLO positions. In the same process, Israeli forces (in tandem with Lebanese Christians) massacred many hundreds of Palestinians living in Israeli-controlled concentration camps.

Since World War II the United States had done much to establish its hegemony over the Middle East—for its oil and its strategic location. But as so often happens, the means used to achieve particular ends often created other problems. That has been the case with U.S. assistance in the creation and support of the State of Israel, as the linchpin of U.S. aims in the Middle East. A linchpin it has been, but its creation and its existence proved to be a force for great instability, regarding both oil and strategic matters.

In 1982 the situation in the area was threatening—once more—to get out of hand; and the Reagan administration intervened to keep the growing violence within bounds. When we moved in fewer than 2,000 troops, their meaning was almost entirely symbolic:

to try to protect Palestinians, encourage Israeli withdrawal, and keep peace between Christian and Moslem factions inside Lebanon. In April, 1983, [some] lives were lost when the U.S. Embassy in Beirut was bombed. Meanwhile, U.S. troops, hunkered down near the Beirut airport, were not only open to sniper fire but were never clear about their mission. On October 23, 1983, a terrorist bomb killed 239 U.S. soldiers in their barracks . . . [and] Reagan declared that keeping troops in Lebanon was now "central to our credibility on a global scale."[41]

And two days after all those marines were killed in Lebanon, the United States mounted an invasion of Grenada, its most heroic military assault ever, in order to preserve not just our credibility but our very survival.

Announcement

I have been appointed as Judge in the First Grenada Competition, the winner of which will receive a copy of Ronald Reagan's *An American Life.* Now—taking the form of multiple-choice, to insure against unfair interpretation on the Judge's part—the questions (to which more than one answer may be correct):

1. Grenada is in the a) northern, b) southern, c) western, d) eastern hemisphere.

2. The population of Grenada is (or was, before the war) a) 800,000, b) 14 million, c) 94,500, d) angry.

3. The U.S. invasion of Grenada was necessary in order a) to pre-empt an expected invasion of the United States by Grenada on the coast nearest the two hemispheres (N, S, E, and/or W) in which Grenada sits, b) to gain additional *lebensraum* for our burgeoning population, c) to assure our continuing access to Grenada's vast mineral resources, d) for reasons to be announced at a time to be announced.

4. When Reagan described the consequences of the Battle for Grenada in his subsequent State of the Union Address as follows (no kidding): "Our days of weakness are over. Our military forces are back on their feet and standing tall," a) he was sober, b) he was drunk, c) Ollie was pointing his gun at him, d) he was running for re-election.[42]

One shouldn't joke about such things, of course. In fact, eighteen U.S. soldiers were killed, as well as 45 Grenadans and 24 Cubans. The Cubans were not soldiers but construction workers enlarging an airstrip, presumably to enhance tourism's possibilities for that tiny and poor island. The State Department and Pentagon told us the airstrip was not for tourism, but for military purposes, neglecting to tell us whom and how the Grenadans were going to attack; or, if the Cubans were going to attack us (presumably) from there, why they couldn't attack from their own stinkin' airstrips, much closer to our shores. But we have all learned by now that these are questions only trained military experts can answer.

Or, how about Michael Deaver—Reagan's closest and most trusted advisor, from an interview with Mark Hertsgaard:

> Deaver himself denied having engineered the invasion of Grenada, but volunteered that he had wholeheartedly supported it, partly because, in his words, "it was obvious to me that it had a very good chance of being successful and would be a good story." Asked whether he did not fear that attacking such a weak and tiny country would in fact expose the President to ridicule, Deaver replied, "No, because I think this country was so hungry for a victory, I don't care what the size of it was, we were going to beat the shit out of it. You know"—he chuckled—"two little natives someplace, if we'd staked the American flag down and said, 'It's ours, by God,' it would have been a success." [43]

Pretty cynical stuff for the chief advisor to the President to be saying, you might like to think. The larger problem, however, is that Deaver knew what he was talking about: "Reagan's overall popularity rating jumped sharply after the invasion, [as did] public sentiment on his handling of foreign policy. . . ." (ibid.) And, given the way the media was kept from the story, and then cooperated in obscuring the origins, nature, and double-dealing connected with it, you'll not find more than a handful who have even heard of what now follows:

> Almost everything went wrong, in the invasion of Grenada, that could have. The war was won because it could not be lost—the American invaders had a ten-to-one superiority over the defenders, and *all* of the air and artillery weapons used in the "war." Two thirds of American casualties were inflicted by other Americans or by accident. The exclusion of reporters from the scene helped suppress knowledge of these facts, as has classification of some information to this day and the suppression of several court martial complaints. [44]

The Grenada invasion was a large matter for the people hurt or benefitted by it, but can't compare with the damage done (and still being done) in Central America, where the United States has occupied itself greatly throughout this century, of course—taking territory to build canals (whether in Panama or Nicaragua, built or not), to make money out of bananas and coffee, other investments or, more recently, to pursue some or all of that in conjunction with presumably strategic objectives. In the process we have corrupted almost all of the governments in all of Latin America, but especially the smallest among them: such as El Salvador and Nicaragua.

The important and appalling history of our involvement is not difficult to find. Before and since fascism entered the world scene, the United States was creating and/or supporting fascist-type governments in all of Central America (Costa Rica the sole exception) and those parts of the Caribbean—notably Cuba—within our reach.

Now that "the Cold War is over," it has become easier to see how, for about fifty years after World War II, the Soviet Union could not realistically be viewed as the kind of threat it was taken to be—whether by the CIA, the military, politicians at all levels or, in large numbers, academics. But the key word there is "realistically." And so must it be when we view the rationales given for heavy U.S. intervention in El Salvador and Nicaragua during the Reagan years.

Both were in our "backyard," putatively oozing with dangerous intent—although taken together they didn't have a third of the population of California or the economic or military resources of San Jose. What got those two—and Cuba, and Guatemala, and others—in trouble was that either for the first or an additional time, they were trying to break free from the de facto colonial rule of the United States. In doing so, they were not only violating a code sanctified by usage, but setting a terrible example for other societies with equally sufficient reason: dominoes, dominoes, dominoes.

Now a closer look at the intertwined tragedies of El Salvador and Nicaragua, and then, holding the nose, at the violations of the Constitution and the laws of the United States by "the amiable dunce" and his cohorts that came to be called Iran-Contra.

xi.

Danger: Brutes at Work

Once more, as another sordid story is told, a reminder that the kinds of criminality, duplicity, and rhetoric that the Reagan gang was guilty of in Central America began neither there nor then: it began with the Spanish "discovery of America" and was spread by the United States over the entire continent and thence to the Caribbean and the Philippines, getting the twentieth century off to a running start. By the time Reagan had mounted his portrait of Calvin Coolidge on the wall of the Oval Room it had become an ingrained habit for Presidents.[45] That's no excuse for what he and his cronies did, merely a way of saying neither should it have been a surprise.

In 1980, Walter LaFeber says, "with one of the most inequitable societies and brutal militaries in the hemisphere,"—in a hemisphere famous for such governments—"El Salvador was ripe for revolution."[45a] The group that came into existence to achieve that desirable end was the Farabundo Martí National Liberation Front (FMLN). The FMLN spoke very much to the needs and desires of the largely peasant, terribly oppressed and exploited population of their country. The group was also quite capable of moving toward the overthrow of the unpopular Salvadoran government without help from any foreign source, had the government not gotten considerable help from its foreign source: the United States.

Just as in Vietnam, these similarities: a) the (literally) overwhelming sources of information for the people of the United States were the media, which in turn (except for a few at risk investigative reporters), got their ongoing information from the U.S. and Salvadoran governments; b) the inevitable violence accompanying a revolutionary process was treated with the usual double standard (also in Nicaragua), so that civilian deaths done by "our side" were either denied or given facile justification and civilian deaths caused by the FMLN were treated as terrorism;[46] c) when the rebel forces in El Salvador got arms with the help of Nicaragua (perhaps from Cuba), that constituted "foreign intervention"—do I have to go on with the next clause?—but when the armed forces and arms of the government were trained and supplied by the United States that could be seen as divine intervention. To which must be added that the arms with which the FMLN fought in El Salvador and the Sandinistas had in Nicaragua were at the simplest level (rifles, machine guns, mortars), whereas the U.S.-supported Salvadoran government and Nicaraguan "contras" were getting the best of all that—plus air support craft, artillery, etc.

But quite apart from and in addition to the fulsome acceptance of such double standards by the media and the country and, of course, by those propagating them, there was in Central America as elsewhere this much larger problem to be dealt with by the people of the United States: what kind of crooks' game are We the People playing with ourselves, or letting be played upon us, when we consistently take the wrong side in struggles in the imperialized world (or for that matter, at home)? And what might be meant by the right side? For people whose country has the longest-standing set of democratic political institutions in the world, since when has democracy supposed to have meant rule by the few, rule by foreigners, rule by force and violence and terror? That is what rule has been in virtually every nation we have supported in the struggles circling the globe in (at least) the past half century: in Asia, Latin America, and Africa; in Indochina, in Central America, in South Africa, and in key areas of the Middle East.

And when even the forces normally associated with conservatism such as the Catholic Church are gunned down, as in El Salvador, how do we find the ability to twist or close our minds? Only the best publicized cases in El Salvador—the rape and murder of four U.S. Catholic nuns and the young American college student with them, the gunning down in his church of the Archbishop Romero, the murder of six Jesuits, the murder of the head of the Salvadoran land-reform agency and his two U.S. aides in downtown San Salvador—all the work of Salvadoran death squads—got even a moment's attention; and, in the worst case of all—El Mozote—every effort was made to forestall even that attention. So we'll give it a long moment.

In the Name of Freedom

In 1981, in the tiny village of El Mozote, El Salvador, over 900 civilians—men and women, babies and old people, a whole village, plus others dragged in from surrounding Morazan province—were slaughtered in My Lai fashion: lined up, machine-gunned down. And worse. News of it trickled out, and two U.S. reporters and a photographer sought to pursue and uncover the story. They got enough to cause trouble up to today, but faced finally effective obstacles at the time from both the U.S. embassy in El Salvador and from their employers. Raymond Bonner, the *Times* reporter, was quickly removed from the story by the then Managing Editor of the *Times,* and Alma Guillermoprieto and her photographer Susan Meiseles, suspect as "non-Americans"—non-*North* Americans—were dismissed as unreliable, while the U.S. and Salvadoran governments cooperated in suppressing the story; at the same time, in the common dodge, they argued that all "rumors" concerning El Mozote, to the degree that the carnage pointed to had happened at all, was the work of the rebels.

Three years later, Bonner had a book on the matter: *Weakness and Deceit: U.S. Policy and El Salvador* (New York: New York Times Books, 1984). Useful though the book was in bringing attention back to the massacre, the Cold War was still raging, Bonner had been prevented from following the trail of facts adequately, and it all quieted down again. Until a persistent young man, Mark Danner, aided by the release of documents and the lessened pressures of post-Cold War, prodded and pushed and was able to get what is as much of the whole story as now seems possible. He published it first as an eighty-three-page essay in *The New Yorker* (December 6, 1993), and later as a book. [47]

It is a story of which all of us should be as much ashamed and angry as horrified. Bonner, prevented from seeing the evidence fully, had thought several hundred were murdered; Danner proves it was over 900—at least. Bonner could not pin down who did what and why; Danner proves that the action was devised and led by Lt. Colonel Domingo Monterrosa, commander of the elite Atlacatl Battalion—U.S.-trained, equipped, and admired: as one embassy person put it, "that rare thing; a pure, one-hundred percent soldier, a natural leader, a born military man." Indeed: the facts are that he was utterly involved, determined, and ruthless in the massacre of the inhabitants of the area, even though they were demonstrably *not* supporters of the rebel cause—not that anything could have justified such a slaughter. And, among other important matters, Danner traces out the years' long and complicated coverup by, especially, our government.

And one wonders once more about how many hundreds, thousands of other bloody lies our government has fed us over the years, about so many other disgraceful and dangerous actions; and what it has done to us that may never be undone.

Had all the foregoing (and innumerable other) atrocities been done by the FMLN, then our President, the State Department, and the media would have given it Super Bowl attention—and the U.S. public would have risen up in horror.

As for Nicaragua. A minuscule percentage of our people have but a foggy (if any) notion of that tiny country's history, know even less about how the United States dominated and distorted Nicaraguan development throughout the entire century, have no idea at all as to the whys and wherefores of our role there, and zero knowledge that we occupied it from 1911 to 1933 and then placed and kept in power (until 1979) the Somoza family and its National Guard, the most brutal of thugs—and who became the hard core of the "contras" (contrarevolucionarios)—the rebel forces trained and supplied and controlled by the CIA to overthrow the Sandinista government: called "freedom fighters" by our not very amiable dunce of a President.

After taking power in 1979, the Sandinistas, led by Daniel Ortega, found themselves attacked on all fronts. The following long quote from LaFeber tells the story as briefly as possible:

In 1981 [Reagan] signed the secret National Security Decision Directive 17, which authorized the CIA to spend millions to train and to equip Nicaraguan exiles, or "contras," who would fight the Sandinistas. In clear violation of U.S. neutrality laws, the CIA trained contras in the southern United States, then shipped them through Honduras to fight in Nicaragua. The Sandinistas, however, responded by building a force of 65,000 troops, strengthening their political hold on the country, and obtaining help from Western Europeans as well as the Soviet bloc. By late 1983, the contras' failures led the CIA to take over operations that destroyed oil refineries, mined Nicaraguan harbors, and aimed at assassinating Sandinista officials. A stunned U.S. Congress discovered these secret CIA missions, cut off military aid to the contras, and—as public opinion polls indicated—received support from a large majority of Americans. U.S. military leaders again wanted no policy that might force them to fight an unpopular war in Nicaragua. Reagan's economic sanctions proved more effective. They helped make Nicaragua an economic basket case that lacked many necessities and, by 1989, suffered an unbelievable 33,000 percent inflation rate. The Sandinistas nevertheless held to power, despite the 40,000 killed by the contra war, until 1990 when peaceful elections voted them out of office.[48]

The congressional cutoff of contra financing (through the "Boland Amendment")[49] did not of course daunt the Reagan gang; quite the contrary, it led them to find other ways to break the laws and flaunt the Constitution. The energetic cheerleader and de facto dynamo of the operation—become so by his total lack of scruples—was the "Chief Action Officer" of the NSC, Lt. Col. Oliver North. As so often happens, one crime led to another: and thus was Iran-Contra born.[50]

xii.

Iran-Contra: Foul Means for Filthy Ends

The substantial attention paid to violations of the Constitution and associated law-breaking in Iran-Contra has certainly been warranted; equally warranted would have been considerably more attention to why it was all done—why so many laws had to be broken. The answer is not entirely negative. Our political system had not deteriorated so fully by 1981 that its safe-guarding separation of powers had been completely replaced by an imperial presidency. Congress, or at least a majority of it, had not yet forgotten how easily a president can and will twist the truth when his intent is to pursue military ways and means that would otherwise be frustrated: the Vietnam Syndrome (at least in the early 1980s) still functioned.

But the rest of the answer to that "why" is largely ominous. After all, with whatever effort and ingenuity at least some members of the Congress might exert, arms were traded for hostages, profits were made from the sale of the arms, the gains were diverted for the secret purchase and delivery of arms to the contras—despite a law passed specifically to prevent that. And, to top it all off, it became—or was made—virtually impossible for a real trial of all the criminals and crimes involved. And one of the criminals, North, came too close to becoming a Senator from Virginia and, with just a little help from the social process over the next few years, could become the President of the United States.[51] That's going scot-free in the grand style.

In his *A Very Thin Line*, Theodore Draper rightly finds the enabling possibilities of Iran-Contra in the creation in 1947 of the CIA, the Department of Defense, and the NSC—all, properly or not, viewed or used as an exfoliation of presidential powers. It might be said that the imperial presidency began when Thomas Jefferson—of all people!—presided over the Louisiana Purchase (1803), even though it was "boughten land" (by one thief from another, so far as the Cherokee and others were concerned). But its contemporary roots were much deepened as our empire stretched overseas at the turn of the century; and the presidential tree that now is so strong became that way as U.S. hegemony took hold after World War II—Vietnam its most clamorous manifestation.

A major problem facing the United States now and for the future is whether or not there are ways to bring that imperial presidency to heel, to reverse the processes of its cancerous growth and in doing so to regain the possibilities of being a decent nation both abroad and at home.

What was wrong about Iran-Contra was not so much that arms were sold to Iran (violating a law), that they were traded for hostages (violating a promise), that the gains from the sales were used to finance the contras' efforts to overthrow the government of Nicaragua (violating our own and international laws), or that private funds were raised from various potentates (of Brunei, of Saudi Arabia) for the same purpose (and violating some of the same laws). All that is terrible, and the President and his associates who were responsible should have been impeached, jailed, or whatever punishment fit their crimes. But there were two considerably larger problems.

The first of these was the deliberate, conscious, systematic, and enduring (years-long) misuse of the powers of the Presidency. Draper aptly
quotes Justice Louis D. Brandeis on this matter:

> The doctrine of the separation of powers was adopted by the Constitution of
> 1787, not to promote efficiency but to preclude the exercise of arbitrary power.
> The purpose was, not to avoid friction, but, by means of the inevitable friction
> incident to the distribution of the governmental powers among three depart-
> ments, to save the people from autocracy. [52]

The second major problem whose existence predated but whose dangers and visibility were much increased by Iran-Contra takes us to the
nature of our society and its people. In mid-January of 1994, Lawrence
Walsh issued his final report, after seven years of, finally, futile investigation. His conclusions were anything but insubstantial; indeed they were
damning: [53]

> U.S. policy in Iran and Nicaragua was all but turned over to and carried out by
> a secret band of international arms dealers and private operatives.
> The small number of people in the government who knew about these policies
> misled Congress and lied to other top officials and even to each other so that
> no one knew all the facts.
> The president, Ronald Reagan, who maintains that he paid little attention to
> these offenses at the time, neglected his constitutional duty to ensure that the
> laws are faithfully executed.

The *Times* story goes on to point out that:

> Presented so starkly, these matters may seem grave enough to bring down a
> government, but they were basically lost on the American public . . . ; and two
> primary offenders, Oliver L. North and John M. Poindexter, were seen as
> patriots.

Where does that leave us as a nation, for the next time around? Or are there
those who think there will never be a next time around? It is not easy to forget
the results of a poll taken in the mid-1950s (I cannot provide documentation,
but it happened and was widely-publicized): when those polled were shown
a simple copy of the first ten amendments to the Constitution (without being
identified as such)—the Bill of Rights—and asked whether they would
approve or disapprove of such principles, more than half disapproved.
Doubtless some members of the Congress at the time—Joe McCarthy only
one of them—would also have found themselves in the latter camp; and to
repeat, because it is so important, what has been said earlier: the Congress
and the Judiciary are the other two powers, and their efforts to halt and reverse

the tides of the imperial presidency in its growing strength have been either too weak—obviously—or non-existent.

And of course "the next time around" has already come and gone—in the Bush years, in Panama and the Gulf—and, with a somewhat different spin, is coming around again in the Clinton years. Like the recession that we may or may not genuinely (in terms of good jobs and stability) recover from, our recent splendid little wars marked the opening of the 1990s: to be looked into in the next chapter.

It was by no means inevitable that either of Bush's two wars would take place; but the recession should have come as no surprise when it became obvious in the second half of 1990; it had been sitting under the table and making warning noises in 1989.

7 THE LONG MORNING AFTER: SINCE REAGAN

BUSH/QUAYLE

We are the hollow men
We are the stuffed men
Leaning together
Headpiece filled with straw. Alas!
Our dried voices, when
we whisper together
Are quiet and meaningless
As wind in dry grass
Or rats' feet over broken glass
In our dry cellar
Shape without form, shade without colour,
Paralyzed force, gesture without motion. . . .

—T. S. Eliot, "The Hollow Men"

Remembering back to the 1980s, when it often seemed that Reagan and we might all go out together with a bang, perhaps we must give thanks that instead we descended into the whimpering farce that was Bush's New World Order.

The elements of the New World Order were put in place with two cheap wars, the invasion of Panama, and the clash with Iraq—the latest species of the genus "splendid little war" whose U.S. birth in 1898 was in the Caribbean. The immediate predecessors of Bush's Two were Lady Thatcher's war to keep the Falklands and Reagan's "rescue" (that's what he called it) of Grenada.

What does it mean, "cheap war"? One that could be quick, *couldn't* be lost, would mean very few (U.S.) casualties and, putting all that together, could be over and done with so swiftly the press could be kept at bay and nobody would ever know—until much later when it wouldn't matter— what had happened.

i.

Where There's a Will, There's a Way

First, a quick summary of the facts presented to the U.S. public that came to constitute the substance of the rationale for the invasion of Panama on December 20, 1989, as reported by Bob Woodward in his book *The Commanders*: [1]

- In 1988, the U.S. Justice Department under Reagan indicted the "strong-man" of Panama, Manual Noriega, as a drug trafficker, to no avail. (In 1980, the Carter Administration had ruled that U.S. agencies could not enforce U.S. laws abroad.

- In April of 1989, "a CIA operative named Kurt Muse had been arrested by the PDF [Panama Defense Forces, controlled by Noriega] for running a clandestine radio network which was part of the agency's covert operation to unseat Noriega."

- On May 7, 1989, Noriega's candidates were defeated in an election, which Noriega—head of the National Guard (which in Panama then meant virtually all else)—nullified. On May 10, the winning candidates (Guillermo Endara [later President] and Guillermo Ford) led a protest march in which they were physically beaten by Noriega's forces, and Ford's bodyguard was killed.

- On December 16, 1989, an off-duty U.S. Marine Lieutenant, out for the evening in civilian clothes with three others, was shot (and later died) after he and his companions, stopped by a Panama Defense Corps (the military force of Panama) roadblock after having made a wrong turn, sped away when they became fearful of the PDF personnel. Some thirty minutes earlier, a U.S. Navy Lieutenant and his wife had been stopped, searched, and detained, and both were "verbally and physically abused."

Those were the principal activities of Noriega and his forces that provided what was seen as abundant justification for what became the largest military operation of the United States since Vietnam: "a total of 24,000 U.S. troops against the 16,000 member PDF, only 3,500 of whom were combat-capable; superior equipment, night capability, surprise, superior soldiers." And (or but), like most everything in politics and business and war these days, it had to be sold—before, during, and for a little while, after.

At first, the Panama invasion did not prove easy to sell; in part because of the general ignorance and lack of concern with distant places that is so common among us. And it was important all along the way for the Administration to distinguish between why it *wanted* to invade and to create—if possible—legal reasons for doing so. [2]

Given that Noriega had become a pain in the neck for the United States, probably the very largest reason for invading Panama was that it was so very small—compared with *any* country, let alone the Colossus of the North. Also, U.S. troops had been there for almost a century and knew their way around, and Noriega, who ruled over Panama, was easy to make look bad and impossible to make look good. Given that Bush was bent on doing something impressive about the drug trade, it didn't hurt that Noriega's large part in it by 1989 was known to all—among whom were those in the CIA and the NSC of the U.S. government who had strewn roses on his path to that position.

Indeed, Noriega was very much *our* man in Panama; bought and paid for. He was lifted to power after its most popular and powerful president— Omar Torrijos, with whom Carter had worked out the treaty providing that Panama might rule itself some day—died in circumstances not totally mysterious: Torrijos's brother claimed to know that the plane crash was arranged by the CIA. [3] (Is *he* still alive?)

Noriega had served as a conduit for U.S. weaponry going (illegally) to the contras in Nicaragua; one of his rewards for these services was the customary one (going back to the Korean and Indochinese wars, noted earlier) of giving him a slice of the drug trade, courtesy of the CIA.

Besides, Bush wanted to mount an invasion in order to *arrest* Noriega for being a drug trafficker, and then take him to the States to be tried. This despite the Justice Department ruling in Carter's years that the U.S. had no power to arrest foreigners in their own countries for violating U.S. laws.

But as administrations change, so do Justice Departments. As many will remember, one of the Bush administration's major domestic efforts was "the war on drugs." *His* Justice Department, on June 21, 1989, issued a twenty-nine-page legal opinion (cited by Woodward), stating:

> the President [has] legal authority to direct the FBI to abduct a fugitive residing in a foreign country for violations of U.S. law. This could be done even if the arrest was contrary to customary international law. . . .

The biggest drug lord of all was Pablo Escobar Gaviria, head of the Medellin drug cartel. (Killed, evidently by some of his own associates, in 1993.) Our people expected him to be in Panama in August of 1989, and Bush wished to have him arrested by the DEA backed up by a small military task force, in Panama. And Bush was going to be making a big speech on drugs, scheduled so as to follow that arrest.

It might have made a good movie, except that Escobar didn't show up, and Bush was left holding his big speech. On September 5, Woodward notes, Bush delivered his big speech on national television, in which—there being no Escobar to talk about—he held up to the camera a sealed plastic evidence bag full of crack and said:

> This is crack cocaine seized a few days ago by Drug Enforcment agents in a park just across the street from the White House. It could just as easily have been heroin or PCP. It's as innocent looking as candy, but it's turning our cities into battle zones, and it's murdering our children.

The Washington Post soon revealed that "the drug buy had been set up," by the Administration not to catch a criminal but as a good photo op for Bush's speech—the sort of thing some other President's Justice Department might have called entrapment, or that you and I might just call sleazy (or "bush"). However, Woodward points out:

> All the publicity on the drugs put the spotlight once again on Noriega, an unpleasant symbol of American impotence in the face of illegal narcotics.

And that had the effect of speeding up the long-brewing plans to invade Panama, capture Noriega, and install our own people there—as we had been doing in Central America for a century or so.

Between April and December 1989 the operational basis for the invasion of Panama was being laid, the number of U.S. troops in Panama was doubled, and there were maneuvers designed to unnerve Noriega; the latter led to the roadblock incident of December 16 which provided the operational justification for the war. [4]

In those same months, seventeen names for the "operation" were developed—ranging from "Maze" to "Blue Spoon" to "Nifty Package" to "Pole

Tax." Finally, Woodward quotes the general in command (James J. Lindsay) asking: "Do you want your grandchildren to say you were in BLUE SPOON?" so they searched until Admiral Lopez found the solution: JUST CAUSE. I would have called it JUST BECAUSE.

Thus: using the media suppressive techniques practiced in Grenada (used even more effectively in the Gulf War), we invaded and, after some time and damage and dealing, found and "arrested" Noriega, and carted him off to Florida. LaFeber sums up the victory neatly:

> Most important, the [Latin Americans] began to refuse to cooperate with U.S. anti-drug efforts. Through it all, Congress only stood by and failed to exercise its constitutional checks on the President . . . [or even to] hold hearings that would have created a record of the invasion. Bush's foreign policy powers consequently approached those of the 1960s "imperial presidency." [5]

And most important to Bush, the invasion of Panama made his popularity rise.

ii.

The Making of the Gulf War

The Gulf War was quite different in both its origins and its nature from the invasion of Panama. The Gulf, of course, is where all that oil sits. Between them, Iraq and Kuwait hold 20 percent of the world's oil reserves; Saudi Arabia holds another 20 percent. George Bush may be ignorant of many things and indifferent to many others, but oil is not on either of those lists.

Iraq had the fourth largest armed force in the world by 1990. That Reagan and Bush had helped it to become that way during the Eighties—secretly, of course, because laws had to be broken to do it and to keep it from Congress—was left undiscussed.[6] But Saddam invaded Kuwait, and could easily go on into Saudi Arabia. When in July Iraqi troops had begun to move toward Kuwait, and the political atmosphere was heated up by Iraqi charges, there was at first disbelief that there would in fact be an invasion.

The first position taken by Bush's inner circle was "to deter and defend"—to deter Saddam from invading Saudi Arabia and to aid in the latter's defense if it became necessary. That meant inducing the Saudis to allow

U.S. troops to be based on Saudi soil. For broader strategic reasons, the United States had for many years sought to gain a military presence there, and the Saudis had always refused. This time, the combined pressure of Saddam and the United States led them to acquiesce—with the understanding that a substantial number (100,000 at first, changed to 250,000 before long) would be necessary if the defense were to be accepted and effective.

It is important to note that General Powell and the Joint Chiefs were apprehensive of any military involvement in the Middle East unless it were clearly sufficient in numerical and qualitative terms to assure victory—with the added assurance of political support at home. No more Vietnams. In turn, it was Powell's judgment a) that it would be best *not* to get militarily involved because, given enough time, the sanctions would work, and b) if we were to develop a military presence that three to six months would be necessary to get the troops and matériel in place.

Bush in the meantime under the influence of National Security Advisor Scowcroft had become convinced not just that Saudi Arabia must be defended from possible attack, but that Iraq had to be pushed out of Kuwait and Saddam overthrown—the first publicly, of necessity, the second covertly—also of necessity, but of a different kind: it was illegal by *our* laws for that to be done.

By October the directions were becoming clear: the United States, having gained Saudi approval, would place 250,000 troops—infantry, artillery, tanks, and other ground forces, plus extraordinary air strength— on the ground in Saudi Arabia and Turkey, and combine all that with extensive naval air and bombardment forces. After much backing and filling among all parties concerned, the United States on January 5, 1991, delivered an ultimatum: either, by January 15, Iraq will have withdrawn its forces from Kuwait, or U.S. arms from the air, the sea, and on land would attack Iraq both in Kuwait and in Iraq. And in the early hours of January 16, a U.S. Hellfire missile struck and destroyed a defense radar position protecting Baghdad.

Before that date and throughout the forty-two days the war lasted, the problem had become how to sell the war. And afterwards there came to be another problem: very early on, Bush had come to characterize Saddam Hussein as Hitler reincarnate, while almost bashfully allowing us to see himself as Winston Churchill. But, as the months and now the years have gone on, Saddam has remained in power, oppressing his own people and continuing to murder the Kurds.

iii.

Operation BOOB TUBE

In the modern world the relationship between the powerful and the relatively powerless has never been one of honesty, and always less so in the United States in this century. That condition is the result in greatest part of the interaction of two quite diverse historical developments: democracy and communications technology.

The problems that might arise from democratic institutions were seen as this nation, the first modern political democracy, was born; and a solution was found in the separation of powers. That separation, referred to earlier (in the words of Supreme Court Justice Louis D. Brandeis) as a means "to preclude the exercise of arbitrary power," also served (as Madison approvingly noted in Federalist Paper #10) to preclude an easy or swift movement toward popular rule. The division of Congress into two bodies with different electoral bases and terms of service, the conserving powers of the judiciary, and the powers of the executive branch (including the veto) effectively replace the exciting possibilities of democracy with the more sedate probabilities of a republic.

Despite such provisions, the exercise of arbitrary power has not been fully precluded, as we have seen—nor, to come to the present point, has the threat of popular rule ever been permanently stifled. It must be dealt with on a continuing basis, and most critically when matters of life and death—like war—are involved. The most effective and acceptable way to do that in a political democracy is through persuasion.

Modern communications techniques—given the structures of economic, political, and social power—are not only the best but the most accessible means to that end, for those who preside over those structures. [7]

Although the term "propaganda" may be found too strong a term when used in connection with business and political public relations, it is difficult to withhold from using it if it is defined as those "communications" whose form and content are selected with the purpose of bringing the attitudes of an audience to harmony with those who sponsor the messages. (Education, in contrast, is—or should be—meant to strengthen independent thinking on the part of those receiving it.)

A major asset for a governmental apparatus that wishes to act in illegal and/or unjustifiable ways (militarily or otherwise) is a public whose concerns are more individual than social, and whose knowledge and understanding are dominated by some combination of misinformation, disinformation, and no information—most especially and scandalously true as regards foreign affairs. Thus we are a people easy to fool, or often so indifferent to social realities we can be ignored.

The responsibility for our having arrived at such a state may be located in the nature of our formal and informal schooling—the media, entertainment, our socialization process. Strong though those obstacles to understanding may be, however, it is also true that anyone who, despite all, seeks to gain factual information and at least some relevant analysis, can easily find ways to do so. Although most U.S. newspapers (by comparison with their French or Italian counterparts, for example) are sadly lacking in serious domestic information, and considerably worse as regards the rest of the world, there *are* newspapers (no more than half a dozen, to be sure) and other periodicals available on the newsstands (or at least in public libraries) for those who wish to know. The problem is that as a people we are always more effectively socialized *not* to have that "wish to know"—if anything, the opposite.

To the degree that the foregoing applies, some of the responsibility is taken from the shoulders of the politicians and the media, who are then just "selling" what the voters, readers—and advertisers—want and who, in any case, were reared in very much the same socialization process. Still, it is also true that many politicians and many journalists do know better but adapt or become silent at strategic moments (which often last a lifetime); and those who don't know better could—or should, if they were to deserve the respect that their occupations would like to enjoy.

Given all that, a basic "finding" of the White House (among others with power) that strengthens over time is that the media must be controlled. It has been taken for granted in the White House and in the Pentagon that the major—for some, the only—reason we lost in Vietnam was the behavior of the media.[8] That belief came to be translated into tight restrictions on media access in the Grenada and Panama wars, a policy honed to a fine art by the time of the Gulf War.

Hedrick Smith, who spent many years as foreign correspondent for the *New York Times* in Moscow, wrote in his preface to his book, *The Media and the Gulf War:*

> In the Persian Gulf War, hundreds of American reporters protested that they were being forced to work under similar or worse conditions than those my compatriots and I had known in Moscow. For one thing, the war reporters actually faced

censorship—that is, military officers reviewed, delayed, or edited their stories, changing words or simply holding up the dispatches until they were no longer timely and thus no longer worth printing. They posed more interference than my Kremlin gremlins. But more important was the basic parallel to Moscow: access was radically confined, gingerly rationed to a tiny fraction of the press corps. Freedom of movement, opportunities for independent conversation and reporting, for simply developing one's own view of reality were all severely restricted. Press movements were controlled; reporters and camera crews had to travel with official escorts or risk losing accreditation to the entire war zone or even being shot at by "friendly" fire. [The reporters'] main view of the conflict in Iraq—like the public's—consisted of the videotapes the Pentagon chose to release. [9]

The Pentagon of course chose to show only the successful gaming of its pilots; they did not show the 70 percent misses—or, more importantly, what the bombs and missiles hit when they missed their assigned targets in Baghdad.[10]

Nobody denied that there were also many tens of thousands of Iraqis dead. But who among us knows how many more were wounded, how many schools, hospitals, homes, and factories were destroyed, how much war-created illness raged in the aftermath? And who knows *why* there was such a war? That among the principal causes of all those troubles has been the centuries' long process of intervention by, most notably, the British, the French, and (most recently) ourselves to control and gain from the location and resources of the Middle East?

No surprise then, that after the Gulf War ended and Saddam stayed in power, few of us had the foggiest idea of what then transpired—although it was in human terms a variation on the horror of the war just ended. I refer in part to the continuation of authoritarian rule in Kuwait (as well as in Saudi Arabia and Iraq), and, more to the point, to the resumption and deepening of the deadly war against the Iraqi Kurds (and, by the Turks, against *their* Kurds). You could read about it, but it took an effort; and you, if not Bush, were more likely to be reading about undesirable developments at home.

iv.

"What's that Awful Smell?"

The recession had begun in June or July of 1990, just before Saddam started to roil the waters of the Gulf. Bush didn't cause the recession, of course; but as it unrolled and became obvious and painful to the people at large, Bush remained oblivious—had to be induced even to comment on it; and when he did, it was always awkward and lacked a sense of sincerity: "I really feel for you folks out there hurt by the recession." Thanks.[11]

As noted earlier, Bush's was the first presidency since the 1920s in which the federal government did not use fiscal policy (taxes and expenditures) to turn things around—indeed, due to the continuing federal cutbacks for social expenditures, and thus of federal grants-in-aid to states and localities, the net impact of the State was a *reduction* of expenditures "out there" in order to keep tax *increases* to the minimum: worse than nothing.

Bush's anti-recession policy, like its counterpart in the Twenties, was "laissez-faire": it's best to leave things alone (except, perhaps, for diddling the supply of money) and let the chips fall where they may—on those below, of course. That such would be Bush's way came as no surprise, and certainly not to me.

Story: Plumber

During the 1988 election campaign, I was asked to participate in a talk show on the PBS-TV station in Silicon Valley. It was to be a Stanford economist, Prof. T., and me, and we were to discuss the state of the economy. He is a monetarist, I am something else. My analytical position was (and is) that there were grave structural problems facing us, at home and abroad, and that they required an appropriate set of qualitative responses. Prof. T. was pleasant, relaxed, confident, and, it seemed to me, not so much opposed to my analysis as mystified by it: I was not "speaking economics" as he understood it. No matter what economic area or process we discussed, his solution was a) leave it alone, or b) increase—or decrease—the money supply. Tough job.

The next day, I met my graduate seminar in the history of economic theory. Many of the students, knowing in advance of the program, had watched it. Their unanimous reaction to Prof. T. was to ask "You mean that fool is an economics prof at Stanford?!" Shortly after the election, "that fool" was appointed to Bush's Council of Economic Advisors. And almost broke his pliers turning the money supply on and off. ("That fool" was also the chief economic advisor for the Dole presidential campaign.)

There have been times when it has been difficult to understand why one candidate won and the other lost a presidential election. Not in 1992. Bush seemed to have (and thought he had) everything going for him: he had made all the right moves with wars and mind management; the Soviet Union fell apart; his opponent was an inexperienced hick from the sticks who was being torpedoed by gossip and confusion. But that silver spoon of Bush's life, as they say in Texas, jes' plain must have wore out: not only did he get what came to be seen as a serious recession blindsiding him, but he and his chums were only gung-ho when it came to wars against the relatively weak, whether overseas or at home; from the Chief on down they were bored and cretinous about the economy.

After the lost election, and as proof positive that the silver spoon had turned to dross, the official data seemed to reveal that the recession had already begun to turn around while Bush was still in his campaign mode— just what he had insisted upon in October. But in one of those rare instances when justice visits the earth, nobody believed him, and B/Q got the heave-ho they so richly deserved.

v.

Up the Down Staircase

This is a good place to review some fairly reliable generalizations concerning the nature of past and present recessions. First, what we now call a "recession" used to be seen as the down part of "the business cycle." The theory concerning such processes developed in the nineteenth century, as its relevant developments were becoming a normal part of economic history—that is, of nineteenth century capitalist history. "Cycles," by definition self-reversing, were seen as having two "life spans"—"minor" (peak to peak or trough to trough from two to less than five years) and "major" cycles (roughly twice that duration). A downturn of the minor cycle before World War II was what we would call a recession today; a depression was part of a major cycle. The depression of the 1930s was so severe in every way that it ended the usage of that terminology—until recently.

Since World War II, every industrial capitalist society has practiced various forms of governmental intervention to prevent contractions from going too far down or lasting too long, and to stimulate economic growth while seeking to keep it from becoming harmfully inflationary. Whatever their varying degrees of success and/or failure, this has meant that the processes of expansion and contraction have been significantly altered— comparable (up to a point) with the consequences of using drugs to contain pain or anabolic steroids to enhance strength: the body treated in that fashion often suffers side-effects that change it unpredictably and undesirably, and sometimes seriously so.

Looking at the United States with the above generalizations in mind, herewith an overview of recent decades:

1) In the years since World War II there have been nine recessions (including that beginning in 1990);

2) In only one of those (1953-1954) was the official unemployment rate below 6 percent (5.8 percent); in the other eight recessions the unemployment rate has varied between 6.1 and 10.7 percent. The stated goal of the Employment Act of 1946 was to maintain full employment (defined then as unemployment of no more than 3 percent);

3) In all but the 1990s recession, the State has intervened significantly with specific anti-recession fiscal measures (in addition to ongoing massive expenditures).

4) One consequence of such intervention—and the general persuasion that the State would not *allow* a recession to become a depression—has been that the very nature of a recession (that is, of a "minor cycle") has been transformed from a process that earlier *was* self-reversing to one that *is* not, whose onset is delayed, whose depth and severity are lessened, and whose duration is uncertain and accompanied by some degree of inflation: the "stagflation" that is very much unique to the years after 1970, in its turn meaning,

5) That the State has become seriously handicapped in developing anti-recessionary remedies, because policies necessary to produce the desirable rate of expansion are also likely to produce an unacceptable rate of inflation.

That is the way things have been and remain, very much exacerbated by a preoccupation with annual deficits of $250 billion, give or take a small or large handful of billions. Such worries are justified—but *only* if one assumes that current structures (of production, consumption, investment, and trade on the one hand, and of income, wealth, and power on the other) are and should remain inviolate. If such structures are seen instead not only as changeable but also as a main source of present problems, new and more cheering possibilities come into view—assuming also a new politics to move such possibilities toward realization. Quite the opposite of which has been underway since the election of 1994, of course.

The recession that began in the summer of 1990 in the United States had shown its ugly head somewhat earlier in English-speaking "cousin" countries: Britain, Canada, Australia, Ireland, and New Zealand, with Britain, of course, dominating the other four—and Thatcherism dominating Britain. The past several decades have of course seen an always tighter intertwining of all those and other nations' economies with the world economy. Britain and Canada are among our most important "customers" (Canada our largest), and are two of the Group of Seven—which in turn produces two-thirds of global output.

It has been mentioned earlier that Thatcher set off the first stages of what has become a stampede back toward the political economy of the past by (among others) the Group of Seven: "privatization," deregulation, reduced expenditures on education and health and job training, and, among other changes meant to strengthen but which have instead weakened their economies, an obsession with inflation and a diminishing concern with stubbornly high unemployment.

Essentially, Thatcherism and Reaganomics meant that the political economy of the nation would be monetarist, plus using the State's always growing power—in itself a contradiction to traditional monetarist principles—to make the rich much richer through one free-swinging policy or another. Its bottom line for the average person in Britain, as also in the United States (if with somewhat different measures) is summarized neatly by the British economist Michael Stewart:

> Unemployment, the fundamental touchstone of a satisfactory economic policy from 1945 until the mid-1970s, averaged 9 percent between 1979 and 1992. On the old definition of unemployment, however, it would have averaged about 11 percent—compared with a figure of less than 2 percent between 1945 and 1970, and 4 percent in the 1970s . . . The economic waste of having more than a tenth of the labour force out of work is self-evident.[12]

Or should be.

But inflation, interest rates, and finance—as distinct from the production of goods and services—were the obsessive focus of policy in Britain in the Eighties as, with variations, became so in the three largest economies of the world economy: Germany, Japan, and the United States. The financial sector is where most or much of the money was being made in the Eighties; by the Nineties, that's where most problems getting attention were being found: enormous and always rising deficits and debts—private, public, consumer, business, local, national, and global; high real interest rates acting to obstruct what was in any case inadequate ability or incentive to buy consumer and capital goods and to finance social needs, and financial fragility everywhere.

Conventionally viewed it is not surprising that a downturn began in the U.S. in mid-1990; the more appropriate consideration would be why it had not taken place earlier, in the Eighties. The puzzle disappears when one remembers how "unconventional" the Eighties were: the years in which deficit spending broke all records.

There had *never* ever been such a spending spree of such quantitative dimensions or qualitative wastefulness. The analytical surprise is that there could *be* a recession—with the Gulf War going on, no less—with so many stimuli coming from the State. That nevertheless a recession there was is to be explained by the existence of a) widespread and long-persisting excess capacity (extending back into the Seventies), combined with b) the accumulating downward pressures on average purchasing power that had been worsening since the early 1970s: almost, but not quite, two sides of the same coin.

What has just been noted in (a) and (b) has been the origin of several sources of such downward pressure: an always more integrated global economy with always more worldwide excess capacity (a consequence of duplicative facilities *and* increasingly unequal distributions of income limiting purchasing power), leading to softer markets and the felt need of business to lower labor costs by "outsourcing and downsizing." This in turn meant the "hollowing out" of industrial production in the leading countries and a substantial and continuing alteration of the occupational structure away from skilled high-paying and secure jobs to relatively unskilled low-paying and insecure jobs (in *all* the major economies), thus exacerbating the already inadequate purchasing power. And, as noted in an earlier chapter, the declining reliance on production and the increasing emphasis on finance as a source of ready gains contributed to rising interest rates and to rising financial instability, everywhere.

In noting these elements making for a recession—no matter what the quantitative stimuli from the State, no matter what the endless negotiations on global trade and investment—the aim is once more to underscore *structural* rather than cyclical processes as the core problem. Doing so, in turn, implies seeking remedies that change structures rather than—or, more properly, in addition to—"simple" quantitative changes in the level of taxes and expenditures, plus international trade agreements.

When Clinton took office in 1993, one of his first acts was to propose a set of fiscal stimuli which, altogether modest though they were in dollars (about $30 billion) and programs, was not passed—defeated by a Congress whose basic conservatism and professed fears of mounting deficits mixed conveniently with its usual scrambling for political advantage.

Subsequently, what would become the true economic tone of the Clinton Administration came on loud and clear when the "deficit reduction package" sought to make its tortuous way through the congressional maze. In that package, Clinton revealed his own basic conservatism both in the economic policies he proposed and the bottomless well of compromise within which those already mild aims were allowed to drown, no matter what the accompanying uplift rhetoric—just as Reagan had revealed his true recklessness with his annual budgets, despite *his* rhetoric of taking care.

Be all that as it may. Clinton's budget passed, festooned with innumerable ribbons recording deals of all sorts—with we'll never know what promises of what and to whom, with what consequences to be paid for by us down the road a piece. But it passed and Wall Street liked it: interest rates headed down, stock prices headed up and, with or without substantial reason, business confidence began to rise—as did, with or without substantial reason, consumer confidence.

Thus, among other welcome changes as Clinton's first year ended, GDP was rising, unemployment had moved down closer to 6 than 7 percent, and auto and home sales—encouraged by lower interest rates and growing optimism—had begun to rise. A consensus began to spread that a genuine recovery was underway.

Recovery, yes; "genuine," perhaps; fraught with wobbles and worries, for sure; for how long, going where, who can tell? An examination of these whys and wherefores moves us away from the Bush/Quayle ooze into . . . what?

CLINTON/GORE

---

i.

Welcome Back to Mudville

Economists and meteorologists have rightly been the butt of innumerable jokes concerning their murky crystal balls. All predictions are tricky. Those concerning what lies ahead even for the next year are iffy enough; anything beyond that is an informed guess at best.

Still, it *is* close to analytical certainty that two interacting and volatile developments are now causally central for the economic and social well-being of each and every nation and their peoples: 1) quantitative and qualitative changes in the world economy, and 2) the closely-connected processes of technological change. Provisionally accepting the conventional view that the latter processes have in the past been largely positive in their effects, it must be said that recent and expected consequences fall increasingly on the negative side, increasing both joblessness and income inequalities—and therefore economic and social instability—over the globe.

We begin with the world economy, which has taken on critical importance in the functioning of every national economy. Any expectations about continuing recovery or looming recession must begin there; more now than ever, it is inescapably true that no one major economy can prosper for long unless the world economy is expanding.

Making the realization of that global expansion always more problematic, however, is a new and troublesome reality—the spectacular growth of transnational corporate giants, and their means and ends. Their very existence was a novelty when the 1960s began; by the 1990s they were already the dominant actors in national and world economies—whether at stage center or behind the scenes. After an examination of the current recession/recovery in "macroeconomic" terms, the analysis will move beyond that to see how the rapidly growing and already worrisome economic and political strengths of the transnationals complicate the expansion process and, as well, much else that is important.

The global recession that became apparent in 1990 was seen as ended in 1994, but in 1996 mutterings and whispers of slowdown once more filled the air: already in mid-1995, a piece in the *New York Times* (June 23, 1995) led off with the subheadline "Some Consumer Goods Makers Are Now Using the 'R' Word." As well they might, given the focus of another major article on the same day, next page: "Americans' Real Wages Fell 2.3% in 12-Month Period," which went on to note this as "the worst outcome in 8 years, worse yet if counting benefits."

And what about the U.S.'s major trading partners of the Seven? The answer here will be confined to a summary statement concerning each of them which, were it to be more detailed would, if anything, be gloomier.

Japan. In 1996, it had been in recession for almost five years, its average rate of growth over that period under 0.5 percent, its financial system in trauma, its unemployment rate continuing at its highest postwar level, both capital and housing investment falling, its government in what seems to be an interminable state of weakness and confusion.[13] As 1996 ended, a 40 percent fall of the yen in dollars terms was seen as good news for Japan's exporters; for the same reason, it was seen as bad news for U.S. exporters.

Germany. In the recent past its long-term 9 percent unemployment rate has risen to over 10 percent, its rate of GDP growth is stuck under 2 percent, its export markets weaken as strife between unions and companies continues, and both its internal and external political relationships become always more problematic.

France and Italy. Similar in more ways than one: unemployment rates of 12 percent or more, deficit and budget conditions provoking political crises that seem bound to deepen, given that their resolution depends upon draconian cuts in social benefits and greater unemployment—bringing back to life a strong but until recently a dormant labor movement.

Great Britain. The likely end of Tory rule is more than coincident with a political economy such as that just noted for France and Italy, along with a recession whose end is regularly predicted but yet to arrive—in what must be seen as a faltering world economy.

Canada. Our best trading partner, and vice versa; it, like ourselves, adversely affected by a NAFTA which, as predicted by those who resisted it, as noted by the *New York Times* (December 5, 1995), has sped up the loss of good jobs for both countries, while increasing jobs in Mexico—averaging $10 to $20 a *week*—which "kill us with work." Canada now struggles with the deficit/budget bugaboo besetting the other six of the Seven—and Spain, and Ireland, and Sweden, and Greece, and. . . .

Not much in the way of cheer from that bunch.

The world economy includes more than the G-7, of course: the countries to the east in Europe, the Middle and Far East (other than Japan), Africa, Latin America, and the economies of the Western Pacific—Australia and New Zealand, and the "Four Tigers" (Taiwan, South Korea, Singapore, and Hong Kong) and, more recently, China. All are in trouble, even the little Four (whose expansion slows) and big China (whose non-economic trouble is at least in part due to its repressive politics), which continue to expand.[14] Their expansion is dependent mostly upon exports to countries whose imports are more likely at best to stabilize (or fall) than to rise in the foreseeable future; and none of them nor all taken together can, by their imports, do much for the Group of Seven, let alone the world economy as a whole.

The United States. It is possible for a few of the largest economies (and most especially ours) to find ways to a solid and lasting recovery without the principal stimuli coming *initially* from an expanding world economy. But that clearly implies policies directed squarely at the national economy, and such policies must have at their center significant structural changes.[15]

The United States, better able than others to initiate such an expanding process, is at this time among the least inclined to do so. The Clinton Administration is instead training all its guns on opening up foreign markets to U.S. trade and investment, making us always more dependent upon the world economy while continuing the deterioration in the material lives of at least three-quarters of our own people, as though, like a Latin American economy, we were living under IMF austerity rules in order to be eligible for loans. Which, in a real sense, we are.

Neither the White House nor Congress, neither the federal nor state and local governments, show any signs of even beginning to *think* along lines that would—through structural changes at home—simultaneously meet deep domestic needs *and* contribute to a healthier world economy.

Explanations of the structural and institutional deterioration of the United States in recent years are placed on the shoulders of the $5+ trillion national debt and an always rising foreign debt (moving ever closer toward $1 trillion) with, thus, an associated need to reduce (or eliminate) deficits. Therefore, cut expenditures at home and increase exports. Don't cry for me, Argentina.[16]

ii.

Power, Power, Who's Got the Power?

From no later than the seventeenth century, the dominant players in the structures of the world economy were increasingly nation states; in a dramatic process of transformation, however, born in the 1960s and burgeoning ever since, the powers of nation states have been fusing with those of transnational corporations (TNCs), both within and between nations. This small group of companies—many fewer than a thousand—the most numerous and among the most powerful those of the United States, are the principal energizers of regional and global trade pacts: NAFTA and GATT, the EEC/EC/EU, and APEC, most notably. [17]

Politicians in the United States—and, of course, elsewhere—must and do heed the call of these mammoths, increasingly so, as the political power of and pressures from liberal/left political forces, once energized by social and economic concerns, have been replaced and weakened by waning trade unionism and, among other influences, the mind bending of the media ushering consumerism in and other concerns out.

Throughout modern history the owners and controllers of the means of production have naturally had disproportionate power in both their own and in weaker societies. In that sense, "modern" history has revolved around "capitalist" history. But the phenomena of power today have verged off in a new direction. It is not the capitalist class as such that wields this increasing power, it is an always shrinking percentage of its members: the giants among the TNCs (themselves a complex mixture of vertical, horizontal, conglomerate, and cross-sectoral combinations).

Power is by definition a zero-sum game. This means not only that ordinary people (as workers, consumers, citizens) have lost power and are accordingly damaged, but that the same is true of lesser capitalists: where "lesser" in the United States would mean all but the very most powerful corporations straddling industry and finance. And there is good reason to believe that a critical share of support for the *economic* policies of the current rightwing Congress comes from a small business sector that sees its interests as in conflict with those of the TNCs.[18]

This emerging new reality has come to be called "global capitalism," to distinguish its structures and processes from the postwar system of "monopoly capitalism." The latter (as was discussed in chapter 4), had its core relationship in the tight interaction of supercorporations with the superstate, and the dynamic interdependence of those with the Cold War and militarization, neocolonialism, surging waves of debt accumulation, and, not least, consumerism and the persuasive commercial and political powers of mass communications.

The *sine qua non* of the global monopoly capitalist system was the Cold War. Its dissipation as a set of stimuli and controls, along with a swift strengthening of communications technology throughout the 1980s,[19] has made it all the more necessary *and* possible for monopoly capitalism's super-corporations to become global behemoths and, in the process, for their ways and means and their powers to be transformed. What is already emerging constitutes a qualitatively new economic and political phenomenon, a new political economy.

Caught up in an always tighter swirl of global rivalry—for sales and profits, for assured access to resources, capital, tax breaks, and an expanding supply of cheap labor—the immensity of function and power of the TNCs puts other actors in their national economies in a darkening shadow and increasingly bends their national governments to their beck and call. This of course implies the growing relative weakness of all other petitioners of the State: claimants seeking more or better education, health, social security, infrastructure—that is, the bases for social efficiency, socioeconomic strength, and social decency.

In the birthing period of industrial capitalism, John L. and Barbara Hammond note, if capital was to flourish the critical need was to break down the walls of social tradition that protected human beings from becoming commodities; and the deed was done:

> An age that thought of the African negro, not as a person with a human life, but as so much labor power to be used in the service of a master or a system, came naturally to think of the poor at home in the same way. In this sense it was true . . . that the steam engine was invented too soon for the happiness of man; it was too great a power to put in the hands of men who still bought and sold their helpless fellow creatures.[20]

Long and painfully in this century, institutions have been created—shorter work days, safety conditions, pensions, health care benefits, paid vacations, child care. These successes have "rehumanized" or decommodified labor's condition, if not by any means for *all* workers and not completely for any, in important ways: important to workers and to the stability and well-being of modern economies, but costly to their employers' power and profits—and probably more so to the former than the latter.

Such successes as there have been were wrought through the power of organized labor and the State, under pressure from various constituencies other than, simply, business. Today's new "global capitalism" places such of those achievements as have endured at great and increasing risk, and it does so attacking on the same front—now global—as in early capitalism: the creation and maintenance of profits first and foremost by exposing workers (and nature) to the raw forces of the market. Just as in the deep past, when that decisive battle that made human beings into pawns of capital was first won, all other battles—against adequate education and health care for ordinary people and against nature, for example—become easier.

Therefore, global capitalism—a global economy run by giant firms using national polities as their levers—has had as its key functional characteristic that of a never-ending search for ever-cheaper labor abroad, which entails the inexorable cheapening of labor at home.

The appetites of these ever-growing giants is insatiable, and as they are fed and their strengths continue to grow, so do their appetites and their ability to feed them. Thus, and although the numbers of transnational corporations continue to increase, the concentration of power within that rising number also increases. The data are forbidding: in 1970 there were about 7,000 multinationals; by 1990 there were some 35,000. However Richard J. Barnet and John Cavanagh write:

> The emerging global order is spearheaded by a few hundred corporate giants, many of them bigger than most sovereign nations. They are becoming the world empires of the twenty-first century.
>
> The four intersecting webs of global commercial activity on which the new world economy rests [are]: the Global Cultural Bazaar; the Global Shopping Mall; the Global Workplace; and the Global Financial Network. . . . driven by the same few hundred corporate giants in the United States, Japan, Germany, France, Switzerland, the Netherlands, and the United Kingdom. The combined assets of the top 300 firms now make up roughly a quarter of the productive assets of the world.[21]

Those companies are becoming, in a real sense already are, the feudal baronies of today's national and global economies, demanding and receiving with each passing month more control over both economic and political processes. As the tendency toward concentrated power among and between the giants continues, doubtless means will be found along the way to lessen the harm they might do to each other through rivalries while, through their mergers, increasing the harm done to us, our societies, and our planet. If the past is any guide, however, conditions might well arise in which internecine conflict will be hard to contain, allowing global economic anarchy, as in the 1920s, to emerge once more. But all that is truly unpredictable.

After this long detour, back now to that which is less though still problematic: the likelihood of a renewal of sustained expansion in the United States and of the world economy. Because that will be determined by the intersection of economic with political processes, the stultification that has descended on the political process in the United States, and is worsening, bodes ill for the maintenance or strengthening of economic recovery. For reasons to be noted shortly, most probable is that the present recovery in the United States will slowly turn back on itself, and slide once more into a recession: bad news for the global economy, especially with its Las Vegas financial system and its $2.6 trillion daily of speculation.[22]

The foregoing does not constitute a warning that the 1930s are once more around the corner; that is not only unlikely, it is very close to impossible—if only because of all the changes in economic thought and institutions that the earlier depression produced. But what can happen—a strung-out process of debilitating and painfully high unemployment, the continuation of static or falling real incomes for most, increasing difficulties for small businesses and farmers—sooner or later could transform continuing and widespread national and global financial fragility into a financial "crack" with fearful consequences. In turn, that means that the political processes in all the major nations—not least that of the United States—have become critical.

And those in the United States are worrisome indeed. For in addition to economic developments that have made the formulation of economic policy a game dominated by a tiny group of big corporate players has been the transformation of Congress into that gaggle of geese tightly led (until recently) by Newt Gingrich, nicely targeted by Molly Ivins as "YAFers,"

> the Young Americans for Freedom—who used to bustle around campuses in those dorky suits, like Mormons on speed. . . . Boy, are these people followers. Lockstep, in line, march in unison, chant in unison, don't think, don't learn, follow the leader.[23]

Rumbling along in that same march have been those related developments which, in shifting U.S. politics always to the political right on "social" matters—abortion, guns, laws against gay people, resurgent racism, school prayer—have facilitated the increasing domination at all levels of government by harsh conservatism. In this process, those whose real incomes have steadily deteriorated for more than twenty years have learned to waste their energies by bashing the wrong enemies: immigrants, blacks, the poor, the homeless, pro-choice supporters, those on welfare, et al.

Consequently, when Clinton moved into the Oval Office he had so much cherished, he was walking into a bramble bush created in preceding decades: mountains of debt and deficits, mostly accumulated for wasteful expenditures and "corporate welfare"; a teetering world economy dominated increasingly by greedy and reckless titans; a disappeared Cold War whose vital role in supporting U.S. "prosperity" and power dwindles; accumulating social fears combined with economic apprehensions, and an electorate weaving together apathy with irrationality and a spreading pessimism. Who would want such a job? And now that he has it, why does he keep smiling?

iii.

Billy: the Kid

In experiencing and reading about all this century's presidential administrations, one cannot find anything even remotely approaching the almost palpable disappointment, disillusionment, and anger generated by Clinton's, most especially among those who voted for him. The puzzle becomes all the more confusing when it is noted that the economy has improved noticeably in those years (although wages continue their long decline), that there have been no costly or shameful wars, that he is—on the face of it, at least—easier to like than almost everyone except FDR and JFK, and he should be more difficult to hate than Nixon. Such a list could be lengthened.

I include myself among the Clinton critics, so I'll start with how he lost me. I expected leadership out of the mess he had inherited, from him and from Hillary, who initially struck me as having more to her than Bill. Although I didn't see him as even a basic liberal, it was such a relief to get rid of B/Q, and Clinton did come on as decent, bright, personable, thoughtful, informed, and flexible. A bit of this and that has come through—but first and foremost, of course, he has been flexible: *really* flexible.

After the hoopla of the inauguration was over, almost the first thing Clinton did struck me as hopeful: his order as Commander-in-Chief to stop all the brutish nonsense about gays and the military. But he drew back from that as swiftly as though stung by a yellowjacket. And then made matters worse by dithering about showing and telling.

That policy failure looked bad, but early on it also had its positive signs— at least he had made a *try* at something sensible and decent. But now we know: what he tries doesn't add up to much even at the beginning; he relents at the slightest opposition, and ends up looking like a horse's ass.

Lingering hopes were shredded with the betrayal of Lani Guinier. But it was not only Guinier but the cause of civil rights and those who had fought for and supported and continue—and still need—those struggles who were betrayed. When the news came out that he had dumped Guinier (and the way he had done it), I thought then what I know now: "He's big trouble."

So, far from leading the country to at least a somewhat better state of affairs, Clinton has allowed a steady if sickening descent to become a plunge—and to demoralize a large number of those who had seen him and the Democratic Party as source of change for the better. What we got instead were changes for the worse, even worse than the Reagan years, with the worst yet to come.

Of course Clinton has had to deal with a Congress which, over the past twenty years and more, has moved from a composition of liberals, moderates, and conservatives to one of moderates, conservatives, and right-wingers; has had to face, moreover, a population a significant percentage of which has moved in the same directions and at least the same speed.

That makes life difficult for a President who would doubtless choose to be a moderate with a tinge of social liberalism, if it didn't keep him from being President. Instead, he has responded to our regressing national political condition by bending to its winds and (mixing the metaphor) feeding the voracious beast, almost political suicide for him and worsened socioeconomic damage for the nation. The only matters on which Clinton has stood fast—his first budget and NAFTA, even the crime bill and, for a while, health care—we would have been better off without. [24]

The larger problem is that he won the office at a critical time—*another* critical time—in our history. In such times presidential leadership has more than once reminded our people of what in us is worth encouraging or discouraging, worth preserving or bringing back to life in the United States. Doing that is what made Lincoln and FDR worthy of our respect, both having faced a profound crisis, both having grown in office to meet it. More often than not, of course, our presidents have not led the nation to a better fate but have made their deals, moved us a bit back or sideways or, like Reagan and Bush, flung wide the doors to greed and glitz combined with hate and fear. It would have taken someone with more strength and talent than Clinton's to have placed that process in reverse; but had he been resolute about *that*, instead of whatever he has been resolute about, he would have found enough allies both in and out of government to have slowed down, or even stopped and reversed the foul torrent now swamping us.

Instead, Clinton has discouraged his potential allies and encouraged his relentless enemies and made it easier for political plug-uglies to rise to positions of overweening power. Nor is it irrelevant to note that when, a week before the election of 1994, the man who became the Speaker of the House of Representatives characterized the Democratic Party as "the enemy of the American people," the media reported it not at all or as though it were a playful belch at a ball game. My fellow Americans, we're in real trouble.

And, my fellow Americans, we're going to have dig ourselves out of that trouble, from the bottom and middle up; there's nothing but more trouble to be had from the top down. We must work very hard to bring back to life the liberalism and the radicalism that sit below the surface, waiting for the rain of leadership—reminding us, once more, that it's up to us to save ourselves alive, up to us to *be* that rain of leadership. We must; but *can* we?

iv.

Where There's Life There's Hope
(And Where There's Hope There's Life)

It may seem strange indeed to those who have read this far that one as critical as I of the past and so dour concerning the present of the United States would have either the hope or the energy to think about changing this society for the better. But it is frequently true that it is among those who are most critical that one also finds the most hopeful. It is from our hope and our anger that our energy derives.

Will Rogers, the droll popular "philosopher" of the Twenties and Thirties, used to say "I've never met a man I didn't like." Well, I have, and more than a few. But after a long life bringing me into contact with many thousands of students, fellow soldiers, and blue and white collar co-workers, I am convinced that some substantial percentage of our people yearn to believe that this can be, even must be, a good society.

The other side of that hopeful belief is the conviction that without the steady participation of ordinary people in the political process—which means much more than voting once in a while—the truth of the adage that "for evil to triumph it is necessary only that good people do nothing" will continue to be affirmed. We the People, as Lincoln said as his United States of America was disintegrating under his feet, "must disenthrall ourselves."

I have been one of those who has "steadily participated" in the political process, and have had my life enriched thereby. It is necessary to remark, however, that a very large proportion of that political work (for me and most others) has been involved in fighting *against*—against racism, against war, against poverty, against oppression. All of that was necessary, all of it must continue. But for victories won there to endure, they must also be part of a larger and *positive* effort which goes beyond struggle against and toward social transformation.

Thus, and only as one important example, it should be clear by now that we cannot end (or even much mitigate) racism just by fighting against it, by making it illegal, by robbing racists of their arguments/beliefs, and the like, vital though all that may be. It is also necessary to make good education and good jobs and good housing and good health possible for all, all of those abundant rather than scarce. Moving in that direction will reduce and finally end the competition between us and, over time, render racism and its accompaniments harmless.

Such an effort must be not only positive, that is, but comprehensive and inclusive; and such an effort would succeed only if it were seen by large numbers of us as a natural, normal part of our lives. What its components might be, its ways and means and whys and wherefore, are of course and necessarily controversial. In these dark days, many have been putting forth their proposals along such lines, it is cheering to know.

My own suggestions—anything but a "blueprint"—take up the next chapter. There proposals will be put forward (most of them following those "others" just noted), and arguments made to show that what is desirable is also necessary; and that what is necessary is possible.

EPILOGUE: INTO THE TEETH
OF THE STORM

This book began with the argument that the spread and deepening of greed and racism have been our undoing. Their pernicious interaction has always narrowed, and may yet completely finish off "the American dream."

A program for a good society must be comprehensive and inclusive: we must all work for the many changes needed for all and, as well, for those that some of us do not need but others do. Much to our peril, we seem to have forgotten that our common needs as human beings can be at least as important as—at times more important than—those particular to us in terms of our social "categories."

Greed and racism are fueled—and in many ways created—by our contemporary exultation in consumerism run amok. Consumerism has very little to do with the satisfaction of our or other people's needs for goods and services; it has everything to do with the need of a business system to create insatiable wants in order to become or remain profitable: it is the socialization of greed, a product of how advertising leads us to feel and behave, not of our "human nature."

Consumerism has several socially toxic by-products: the infantilization of the society, the trend of increased hours of work and multiple jobs (by one or more members of a rising number of families), the accelerating erosion of an already fragile sense of human solidarity—and, not least, the accelerating proliferation of wasteful and often environmentally dangerous products and processes for the already slender prospects for a "sustainable industrialism."

Consumerism as a dominating social tendency would be harmful enough were it confined to the United States—where in the 1920s, as was pointed out in chapter 1, it first took hold. But since World War II consumerism has spread in one degree or another all over the globe: it is a central part of what is meant by "the Americanization of the world." It is highly desirable and quite feasible that all the peoples of the world develop economies that enable them to have a decent level of life; it is quite simply impossible for the lives of any people in any society to become or remain comfortable if consumerism continues to spread and deepen.

The kinds of proposals made in this chapter entail a restructuring of production and consumption to allow an *increase* of good jobs along with reasonable profits.

As is also true for the conversion of military to non-military production, there is no conflict between jobs and profits, on the one hand, and a safe and sane and decent economy, on the other. There are problems of conversion in both cases, but these can be worked out, usually with governmental assistance (as happened on a grand scale after World War II). What has to change, along with the structures of production and consumption is the structure of decision-making; that is, of power.

That structure already changed significantly in the postwar period in the United States, as unions strengthened and social legislation moved ahead on all levels, taking the form of social democracy in Western Europe. But now, at a moment of great social and ecological dangers, we and others are devolving to a kind of social dinosaurism. [1]

The restructuring of production, consumption, and power entailed by a substantial reform program carries with it also the restructuring of income and wealth to a significant degree: it means moving back away from rather than always more deeply into a "winner take all" society. And that necessitates an overhaul of the present educational process and its content at all levels.

No program for beneficial social change in the United States can make headway or endure unless it is recognized how very strong the hold of capitalist ideology has been and remains on the "hearts and minds" of all of us. We must find and encourage ways of ridding ourselves of the dense ideological fog that suffocates our humanity, that leads us casually to waste countless lives and natural resources while destroying nature's bounty.

That stifling ideology embraces more than capitalism, of course, but capitalism provides its steely center; nowadays, an attractive velvet cover for the capitalist fist is the rendering of today's benign and selfless Holy Family—"the free market," economic growth, and world trade. Taken separately or together, these constitute the theoretical basis for the "trickle-down" theory, or as it was put in the 1950s, "What's Good for General Motors is Good for America."

The arguments supporting this now deified trio were put forth first in the seminal works of Adam Smith and David Ricardo, seen by them, however, as means, not as the social *ends* in themselves they have become at present. That is not new to the postwar world; what is new is the sudden rebirth and widespread acceptance of nineteenth century brute capitalism and the anointed offspring of the Holy Family: balanced budgets and the demonization of deficits, deregulation and privatization, cuts to the bone of social expenditures, the application of IMF monetarism to the leading as well as the led economies, and so-called trading agreements (NAFTA, GATT), which serve to rationalize and facilitate production "outsourcing" to lands of cheap labor and no ecological safeguards while decimating job possibilities at home.

All this has been accompanied by an associated redistribution of income zooming upward—unprecedented in either its rapidity or its dimensions—unknowingly cheered on by millions whose own incomes are stagnant or falling. In an earlier chapter, using census data from 1990, it was noted that from the 1970s the top 20 percent of income receivers gained as the bottom 80 percent lost in their share of the national income. Data from 1992 showed that after 1989 it was *the bottom 90* percent that was losing share; and the 1994 data are even more astounding: since 1989, as was shown in chapter 6, all but the top 5 percent of income receivers have seen their incomes go down in both real and percentage terms. In those same years, the top 1 percent had its share rise by over 50 percent.[2] Meanwhile (as shown in the UN Development Report of 1994), from 1960 to 1991 the share of world income for the richest 20 percent rose from 70 to 85 percent; that is, the other 80 percent—a quarter of whom try to survive on a daily income of $1—suffered a decline in their share.

i.

Aux Armes, Citoyens!

What do we need and want? Jobs. Health Care. Education. Housing. Security. Freedom. Respect. More exactly: more and better jobs, and a livable income for those who can't or shouldn't seek one in the market;

suitable health care for life for all, preventive and otherwise; education—before the job, on the job, along with the job, after the job, irrespective of the job—education, not just training, not just discipline; decent housing for all; daily and lifetime security; freedom to *be* for all, and for anything that does no harm to others; and the respect for all that marks a society living in accord with its first and finest idea: we are all created equal. All that combined will move us toward genuine democracy. And peace. And sustain our planet's riches.

Each and every element of what we need and want must be worked for as part of an organic whole; that is, difficult though it may seem to work for *any* positive reform now, none can take secure hold and function as designed unless each is part of a broad pattern of *linked* reforms. Such a strategy, far from making any or all reforms impossible, is the very basis for their economic and political feasibility. That will become evident from the first, as we take a closer look:

Jobs. Item: between 1978 and 1995 production jobs fell by 12 percent. Quite apart from the fact that the official unemployment rate is an understatement by about 50 percent of reality, the wages of the fully-employed have either been stagnant or in decline since 1973, and that process is accelerating. Equally important is that the average quality of jobs has also fallen in the same period, that all levels of work are now threatened, and that both processes worsen—along with a mounting loss of benefits: health care, pensions, paid vacations.

All those trends took hold first in the 1970s and have continued through periods of normal as well as low rates of economic growth; indeed, the *kind* of economic growth we have had in this era—ushered along by downsizing and outsourcing and megamergers—has been more a cause than remedy for the jobs problem.

The quantitative standard to be worked for should assure that everyone seeking work is *entitled* to a job, with the local, state, or federal government as employer of last resort; that the wages of such work, irrespective of employer, should yield a living—be a livable not a minimum wage (which, today, leaves one below the poverty level). And if that means governmental subsidies for the private sector to provide a living wage: so be it. If businesses cannot function satisfactorily without the economic mistreatment of labor (or natural resources), those businesses should cease to exist or be subsidized. Period.

In that connection, it is worth pointing out that in the early 1970s, as average incomes peaked and were just beginning the slide that takes us to the present, the Bureau of Labor Statistics compiled data showing that less than half of the people enjoyed "a moderate but adequate level of income"—representing, it seems, "the American standard of living."

And was that level so high as to constitute affluence? Not quite. High enough to make four-fifths of the world's people envious, to be sure; but not exactly living high. *Item:* it allowed one suit every three to four years for the father, and three street dresses for the mother every two years. *Item:* big ticket purchases included a *used* car every four years, a new TV every ten years, a new fridge every seventeen years, and a toaster every thirty-three years. There were also nine movies a year for the parents, but none for the kids. The budget allowed *no* savings to meet unemployment, illness, or higher education for the children; and from it social security and other taxes had to be paid. Even assuming the durable goods were better made in the past than now that's pretty slim pickings; and not even half of the people had that. Others had what the Bureau called a "lower" or "austere" level of consumption—in other words, were "poor." [3]

Those data are for our economic heyday, the early 1970s, after twenty years of the greatest and most sustained and widespread well-being the people of the U.S.A. had ever had. And from this moment on?—after slashes in everything but military and corporate welfare—and by the fabled year of 2002? By then, the wrecking ball of current policies should have further lowered the purchasing power of most of us and further weakened the already mushy economy; by then, perhaps, the business world may come to realize that once again it has supported a bunch of false prophets.

That's some of the quantitative side of "jobs." Of course quantities and qualities exist side by side and also interact. One can work at a low income and still take satisfaction in one's work and skills, have hopes for the future, preserve one's dignity, and be able to provide for the kids' education, housing and morale, with discipline and sacrifice. One can and some do, but most cannot, try though they might. It's not a level playing field in a society where the average C.E.O. gets 175 times the income of the factory worker over whom he rules.

As many jobs as possible—and that means most—should be "good jobs"; that is, jobs with decent pay and prospects, job security, no threat to health or safety on the job, ample opportunities for training for advancement on the job and for educational leaves, declining not rising hours, assured child care for those needing it, paid vacations and—so long as we lack universal health care and adequate social security—health and pension benefits.

But wouldn't that simply drive businesses into bankruptcy?

It didn't when—between 1955 and 1975—some approximation of all that was achieved in the United States for many workers in many jobs. Some or all of those reforms are now declining, and all are threatened— not least because the unions and the politics that created them no longer exist, or are lying low.

There are, of course, jobs that must be done that cannot be called good jobs: jobs that deserve the name "shit work." What about them? At least three points: their nastiness should be compensated for by high, not the lowest wages; those doing them should have easy access to training for better work; meanwhile, our technological wizardry should be applied to find ways of automating such jobs: machines have no dignity to lose.

But we're having hell's own time finding enough jobs as matters now stand; how could we create more jobs and have more of them be *good* jobs? That's exactly why we need to link reforms: as programs for health and housing and education (and, to be noted, for "infrastructure") get under- way, there will be a) more jobs *and* more good jobs, b) doing useful work while also increasing real incomes, and c) paying for themselves with increased socioeconomic productivity and taxes. There would also be another and substantial source of their financing: such steps ahead would have the effect of reducing poverty and crime and the financial and human costs associated with them.

Health Care. Instead of the pathetic, disgusting, and destructive bum- bling of the Clintons on health care reform, with its hundreds of pages, witnesses, experts, companies, and proposals for "managed competi- tion"—a euphemism for big business control of our health care—suppose Bill or Hillary had begun with a statement something like this:

> Health care must never be seen as a commodity, whose provision is deter- mined by income, but as a human need that must be provided, for social and individual well-being. There should be no distinction between the health care needs of the poor and the rich: pain and suffering make no such distinctions.
> Therefore, I propose that the Congress pass a single-payer national health care system, similar to that of Canada (and that proposed by President Tru- man), to be financed through a progressive income tax. In this way the needs

of our people and the standards of the medical profession will be met and, at the same time, the costs of doing so will be substantially reduced.

Instead, of course, the whole Clinton effort collapsed of its own weight [4] and the coyotes and vultures descended for the corporate feast that has ensued: the emerging triumph of the Big Five insurance companies (Prudential, Travelers, Cigna, Aetna, and Metropolitan), the HMOs and "for-profit" chains, the giant pharmaceutical and equipment manufacturers.

Well-financed lobbyists and Congress have insured that our inadequate system will become considerably more so—as Medicare and Medicaid are downsized, as public hospitals such as the Los Angeles USC complex shut down and their emergency rooms disappear (private hospitals tend now not to have emergency facilities), as the quality and time given to health and medical care are meted out in terms of business not medical criteria, as the number of those not covered by any, let alone adequate health insurance grows apace, as more horrors yet unthought of become commonplace. There are now over 42 million people with *no* health insurance in the United States, and another 40+ million whose coverage is wretchedly narrow. That things had come to a pretty pass already in 1994 is encapsulated in this news item:

> During 1993 and 1994, for-profit health maintenance organizations grew so fast that they overtook nonprofit organizations as the dominant force in managed care. . . . Today the majority of all people enrolled in HMOs are in plans operated by for-profit companies. Among doctors who work in group practices, the share of such managed-care contracts was 89 percent by 1992, up from 56 percent (in 1991). . . .[5]

Glooming to myself as I ponder these scandalous conditions, my mind wanders back to 1940, when I was a part, however humble, of the prewar health care complex. Conditions are likely to fall back to a level worse than 1940 if present trends continue.

Story: Never Give an Inch

One of the jobs I had while attending San Francisco Junior College was as an orderly in surgery in San Francisco County (now General) Hospital—the major source of health care for the poor in the city then, as now: one didn't have to pay, which would have added insult to injury, given the problematic quality of treatment.

I worked the night shift (4 p.m. to midnight), when only prolonged surgery was scheduled; the rest of our cases were emergencies. Surgery was just above

Emergency, and when I heard an ambulance siren approaching I would hustle down to see if anyone had to be brought to us to be sliced up.

One night, the siren sounded, I popped downstairs and arrived as a middle-aged man, screaming in pain, was being lifted from the ambulance. He had a ruptured appendix—let it be too long and you've got peritonitis. Make haste!

I had to wait quite a while, however, for the rule at Emergency was (is again?) first things first. Answer the following questions Mr. Luckless, the most important one being: "Do you have any savings?" Demented by pain, lacking good English, wailing all the while, the man could not comprehend at first. That question *had* to be answered, first things being first, and it was asked repeatedly until it was: and he had $300 in savings. And so help me Milton Friedman, zip! back into the ambulance he was plopped and whisked away to a private hospital some twenty minutes away. There he lost his appendix and his savings—in which order I am unable to say.

A couple of nights later when I was in one of the wards, there was Mr. L., still breathing, praise Uncle Miltie, but flat broke. But one more misguided soul had been pulled back by a vigilant health care person from the precipice of economic transgression—and Franklin Hospital was richer by $300. Praise the Law of Supply and Demand!

The United States does have the best health care in the world: for the rich (and the Congress and the military); it has one of the very worst health care systems for the bulk of its population—as measured, for example, in infant mortality and longevity rates. And if there were a measure for health care anxiety rates, we would be Numero Uno among the industrial countries.

A strong political effort to change that—and to counter the health care empire's lobbyists—is necessary, possible, and politically feasible; and such an effort must and could be a vital building block for a movement creating a far better society.

Education. The public schools in a safe and sane and decent society would—as little else can—provide an experience in which youngsters could begin to realize their constructive and creative possibilities, begin to understand and appreciate nature, their culture, their society, and themselves, begin to develop into citizens fit for a vibrant democracy; their schools would be among the most positive of their experiences. Just writing those words makes the teeth to gnash: the reality, except for a privileged few, is of course a tragic failure in all those respects, schools as hellholes of coercion and discipline and fear (for teachers and students).

For the last thirty years or so one of most astute and concerned students of our public schools has been Jonathan Kozol, once a primary school teacher in Boston. His experience and his emphasis have always been in and on urban schools—where most of our children are—especially with poor children in the inner cities and the poorer suburbs, those whose educational needs are the greatest, for whom a good education is the sole means of climbing out of the ditch of poverty and despair. But their educational opportunities have always been the worst. Kozol's most recent book details how very much worse the worst has now become:

> Liberal critics of the Reagan era sometimes note that social policy in the United States, to the extent that it concerns black children and poor children, has been turned back several decades. But this assertion, which is accurate as a description of some setbacks in the areas of housing, health and welfare, is not adequate to speak about the present-day reality in public education. In public schooling, social policy has been turned back almost one hundred years. [6]

The decades-old emigration from city to suburb, leaving the cities and their schools (and other services) to their fate, of course has made it close to impossible to prevent an accelerated process of manifold deterioration: the very essence of a vicious circle. The costs of all this to the cities' children—and of course a very large majority of children live in our cities—are heartbreaking, deeply harmful to and wasteful of their lives. The social process is harmed just as deeply, as its politics become increasingly surly, dominated by fears and resentments coming from all quarters—with, again, the worst on its way. [7]

Curriculum aside, among the most essential changes to the existing system would be: smaller classes for all; more power to teachers, parents, and (get this!) students, and considerably less to bureaucrats and politicians; school facilities and grounds that are pleasurable to behold and work in; serious consideration to getting rid of the agrarian age's summer vacation and replacing it with, say, an 11-month year; and courses and content (varying with age levels) that will make it a joy forever for young people to study what makes their society, nature, and themselves tick, and gives serious time for the appreciation of beauty.

What's wrong with our schools and universities needs a book or two instead of the few words proffered here; they are meant to be suggestive of a broad range of other needed changes.

Story: Western Justice

In 1951, I was a Lecturer at Berkeley and one of my courses was the introductory course. I had about 1,000 students and exactly twenty-two teaching assistants. By the end of the year I had just barely gotten to know *their* names, and had virtually no contact with the students—until one day.

It was just after the final exam, and as I was walking through the campus I was stopped by a student who said he was in the big class, and wished to speak to me. He told me he was from Persia, that he had a scholarship that depended upon his maintaining a "C" average, and that he had just received his grade from his T.A. and it was a "D." He had to have a "C" to hold his scholarship the following year, and was there any chance it could be changed?

I spoke to him for a few minutes, decided that he was not totally without virtue, and told him OK, I would change his grade, but to an "A." "I don't deserve an 'A,' he said, clearly upset. "You don't deserve a 'C' either," I said. "I won't haggle with you. If you need to raise your average and are asking me to help I might as well help a lot as a little, since principle is being violated anyhow." For some minutes he tried to persuade me to do as he asked rather than what I had decided. But I used my power and privilege to prevail. (I believe he is now a ranking general in the Iranian Army. A lesson to contemplate.)

Nobody can teach or learn properly in very large classes—that is, classes over twenty to twenty-five students. Getting rid of large classes, along with other desirable changes in education, apart from being good in themselves, would also be a source of lots of good jobs.

To say nothing of how many good jobs would be generated if we were to move toward decent housing for all:

Housing. We surely don't have that now—whether that means home ownership, whose costs are rising out of reach for most families and declining as a percent of the population, or reasonable rents for apartments, which are decreasing (the reasonableness, not the rents). *Items:*

- In 1983 it was estimated that "approximately 50 million people still live in the deteriorated and socially dysfunctional areas called slums."[8]

- In 1952-53, the average household spent 34 percent of its budget on housing; by 1982-84 it had risen to 42 percent.

- For the poor, matters are worse: in 1985 it was estimated that half of low-income renters spent at least 65 percent of their income on rent (which pushes the official poverty line up considerably, for it assumes 33 percent).

- And then there are the homeless, of which there are . . . ????

The federal government began to move in a sensible way on housing in the 1930s, spurred on by the depression. In addition to privately-constructed public housing (whose interest costs were subsidized, allowing low rents), private home purchases were eased by keeping interest rates down, and by the creation of "neighborhood" savings and loans banks (specifically for home mortgages); and later, countless GIs (myself included) could get a subsidized veteran's loan. More recently, however, the subsidies of much-reduced public housing is for *upper*-income apartments, the S&Ls became gambling casinos, GI housing loans a pleasant memory, and both rents and home prices have gone toward the ceiling.

We can start over again with the useful steps of the 1930s, and improve on them. Doing so would stimulate a construction boom, many good jobs in construction itself and in the industries supplying goods and services for building, rising incomes and taxes to handle the fiscal costs, and—lest we forget—decent housing. Good jobs there, just as in the proposals for health care and education; and those now to follow.

Infrastructure. The term has no precise limits on its meaning, but for present purposes let it refer to the "structure" within which both businesses and people function but that neither can nor should provide (except as regulated utilities): roads, bridges, water supplies and sewers, gas and electricity systems, mass transit, and, among other items some or most educational and health facilities.

In 1981 the dollar amount of infrastructural renewal seen as desperately needed came to $3 trillion. It may have doubled since then. [9] But where would we *get* $3 trillion? A place to begin—for this and other improvements—is the military budget. Try these numbers on for size:

In the United States, from 1947 to 1991, the sum of military budgets (in dollars of 1982 value) amounted to $8.7 trillion. Compare this to the total value of U.S. industry and infrastructure—again for 1982—of $7.3 trillion. During the Cold War the U.S. military used up more than enough resources to rebuild nearly all of its civilian asset base. . . . This is the physical "using up" that lies behind the lack of government money for infrastructural repair. [10]

Governmental intervention to provide needed infrastructure was vital first in our transportation system: the canal system completed before and the railroad system completed after the Civil War depended squarely upon state and federal subsidization, and in their time each was vital to our process of economic development. Although the national highway system has not served such vital purposes, it too was financed by the now scorned "gummint."

The word "financed" is important to emphasize here: whether for infrastructure or any of the many programs proposed above, while their financing is wholly or in part by the government, the work of building and using the schools, hospitals, bridges, etc. is done by the private sector, which gets the jobs and profits. (And which, like other governmental expenditures, should be paid for through a progressive income tax.)

That there is nonetheless so much opposition to government having a positive role to play in the economy, despite its obvious benefits, is due to two major attitudes: one is sheer ideology, the deification of private enterprise, and the other is cousin to greed, the belief that there is more money to be made if, as Milton Friedman and his Munchkins propose, *everything* is done by business for profit, and if it isn't seen as likely to be profitable by them—let's be clear—it's not worth doing.

Quite apart from the social cruelty and economic stupidity involved in that position it is stupid also from a business point of view, to say nothing of the social explosiveness it fuels.

ii.

All Together Now: Unlearn!

High on the list of what must be unlearned if we are ever to find our way out of today's enveloping fog are the siren songs that celebrate "the free market." As was discussed in the prologue, it was essential to the very birth of capitalism that "commodification" be accomplished: first and foremost of labor and the land; the subsequent development of capitalism has moved society toward the commodification of everything. It is becoming always more difficult to locate a thing, a service, an activity that has *not* been commodified, that doesn't have its price, that does not have to meet the "bottom line" market standard of profitability. Thus, what would have been unthinkable even a generation ago—"for-profit hospitals, parks, prisons, even the military," is now already in existence or on the books.

To commodify a thing or a service—and in "the free market" *everything* is commodified—is importantly and among other undesirable consequences to make access to it a matter solely of purchasing power. Given the intrinsically unequal patterns of income, wealth, and power of capitalism, the very largest percentage of the world, including a substantial part of the U.S. population, is denied access to whatever has been commodified. It is not autos and VCRs and computers that count most in this respect, much though they may count in the passions of those who have been taught to want them. It is, rather, the very stuff of life: adequate food, clothing, shelter, health care, and education—without all of which, it must be recognized, all but the most exceptional will be denied the opportunity to realize their productive and cultural needs and possibilities. A closer look at "the free market" will support that generalization.

The textbook model of perfect competition has the following characteristics: 1) there are so many small firms that no one of them can conceivably affect the market significantly by restricting its own output in order to hold up price, 2) each of those firms produces a product identical with that of its competitors (and thus, among other virtues, there is no point in advertising); and, 3) there are no significant barriers to the entry of new firms in the industry, so if by chance firms were making an excess profit in the industry, new capital would be attracted, supply would increase, prices go down, and the excess profits (Ricardo's "rent" again) disappear.

Once upon a time, these conditions were in fact met in staple agriculture (wheat, cotton, and the like), in the cotton textile industry, and in bituminous coal mining. In all three of these very large cases, one or another disaster was the outcome: a disaster for the workers and/or the owners, for nature and/or society—or for all the above. As free marketry comes to be the byword in Congress, in corporate boardrooms, and in economics classrooms again, just as though this were, say, 1880, it is vital to look at some of the leading historical facts of the matter: [11]

1. *Wheat farming.* The cultivation of wheat in the states between the Mississippi and the Rockies was extensive, despite what an agronomist— noting the sparse rainfall of much of the area—would have advised. Falling

prices in the last decades of the nineteenth century and regularly inadequate rainfall went along with expanding acreage. By the end of the Twenties, economics and nature combined to make a large part of the area (and not just Oklahoma) in the 1930s into "the Dust Bowl." The farmers and the land were both ruined. The free market in that and other areas of agriculture began to be abandoned in favor of governmental controls in 1928—at the behest of the farmers, and in the name of saving the family farm—under free marketeer Herbert Hoover. After many twists and turns, all of them finding ways to substitute controlled for free markets, agriculture now finds its stability in market control by giant agricultural corporations ("agribusiness"), still aided and abetted by the State. There were over seven million family farms in 1935; there are fewer than two million now. R.I.P., free market.

2. *Cotton textiles.* It was the classic industry of early industrialization, taking hold in New England. By the turn into this century, capital began to migrate to the South, in search of cheaper labor. (The first great "restructuring.") By the Thirties the industry had been "perfectly competitive" for close to a century; it (along with much of staple agriculture and coal mining) was in depression already in the 1920s. The long-impoverished "poor white trash" who had attracted northern capital found their lives sinking to even lower levels: at least earlier they had not lived in a "company town" (houses, stores, banks, cops, everything, owned by the one company, whose power may be imagined), with all the viciousness associated with that institution. The solution materialized after World War II: the cotton industry was taken over by giant chemical companies, as textiles became dominated by synthetics. R.I.P., free market.

3. *Bituminous coal.* By the 1930s there were about 5,000 "soft" coal mines in the United States. Perfect! It was the most dangerous job in the economy—broken backs and limbs for many, black lung disease for most. Wages were as bad as working conditions and (un)employment was intermittent. The miners too lived in company towns, and the small coal owners were their feudal barons—and most of them losing money. What saved the miners, for a while, was the emergence of what became, for a while, the toughest union in the country: the United Mine Workers, led by the sharpest and most interesting of all such leaders, John L. Lewis (discussed in an earlier chapter). Many owners were saved when they were bought out by big steel and chemical and energy companies, who were vertically integrating to save money and gain market power. R.I.P., free market.

In sum, nobody who produces and sells any good or service believes in the free market—except for one side, the side on which they're buying. The more competition there is among those selling you something, of course, the more likely you are to get a good deal. Conversely, the more competition there is among those selling what you're selling, the worse off you are—whether you are a farmer, a worker, an auto company, a doctor, whatever.

That has been so since buying and selling began, and it still is. But what about GATT and NAFTA and all the pressures by the big corporations on our and others' governments to sign agreements for freeing up markets, in those and other such arrangements?

NAFTA (the United States, Canada, and Mexico) and GATT (most of the world) are touted under the flag of free trade, and how much cheaper all goods will be for all of us, and how, over time (in the sweet bye and bye) also more (and better!) jobs—though there could be a brief decline. In fact these policies are much more concerned with business investment than with trade.[12] The lobbyists for the agreements represent (usually giant transnational) companies already producing abroad or eager to do so.

In the case of NAFTA, not the only, but the principal basis for the desire to widen the door to Mexico is to have easier access to its very cheap and unprotected labor and environmental laxity. The case of Canada is wryly different: Canadian industrial wages are on average higher than those in the United States. But two-thirds of all industrial capital in Canada is U.S.-owned, so Canadians lose jobs to U.S. workers—and U.S. workers (not the same ones, yet) lose jobs to Mexico, to workers receiving a tenth of their U.S. counterparts. And the U.S. corporations who preside over these moves make out like bandits: the financial news regularly has reports in the same day's news that profits and layoffs have risen simultaneously for this or that corporation.

Good for business, and what's good for business is good for—business? The most important "free market" for business is the labor market. That means they want weak unions or, better, *no* unions. With new jobs going to the desperately poor (who remain that way) in the poor countries while the once better off lose theirs in the rich countries, the implications are for a steady decrease in average purchasing power over the globe.

The foregoing is not meant to suggest that a functioning world economy is bad for ourselves or others, even though that is often so, nor is there an implicit notion that we should withdraw from or erect high barriers to world trade. That would be a combination of the undesirable and the impossible. We must and can beneficially import and export a broad variety of consumer and capital goods and raw materials, to the benefit of consumers and businesses and jobs. But we cannot allow our structures of production and consumption and jobs to be decided by the needs and standards of giant transnational corporations which, as they evidently see them, mean investment and production processes that advantage the very few at the expense of the very many and that threaten our future. Acceptance of the goal of maximum growth and world trade is the main trend of all economies today, the consequence of what amounts to a giant and persisting ideological hoax.

A lessening of our dependence upon and devotion to economic growth would permit us to increase the flexibility of the ways and means of our domestic economy. A close examination—closer than this book allows—would show that the fulfillment of the reforms argued for in this chapter would both enable and require that lessened dependence while fostering rising living standards for our population and less harm to others.

In sum, virtually all the long-standing support of business for the free market is one-sided, is designed and accordingly functions to meet the interests of capital and to increase the incomes and wealth of the world's top 10 percent. The rhetoric supporting and accompanying these processes is in the name of benefitting the economy, thus the society, thus all of us. To those who argue that way, as always, the interests of capital *are* the interests of the economy and the society; their position and their power make it seem obviously so, to them. For the rest of us—because of *our* position and individual powerlessness—good sense and reflection point in different directions.

iii.

No Time for Comedy

Not least daunting of the challenges facing us is that for there to be substantial social change in a positive direction, there must be solidaristic political efforts. The economic individualism that capitalism has bolstered and embellished also eschews solidarity, of course; and the postwar creation of an almost manic consumerism among us threatens to be the straw that breaks the camel's (that is, our species's) back.

But if both the difficulties of and the needs for achieving an even minimal human solidarity in our world are formidable, equally impressive are the material possibilities for doing so—offered by our great production and productivity, especially when combined with the positive possibilities of modern education and communications.

Precisely because the socially-created difficulties of doing what we need to do continue to rise, it becomes always more essential for the effort to be made before time runs out. Michael Ignatieff warns us that

> the allegiances that make the human world human must be beaten into our heads. We never know a thing till we have paid to know it, never know how much is enough until we have had much less than enough, never know what we need till we have been dispossessed. . . . Our education in the art of necessity cannot avoid tragedy.[13]

But how much tragedy can be endured in our nation and our world before we reach a point of no return? Being beaten over the head can awaken one; it can also make one senseless. If all those not yet too seriously diminished by the callous social institutions of capitalism must be so afflicted before suitable steps are taken to regain our dwindling humanity, we may have to pass through disasters amounting to the social equivalent of Hiroshima. We cannot take that chance, for neither the people nor the earth can afford much more damage.

In the United States one should not need to be told these things; only to be reminded of them. It would be hard to find a society in which people's shame is greater over their poverty, unemployment, hunger, poor housing, or homelessness, even over their old age, disability, and illness; or one in which the attitude of those who are not in basic need toward those who are is more scornful, insulting, hateful, and—as well it might be—fearful. Nor is it even grimly satisfying to note that many who were recently in the scorning category have found themselves placed by unemployment (or "downsized" jobs) among the scorned, standing in the lines for assistance where now it is *their* dignity that is shredded.[14]

iv.

We Can Get There from Here

A great paradox of our society is the almost palpable social despair of most of the people you and I know and believe we know about; side by side with that, however, exist literally thousands of groups over the land that are fighting for policies that harmonize with our own felt needs and hopes (and against those that don't). Complicating the puzzle is that many of us know of those ongoing efforts, having learned it from our own participation in such groups, from friends and acquaintances, from the periodicals we read, from occasional mainstream news stories.

Doubtless a full explanation of the paradox would have several dimensions to it; surely at their center is the political crux of what it means to be an "American": individualism taken so far as to virtually obliterate solidarity. That stance is the product and residue of a socialization process teaching us that our own efforts in an effectively business society will suffice to carry us toward the good life—if, that is, we are worthy. In the same process, we have learned not to trust others (nor ourselves?), not to see others as being in the same boat as ours (and even less often, ourselves as being in theirs), except as competitors for space.

Principles. What we seek to achieve should be compatible with the main foundations of the "American dream," because that dream is in our bones and is largely valuable in itself—and also to remind ourselves of how far we have strayed from what has been precious in our society.

Our aim should be one of continuous evolution toward and the maximum feasible practice at all times of economic, political, and social *democracy*, social *equality*, personal *freedom*, and *peace*. And though it must start with the focus on our here and now, it can neither succeed nor endure if "our" means only the people of the United States and the other rich countries, or pays insufficient attention to the social and physical environment that will—or will not—sustain us through time.

Much of that is very familiar, to be sure; but too often as empty or even deliberately deceitful rhetoric. If such principles are to be more than rhetoric, and such aims to be realizable, we must also take explicit account of what needs to be offset and undone: economic and political oligarchy, institutionalized racism and sexism, numerous de facto and legal constraints on the freedom of individuals to live as they choose even when such freedom would be harmless to others, the leukemia of militarism and violence in our system, the continuing violation of the land and the peoples of the "periphery" and of the planet itself—and a broad range of encrusted and supportive attitudes toward all these matters.

Necessary for and contributing to the realization of democracy, equality, and freedom is the maximum *decentralization* of power in the economy and in government, and a connected maximum *debureaucratization* of all functions, not just in the obvious areas of economy and government, but also in education, health care, and in the informational, entertainment, and cultural functions of the media. Living in a consumeristic and oligarchic society, we have become the passive users instead of the active producers of our own lives.

Structures. This takes us to the next area, ground partially covered earlier, where recommended policies were seen as implying changes in the structures of production, jobs, education, consumption, income, wealth, and power, all of which are in continuous and dynamic interaction. Each structure must be changed substantially and qualitatively, but none can be without concomitant changes in all the others. Furthermore, although the foregoing refer most directly to structures of the economy, they of course intermingle with and act to shape political, social, and cultural processes and relationships.

A sustained generalization in these respects may be useful to support the point. What is produced, and by whom, and how, is also the principal set of determinants of what and how much can be consumed, and by whom; in turn, that is all directly and indirectly set by those with the wealth and the connected power to make decisions. Their decisions have led to a structure of production in which we produce too many of certain commodities and services and too few of others—too many automobiles and guns, not enough mass transit facilities and housing; too many advertising, financial, and military services and too few health and educational services.

All this is reflected in the occupational structure. In addition to those who labor at producing commodities that do not satisfy real needs and cannot satisfy created wants, there are many millions of able-bodied people who either don't work at all, don't work full time, or who work at socially useless, trivial, or distasteful occupations. Almost all such people could and would give their energy to full-time and meaningful work if available, which, as noted earlier, would greatly expand the national income in terms of needed and desired goods and services and more than "pay for itself."

Engraved on my memory, in this respect, is a news item from the 1954 recession. A roving reporter developing a story about the recession for (as I remember) the *New York Times* asked people in the street about their status, their attitudes, etc. A man interviewed in Harlem, middle-aged and black and unemployed, said he just couldn't understand why all this was happening: "Before I came here," he said, "I used to do building work in the little town I grew up in, and I could do it now. But I can't get into the union, there aren't any houses or apartments going up, and I live in a dump. It seems to me that some apartments could be built hiring people like me and others to build them, and some of us could live in them and pay the rent with our wages." And to think they let crazy people like that run loose in the streets!

Our business community has long seen its system as the most efficient possible, and has taken credit for having made it so. It is, rather, a system that has used much of its ingenuity in finding ways to waste—deliberate obsolence of products and restricted output in industry and agriculture, powerful support of military expenditures (the most wasteful of all), bloated, highly-paid and unproductive financial and advertising sectors, counterproductive bureaucracies, and much resource-expensive, unsatisfying, and unnecessary consumption—for which that same business community (and its supporters) must also take the "credit." [15]

The point of all the foregoing is to reveal how much flexibility for desirable change exists in the economy. And it is a way of underscoring that qualitative change (socioeconomic development) rather than quantitative change (economic growth) is the best solution to our economic and social needs. This is not an argument against growth as such, but against growth for its own sake, growth no matter what: the worship of growth.

But significant structural alterations in the economy are impossible so long as decision-making processes are totally in the hands of (or acquiescent to) those who control and benefit from the existing patterns of production, consumption, income, and wealth: the hidden bottom of the iceberg that sinks liberal reforms. It will continue to do so until the majority of our people organize and activate themselves—and in doing so change the structure of power. Which takes us to our politics.

Politics. The United States never became the small-holders' democracy of Jefferson's dream (even setting aside slavery), but its power structure was considerably less concentrated for most of the nineteenth century than it has been since, say, the 1890s. The processes of ever-increasing concentration moved synchronously with industrialization and its inexorable domination by big business. "Plutocracy" began to vie with "democracy" in the same process, and won big: how much was controlled and by how few a century ago, a half century ago, pale by comparison with now—how much wealth, income, and power—how much power, mind, not just over the economy, but the entire social process.

Neither the Democrats nor the Republicans have ever wavered in their support of capitalism, of course; but there have been times when that support was mixed in with some concern for the needs and possibilities of (what Veblen called) "the underlying population," with now and then a gadfly causing a social itch. No longer, of course; now we are faced with two parties arguing essentially about which of their respective social ruination programs can do the job most efficiently—or rather, most cheaply.

This does not mean there are no differences between the two parties, that they can or should be ignored; especially it does not mean that in local and state elections. But it does mean that something more than politicking for or against a particular Democrat or Republican is essential. Does *that* mean a third party?

v.

Of Two Alternatives, Take the Third

I cannot fully make up my own mind yet, but I am sure that the matter is worth discussing and, probably, trying—for all its difficulties and perils (and I am working with more than one of the groups). After all, think of the difficulties and perils of going on as now? Herewith, first, a few considerations that make a third party seem worth doing.

A long-time friend whose judgment I respect responded recently to the notion of a third party by saying "OK, as a tactic, but not as a strategy." We didn't have time to talk it out, but I took it that he meant such a party's existence and work could constitute a threat sufficient to make GOP and (more likely) Democratic candidates take somewhat better positions.

I think that's wrong. Unless a third party takes itself seriously—as a strategic development with the indefinite future as its horizon—it won't be taken seriously by others. However, I also think that to be taken seriously by its followers as well as by its opponents it has to recognize its limits, and therefore its possibilities; and know that both evolve over time—for the better, if the party is, so to speak, "behaving itself."

One frequent form of misbehavior of such parties—with which I have had some experience, as noted earlier—is to be indiscriminately electoral in orientation: at the extreme of such foolishness, to field a candidate for the presidency. Voters should not be too easily convinced that they are "throwing their vote away." To know you're going to lose should not exclude any particular effort; but when the effort appears as ludicrous: no. ("Been there, done that," I am able to say. See the earlier Story on the '68 election, and my third party candidacy.)

One important reason for developing a third party—always with some combination of patience and impatience—has to do with the virtual absence of sustained political work in this country, except by the pros of the two parties. Having our own party would provide both the need and the opportunity for getting the habits and doing the work that constitutes being a political being—for the "institutionalization" of our efforts.

Another good reason is that it is considerably easier to work for a broad program within a party than on separate issues, when each group is usually seeking temporary coalitions (often with its own agenda mostly or entirely in mind—and obviously so). Rather than working on separate issues for a particular group being the best way to succeed, it is almost always the assured way to fail—in reality if not in appearance.

Part of the problem: in only a small minority of states is there anything like a good possibility of creating a viable third party—a few in the northeast (New York, New Jersey, Pennsylvania, Massachusetts, maybe Vermont and Maine); in the midwestern states of Michigan, Wisconsin, Minnesota, Illinois, and perhaps Ohio; and in Hawaii, California, Oregon, and Washington—perhaps New Mexico and Colorado? Ten to fifteen out of fifty.

Doesn't sound like much, not if you're thinking of the White House or the Senate. But it could have a spreading and lasting educational effect on realities and possibilities in those states and, not too long after, in many others; soon it could have a meaningful effect on elections for city and state offices, referenda, and the like. If I were in either of the major parties, it would make me stop and think: especially with the Perots and Powells running on and off the stage. As for me—and I hope you—I would find it a welcome change from sitting around and, as my mother used to say, *kvetching*.

This has been my roundabout way of saying that I don't think of a third party as a tactic but as a strategy; or, better, as a lifelong effort—win, lose, or draw. So do an interesting number of others, these days: the Greens, the Labor Party, the National Committee for Independent Political Action, Democratic Socialists of America and the New Party, among others. [16]

vi.

Now or Never?

There is something to be learned from Germany—which, it needs reminding, was seen in the mid-1920s as the peak of Western Civilization, drawing to it the world's scientists, writers, artists, students of politics and economic organization, and more. Within less than a decade, Germany had become ineffably monstrous, history's pit.

Nowadays we seem to be accelerating toward a society that a mere generation ago most of us would have thought loathsome and dangerous: "two nations"—one seeking to fight off racism and poverty and prejudice and repression, the other, indifferent to or complicit in all that, some of it rolling in money some of it not, all motivated by fear and scorn and hate and ignorance and greed. As both those "nations" grow, the social space between them shrinks.

The Germany of the 1920s and early 1930s had many more differences than similarities with the United States of the recent past and present. But like us now, it was divided and dividing, and its political center was eroding swiftly. At the heart of that, Germany's split was a struggle between left and right, its origins in the conflict between labor and capital. But as the Twenties drew to a close, what was taking on the signs of a civil war had been successfully submerged by the ultimate winners in a froth of nationalistic vanity and anger, mixed in with whipped-up hatred against Jews, Gypsies, and gay men and women. As the 1930s opened, support for Hitler grew rapidly, even among workers; while always smaller numbers—workers, artists, people of all types—soon outlawed politically, undertook and endured the dangers of resistance.

Those upon whom I wish to focus were in neither of those solidifying groups; rather they were the many millions—very probably the majority of the population in the early stages—who feared or disliked the trends and the unfolding realities of what became the Third Reich but who stood by, watching, waiting, and hoping for the best. They came to be called "The Good Germans."

One can perhaps understand those who supported Nazism, while also despising them;[17] and one can understand and admire those who sought to stop the madness. The critically most important group, however, ultimately despicable but never admirable, was that of those "Good Germans." Their numbers were very large in, say, 1928, but unknowably smaller by 1938, the tidal wave of fascism having drowned whatever doubts they may once have had the good sense and decency to hold. The Good Germans were crucial not just in Nazism's triumph, but in the unspeakable depths of its policies. Had their silence found a voice early on and taken them to politics, history could have taken a different turn; it couldn't have been a turn for the worse.

The class conflict that shook Germany in the 1920s will not occur here (however much it might be warranted); but each year that passes makes terrifying racial conflicts in the United States always more probable—whose path, whose resolution, whose consequences, one shudders to ponder.

Recent, current, and likely policies have done and will do nothing to mitigate and much to exacerbate the causes of such conflict, from any and all standpoints. We do not have to match Nazi Germany to create our own version of Hell on earth. Those of us who dislike and fear what is happening to the United States—and who want very much to see our country alter its direction for the better—cannot permit ourselves to enter the history books as "The Good Americans."

In the midst of World War II, when I was on R&R in Sydney, I was given a book of poems by my friend Carl (he who had persuaded me to go AWOL for a few weeks). It included W.H. Auden's "September 1, 1939." I was much affected by it then; unfortunately, it resonates still:

> All I have is a voice
> To undo the folded lie,
> The romantic lie in the brain
> Of the sensual man-in-the-street
> And the lie of Authority
> Whose buildings grope the sky:
> There is no such thing as the State
> And no one exists alone;
> Hunger allows no choice
> To the citizen or the police;
> We must love one another or die.

Defenceless under the night
Our world in stupor lies;
Yet, dotted everywhere,
Ironic points of light
Flash out wherever the Just
Exchange their messages:
May I, composed like them
Of Eros and of dust,
Beleaguered by the same
Negation and despair,
Show an affirming flame. [18]

Auden did not of course believe that loving one another would make us immortal; he did believe that if we do not we lose our humanity. Then nothing separates us from the beasts, except that they are less adept at killing and neglecting their own than we. Our "own" is our species. But have we not come to feel that our "own," except for wars and athletic events, is our family (if that), plus a few friends (and not always them)? That is more than just a socially dangerous stance; it is one of self-deprivation.

On the way to becoming an old geezer I have in one degree or another come to know innumerable people of very different persuasions and character—in school, in business, in the army, in the university, in politics, and in my smaller personal and family circles. What is interesting and relevant is how many I have known and barely liked but with whom I could work usefully and well—in the war, at my jobs, and in my political efforts, for example. Very important in my memory is how much change I saw in the young and in the older (and, of course, in myself) as they and I learned, worked on our jobs, worked at politics—and as we participated in shaping, not just accepting, our lives.

In the sense in which Auden meant the word, I "loved" them: that is, I came at least partially to understand them, to be concerned for them, to care for them—and, sometimes, to like and, for a splendid few, even to *love* them. I came to see my life intertwined with, in important ways interdependent with, theirs, as we all were learning to do regarding unknown others—others whom, in that same sense, we learned to love. [19]

Over time, with a little help from books, friends, and life, I have come to know that the interdependence exists on a global scale; have found that working with others to keep hell away from the door (and let a bit of heaven in) is an expansion of the good life.

It would be wonderful indeed if the efforts of all of us—everywhere and always—would achieve our goals, or even move us noticeably closer to them: but that cannot be the *condition* for political effort. After a long political life, in fact I can remember no clear instance of a *lasting* political success, though I could note many clear failures. We have been taught to believe that what makes efforts worthwhile is the success that sits at the end of the road, that all else is sacrifice. But none of the many people I have worked with politically—including those who have gone to prison as a consequence—has ever seen those acts as sacrifices; all would do it again.[20]

One of the epigrams that came out of the American Revolution was "it's better to die on your feet than live on your knees." The political work we all can and must do does not require our deaths; but not doing it does rob us of our lives.

That's the way it is. To do nothing is to be a spectator of the continuing disappearance of "America." To learn and unlearn as we must and can, and to put our minds and energies and hearts into staving off the dark and letting in some light gives our society and ourselves the chance and the right to live up to our uncommon possibilities.

NOTES

PREFACE AND ACKNOWLEDGMENTS

1. By the British writer Penelope Lively.
2. See Andrew Hacker, *Two Nations: Black and White, Separate, Hostile, Unequal* (New York: Macmillan, 1992), and, more briefly, on the vital role of racism in our politics, Thomas Byrne and Mary D. Edsall, "Race," in *The Atlantic Monthly* 267, No. 5 (May 1991). Also see my 1967 article "America Fouls Its Dream," *The Nation*, 13 February 1967. Unhappily, to the degree my argument was applicable then, it is even more so now.
3. Also see William Manchester, *The Glory and the Dream: A Narrative History of America, 1932-1972* (Boston: Little, Brown, 1974). Most recently, and in considerably greater detail, David Halberstam has done something of the sort in *The Fifties* (New York: Villard Books, 1993).

PROLOGUE

1. The poem is entitled "The Second Coming." It may be found in many collections including Richard Ellmann and Robert O'Clair, eds., *The Norton Anthology of Modern Poetry*, 2d ed. (New York: W.W. Norton and Co., 1988).
2. From *Paradise Lost*.
3. The most searching and illuminating historical study of this process of commodification is Karl Polanyi, *The Great Transformation* (New York: Holt, Rinehart and Winston, 1944), a book whose value rises as the market "ethic" continues its spread.
4. In 1986 UNICEF estimated that 40,000 children were dying *every day* from malnutrition-related diseases. In 1993 the UN estimated that over 700 million people in the world are subject to famine, and that 2 billion or more are malnourished. And such conditions worsen steadily.
5. *An Inquiry into the Nature and Causes of the Wealth of Nations* (London: McCulloch Edition, 1869; originally 1776), p. 215.
6. William Blake (1757-1827)—poet, artist, engraver—celebrated life lustily, and attacked evil in the same manner. For Bentham's remarks on the newly achieved usefulness of children, see W. Stark, ed., *Jeremy Bentham's Economic Writings* (London: Allen & Unwin, 1954).

7. See Ronald Wright, *Stolen Continents: The Americas Through Indian Eyes Since 1492* (Boston: Houghton Mifflin, 1992), which studies what happened to just three groups (the Maya, the Aztec, and the Cherokee)—first in the early days of their colonialization, and then in the very recent past. Also, Noam Chomsky, *Year 501: The Conquest Continues* (Boston: South End Press, 1993), which takes us from Columbus to our own time, from the Spanish to ourselves, from this to the other hemisphere.

8. Jerry Mander, *In the Absence of the Sacred: The Failure of Technology & the Survival of the Indian Nations* (San Francisco: Sierra Club Books, 1992).

9. See E.J. Hobsbawm, *Nations and Nationalism Since 1780: Programme, Myth, Reality* (Cambridge: Cambridge University Press, 1990).

10. Maurice Dobb, *Political Economy and Capitalism* (London: Routledge, 1937), pp. 239-40. Also, more thoroughly in Tom Kemp, *Theories of Imperialism* (London: Dobson, 1967).

11. John Maynard Keynes, *The Economic Consequences of the Peace* (London: Macmillan, 1921), pp. 6-7.

12. See Paul Fussell, *The Great War and Modern Memory* (London: Oxford University Press, 1975). Also see two novels: Erich Maria Remarque, *All Quiet on the Western Front*, and *The Enormous Room* by the poet e.e. cummings.

CHAPTER 1 PROSPERITY AND ALL THAT JAZZ, AND INTO THE BLACK HOLE: 1920-1930

1. The story of Cleophas Dowd is to be found in two books: Bruce Chatwin, *In Patagonia* (New York: Summit Books, 1977), p. 44 ff., and in the book by, of all people, Robert Redford, *The Outlaw Trail* (New York: Grosset & Dunlap, 1978). On the unnecessary Irish famine, see Cecil Woodham-Smith, *The Great Hunger: Ireland, 1845-1849* (New York: Harper & Row, 1962).

2. That was a song that became very popular in the United States as World War I ended (and I began). It was in the films "For Me and My Gal" and "The Eddie Cantor Story." Written in 1919 by Sam M. Lewis and Joe Young, music by Walter Donaldson.

3. Two invaluable economic histories of the interwar years in the United States: George Soule, *Prosperity Decade: From War to Depression, 1917-1929,* and Broadus Mitchell, *Depression Decade: From New Era Through New Deal, 1919-1941* (New York: Holt, Rinehart and Winston, both 1947. Republished in paperback by M.E. Sharpe, Armonk, NY, 1993).

4. Thorstein Veblen, *The Higher Learning in America: A Memorandum on the Conduct of Universities by Businessmen* (New York: B.W. Huebsch, 1918), pp. 135-36. His original subtitle, disallowed by the publisher, was "A Study in Total Depravity." For Veblen, the most precious characteristic of our species is what he called our "idle curiosity," the basis for science, the arts, technology, and of all learning, whose principal seedbed is the university.

5. The relationship between mass production and mass consumption is one of several that constitute what has come to be called the "new productive forces"—in effect a third "industrial revolution"—that emerged early in this century and which required, if those forces were to contribute to increased well-being rather than disaster, a complex of socioeconomic changes that did not evolve until some years after World War II. The failure of those changes to take shape earlier was one of

the decisive factors causing the Great War and the ensuing decades of chaos and convulsion. Only in the United States, in the 1920s, were some—but by no means all—of the necessary steps achieved.

6. See Stuart Ewen, *Advertising and the Social Roots of the Consumer Culture* (New York: McGraw-Hill, 1976). For the larger historical background and social consequences for the United States see David M. Potter, *People of Plenty* (Chicago: University of Chicago Press, 1958). See also the memoirs of the acknowledged single most important creator of the technique of business propaganda in the 1920s and 1930s, Edward L. Bernays, *Public Relations* (Norman, OK: University of Oklahoma Press, 1952). Bernays's uncle was Sigmund Freud. Bernays died in 1995 at the age of 103.

7. For illumination on this (and similar) matters, see E.J. Hobsbawm, *Primitive Rebels: Studies in Archaic Forms of Social Movement in the 19th and 20th Centuries* (New York: W.W. Norton & Co., 1959), chap. 3 ("Mafia").

8. That is, Charles A. Lindbergh. He was not the first to fly the Atlantic, though he was the first to go solo. His luster was substantially dimmed in the 1930s when he seemed to be flirting with fascist Germany.

9. One of Sinclair Lewis's finest novels, which may be read as a synthesis of Billy and Aimee, is *Elmer Gantry.*

10. The quotations are from a very long article by Frankfurter in *The Atlantic Monthly,* March 1927, "The Case of Sacco and Vanzetti," part of which is reproduced as "The Crime of Radicalism" in Loren Baritz (ed.), *The Culture of the Twenties* (New York: Bobbs-Merrill, 1977), pp. 110-36.

11. Philip Strong, of the North American Newspaper Alliance, who interviewed Sacco and Vanzetti in the Dedham jail after the death sentence, later admitted in a letter to Upton Sinclair that "it was out of the question to take notes": "[Strong] said he got 'a bit more oratorical' than Vanzetti in reconstructing the conversation and had made up the phrase about the 'lives of a good shoemaker and a poor fish peddler.'" See Roberta Strauss Feuerlicht, *Justice Crucified: The Story of Sacco and Vanzetti* (New York: McGraw-Hill, 1977), pp. 344-45.

12. See Dudley Dillard, *Economic Development of the North Atlantic Community* (Englewood Cliffs, NJ: Prentice-Hall, 1967). Also Alfred E. Kahn, *Great Britain in the World Economy* (New York: NYU Press, 1946) and Richard Du Boff, *Accumulation and Power: An Economic History of the United States* (Armonk, NY: M.E. Sharpe, 1989), including its comprehensive references.

13. Harold U. Faulkner, *The Decline of Laissez-Faire, 1897-1917* (New York: Holt, Rinehart and Winston, 1947; republished by M.E. Sharpe, 1993), pp. 31-32.

14. See Paul Baran and Paul Sweezy, *Monopoly Capital* (New York: Monthly Review Press, 1966), pp. 228 ff.

15. See Du Boff, *Accumulation and Power* for details.

16. It was in 1928 that Hoover, so staunchly free market and anti-governmental intervention, presided over the creation of the first price support program in our history. It was in farming, of course, which had become the first populous (but no longer "populist") economic pressure group, in clamorous reaction to excess farm productive capacity, falling world markets, and consequent falling prices. The Federal Farm Board collapsed after 1929, unable to go on buying the ever-rising output of farmers, encouraged by a legislated profitable price.

17. Herman P. Miller, *Rich Man, Poor Man* (New York: Crowell, 1971), p. 29. At the time he wrote the book, Miller had been working on such matters for the U.S. Bureau of the Census for over thirty years. Du Boff, op. cit., p. 87, provides

different but compatible data when (quoting a Brookings Institution study of 1934) he states that in 1929, 12 million families (40 percent of the population) had incomes below $1,500, at a time when $2,000 was "sufficient only to supply basic necessities."

18. If one has been seeking work so long as finally to give up, one is jobless but not "unemployed"; npr does the "unemployed" category apply if one has a part-time (even an hour a *week)* job, but wants (and needs and formerly had) a full-time job. An example of what that meant sixty years later: in March 1993, when the official rate was 7 percent (about 9 million people), if one added the "hard-core" and involuntarily part-time out of work, the number of unemployed was 16 million—close to double the official number. It was not until the depression began that systematic attempts to gather and analyze aggregative data (jobs, investment, consumption, savings, etc.) were institutionalized: why bother, if there couldn't *be* a depression?

19. Unemployment in the 1920s had a harsher meaning than it has today, harsh though it remains: in those years there was very little in the nature of a "safety net" to break the fall into joblessness—no unemployment compensation, no social security system or Medicare or Medicaid, no foodstamps, no meaningful welfare programs. In the major cities—New York, Chicago, St. Louis, San Francisco, Pittsburgh, etc.—the various political "machines" in effect traded some minimal support (in dollars or in kind) for votes, but it was sporadic at best, and minimal indeed. The "homeless" and long lines of people hoping for food were common in the Twenties, and considerably more so in the Thirties. The kinds of cardboard shacks (and the like) now so easy and awful to see in all the major cities of the United States could be seen in San Francisco when I was a boy, especially after 1929; they came to be called "Hoovervilles."

20. See Soule, *Prosperity Decade,* p. 286, and Du Boff, op. cit.

21. Quoted in Andrew Hacker, *Two Nations: Black and White, Separate, Hostile, and Unequal* (New York: Macmillan, 1992), p. vii. Benjamin Disraeli was Prime Minister under Victoria, and an "enlightened conservative."

22. This was the title of a book by Henry George, published in the years 1877-79, that became influential in the early years of this century and continues to be so, although among a dwindling number.

23. The society that requires millions of its children to live as heroes will never be able to build enough prisons to hold those who cannot. For the many who are unclear as to just how heroic such young people must be in our day, it would be chastening to read "Children of the Shadows," a remarkable series published in the *New York Times,* 4-25 April 1993.

24. See Amartya Sen, *Poverty and Famine: An Essay on Entitlement and Deprivation* (Oxford: Clarendon Press, 1981), where he shows that "Starvation is the characteristic of some people not *having* enough food to eat. It is not the characteristic of there *being* not enough food to eat." (p. 1)

25. And in late twentieth century industrial capitalism it has become both necessary and possible for the system's and the enterprises' appetites to be internalized and acted upon by the population: one of the larger meanings of "consumerism." All the population has learned the desire to "shop 'til you drop," as the saying now goes; but that the largest part of the population has increasing difficulty in mustering the purchasing power and credit to do so greatly adds to the instabili-

ties of contemporary society. Indeed, the very high percentages of families with two wage-earners (virtually unique to the United States) has changed to include 7 million families with *three* wages: two by the wife and one by the husband, or vice versa, the numbers rising rapidly, fueled by need more than by greed.

26. See W. Arthur Lewis, *Economic Survey, 1919-1939* (London: Allen & Unwin, 1949). As the title shows, the author takes the entire interwar period as his focus, not just the 1920s.

27. Production for profit remains the hallmark of capitalist economies, of course; but since World War II a substantial percentage of goods and services—profitable though their "production" may be—are produced for uses generated in social (including military) policies.

28. Du Boff, op. cit., p. 87. "Disposable personal income" is the best measure of purchasing power; the $10,000 figure in today's dollars would be equal to a minimum of ten times that.

29. For an excellent history and analysis, see David J. Ravenscraft and F.M. Scherer, *Mergers, Sell-Offs and Economic Efficiency* (Washington, DC: Brookings Institution, 1987).

30. See Paul M. Sweezy, "Cars and Cities," *Monthly Review,* April 1973.

31. In recent years, fleet buyers (for rental cars, taxis, governments, etc.) have become quite important; but that was not yet so in the 1920s.

32. Soule, *Prosperity Decade,* p. 288.

33. See John Kenneth Galbraith, *The Great Crash: 1929* (Boston: Houghton Mifflin, 1955).

34. In addition to the stock market's importance being much over-rated then and now, it has never been a reliable gauge to the path of the economy; if anything, quite the contrary. If one were to chart the "Dow Jones index" of leading industrials on a daily basis for, say, three months, it would be seen that the index is going up when the economy is entering trouble just as or more often as it is going in the same direction as the economy.

35. In the late 1920s, as again in the 1980s, as real private net investment—expanded productive capacity and residential and commercial construction—fell off, financial speculation *took* off.

36. Buying on margin meant making a down payment when stocks were purchased, a payment financed usually by borrowing. The loan had to be repaid, of course, the hopeful expectation that it would be easy to do so out of the rise in share prices—the shares themselves having to be fully paid at some specified date. When the market falls instead, and the margin buyer must repay the loan, he and the creditor bank are both in trouble; and when such behavior is the rule rather than the exception, as it was in the 1920s (with even banks buying stocks on the margin), disaster lurked around the corner. Since the banking and securities markets reforms of the 1930s and subsequently, such behavior has been somewhat constrained. One of the aims of the Reagan years was to undo those constraints, most disastrously (up to now) in the deregulation that, along with a large number of crooked types, created the S&L calamity: "All in all," Reagan exulted as he signed the Garn-St.Germain bill opening wide the gates for the criminalizing of the thrift industry, "I think we've hit the jackpot." Stephen Pizzo, et al., *Inside Job: The Looting of America's Savings & Loans* (New York: McGraw-Hill, 1989), p. 12.

37. In other words, two to three years passed before what had occurred was recognized as such. Robert A. Gordon, *Economic Instability and Growth: The American Record* (New York: Harper & Row, 1974), pp. 49-52.

CHAPTER 2 DEATH, DESTRUCTION, AND DELIVERANCE: 1930-1945

1. The title of a book by Studs Terkel which contains more than 200 interviews of people who lived through the depression, some of their children, and others (New York: Avon Books, 1971).
2. W. Arthur Lewis, *Economic Survey*, p. 52.
3. That large a drop is unimaginable for people who came to adulthood after World War II. Though there have been at least ten recessions since the close of the war, industrial production declines have exceeded 10 percent only four times, and never reached 15 percent.
4. Germany was the "decadent" society par excellence of the 1920s, and there was plenty of competition for that honor in the USA and Europe—in its pop and not so pop culture (see Grosz, Brecht, Weill, and films such as "The Blue Angel")—and in its politics. It was an "overripe" society and generally seen as so. The easiest and pleasantest way to confirm this is to see the U.S. film "Cabaret," based on Isherwood's *Berlin Stories* and the play derived from them, *I Am A Camera*, as the '20s ended. That Germany was also seen as the center of engineering and science *and* culturally most dynamic only underscored the decadence.
5. The best and first book in English on the rise and nature of Nazism is Robert A. Brady, *The Spirit and Structure of German Fascism* (New York: Viking, 1937). Also see my memoir concerning Brady (with whom I studied at Berkeley), "Against Decadence: The Work of Robert A. Brady, 1901-63," in *Journal of Economic Issues*, December 1994.
6. See Alexander Gerschenkron, *Bread and Democracy in Germany* (Berkeley: University of California Press, 1943) and Erich Fromm, *Escape from Freedom* (New York: Rinehart, 1941).
7. See *The John McPhee Reader* (New York: Farrar, Straus and Giroux, 1976), edited by William L. Howarth, p. 5, for a 1960s essay on Bill Bradley, then a Knicks superstar (now U.S. Senator from New Jersey): "Bradley is not an innovator. Actually basketball has had only a few innovators in its history—players like Hank Luisetti, of Stanford, whose introduction in 1936 of the running one-hander did as much to open up the game for scoring as the forward pass did for football. . . ." Sorry, Mr. McPhee, Hank began to do that in 1934, at Galileo High, and we watched in amazement as it happened.
8. The late E.Y. (Yip) Harburg, composer of the song lyrics, as quoted in Terkel's *Hard Times*, cited earlier, pp. 35-36. Harburg also did the songs for "Finian's Rainbow" and "The Wizard of Oz," among other musical comedies and films.
9. Donald Streever, "Capacity Utilization and Business Investment," University of Illinois Bulletin 57, no. 55 (March 1960): 65, quoted in Baran and Sweezy, *Monopoly Capital*, p. 242. Unemployment data are from *Historical Statistics of the United States (HSUS)*, part 1, p. 135.
10. These data and others like them are taken from *HSUS*, the annual *Economic Report of the President* (Washington, DC: various years), and Broadus Mitchell, *Depression Decade*, pp. 428-48.
11. See Mitchell, op. cit., p. 231.

12. There were shenanigans of one sort or another in all of that, of course, but they did not rival the larger and more costly "shenanigans" of, say, the "military-industrial complex" of ongoing importance: no PWA worker ever used a $1,500 screwdriver; no WPA employee ever had a $700 toilet seat to sit on. Of which, more in later pages.

13. As was noted in Chapter 1, the farmers of "the family-size farm" were falling into deep troubles already in the 1920s, a period of presumed prosperity. When, on top of that, the depression hit, farmers found themselves under the assault of universal excess capacity, sharply falling prices (on the average, a 50 percent fall, 1929-1933), and foreclosures. And then the Dust Bowl: decades of cultivating lands in the middle states (running all the way north from Texas to Canada, and those surrounding them to the east and west) instead of using them for grazing. The result was disaster compounding disaster, as topsoil turned to dust and was simply blown away. Two extraordinary books of photographs and text keep that catastrophe vividly alive: Dorothea Lange and Paul S. Taylor, *American Exodus* (New York: Knopf, 1939) and Erskine Caldwell and Margaret Bourke-White, *You Have Seen Their Faces* (New York: Viking, 1937). And of course there are John Steinbeck's novel, *The Grapes of Wrath* (New York: Viking, 1939) and the study by Carey McWilliams, *Factories in the Field: The Story of Migratory Farm Labor in California* (Boston: Little, Brown & Co, 1939).

14. I place quote marks around "guaranteeing" because there were no provisions whatsoever for enforcing that right of labor. The key provision of the subsequent National Labor Relations Act (NLRA) of 1935 (the "Wagner Act") was that it provided for a National Labor Relations Board (NLRB) whose function is to provide for enforcement, and for punishments when employers violated the law.

15. Clifford Odets's first play, and the only one of the "agitprop" variety. See *Six Plays of Clifford Odets* (New York: Grove Press, 1979), with a useful introduction by his original director (and theater critic) Harold Clurman.

16. In July and August 1933 "nearly ninety-five percent of the longshoremen in San Francisco joined the International Longshoremen's Union." Jeremy Brecher, *Strike!* (Boston: South End Press, 1972), p. 150. Workers had to show up every morning at 6 a.m. on the Embarcadero (the waterfront) for the shape-up, which they saw as "their greatest grievance."

17. See Charles P. Larrowe, *Harry Bridges: The Rise and Fall of Radical Labor in the U.S.* (New York: Lawrence Hill & Co., 1972).

18. In addition to Brecher, *Strike!,* I have relied upon the excellent book by Irving Bernstein, *Turbulent Years: A History of the American Worker, 1933-1941* (Boston: Houghton Mifflin, 1971), pp. 252 ff., for some of the material on Bridges and on the strike of 1934.

19. It is of interest that the first five times, the instigating party was the Waterfront Employers' Assocation, using the Immigration and Naturalization Service (INS) as its agency and (subsequent sworn testimony showed) hiring paid informers to suborn themselves. When, after World War II and in the midst of the Cold War, Bridges was for the sixth and last time accused of Communist Party membership (notwithstanding the acquittal by the Supreme Court in 1945), it was the government that was the instigator, and the Waterfront Employers, having found the ILWU to be a stabilizing influence on the docks, that sought to avert the trial.

20. Brecher, op. cit., p. 151.

21. The description of the procession is that of the novelist Charles G. Norris, as quoted in Bernstein, op. cit, p. 281.

22. Bernstein, p. 516. (The "Cheka" was the secret police of Czarist Russia.) As for profits: "It had made money in every year since 1921, including 1932. In the worst years of the depression, when the losses of other motor companies were subtracted, it accounted for more than 100 per cent of the industry's earnings, and in 1937 its share was 78 per cent (and its net profit $196 million). Its rate of return on net capital investment over an eighteen-year period, including the early thirties, was 18 per cent" (ibid.) Not satisfied with this performance, in 1935, GM—like so many other companies in that period (and since)—initiated a speed-up, in an industry where workers were already working at literally maddening rates of speed. The basic book on the GM strike is Sidney Fine, *Sit-Down, the General Motors Strike of 1936-1937* (Ann Arbor: University of Michigan Press, 1969).

23. Fine, *Sit-Down*, op. cit., p. 75. Also see Harvey Swados's illuminating short stories about the kinds of lives led by those who are chained to an assembly line: *On the Line* (Boston: Little, Brown, 1937).

24. See Bernstein, op. cit., pp. 528-51, not only for the ins and outs of the conflict, but also for the manner in which FDR, Secretary of Labor Perkins, John L. Lewis of the CIO, and Governor Frank Murphy (later Supreme Court Justice) behaved: an interesting "civics lesson."

25. The victory over GM did not imply an automatic victory over Ford by the UAW. For the gangster tactics of Ford Company's "Industrial Relations Department" (under the leadership of ex-pug Harry Bennett), see Keith Sward, *The Legend of Henry Ford* (New York: Holt, Rinehart and Winston, 1948).

26. See Bernstein, pp. 479-98.

27. Bernstein, pp. 488-89. It was a massacre committed by brutes, and it was not reported that way by the press.

28. Ernest Hemingway's tale of the Spanish Civil War. For a less romantic view see Ramon Sender's novel, *Seven Red Sundays* (New York: Collier Books, 1961; originally 1936).

29. See George Orwell, *Homage to Catalonia* (New York: Harcourt, Brace and World, 1952) and Andre Malraux, *Man's Hope* (New York: Random House, 1938).

30. *The American Earthquake* (New York: Octagon Books, 1958, 1971), p. 569.

31. That figure is considerably higher than for World War I, when about 250,000 U.S. soldiers were killed.

32. Paul Kennedy, *The Rise and Fall of the Great Powers* (New York: Vintage, 1989), pp. 361-62. If anything, and monstrous though the figures are, they are probably an understatement. For example, Gregory Frumkin, in *Population Changes in Europe Since 1939* (Geneva: United Nations, 1951), estimates that 28 million were lost in the Soviet Union during the war.

33. Samuel Eliot Morison, *The Oxford History of the American People*, vol. 3 (New York: New American Library/Mentor, 1965), p. 342.

34. Still described as "a sneak attack," as though a proper antagonist would have provided ample warning.

35. For the nature and the strength of opposition to U.S. participation in the European (or Asian) war, see Selig Adler, *The Isolationist Impulse* (New York: The Free Press, 1957).

36. A week earlier, on August 23, 1939, Ribbentrop and Molotov had signed the Nazi-Soviet Pact, a treaty of mutual non-aggression. The pact secretly gave a free hand to both countries for movement into various portions of northeastern Europe (Poland,

Lithuania, Latvia, etc.). The Soviets, who had sought an alliance with Britain and France both before and after Munich, and on top of the aloof position the latter and the United States had taken regarding German and Italian military involvement in the overthrow of the elected government of Spain by Franco, had good reason to believe they had better make a strong bid for time, irrespective of its short-term meaning.

37. Kennedy, op. cit., p. 354.

38. Op. cit., p. 356. The most vital of the contents of the "purse" was oil. The Japanese and Germans have no domestic oil supplies, and the superior air power of the Allies made it relatively easy over time to destroy and/or cut off supplies brought in from outside. Even before the summer of 1945 Japan had effectively run out of oil. Consequently, it was virtually unable to fend off our bombers with fighter planes or—as our planes flew at increasingly "stratospheric" levels—with anti-aircraft.

39. Mitchell, op. cit., p. 371.

40. Mitchell, pp. 396-97. The "eleven million" noted by Mitchell is for one particular year; over the course of the war, over 16 million served in the armed forces. The data in the text immediately preceding this quotation are drawn from Mitchell, chap. 11: "War to the Rescue," and from *HSUS*, part 1, pp. 130-31. And contemplate how much was produced: "In the five years following the French collapse [1940], America turned out almost 300,000 warplanes, over 100,000 tanks, 372,000 artillery pieces, 2.4 million trucks, 88,000 warships and, among other things, 5.8 million tons of bombs and 44 billion rounds of rifle ammunition." Paraphrased from Manchester, *The Glory and the Dream*, p. 362.

41. The figure (in 1982 dollars) for military expenditures is from Seymour Melman, "*The U.S.-Russian Conversion Crisis,*" *In These Times*, 11 July 1994. Compare the figure of $8.7 trillion on the military with "the total value of U.S. industry and infrastructure—again for 1982—of $7.3 trillion," in Manchester, ibid.

42. Mitchell, *Depression Decade*, pp. 384-385. The data preceding the quotation are from the same pages. Also see Harold G. Vatter, *The U.S. Economy in World War II* (New York: Columbia University Press, 1985).

43. As cited by Vatter, op. cit., p. 96, the actual percentage change in the consumer price index between 1940 and 1945 was 22.9 percent; but from 1942 to 1945, when "General Max" price controls were put into effect, and, more significantly, when the percentage of GNP going solely to the military was doubling and tripling, the rise was only ll.6 percent—over four years!

44. Widely understood by *most* generations, that is, as "Not in my backyard."

45. Quoted in Barton J. Bernstein and Allen J. Matusow, *Twentieth-Century America: Recent Interpretations* (New York: Harcourt Brace Jovanovich, 2d ed., 1972), pp. 395-96.

CHAPTER 3 CREATING A COLD WAR AND A GLOBAL ECONOMY: 1945-1960

1. Reference has already been made to Howard Brands, *The Devil We Knew: Americans and the Cold War*. On narrower—which is not to say unimportant—matters, see Frank Kofsky, *Harry S. Truman and the War Scare of 1948* (New York: St. Martin's Press, 1993), and Christopher Simpson, *Blowback: America's Recruitment of Nazis and Its Effects on the Cold War* (New York: Weidenfeld & Nicolson,

1988). Kofsky, like almost all recent students of cold war deceptions, depended on recently declassified government documents (made so through the Freedom of Information Act, following upon Watergate) to show how Truman and the heads of the Defense and State Departments knowingly and systematically led us to believe what they knew was *not* true, that the Soviet Union was on edge of initiating a new world war: in 1948, yet! The Nazis of the Simpson book comprise two groups, one widely known about—the rocket specialists—the other covertly transported here and much more important for shaping and inflaming the Cold War: "political Nazis," whose "intelligence" concerning Europeans to the left of center was as poisoned and as dangerous as their racial theories.

2. Stalin was a merciless ruler, of course, but his main concern in that period for the Soviet Union was survival, not expansion; and wishful thinking was not one of his habits. The story of his refusal to help the Greek Communists, soon to be related, illustrates the point. The quotations from Churchill are found in Lawrence Wittner, *Cold War America: From Hiroshima to Watergate* (New York: Holt, Rinehart and Winston, 1978), p. 18.

3. Wittner, *Cold War America*, pp. 8-9.

4. A fearful menace of which I was evidently a significant part. When my FBI dossier is discussed later on, it will be seen that they used three classifications for their files: I, II, and III—in ascending order of danger to the Republic. Stamped on my files was III, which led me immediately to wonder how ineffably innocuous those of II, to say nothing of the wimps of I, must have been.

5. The agreements carved up parts of Europe in such fashion that Bulgaria, Poland, and Rumania would be in the Soviet sphere and Greece in the British. Churchill never departed from his position that the Soviet Union had "adhered strictly and faithfully" to the agreements. See Howard Zinn, *Postwar America: 1945-1971* (Indianapolis: Bobbs-Merrill, 1973), pp. 42-45. Tito's Yugoslavia—not the Soviet Union—was the source of small arms for the EAM forces. In early 1948, Stalin informed Tito that "the uprising in Greece must be stopped, and as quickly as possible." Subsequently, for that and other reasons, Stalin expelled Yugoslavia from the Comintern.

6. Quoted in Zinn, op. cit., pp. 42-43. See the film "Z" for the murderous means used in Greece to maintain fascist rule there—very much as a connected outcome of the Truman Doctrine.

7. For those whose geographic studies never began or have not endured, Turkey sits at the southern half of the Black Sea, and the ex-Soviet Union at its northern half (except for the western shores, which are Rumanian and Bulgarian). And the Black Sea is reached by going through two straits: the Dardanelles and the Bosporus, both in Turkey.

8. Melvyn P. Leffler, *A Preponderance of Power: National Security, the Truman Administration, and the Cold War* (Stanford: Stanford University Press, 1992), p. 123.

9. Ibid.

10. It was sold to the U.S. public even more as the milk of U.S. kindness, but it concerned oil more than milk, and was a shrewd use of economic and state power. See Michael Tanzer, *The Energy Crisis: World Struggle for Power and Wealth* (New York: Monthly Review Press, 1974), p. 16. Tanzer once served as an economist for Standard Oil in the Middle East.

11. For an excellent history of the bomb's development, see Robert Jungk, *Brighter Than a Thousand Suns: A Personal History of the Atomic Scientists* (New York: Harcourt Brace, 1958). Also see the excellent novel concerning Los Alamos and

the first nuclear fatality—*The Accident* by Dexter Masters (New York: Knopf, 1955, reissued by Viking Penguin, 1985).

12. From an interview with former Secretary of the Interior Stewart Udall in the *New York Times*, 9 June 1993. Also see his book *The Myths of August: A Personal Exploration of Our Tragic Cold War Affair with the Atom* (New York: Pantheon, 1994), and Carole Gallagher, *American Ground Zero: The Secret Nuclear War* (Cambridge: MIT Press, 1993).

13. In her column (reprinted in the *San Francisco Chronicle*, 10 August 1993) entitled "Government Lying," Molly Ivins of the *Fort Worth Star-Telegram* reports on an incident for which she was present in the 1970s: "One fine day, some unpleasant chemical drifted out of Dugway (Utah) and killed hundreds of sheep [causing] concern among the locals. Reporters arrived. . . . The military issued denials as only the military can. What about the dead sheep? we asked. The briefer looked at us all in perfect seriousness and said, What dead sheep? Now you understand that just downwind from Dugway, there were at least 400 sheep lying on their backs with their bellies distended and their little sheep feet pointing straight up in the air. What dead sheep? asks this guy. They couldn't even open the windows in the briefing room because these sheep smelled so bad. What dead sheep? So whenever I listen to a government spokesman engaged in earnest, pathetically obvious lying, that wonderful question comes back: What dead sheep?" Perhaps the government briefer had been inspired by the wonderful musical comedy of the 1930s, "Jumbo!" It was about a circus, and was held in Madison Square Garden. In one scene, Jimmy Durante is stealing an elephant, leading it out of the tent by a rope. He is accosted by a guard who demands: "Where're you going with that elephant?!" "What elephant?" asks Jimmy.

14. The quotations may be found in the essay by Gar Alperovitz, "Why We Dropped the Bomb," in Bernstein and Matusow, op. cit., pp. 400-402. That essay is taken from a book by Alperovitz, *Atomic Diplomacy: Hiroshima and Potsdam* (New York: Vintage, 1965), a new version of which (updated in keeping with recently released documents) has been announced.

15. From John Hersey, *Hiroshima* (New York: Vintage Books, 1989), adapted from pp. 1-6. This small book was originally printed as a magazine-length article in the *New Yorker*, 31 August 1946. That issue contained nothing but this essay: no ads, no cartoons, no stories, only the essay. In furnishing detailed information on the previously well-cloaked catastrophe, Hersey's article deepened and provoked horror among the public at our use of the bomb—and consternation in the higher circles that had decided to use it. Among the highest of the high was James B. Conant, president of Harvard University. As a chemist, Conant had supervised the invention and production of "lewisite," a poison gas for World War I (not used). He was called upon again in 1941 to be the chief civilian administrator of U.S. nuclear research—and he was one of the small group that decided to drop the bomb: not once but twice. (No Milquetoast professor, he.) Conant's reaction to Hersey's essay was to go to work immediately with Henry L. Stimson (retired Secretary of War) to produce an article largely written by Conant to be published under Stimson's name in *Harper's Magazine* in February of 1947: "The Decision to Use the Bomb." The intent of the article was to cause its readers to believe that the bomb was used solely to meet military needs, which both Conant and Stimson knew not to be true: Conant in particular was much concerned when the decision was made—with his critical support—that the explosion serve as an admonition

to the Soviet Union and, as well, to cause our own people (à la Strangelove) "to learn to love the bomb." The Soviet Union is not mentioned in Stimson's article. Nor has Conant or anyone else ever provided a justification for dropping it a second time, on Nagasaki. See James G. Hershberg, *James B. Conant: Harvard to Hiroshima and the Making of the Nuclear Age* (New York: Knopf, 1994) and, for an extended discussion on the Nagasaki bombing as a "terror" bombing see the book by, of all people, McGeorge Bundy, *Danger and Survival: Choices About the Bomb in the First Fifty Years* (New York: Random House, 1988). "Of all people," because Bundy was Secretary of Defense under JFK, and also helped to write the Stimson piece.

16. It had been agreed at Yalta that the Soviet Union would enter the war against Japan three months after Germany was defeated, and move in from west to east. The U.S. Strategic Bombing Survey concluded "Japan would have surrendered even if the atomic bombs had not been dropped, even if Russia had not entered the war, and even if no invasion had been planned or contemplated." This and the quote in the text are from Wittner, op. cit., p. 12.

17. *New York Times,* 11 August 1993, emphasis added. Here it is pertinent to point out that Truman's position was "unconditional surrender," and that the only item of difference between his position and that of the Japanese in the secret messages that were going back and forth had to do with the Emperor: Truman wanted him out, and the Japanese didn't. So *that's* why we dropped the bombs. Except that the Emperor still sits on the throne of Japan.

18. Japan was occupied only by the United States (with MacArthur as resident emperor), Germany by the British, French, the Soviet Union and ourselves until 1949. After that, Germany was divided into the German Democratic Republic, under Soviet domination, and the German Federal Republic, under the other three powers until 1955, when it became part of NATO—which in turn was dominated by the United States.

19. The usual view of our involvement in Vietnam sees it as beginning with JFK's dispatch of the Green Berets to South Vietnam, or LBJ's Tonkin Gulf Resolution of 1965. Those who followed the area closely during the Truman years—as already partially suggested in earlier pages—know our involvement began to deepen soon after FDR's death. By 1952 the United States was funding fully 80 percent of France's expenditures in the war against the Vietminh (largely motivated, as earlier, by the need to bribe France to play its role in the cold war in Europe). See George McT. Kahin and John Lewis, *The United States in Vietnam* (New York: Dial Press, 1967), pp. 157-59, but also chaps. 1-7.

20. Richard M. Freeland, *The Truman Doctrine and the Origins of McCarthyism: Foreign Policy, Dolmestic Politics, and Internal Security, 1946-1948* (New York: Knopf, 1972), p. 360.

21. Many, but not all readers will know that the "Solid South" was the assured stronghold of the Democratic Party until after the 1960s. What was assured was that only whites could vote, that they would vote almost always for conservatives (and racists), and that those easily gained and held seats would, in both houses of Congress, give the conservative Democrats seniority and substantial control of congressional committees. The civil rights movement, to the degree that it helped to break that pattern, thus went beyond matters of race in its potential for beneficial social change.

22. Freeland, op. cit., pp. 89, 93.

23. The quotations to follow are from Merle Miller, *Plain Speaking: An Oral Biography of Harry S. Truman* (New York: Berkley, 1974), with pages as indicated in parentheses. Of the many books written about Hoover showing how his personal life as it connected with his working life should have awakened his boss's interest (not least that the expert at blackmailing others was being blackmailed by the Mafia into "laying off" their activities, being able to do so after having come into possession of a film of Hoover in a compromising position with a male sexual partner, the number two man in the FBI), see Anthony Summers, *Official and Confidential: The Secret Life of J. Edgar Hoover* (New York: Putnam, 1993) (illustrated!). Or, for a sport/synopsis, see John Updike in the *New Yorker*, 1 March 1993, entitled "Glad Rags" on the crossdressing of the entire Eisenhower administration.
    24. Harold G. Vatter, *The U.S. Economy in the 1950s: An Economic History* (New York: W.W. Norton & Co., 1963), p. 3.
25. As made clear a year earlier by Michael Harrington in *The Other America* (Baltimore: Penguin, 1962).
26. The data supporting the foregoing generalization are overwhelming. For those wishing to study them before proceeding further the most convenient reference is Lawrence Mishel and Jared Bernstein, *The State of Working America, 1992-93*, Economic Policy Institute Series (Armonk, NY: M.E. Sharpe, 1993), especially chap. 6. "The number of poor Americans increased to 36.9 million last year [1992], more than at any time since John F. Kennedy was president, the U.S. Census Bureau said Monday" (*International Herald Tribune*, "Number of Poor Hits 30-Year High in U.S.," 5 Oct. 1993).
27. The single most insightful and penetrating analyst of these developments, analytically and in factual detail, has been James M. Cypher. See, for example, his "Capitalist Planning and Military Expenditures," *Review of Radical Political Economics* 6, No. 3 (Fall 1974); "Back to the Bomb: The Ebb and Flow of Military Spending" in Union of Radical Political Economists (eds.), *U.S. Capitalism in Crisis* (New York: Monthly Review Press, 1978); "Ideological Hegemony and Modern Militarism: The Origins and Limits of Military Keynesianism," *Economic Forum* 13, no. 1 (Summer 1982); "The Basic Economics of 'Rearming America'," *Monthly Review*, November 1981; "A Prop, Not a Burden: U.S. Economy Relies on Militarism," in *Dollars and Sense*, January 1984, and, among other essays, "Military Spending, Technical Change and Economic Growth: A Disguised Form of Industrial Policy?" in *Journal of Economic Issues* 21, no. 1 (March 1987).
27A. Gordon, *Economic Instability and Growth*, pp. 110-12.
28. Kemp, *The Climax of Capitalism*, p. 125. The "automatic stabilizers" Kemp notes consisted of some combination of "automatically" reduced income taxes plus increased unemployment compensation benefits or welfare payments. Not quite automatic, but by then becoming virtually so, were rising military expenditures— "going against the cycle."
29. Most have forgotten or never knew that McCarthy's initial election was importantly based on his public position that lies had been spread about Nazi Germany. He was a precocious "revisionist" concerning the Holocaust—explicable in part by the fact that McCarthy, three-quarters Irish, was one quarter German, and the substantial German population of Wisconsin (rural and urban) "regarded McCarthy as their champion against Anglo-Saxons." See Morison, *Oxford History of the American People*, p. 443, text and footnote.

30. It is not known if McCarthy ever told the truth about anything. "Tail Gunner Joe" was a name he allowed and encouraged to be used about him as his career developed, though a tail gunner he never was. He was an information officer in the Pacific war. Even less inspiring was the military career of Ronald Reagan, who became an army captain for talents used exclusively in films during the war. Reagan often suggested—possibly even had come to believe—that he spent the war in bloodier settings, rather than, as a matter of record, in Hollywood. At least Joe got outside the continental limits of the United States. George Bush did also, and flew combat, if also with at least two shifty incidents: 1) evidently, having bombed some Japanese cargo ships, he and his wing leader saw fit to strafe the survivors in their lifeboats—a war crime, by official definition; and 2) on another occasion, when his plane was shot down, *he* bailed out successfully, but his two crewmen went down with the plane: not the desired sequence for pilots and crew. For the strafing incident, see *Harper's Magazine*, September 1993. The bailout story (furnished by men in his outfit) was in the newspapers during the 1988 election campaign but nothing was made of it.

31. Up to here, the quotation is from Samuel Eliot Morison, op. cit., pp. 442-43. The rest of the "snapshot" is derived from my own essay "Militarized Economy, Brutalized Society," in *Economic Forum*, op. cit. (the same issue in which Cypher's essay appears, in an issue dedicated to "Militarism and the American Economy," summer 1982).

32. Although, as subsequent references will show, there has been an interesting and useful spate of books concerning Korea in the past ten years or so—facilitated in part by the Freedom of Information Act, in part by the diminution of the Cold War itself.

33. Our first serious commitment in Vietnam took place during (and partially as a response to) the Korean war, as increasingly from 1950 on we undertook to finance the hopeless effort of the French to hold on there and in the rest of Indochina. By 1952 we were paying four-fifths of the French bill; and when they were defeated in 1954 we began our long military involvement, succeeding in keeping it covert and camouflaged in one way or another for another ten years. And then ten years of war.

34. The weaponry provided to North Korea by the Soviet Union (which clearly stood aloof from the war) was paltry, apart from matériel left over from World War II. It was the Chinese entry that altered the balance between North Korea and the United States; but that entry would not have occurred had Truman not sent MacArthur "across the 38th parallel" in September, despite an explicit warning from Premier Zhou Enlai that China would enter the war if that happened. Acheson worked on the assumption that China was controlled by the Soviet Union and that Stalin's withdrawal from involvement meant China was bluffing. See Walter LaFeber, *America, Russia, and the Cold War, 1945-1990* (New York: Macmillan, 1991), pp. 114 ff. Among the many differences and similarities between the wars in Korea and Vietnam: 1) in neither case was what had been a colonialized society allowed to find its way toward independence; 2) attempts to achieve the latter were accompanied in both countries by considerable internal conflict—between bottom and top, those who had resisted and those who had worked with the former colonial power, between what were or became left and right forces; 3) both were victimized as pawns in the Cold War; 4) both societies, if at different times and in different ways, found themselves arbitrarily divided in

two (at the 38th parallel in Korea, at the 17th in Vietnam); 5) for both the war was a tragedy of limitless dimensions. Korea is still divided; and South Korea still has over 40,000 U.S. troops in place, equipped with nuclear weapons (as this is being written).

35. Jon Halliday and Bruce Cumings, *Korea: The Unknown War* (New York: Pantheon Books, 1988), pp. 200-201. Bruce Cumings, *The Origins of the Korean War* (Princeton, NJ: Princeton University Press, 1981), provides full documentation and references. The present book has many illuminating and wrenching photographs. For purposes of comparison: just under 60,000 U.S. troops died in Indochina and over 3 million Vietnamese died. The numbers for Laos are impossible to pin down. As is well-known, however, at least one million died in Cambodia in the 1970s, killed by the Khmer Rouge—which, it is vital to note, the United States (along with China !) supported (and supports still?), as a means of continuing to oppose Vietnam (which opposes the Khmer Rouge): a more horrendous combination of national madnesses and mass murder would be hard to find. The people of the United States are almost entirely ignorant of the heavy responsibility we bear for the tragedy in Cambodia, despite available essays and books that tell the story. See, for example, William Shawcross, *Sideshow: Kissinger, Nixon and the Destruction of Cambodia* (New York: Pocket Books, 1979).

36. As LaFeber points out in his authoritative study, there was "no indication that the President consulted his European or Asian allies before committing American air and naval units on June 27 [1950]. This was not the first nor would it be the last time the United States would take unilateral action in an explosive situation without consulting its Western European partners. As for the sudden American concern to bolster the United Nations, this had not been apparent when the United States acted unilaterally or with some Western powers to establish the Truman Doctrine, the Rio Pact, the Marshall Plan, and NATO. American actions in Korea were consistent with this history, for the United States. . . . establish[ed] a military command in Korea that took orders not from the United Nations but from Washington." *America, Russia and the Cold War,* pp. 103-105. LaFeber goes on to remark that "although the war was limited to Korea, Truman and Acheson used the war as the opportunity to develop new American policies around the globe. Because of these American initiatives, the six months between June and December 1950 rank among the most important of the Cold War era."

37. Halliday and Cumings, op. cit., p. 108. Those who were politically attentive in 1951 will remember how electrifying the period was after MacArthur—who had been the *de facto* emperor of Japan since 1945—was removed from his command and then returned to the States. He was greeted with triumphant parades and enormous hullabaloo, and he made a dramatic attempt to gain the GOP nomination for president in 1952—which went instead to another general.

38. The economic development of Japan after 1950 had sitting at its center the direct and indirect economic stimuli provided by the U.S. military and paramilitary efforts in East and Southeast Asia. Japan served many useful military purposes for the United States: weapons and other military manufacturers, vital army and navy bases (and nuclear weapons, illegally), and r&r areas, all of these in Japan proper, or in Okinawa.

39. "[F]rom the first days of the war the Americans contemplated the use of atomic weapons in this 'limited' war. On July 9—a mere two weeks into the war...—MacArthur sent [General] Ridgeway a 'hot message' that prompted the Joint Chiefs

of Staff 'to consider whether or not A-bombs should be made available to MacArthur.' General Bolté, Chief of Operations, was asked to talk to MacArthur about using atomic bombs 'in direct support [of] ground combat'; some ten to twenty bombs could be spared without 'unduly' jeopardizing the general war plan.... At this point in the war, however, the Joint Chiefs of Staff rejected the use of the bomb." Halliday and Cumings, op. cit., pp. 49-50. After U.S. troops crossed the 38th parallel, despite China's warning that it would enter the war if that occurred, the war heated up considerably and dangerously. Truman changed from trying to restrain MacArthur to announcing, at a press conference on November 30, that the United States would use all its power, not excluding atomic bombs, to contain the Chinese. Within four days, the Prime Minister of Great Britain (Attlee) arrived in the United States (evidently speaking for other countries in Western Europe as well), seeking to prevent what would have been an irreversible first step toward the nuclear devastation of Europe. See LaFeber, op. cit., pp. 116-17.

40. Halliday and Cumings, op. cit., pp. 203-204. The authors point out that Dean Acheson (Truman's Secretary of State), after stating that the Korean war "destroyed the Truman administration" went on to observe that it also "came along and saved us"—where "us" is clearly not the Truman administration but the larger economic and political scene in which Acheson saw himself as moving. And then they add that the war "was the key factor behind the military build-up of NATO and the vast expansion of military budgets in all the major Western countries. The U.S. army expanded from 1.5 million to 3.5 million during the war, and the military budget rose from about $15 billion in 1950 to some $50 billion a year ... [and] led to a world economic boom...."

41. Not least in forcing estimated hundreds of thousands of Korean girls and women into prostitution for the military—called "comfort ladies"—of course a very well-known fact in both Korea and Japan—but, as is the custom of governments, blandly and officially denied until the 1990s.

42. LaFeber, op. cit., p. 99.

43. James I. Matray (ed.), *Historical Dictionary of the Korean War* (New York: Greenwood Press, 1991), under the entry "Thirty-Eighth Parallel," pp. 452-53. This massive "dictionary" covers all aspects of the Korean war and its relevant prior history.

44. Ibid.

45. "1945" of the "In Our Pages: 100, 75, and 50 Years Ago" subsection, *International Herald Tribune*, 24 November 1995.

46. Cumings, *Origins of the Korean War*, p. xxi.

47. A term that became part of GI vocabulary during the war against Japan, widespread in Korea, and institutionalized in Vietnam.

48. In all three cases, nationalization of the resources of the three societies was the central issue: oil in Iran, agricultural land (plus shipping, railroads, and communications) in Guatemala, the Suez Canal for Egypt. The United States was critical for the overthrow of the democratically elected (1951) nationalist Mossadegh in Iran, by supplying the military force and CIA guidance that placed our man the "Shah of Shahs" on the throne in 1953 (thus planting the long-growing seeds of the Khomeini "revolution" of 1979). The United States, Dulles using the Monroe Doctrine (1823!) as the official pretext, airlifted arms and CIA-trained Guatemalan exiles to overthrow the duly elected government of Arbenz in 1954 (which had confiscated 178,000 acres of United Fruit Company land, the real ruler of

Guatemala throughout this century); and Britain and France, the owners of the Suez Canal Company, were seeking to overthrow the nationalist Nasser. For these, among other such moves of the Eisenhower-Dulles years, see LaFeber, op. cit., chap. 7 ("A Different Cold War. 1953-1955"), esp. pp. 152 ff. For oil and Iran (among other places) see Robert Engler, *The Politics of Oil: Private Power and Democratic Directions* (Chicago: University of Chicago Press, 1961), especially chap. 8, and Michael Tanzer, *The Political Economy of International Oil and the Underdeveloped Countries* (Boston: Beacon Press, 1969).

49. It may be of interest that in 1958 I wrote an essay arguing that the only hope for a decent evolution for the Soviet Union was a diminution of the Cold War. See my essay on the Soviet Union and Japan in Douglas F. Dowd (ed.), *Thorstein Veblen: A Critical Reappraisal* (Ithaca: Cornell University Press, 1958).

CHAPTER 4   *THE SIXTIES: FASTEN YOUR SEATBELTS*

1. Much of the following chronology is adapted from Gerald Howard (ed.), *The Sixties: The Art, Attitudes, Politics and Media of Our Most Explosive Decade* (New York: Washington Square Press, 1982), pp. 505 ff. The book is very much worth reading for its more than two dozen selections of essays and excerpts from books written in the Sixties which, taken together, provide a fine introduction to—or memory of—the decade. See also Todd Gitlin's *The Sixties: Years of Hope, Days of Rage* (New York: Bantam Books, 1987). Gitlin was very much a participant in those years, having been an early leader of SDS. When Todd was a young student at Harvard and I a prof at Cornell, in 1960, we shared a "ban the bomb" platform at a meeting at Brown University.

2. From his foreword to Lawrence Chang and Peter Kornbluh (eds.), *The Cuban Missile Crisis* (New York: New Press, 1992).

3. For the full story of that tragedy, and much besides, see the wrenching book by Elizabeth Sullivan (ed.), *Letters from Mississippi* (New York: McGraw-Hill, 1965), dedicated to James Chaney, Andrew Goodman, and Michael ("Mickey") Schwerner.

4. The first systematic treatment in English of "monopoly capitalism" appeared in 1966: *Monopoly Capital: An Essay on the American Economic and Social Order* by Paul Baran and Paul Sweezy. Note that in the title the authors center on the United States, and are concerned with both the economic *and* the social order. Baran and Sweezy were the leading Marxists in the United States at the time, but Marx had mid-nineteenth century Britain as his principal focus, and had reason to conduct an analysis that paid little explicit attention to the "noneconomic" process. The authors of *Monopoly Capital* were thus embarking on a major revision of Marxian theory, the "competitive capitalism" of Marx's time having been replaced by today's "monopoly capitalism." As they wrote, that system was becoming a *global* system; by now it is in process of becoming a global system dominated by transnational corporations as much as or more than various national states.

5. See *Monopoly Capital*, chap. 1, where the economic surplus is defined as "the difference between what a society produces and the costs of producing it. The size of the surplus is an index of productivity and wealth, of how much freedom a society has to accomplish whatever goals it may set for itself. The composition of the surplus shows how it uses that freedom: how much it invests in expanding its productive capacity, how much it consumes in various ways, how much it wastes

and in what ways" (pp. 9-10). The headings of their chaps. 3-7 on the absorption of the surplus constitute an introduction in themselves: "Capitalists' Consumption and Investment," "The Sales Effort," "Civilian Government," and "Militarism and Imperialism." For the capitalism of his time, Marx would have needed only chap. 3. For identification and measurement of the components and size of the economic surplus see the appendix (by Prof. Joseph D. Phillips), which shows it as about 50 percent of GNP in 1963 (and, during World War II at over 70 percent.) This conceptual apparatus was developed by Baran in his path-breaking *Political Economy of Growth* (New York: Monthly Review Press, 1957). Baran died in 1964, and *Monopoly Capital* was completed by Sweezy. In the spring of 1974, the Economics Department at Stanford University—where Baran had taught for over a decade before his death, and where he had been treated shabbily—belatedly held a symposium on his life and work, at which I delivered the paper "Social Commitment and Social Analysis: The Contribution of Paul Baran" (published in 1975 in *Politics and Society*), a tribute to Baran and a critique of our profession, wherein I pursued some of the implications of his analytical achievements.

6. These and related notions are put forth in the last chapter of his *Theory of Business Enterprise* (New York: Scribner's, 1904). Veblen's expectations concerning Germany (now to follow in the text) are to be found in the second part of his long essay "The Socialist Economics of Karl Marx," in *The Place of Science in Modern Civilization* (New York: B.W. Huebsch, 1919).

7. This kind of argument, richly put, is very much a main theme of Jerry Mander's *In the Absence of the Sacred: The Failure of Technology & the Survival of the Indian Nations* (San Francisco: Sierra Club Books, 1992).

8. An old but still a valuably comprehensive and lucid presentation of Keynesian analysis and policy is Dudley Dillard, *The Economics of John Maynard Keynes* (Englewood Cliffs, N.J.: Prentice-Hall, 1948).

9. The data in that paragraph are taken from the deeply disturbing book by Richard Barnet and John Cavanagh, *Global Dreams: Imperial Corporations and the New World Order* (New York: Simon & Schuster, 1994), pp. 423 ff.

10. Usually called "neocolonialism" in recent decades. The initial public steps were taken in 1949 when President Truman in his inaugural address made as his fourth point a "technical assistance program" for the "underdeveloped areas" of the world. The program came to be called the "Point Four Program" by its proponents (and something more colorful by those for whom its "assistance" was seen as imperialism). It fitted in smoothly with the recommendations made shortly thereafter by the International Development Advisory Board's *Partners in Progress* (1951, "The Rockefeller Report") and the President's Materials Policy Commission's five-volume report entitled *Resources for Freedom* (1952), both of which made the connection between the growing dependence of the United States on imported raw materials and the need for a congruent foreign policy. Harry Magdoff, in his *The Age of Imperialism: The Economics of U.S. Foreign Policy* (New York: Monthly Review Press, 1969) shows in detail just how rapidly raw materials imports were growing after World War II and into the 1960s—to say nothing of since then.

11. The literature is vast. For an early analysis, see Seymour Melman, *Pentagon Capitalism* (New York: McGraw-Hill, 1970); for an informative analysis complemented by wise policy suggestions, see the recent book by Ann Markusen and

Joel Yudken, *Dismantling the Cold War Economy* (New York: Basic Books, 1992). There you will also find a comprehensive bibliography for the whole matter.

12. The figures for the United States are those noted earlier, from Seymour Melman; for the rest of the world and the Third World figures see R.L. Sivard, *World Military and Social Expenditures* (Washington, DC, 1983, et seq.) and Saadet Deger, *Military Expenditures in Third World Countries* (London: Routledge and Kegan Paul, 1986).

13. Richard Ned Lebow and Janice Gross Stein, *We All Lost the Cold War* (Princeton, N.J.: Princeton University Press, 1994).

14. A fine book about the varieties of resistance is Michael Ferber and Staughton Lynd, *The Resistance* (Boston: Beacon Press, 1971). Ferber, along with Dr. Spock and others, was brought to trial for having publicly—and frequently—encouraged draft resistance. After their indictment, we held a large event at Town Hall in Manhattan to raise money for their defense and to have some 1,500 others sign the very statement for which they were being prosecuted. None of us was ever indicted; nor were they convicted. The resulting political group, called "Resist," still functions.

15. The summer's work is told in a book, by myself and Mary Nichols (eds.), *Step by Step* (New York: W.W. Norton, 1965).

16. The most recent book on the antiwar movement is, in my judgment, also the best and most comprehensive: Tom Wells, *The War Within: America's Battle Over Vietnam* (Berkeley: University of California Press, 1994). Also excellent is the detailed study by Nancy Zaroulis and Gerald Sullivan, *Who Spoke Up? American Protest against the War in Vietnam, 1963-1975* (New York: Doubleday, 1984). Both books treat an incredible amount of politics and people, with considerable dependence upon interviews with virtually all of those most heavily involved.

17. See, among other publications, Daniel Ellsberg, *Papers on the War* (New York: Simon & Schuster, 1972). On the same question see chap. 3 of the fine book by Jonathan Schell, *The Time of Illusion* (New York: Vintage, 1975). See also *The Pentagon Papers* (New York: Bantam, 1971) for the cat's meow. And also see H.R. Haldeman, *The Haldeman Diaries: Inside the Nixon White House* (New York: Putnam, 1994), especially pp. 299-315, for entries on the Ellsberg case and related matters.

18. There were two big demonstrations in 1967, the first of which—the "Spring Mobilization" in San Francisco and Washington, D.C.—I missed, for I was out of the country from September 1966 until August 1967, teaching as a Fulbright prof in Bologna.

19. The title of Norman Mailer's book (New York: New American Library, 1968), which centers on the events now to be described.

20. The one just noted is to be found in Halberstam's *The Best and the Brightest*, p. 647.

21. Trillin's remarks on the matter may be found in "Shouts and Murmurs," *The New Yorker*, 25 January 1993.

22. See Zaroulis and Sullivan, *Who Spoke Up?*, pp. 275-300.

23. In his excellent *The Whole World is Watching: Mass Media in the Making & Unmaking of the New Left* (Berkeley: University of California Press, 1980), Todd Gitlin describes and analyzes the ways in which the media over time provided a portrait of protests and demonstrations that made it easy to dismiss us (or worse).

24. A very good film of 1962, its title adapted from Faulkner's *Requiem for a Nun*, probably. The excellent teleplay by Rod Serling for *Playhouse 90* from which it

adapted was inspired, I believe, by the career of Primo Carnera, a giant of a man from Italy who became heavyweight champ—but was seen and treated as though a side of beef. Anthony Quinn was the fighter in the film, and Jackie Gleason his manager who (much trusted by the fighter) corrupted himself and ruined the fighter by making deals, etc. Worth getting on video.

25. *Sometimes a Great Notion* was one of Ken Kesey's books, and I have reworked the title to echo LBJ's Great Society, which was only a partial failure, only partial success, Vietnam and capitalism getting in the way a bit.

26. Doris Kearns, *Lyndon Johnson & The American Dream* (New York: Signet, 1976), p. 226. Kearns teaches government at Harvard, had earlier been a White House Fellow in LBJ's years, and is married to Richard Goodwin, one of the key members of LBJ's staff. After he left office, LBJ invited Kearns to interview him often and extensively. The result is a uniquely-researched book revealing much of LBJ's persona, as well as a lot of "inside information" about his years before and during his presidency. Kearns was clearly taken by LBJ as (at least sometimes) an attractive human being; but her book maintains as much of an objective stance as might be achieved.

27. See David Halberstam, *The Making of a Quagmire* (New York: Random House, 1965), for some of the evolution up to LBJ, and the latter's first tragic and critical decisions.

28. My report of this conversation has been published as "The CIA's Laotian Colony," in N.S. Adams and A.W. McCoy (eds.), *Laos: War and Revolution* (New York: Harper, 1970).

29. Halberstam, op. cit., p. 620.

30. Quoted in Robert Sherrill, *The Accidental President* (New York: Pyramid Books, 1968), p. 232, who adds, "so much for the Congressional mastermind." The whole terrible story, from beginning to today, is put forth excellently in Marilyn B. Young, *The Vietnam Wars, 1945-1990* (New York: Harper Perennial, 1991), whose very title is illuminating.

31. Kearns, op. cit., pp. 252-53. Sherrill recounts an Oval Office press meeting during which, the subject being power, LBJ opened his pants, placed what we shall call his member on the desk, and said, "That, boys, is *power!*"

CHAPTER 5 PRESIDENT QUEEG AND HIS MERRY MEN; AND THE REMAINS OF THE DECADE: 1970-1980

1. Queeg, Captain of the U.S.S. Caine, a man whose competence and character were done in by his obsessions and his paranoia, but one for whom it was impossible, even while scorning him, not to feel at least some sympathy. But Queeg was played by Bogart in the film. Bogie never could have played the role of Nixon, for whom any sympathy one might have felt would be like that generated for a snake caught in a trap—a trap, in Nixon's case, always of his own making.

2. Kissinger, Haldeman, Erlichman, Mitchell, Agnew, Colson, Liddy. . . .

3. Shawcross, *Sideshow*, p. 396.

4. Prince Norodom Sihanouk, had done everything in his power to keep Cambodia out of the conflict between the French and the Vietnamese after 1946, and that between the United States and the Vietnamese after 1954. For his pains, we participated in his overthrow in 1970. He now presides over Cambodia once

more, a Cambodia whose population was reduced by at least one-quarter as a result of the events beginning in late 1969—in "the killing fields."

5. For the details see Shawcross, op. cit., especially pp. 28-32, 93-95. They were *always* sent off on their missions to a particular coordinate in Vietnam, there to communicate with a radio contact which in turn gave them coordinates which were over the Cambodian border, but not revealed as being so.

6. Noam Chomsky is Professor of Humanities at MIT, and a long-time and profound critic of U.S. foreign policy and much of what occurs at home. The Rev. Richard Fernandez ("Dick") was then head of Clergy and Laymen Concerned, the leading religious coalition against the war. See David Dellinger's autobiography, *From Yale to Jail* (New York: Pantheon, 1993).

7. The title of Alan Paton's book about South Africa, published in 1948.

8. There was, of course, always an Emperor—but his rule was that of a symbol not a reality, lacking even those few real powers held by Queen Elizabeth II.

9. The talk was published under the same title in *Bulletin of Concerned Asian Scholars*, December 1970, and, by means of which I remain ignorant, it came to be reprinted on the Op-Ed page of the *New York Times*, 15 March 1971.

10. R.T. Naylor, *Hot Money and the Politics of Debt* (New York: Simon and Schuster, 1987), pp. 94 and 202. For an overall picture of the political, military, and drug developments in Laos during this period, see Adams and McCoy (eds.), *Laos: War and Revolution* (which contains my interview with Prince Souvanna Phouma), Alfred W. McCoy, *The Politics of Heroin in Southeast Asia* (New York: Harper, 1972), and the illuminating essay by Larry Collins, "The CIA Drug Connection is as Old as the Agency," *International Herald Tribune*, 3 December 1993.

11. See Shawcross, *Sideshow*, in its entirety.

12. Howard Zinn, *You Can't Be Neutral on a Moving Train: A Personal History of Our Times* (Boston: Beacon Press, 1994), p. 94. He goes on to point out that the European war ended only three weeks later, that his raid, which was on a small western city in France (Ruyan) and virtually destroyed it (and its French population), had no military/strategic meaning whatsoever—except as a test for napalm.

13. Shawcross, op. cit., pp. 390-91.

14. The "balance" referred to here is the so-called "basic balance," a summation of the balances of government, commercial trade, direct investment, long-term capital, and the gross liquidity balances. There are other measures, but for present purposes this is the most useful. See Fred L. Block, "Roots of the U.S. Deficit," chap. 6 in *The Origins of International Economic Disorder: A Study of the United States International Monetary Policy From World War II to the Present* (Berkeley: University of California Press, 1977) for a lucid explanation of the technical, political, and economic matters involved.

15. Block, ibid., p. 152. Those facts should be placed against the customary assertions that the relationship between the United States (among other rich countries) and the "developing" countries consists of a beneficial capital outflow from us to them: a gift, you might say. In 1970, 60 percent of the total book value of U.S. foreign *investment* was located in Canada and Western Europe, but two-thirds of the *profit* from U.S. foreign direct investment came from the Middle East and Latin America.

16. See earlier writings of mine: *U.S. Capitalist Development*, op. cit., pp. 172-78, and "Stagflation and the Political Economy of Decadent Monopoly Capitalism," *Rivista Internazionale di Scienze Economiche e Commerciali*, n. 10-11, 1976, re-

printed in *Monthly Review*, October 1976. Also relevant is my essay "Accumulation and Crisis," in *Socialist Review*, June 1975.

17. The data are derived from Du Boff, *Accumulation and Power*, pp. 121 and 124. The unemployment rates cited are "official plus discouraged workers," and plain "official." Had involuntary part-time workers been included, the official rate would have to be increased by a minimum of 25 percent. (I have included some of the data from the Eighties, as a matter of interest.) In 1995 the unemployment rate for the twelve nations of the European Community was just over 11 percent.

18. OPEC was born, it should be noted, in 1960, but had no major effect until December 1973, after which oil prices began a process of quadrupling (doubling again, in 1979). A barrel of oil that cost $2 in 1972 could cost as much as $35 in 1979. Its members include all the major Middle Eastern oil producers, plus some in North Africa, Southeast Asia, and Latin America—but not including Mexico or the two newcomers, Norway and Great Britain.

19. Japan and Italy have one important factor in common that has contributed greatly to their corrupted companies and politics: both nations, if in different ways and for some different reasons, were enabled and required by the United States to have governments with one-party rule for more than four decades.

20. Two things. It is sweet to recall that in the 1920s military expenditures were exceeded by those of the U.S. Post Office. *Those* were the good old days. And, in most published calculations of military expenditures (expenditures since the end of World War II and up into the 1980s), the following are often *not* counted as military expenditures: Department of Energy (almost entirely for nuclear weapons work), space, the military component of foreign aid, that portion of interest payments on the national debt (over $200 billion annually) attributable to past military expenditures and veterans benefits (taken together, at least 50 percent of interest payments). Add to this the ingenious trick played by LBJ in the Sixties when he had Social Security contributions and benefit payments classified as taxes and expenditures—which they are not—thereby raising the grand total of all federal taxes and expenditures and thus reducing the percentage of military to the total. If all this hocus-pocus were gotten rid of, the portion of our federal spending going for past, present, and future military activities would exceed 50 percent.

21. The title of his chap. 3, *Nixon Agonistes: The Crisis of the Self-Made Man* (New York: Houghton Mifflin, 1969). The chapter ends with Nixon "reaping maximum advantage from the troubles of the year, using a coolly orchestrated politics of discontent..., to all who were resentful" (p. 76).

22. The data are from Du Boff, op. cit., p. 94, except for price changes, which are from *Economic Report of the President*, 1981, p. 289. The price changes are calculated using 1967 as the base. The Sixties as a whole saw the Consumer Price Index (CPI) rise from 88.7 to 109.8; for the Seventies the rise was from 116.3 to 217.4, a five-fold increase in the rate. All the more worrisome, given that the Sixties were years of greater economic expansion than the Seventies: a 48 percent rise in real GNP versus a 36 percent rise.

23. Kemp, *The Climax of Capitalism*, p. 183.

24. Or was it "Greed is God?" And then there was the King of the Hill, Michael Milken—carted off a bit later to a very comfortable minimum security joint.

25. The Committee for the Reelection of the President: CREEP. Reality sinks satire.

26. All this abetted by the frequent existence of corrupt and militarized governments, "partners in [our] progress," whose leaders often deposited the largest part (in some cases, all) of the loans in their conveniently anonymous accounts in Swiss banks—the resulting debts to be paid off by their generally very poor citizenry.

27. To the average person in those countries the austerity programs meant that already high unemployment would go higher, already low incomes would go lower; and that defaults (which are to a banker what patricide is to a daddy) could be minimized—and euphemized as "restructuring."

28. For those wishing to inquire more fully: Bennett Harrison and Barry Bluestone, *The Deindustrialization of America* and their later *The Great U-Turn: Corporate Restructuring and the Polarizing of America* (New York: Basic Books, 1982 and 1988, respectively). See also the important analysis of Joyce Kolko, *Restructuring the World Economy* (New York: Pantheon, 1988), which ties together the Seventies and the Eighties, the national with the global, and the economic with the political. Then there is the most useful series of clearly-written small books (collecting their essays from *Monthly Review*) covering pretty much the entire process, Paul Sweezy and Harry Magdoff, *The Dynamics of U.S. Capitalism: Corporate Structure, Inflation, Credit, Gold, and the Dollar* (1982); *The End of Prosperity: The American Economy in the 1970s* (1977); *The Deepening Crisis of U.S. Capitalism* (1981); and *Stagnation and the Financial Explosion* (1987), all Monthly Review Press books. Were you just to read the above, you would be better educated on these particular matters than 90 percent of economists.

29. Kolko, *Restructuring the World Economy,* p. 21.

30. Ibid., p. 23. The quotation concerning "all-systems go" was the conclusion of an OECD study group on the origins of the crisis, OECD *Observer,* July 1977.

31. *Fiscal Crisis of the State* (New York: St. Martin's Press, 1973), p. 255.

32. Of the many factors making the recession that began in 1990 so stubborn, one is surely that the reduction of social expenditures, accomplished in critical degree by the lowering of federal grants-in-aid to cities and states—the main locale for such expenditures—has naturally meant the direct loss of thousands of State jobs, and indirectly a further loss through the consequent decline of purchasing power. Nor is it unimportant that those for whom governmental jobs have been most decisive in getting or staying out of poverty have been those most benefitted by the earlier expansion of such jobs: African-Americans, Hispanic-Americans and, among others, women (irrespective of color)—not least because discrimination is more difficult to maintain in public than in private enterprises.

33. See John Bellamy Foster and Henryk Szlajfer (eds.), *The Faltering Economy: The Problem of Accumulation Under Monopoly Capitalism* (New York: Monthly Review Press, 1984).

34. On this matter, a later book of O'Connor's is helpful: *Accumulation Crisis* (New York: Blackwell, 1984).

35. I thought then and think still that McGovern was a fine Senator and would have made a fine President; but that he was allowed to become the nominee of the Democrats, and easily so, was a convincing sign that the bigwigs of the party had decided *no* Democrat could win, so wotthehell, let's throw George—a staunch liberal—to the wolves (and get rid of him).

36. Wills, *Nixon Agonistes*, pp. 548, 550. The break-in was of the office of Lawrence O'Brien of the Democratic National Committee.

37. Not all of them were "burglaries." The White House hired all sorts of shady types to commit all sorts of "third-rate" crimes: guys like Tony Ulasewicz and Tony LaRocco, on the one hand, and our now successful spy novelist Howard Hunt (and his right-hand man Gordon Liddy) on the other, to spy, to wiretap, to break-in, to smear, to obstruct, to do almost anything.

38. Article IV, charging that the Nixon Administration had "waged a secret war in Cambodia"—which of course it had—was not approved, thus adding to that long list of actions by the House and the Senate that themselves constitute cover-ups of U.S. actions abroad: Iran-Contra (of which, more later), Guatemala, Iran (in the Fifties), Iraq, etc.

39. The hell with the details; suffice it to say that forty U.S. sailors were involved, and that the Kissinger/Ford (in that order) solution was such as to have forty-one GIs killed, forty-nine wounded, and who knows how many Cambodians killed and wounded, for an incident you've probably never heard about and which made a bloody mountain out of a molehill, because, as Kissinger said at the time: "there are limits beyond which the United States cannot be pushed." For the background to that remark and the whole story, see Shawcross, op. cit., pp. 342 ff., but be sure to have eaten lightly before you begin.

40. Walter Russell Mead, *Mortal Splendor: The American Empire in Transition* (Boston: Houghton Mifflin, 1987), p. 90.

41. Just as O'Connor had said. The quote is from Read, op. cit., p. 102.

42. One of the discomfiting facts about the family background of this most recent Shah is that his father, Colonel Reza Pahlavi, after he became Shah by a coup d'état in 1925, came to develop a cozy relationship with Nazi Germany, so much so that the British and Soviets mounted a successful joint invasion of Persia in the early fall of 1941.

43. These were the very hostages freed in the first days of Reagan's presidency and, it is believed (probably correctly), through a deal centering around "the October Surprise" made between Reagan's and the Ayatollah's men that would delay the hostages' freedom in order to benefit Reagan's campaign by harming Carter's in exchange for a string of related deals that came to be Iran-Contra.

44. Mead, op, cit., p. 94.

45. A useful bridge between the Nixon/Carter and Reagan years may be found in the excellent collection of essays put together by Thomas Ferguson and Joel Rogers (eds.), *The Hidden Election: Politics and Economics in the 1980 Presidential Campaign* (New York: Pantheon, 1981).

CHAPTER 6   CLOUD CUCKOO LAND: REAGAN 1980-1988

1. Kevin Phillips, *The Politics of Rich and Poor: Wealth and the American Electorate in the Reagan Aftermath* (New York: Harper Perennial, 1991), p. xi (emphasis in original).

2. The genuinely "silent majority" is to be found in that roughly 50 percent (and rising) percentage of the population that doesn't vote in the United States. For a serious study on the matter, see E.J. Dionne, *Why Americans Hate Politics* (New York: Simon & Schuster, 1992).

3. Reagan was from that part of the nation—"small-town America"—where con men had always had a lively existence: the "snake oil" salesmen, the circus tent revivalists, the "rainmakers." Veblen, in his *Absentee Ownership and Business*

Enterprise in Recent Times (New York: Huebsch, 1923), has a chapter on "The Country Town" that not only reveals the essence of their existence at the very time Reagan was growing up in one of them, it also posits the fact that—and the reasons why—such a disproportionate percentage of our presidents have come from just such towns: for better (Lincoln) and for worse (most of the others).

4. Garry Wills, *Reagan's America* (New York: Penguin, 1988), p. 465.

5. Except, for Reagan, when Hinckley tried to kill him. Even in that really dangerous situation, Reagan played out a role, wisecracking—and played it well. He was a Captain in the U.S. Army Air Force, but in its First Motion Picture Unit: his "war work" was making films, facing dangers confined to Hollywood. As for air heroics, the fact is that after taking one trip by air to Catalina Island (about twenty miles west of Los Angeles) before the war, he vowed never to fly again; and he did not, for about thirty years, induced to do so then only because there was no other way for him to make an effective presidential campaign. See Wills, op. cit., pp. 135, 198 ff, 281, and elsewhere.

6. See Wills, op. cit., chap. 31, entitled BASICO. . . . Goofproofing Reagan was a task requiring eternal vigilance. In our next note, drawn from Mark Hertsgaards's book, you may see that what was accomplished for the California campaign was polished to a high finish for the White House efforts and years. See Mark Hertsgaard, *On Bended Knee: The Press and the Reagan Presidency* (New York: Farrar, Straus and Giroux, 1988).

7. Thorstein Veblen, *The Theory of the Leisure Class* (New York: Macmillan, 1899), pp. 110 and 204. And to make matters worse, he pointed out, "for all but the aberrant, self-respect is gained in society through the esteem in which one is held by others"—which makes endeavoring to *change* society (always a minority operation) difficult not only against the powers that be but against one's subjective needs.

8. In using the term "trounced" I have unwittingly fallen prey to the general attitude of Reagan popularity and invincibility. As Hertsgaard reminds us, Reagan received a bit less than 27 percent of the votes of the eligible voting public in 1980.

9. The two closest to Reagan, both charged with one form or another of crime, from which Meese—Attorney General charged with breaking the law—scampered free but Deaver did not.

10. *Great U-Turn,* op. cit., p. 143.

11. A special word about takeovers. They were induced in part by lack of stimuli for expanded productive capacity (as noted earlier, capacity utilization was around the 80 percent level in the mid-and late Eighties), in part by the tax gains to be made in the process (the new tax laws made interest payments on the associated junk bonds deductible—which means you and I are paying for those high jinks), and in part by the swelling greed of the times and the new business world cowboys—RJR, Milken, Icahn, Boesky, et al. The biggest beneficiaries of the LBO's were those who organized them (who could take in literally hundreds of millions for a single deal, for themselves); those harmed were almost always workers, and sometimes stockholders. And the economy. See chap. 7 in Du Boff, *Accumulation and Power,* op. cit., and Phillips, *Politics of Rich and Poor,* op. cit., appendix H for those and additional data.

12. In the United States the first steps were taken by farmers in the late nineteenth century; more importantly, as noted earlier, the larger and more telling reforms were instituted by big business in the first years of this century—amounting to

what Gabriel Kolko called "political capitalism"—in order to provide for *their* security, stability, and predictability. See Gabriel Kolko, *Main Currents in Modern American History* (New York: Pantheon, 1976), chap. 1.

13. Hertsgaard, op. cit., pp. 126-27, his emphasis. In matters such as these it is important to look at the brass tacks once in a while: in Hearings before the House Committee on Armed Services in 1984, the prices of ordinary tools (screwdrivers, wrenches, pliers, etc.) at the retail level were compared with defense contractors' prices. This was done for twenty-one items. At the retail level sixteen were priced below $5, three above $5 but less than $10, and two above $10, but less than $13. The contractors sold nothing at less than $225 (a screwdriver, for which the retail price was $2.79) and their highest price was $1,150 (a wrench, for which the retail price was $4.88). The total for all twenty-one items at retail was $92.44, from the contractors, $10,168.56. This is only a fleabite on the elephant's backside. All the above data are found in Walter Adams and James W. Brock, *The Bigness Complex: Industry, Labor, and Government in the American Economy* (New York: Pantheon, 1986).

14. See Phillips, op. cit., chap. 6 ("The New Plutography of 1980s America") wherein, among a wealth of other data, you will find that "In April 1988 *Business Week* released a startling statistic: during 1987, a year with just 4 percent inflation, the average CEO compensation at 339 of the nation's largest publicly held corporations rose by 48 percent to $1.8 million. It rose 14 percent more in 1988—to $2.02 million." (p. 178) The difference between the average industrial worker's and average CEO wage, about 1 to 40 in the Sixties, had moved to 1 to 150 by 1995. In Japan the ratio between industrial workers' and executive incomes is about 1 to 7.

15. I began to smoke when I was fifteen, hell bent on demonstrating my manliness. I stopped forty years later, when Kay first tried to stop. She couldn't, but I succeeded, though not without incident. I smoked my last cigarette as the first week of classes began in a new semester. After about two weeks, a delegation of students (who knew me from a previous class) came to see me: "Mr. Dowd, we have to tell you that you are acting crazy. You shout at us when we have done nothing; you seem to be splitting down the middle; you're pretty scary. Is there any way we can help?" Goddamn monsters, I thought, reaching into an empty pocket for a smoke. I was helped at that moment by remembering one of the few stories I think of as truly funny: A man was trying to stop smoking. He had spent a sleepless night, woke up exhausted, his breakfast was a hollering session between himself and his family, he just missed his bus to the suburban train station, arrived late at the office, the boss had been waiting for him, and he had a very bad day indeed. At its end, he rushed out only to miss the bus to the city train station. While standing there waiting and out of his mind with rage, he looked down to see, next to him, a little old lady bent over, tying her shoelaces. "You and your goddamned shoelaces!!" he screamed at the terrified woman.

16. The first time was when he was ten years old. I was separated from his mother and living alone on Lake Cayuga, below Cornell. I had a canoe, which Jeff had never experienced. We went out together into the very deep and very cold lake, and I foolishly sought to show Jeff what we had done as kids: one at each end of the canoe, standing on the tip, pushing up and down, etc. We did that, I went up in the air and fell hard on the sharp side of the canoe, breaking some ribs and putting me in or close to shock. I could barely hold on to the now overturned canoe, and Jeff laboriously pushed us back into shore.

17. William Greider, *Who Will Tell the People: The Betrayal of American Democracy* (New York: Simon & Schuster, 1992), p. 61.

18. The most astute analyst of financial fragility, who had been warning us for a good twenty years of how shaky the ground is upon which the economy stands, is Hyman P. Minsky. His thoughts are brought together in *Stabilizing an Unstable Economy* (New Haven: Yale University Press, 1986), a Twentieth Century Fund Report. The book is rich in analysis and data; a careful reading of it will make your hair stand on end. He passed away in 1996.

19. *Institutional Investor*, December 1995. In 1996, the figure was reported as $2.6 trillion. See chap. 7, note 22.

20. Just how good hands I leave it to you to judge: it is a fact that most of the dealers are in their twenties (like twenty-nine-year-old Nick Leeson, who lost $1.5 bill for Baring Brothers), are computer whizzes, and go at their work as though they were trying out for roles in "Animal House": "'These guys are utterly ruthless. The expression "I'm going to rip your lungs out" comes from foreign exchange,' says one longtime forex executive." Ibid.
Maybe it's better in the staid bond houses, like Salomon Brothers? Read Michael Lewis, *Liar's Poker* (New York: Norton, 1989). He was a trader at that most "conservative" company—until good sense (and taste) impelled his departure.

21. See "The Looting Decade: S&Ls, Big Banks and Other Triumphs of Capitalism," *Nation*, 19 Nov. 1990.

22. An important study of the latter, supplementing Hertsgaard and Greider very usefully, is Ben Bagdikian, *The Media Monopoly* (Boston: Beacon Press, 1983).

23. Greider, op. cit., p. 80.

24. This takes us to the term "tax expenditures." Assuming that government expenditures do not fall, a tax reduction for some necessarily means a tax increase for others (or an increase in the national debt, and interest payments on it—largely to those whose taxes were cut). So cutting the taxes of the rich amounts to an "expenditure" that has to be paid for—an expenditure *on* the rich to be paid for *by* the non-rich: paradise regained!

25. For these and many data like them, see Kevin Phillips, *Boiling Point: Democrats, Republicans and the Decline of Middle Class Prosperity* (New York: Harper Perennial, 1993), especially the appendices, which begin on p. 279 (where the exemption data are found). It is important to understand that when the term "middle class" is used to refer to incomes (as is usually the case), the range is usually about $50,000 to $150,000 for a family of four. In 1990, the median income—half above, half below—was $33,500 for that family of four; and 80 percent had incomes less than $45,000.

26. The following information is derived from the biennial series of income and wealth studies of the Economic Policy Institute (Washington, D.C.) entitled *The State of Working America*, all coauthored by Lawrence Mishel—the first of which (1989) with Jacqueline Simon, the following two (1990-91 and 1992-93) with Jared Bernstein and David Frankel, respectively, that of 1994-95 with Bernstein, and the most recent (1996-97) with Bernstein and John Schmitt. All were published by M.E. Sharpe.

27. Disclosures in 1993 regarding the rich and powerful caught up in corruption scandals in, for example, Japan and Italy, show that one of the politically most powerful men in Japan had *millions* of dollars of both currency and gold in boxes hidden in his house, and the man at the head of the pharmaceutical bureaucracy

in Italy had the lira equivalent of millions of dollars squirreled away in suitcases—both of them quite rich without any such doings. That may not be madness; if not, we need a new definition.

28. *New York Times,* 21 August 1995.

29. "Net worth" includes both financial assets (money in the bank, stocks, etc.) and tangible assets (home, auto, etc.). The figures for the bottom 90 percent require qualification: 20 percent of those families had a zero or negative worth; 54 percent had a zero or negative value of financial assets.

30. Phillips, *Politics of Rich and Poor,* p. 157. See his later *Boiling Point* for more data—which do not, however, change the picture significantly, being only a little more unequal. Also see the excellent essay of Andrew Hacker, "Class Dismissed," *New York Review of Books,* 7 March 1991, with data taken from IRS reports. The essay is a review of two quite different but equally absorbing studies: Benjamin DeMott, *The Imperial Middle: Why Americans Can't Think Straight About Class* (New York: Morrow, 1990) and *Money Income and Poverty Status in the United States 1989: Advance Data from the March 1990 Current Population Survey, Bureau of the Census* (Washington, DC: Government Printing Office, 1990)

31. As mentioned in an earlier chapter, the "official rate" is a significant under-statement, not least of all in that its origin is in LBJ's setting it at $3,000 for a family of four (in 1964), a figure arrived at through the Office of Civil Defense: its guess at the amount it would take for a family of four to survive—get this—after a post-nuclear attack (and adjusted each year for changes in the price level). For that off the wall development see Clair Wilcox, *Toward Social Welfare* (Homewood, IL: Irwin, 1969), pp. 26-27. Quite apart from such political hi-jinks, the United States measures poverty in ways more heartlessly than other industrialized countries.

32. Joseph Pechman, *Tax Reform* (Washington, DC: Brookings Institution, 1989), p. 20.

33. See Emma Rothschild in the *New York Review of Books*: "Reagan and the Real America," 2 February 1981, pp. 12, 13, 18; "The Real Reagan Economy," 30 June 1988; and "The Reagan Economic Legacy," 21 July 1988, pp. 41, 53.

34. And a reading of Harrison and Bluestone's *Great U-Turn* or *Deindustrialization* will show that within those categories, the jobs were principally low-pay, low-benefit, and low-security—the kinds of jobs that required more than one person in the family to work to stay out of poverty, and that were predominantly those available to young people just entering the labor force. Their counterparts in the Fifties and Sixties would have been getting relatively good industrial jobs.

35. Kevin Phillips, op. cit., p. 130. He depended for his data on *The Economist,* 14 January 1989. One of the realities making our trade balance worse than it might otherwise have been was the rapid rise of the dollar in the early 1980s—caused in greatest part by the very high interest rates and the great increase of foreign investment in the United States—both increasing the demand for dollars. Reagan's reaction to the costly dollar was happy and uncomplicated: "the stronger the dollar, the stronger the nation."

36. The figures are from *Economic Report of the President, 1992,* p. 385.

37. But not a fall at all in property income. A reminder that one meaning of the past twenty years or so has been the "financialization" and the "hollowing" of the U.S. economy; in turn that has meant a fall in profits and a rise in interest payments. (Corporate profits were $257 billion in 1979 and fell thereafter, not to arrive again at that level for almost eight years.)

38. Presumably because Libya was behind the bombing of a bar in Germany where U.S. G.I.s were killed. But the accumulating evidence indicates strongly that the culprits were more likely Syrian than Libyan. Ghedaffi's young daughter was killed in that senseless bombing, causing great anger in Libya and shock elsewhere but little feeling of any sort in the United States. One wonders what our country would have done had someone dropped a bomb in Washington, D.C. and killed, for example, Bush's dog?

39. The enormity of the crimes there—the killings, the torture, the ruination of two societies' economies, politics, and future—is suggested when one considers that in El Salvador over 70,000 people are known to have been killed (the largest percentage of them in their villages by the army death squads) out of a total population of about 4 million. That ratio, if applied to the United States, would have meant more than 10 million deaths. Nicaragua has a population a bit more than half of El Salvador's, with even more severe consequences in terms of proportions. The main difference between the two countries is that the United States supported the El Salvador government and its death squads whereas it opposed the Sandinista Government of Nicaragua and supported its rebels. One meaning of that is that the United States did everything it could to destroy the Nicaraguan economy and what it could to support that of El Salvador. As some of the materials to follow will show.

40. This despite the atrocious, numerous, and large-scale activities of the Salvadoran death squads—including the murder and rape of several Catholic nuns—whose leadership had been trained in or by the United States. Carter had begun differently with El Salvador, but not with Nicaragua. LaFeber's *America, Russia, and the Cold War*, chap. 12, tells very well the story of Carter's and Reagan's foreign policies, and I have depended upon him above.

41. Shortly afterward, while floundering and losing public support for what was in fact a non-policy, Reagan withdrew the remaining 1,600 U.S. troops. See LaFeber, op. cit., pp. 309-10.

42. Some of you will be unable to get on with your lives without knowing the answers to the questions: 1) a and c; 2) c and d; 3) d; 4) a and d. If you have peeked at this note, you have disqualified yourself for the prize.

43. Hertsgaard, *On Bended Knee*, p. 211.

44. Wills, *Reagan's America*, p. 422. To add to the madness of this whole matter, consider this: "the country's internal politics could be ignored, for the most part, since the contending factions were both Communist.... The invasion was given ancillary justification as a punishment for the murder of Maurice Bishop by Bernard Coard's followers, despite the fact that Bishop was Reagan's original villain, the recipient of Fidel Castro's support. Castro was not backing Coard [who had taken control after Bishop's murder] at the time America attacked him" (Wills, n. 20, pp. 561-62). After the dust had settled, the United States finished the airstrip, to be used, as had been said earlier, to enhance tourism.

45. See the fine book by a favorite author, Hans Koning, *The Conquest of America* (New York: Monthly Review Press, 1993), a book that has the double virtue of being short (150 pages) and unusually readable. The word "guilty" has been used by me, even though the principals—Reagan, Bush, North, Poindexter, Casey, Weinberger, Abrams, et al.—got off scot-free, some of them, of course, because Bush gave a blanket pardon just before he turned in the keys of the White House (if, in fact, he did turn in the keys). The discussion that follows in the text

concerning El Salvador and Nicaragua is desperately brief. A fuller discussion going back to their early history and into the 1980s will be found of both those and the other tortured countries of Central America in Walter LaFeber's also very readable *Inevitable Revolutions* (New York: W.W. Norton, 1983).

45A. LaFeber, *America, Russia, and the Cold War*, p. 298.

46. This is a good time to refer the reader to some of the substantial efforts of Noam Chomsky and Edward S. Herman to try to bring some element of balance to this question in their several books in the area. Their *Washington Connection and Third World Fascism* was noted earlier. A continuation of that analysis is *After the Cataclysm: Postwar Indochina and the Reconstruction of Imperial Ideology* (Montreal: Black Rose Books, 1979), and although most of it is concerned with Indochina, much that is important is not. Invaluable for the matter of the media is *Manufacturing Consent: The Political Economy of the Mass Media* (New York: Pantheon, 1989). See also Herman's book with Frank Broadhead, *Demonstration Elections: U.S.-Staged Elections in the Dominican Republic, Vietnam, and El Salvador* (Boston: South End Press, 1984). The best single book on "terrorism" is Edward Herman and Gerry O'Sullivan, *The "Terrorism" Industry: The Experts and Institutions that Shape Our View of Terror* (New York: Pantheon, 1989).

47. *The Massacre at El Mozote: A Parable of the Cold War* (New York: Vintage, 1994). Also see Joan Didion, "'Something Horrible' in El Salvador," *New York Review of Books*, 13 July 1994.

48. LaFeber, *America, Russia, and the Cold War*, p. 312. And when the Nicaraguans appealed to the International Court of Justice on the matter of mined harbors and the like, and the Court—including a U.S.-appointed Judge—ruled in Nicaragua's favor, the United States ignored the ruling and went on its bloody way (although supporting the same Court earlier on a favorable ruling).

49. Of which there were two, each an amendment of a defense appropriations bill for fiscal years 1983 and 1984. Both disallowed *any* kind of expenditure by the CIA, the Department of Defense, or any governmental agency for the purposes of "overthrowing the Government of Nicaragua." The principal meaning of the Boland amendments to Reagan, the CIA, and the NSC was the need to find ways around it.

50. Naturally there has been much written about this question. The most definitive—and damning—treatment is noted: Theodore Draper's massive and meticulous *A Very Thin Line: The Iran-Contra Affairs* (New York: Hill and Wang, 1991). See also Peter Kornbluh and Malcolm Byrne (eds.) *The Iran-Contra Scandal: The Declassified History* (New York: New Press, 1993), for documentary support, and for its foreword by Draper.

51. It isn't that we don't know what he did or that he denied doing it: indeed, as anyone who watched the hearings will remember, he was very proud of his law-breaking, and arrogantly so. But he was speaking with immmunity then, and it was subsequently ruled that whatever he said there and then could not be used against him later. That those providing the immunity did not know that such an eventuation was implied suggests that they are either fools, cowards, or crooks: in some cases—no names this time—all three categories would apply. Poor Independent Counsel Lawrence Walsh, facing a whole busload of guilty bigshots—President, Vice President, CIA chief (by then gone to his rest), NSC chief, NSC Chief Action Officer, and many others—all greased up like eels by legal

procedures, impossible to pin down. It's a wonder he survived the frustrations. Anyhow, thanks for the effort, Counselor.

52. Draper, op. cit., p. 598.

53. Here I follow the tight summary of a connected essay in the *New York Times*, 20 January 1994.

CHAPTER 7 THE LONG MORNING AFTER: SINCE REAGAN

1. Bob Woodward, *The Commanders* (New York: Simon & Schuster, 1991). Woodward devotes almost 200 pages to the evolution of the Panama invasion, and an almost equal amount to the Gulf War. See pp. 83, 91, 115, 116, 157, 164.

2. Not least of our motives was that the CIA was eager to get their arrested operative out of prison down there. Inaccurately, the CIA saw Muse as a hostage, and hostages can cause political trouble. The problem was that what Muse was doing, as part of a conspiracy to unseat Noriega, was by U.S. laws illegal. So, Muse had to be rescued—as he was—as part of a larger effort that could be seen as legal—if talked about fast enough.

3. Torrijos's plane crash was in 1981, Reagan's first year. Noriega was head of the National Guard, and "Under the Panamanian constitution, the National Guard is equal in importance to the executive, legislative, and judicial branches of government." See Naylor, *Hot Money*, pp. 191-92, where the plane crash is also discussed. Originally part of Colombia, "Panama" was invented by us in 1903. And Colombia, of course, has been the main home of cocaine production and trade.

4. It is worth noting that Lt. General Thomas Kelly, Operations Chief for Powell, did *not* interpret the roadblock shooting incident that killed the Marine Lieutenant as "a clear-cut incident of unprovoked PDF aggression—the car had sped away from a legitimate roadblock, lending an element of ambiguity" (Woodward, op. cit., p. 157). A rather large "element," Bush might have thought, had the situation been reversed, with a PDF man "speeding away from a U.S. Marine roadblock" under conditions of rising tension.

5. LaFeber, *America, Russia, and the Cold War,* p. 330.

6. All of which created what came to be called "Iraqgate," a set of processes involving the secret furnishing of weapons and sophisticated military techniques (and satellite intelligence) for use against Iran (in the eight-year-long war) while at the same time furnishing much of the same to Iran, as part of Iran-contra, for use against Iraq.

7. TV is the most formidable (though by no means the only one) of these techniques. Jerry Mander shows the hows and the whys of TV—most briefly in chap. 6 of his *The Absence of the Sacred,* and at greater length in his *Four Arguments for the Elimination of Television* (New York: Morrow, 1978). See also the more recent study by Jeff Cohen and Norman Solomon, *Through the Media Looking Glass* (Monroe, ME: Common Courage Press, 1995).

8. Whereas, in fact, the media in general went along with the war for most of its many years, with rare and honorable exceptions. But as the war ground on, just presenting a small percentage of the obvious facts—especially during and after the Tet offensive of early 1968—became devastating. What were the TV folks in Vietnam going to do when showing the GIs, ask them to remove their helmets if, as more often than not, they had peace symbols on them? Or never show the GIs? What do you do in an earthquake, take pictures of the unharmed neighborhoods?

9. Hedrick Smith (ed.), *The Media and the Gulf War* (Washington, DC: Seven Locks Press), 1992, p. xiii.

10. See, in Smith (ed.), ibid., "U.S. Bombs Missed 70 Percent of the Time," by Barton Gellman, reprinted from the *Washington Post*, 16 March 1991.

11. Even when the recession was at its worst point, a year or so later, Bush's chief economist (Michael Boskin) recalls that "he had to threaten to quit to get an interview with his boss. . . ." *New York Times*, 12 February 1994.

12. Michael Stewart, *Keynes in the 1990s: A Return to Economic Sanity* (London: Penguin Books, 1993), p. 68.

13. The official unemployment rate was 3+ percent; if measured as in Western Europe it would be 10+, as would be that of the United States. These and other estimates were made by American Express, as reported in *International Herald Tribune*, 25 January 1995.

14. It is of more than passing interest that the Tigers are usually portrayed as the latest proof of the miraculous powers of free enterprise at work in the free market. The obvious realities for the Tigers, like those of the other ongoing "success," China, are due less to enterprise and more to powerful and ruthless state guidance, making for rapid growth in the short run but massive inefficiency in the uses of human beings, natural resources, and capital in the process. See the essay by Paul Krugman in *Foreign Affairs*, November/December 1994, who finds the organization and functioning of these "miracles" to be more like that of the Soviet economy in the 1950s than any other model—and least of all any free market model.

15. This is not the place to make anything like a sufficient basis for that generalization; it must suffice here to remember that when growth (a quantitative process) languishes for any substantial period the time has come for "development" (a qualitative as well as quantitative process). The latter is another way of referring to structural changes: going beyond (and making possible) the further expansion of what exists through the creation of new stimuli—consisting (among other possibilities) of new techniques, new products, new sources of demand, etc. It should go without saying that the principal policies that might bring about such changes must be *initiated* in the governmental sectors. It not only does not go without saying, but saying it these days can get you locked up as a nut case.

16. See, however, two clear and concise analyses with alternatives to the conventional wisdom: Robert A. Blecker, *Beyond the Twin Deficits: A Trade Strategy for the 1990s* (Armonk, NY: M.E. Sharpe, 1992), and Robert Eisner, *The Misunderstood Economy: What Counts and How to Count It* (Cambridge: Harvard Business School Press, 1994).

17. NAFTA (North American Free Trade Agreement) links Canada, Mexico, and the United States; GATT (General Agreement on Tariffs and Trade) almost all countries; initially the six-member EEC (European Economic Community), became the more comprehensive EU (European Union), now with fifteen and moving toward eighteen members; APEC (Asia-Pacific Economic Cooperation, eighteen countries of the Pacific Rim, including the United States); and other lesser groupings. For an incisive introduction to the matters now under discussion, see *The Case Against Free Trade: GATT, NAFTA, and the Globalization of Corporate Power* (San Francisco: Earth Island Press, 1993), with essays by Ralph Nader, William Greider, Jerry Mander, and many others.

18. One example worth pondering in this connection: General Motors has 50,000 suppliers. Not all, but most of them, are quite naturally beholden to GM, both economically and politically. GM is of course the largest of the large; but the remaining 499 of the "Fortune 500" may be assumed to be power players of the same sort, if in lesser degree.

19. As Jerry Mander puts it, the new technology "'popped' communications capabilities into a global dimension. This made it possible, and inevitable, for corporate powers to rapidly accelerate their expansion beyond national boundaries. In fact, corporate form and technological form *coevolved* in a symbiotic relationship: the corporations pushed the technologies that, in turn, made it possible for the corporations to become *primary* international players, beyond the control of the sovereign states that had spawned them" *(The Case Against Free Trade,* op. cit., p. 14; emphasis in original.)

20. John L. and Barbara Hammond, *The Rise of Modern Industry* (New York: Harcourt Brace and Company, 1926), p. 196.

21. Richard J. Barnet and John Cavanagh, *Global Dreams: Imperial Corporations and the New World Order* (New York: Simon & Schuster, 1994) pp. 14-15.

22. Speculation in the foreign market exchange only. The figures are from the Bank for International Settlements, reported in *International Herald Tribune,* 5 February 1996.

23. Molly Ivins, "YAFers in Lockstep," *The Texas Observer,* March 1995. See Connie Bruch, "The Politics of Perception," *The New Yorker,* 9 October 1995, for an analysis of how Gingrich rose to, and how he used, his great power.

24. By which I don't mean we don't need health care reform. But his and Hillary's proposals for "managed competition" were bound to make the giant insurance companies richer and more powerful and leave us poorer in our already terribly inadequate health care system. Why neither he nor Hillary ever even mentioned, let alone proposed, a single-payer system—which had a minimum of one hundred votes in the House from the beginning—combined political cowardice with tactical stupidity.

EPILOGUE

1. See Paul Hawken, *The Ecology of Commerce: A Declaration of Sustainability* (New York: Harper Business Books, 1993).

2. Except for the most recent data, all these and more may be found conveniently in Kevin Phillips, *Boiling Point.* For annual reports of income data, see U.S. Bureau of the Census Current Population Reports, *Consumer Income,* Series P60-184, *Money Income of Households, Families, and Persons in the United States* (Washington, DC: U.S. Government Printing Office).

3. The data are taken from the *Handbook of Labor Statistics* (U.S. Department of Labor, 1975). As for the durability of durable consumer goods in the Fifties and Sixties, some will remember Arthur Miller's *Death of a Salesman,* and the heart-breaking scene when Willy Loman (the salesman) makes the final payment for his fridge on the day when it also ceases to work. A little schmalzy, to be sure; still. . .

4. For what went wrong with the Clinton "plan," and a discussion of the single-payer proposal, see Colin Gordon, *The Clinton Health Care Plan: Dead on Arrival.*

Why It Failed and What It Means, Open Magazine Series, No. 32, available through P.O. Box 2726, Westfield, NJ 07091.

5. *New York Times,* 19 December 1994. A summary sidebar to the article puts it all aptly: "Health care is increasingly a rich new playing field for Wall Street." See also Robert Sherrill, "The Madness of the Market: Dangerous to Your Health," *The Nation,* 9/16 January 1995, which contains a comprehensive bibliography.

6. Jonathan Kozol, *Savage Inequalities: Children in America's Schools* (New York: Crown Publishers, 1991), p. 4. See also his first book, *Death at an Early Age: The Destruction of the Hearts and Minds of Negro School Children in the Boston Public Schools* (Boston: Houghton Mifflin, 1967).

7. These criticisms of public schools are not meant to suggest that private schools are an—let alone the—answer. In an otherwise healthy society, without the extensive poverty and racism of ours, for example, private schools can have a useful function; in this society their expansion and spread intensifies the several deteriorating processes strangling public education.

8. For these data and related matters consult the excellent studies in John E. Ullmann (ed.), *Social Costs in Modern Society* (Westport, CT: Quorum Books, 1983). The quoted sentence is found in chap. 9, "Slums and Poverty," by Gary Knox. See also *Statistical Abstract of the United States, 1994.*

9. The source of the estimate is S. Walter and P. Choate, *America in Ruins* (Washington, DC: Council of State Planning Agencies, 1981), quoted in Ullmann, op. cit., p. 277.

10. Seymour Melman, "The U.S.-Russian Conversion Crisis," *In These Times,* 11 July 1994. Military expenditures since 1991, in excess of $250 billion annually, have of course pushed that $8.7 trillion figure closer to $10 trillion. To paraphrase Senator Everett Dirksen's famous remark, a trillion here and a trillion there, and pretty soon we're talking big money. Melman, now retired from his work as professor of industrial economics at Columbia University, has since 1961 written dozens of books and articles on the need for and possibilities of conversion, some referred to earlier.

11. Those wishing to pursue many more of the facts, along with analysis, may wish to consult Joe S. Bain, *Industrial Organization* (New York: John Wiley & Sons, 1968), which describes and analyzes the three cases to follow, plus many others.

12. After pointing out that NAFTA "meant more to Mexico because trade barriers between the two countries were already low," Prof. Robert Lawrence (Harvard) goes on to state that "What really distinguished NAFTA was the emphasis on foreign investment, which locked in the rights of American business to compete on equal terms in a country long inclined toward xenophobia" (*New York Times,* 14 October 1995).

13. In his very brief but profound study, *The Needs of Strangers* (London: Chatto & Windus; Hogarth Press, 1984), p. 50. Among the many important problems discussed with wisdom in this book is that indicated by the title. In our world, the deepest needs—for food, clothing, shelter, education, and health, which, Ignatieff reminds us, should be seen as human rights—are faced by multitudes of people who are and will always remain strangers to those who must see as their responsibility the fulfilling of those needs: the ultimate in human solidarity.

14. On the last point, see the excellent study by Barbara Ehrenreich, *Fear of Falling: The Inner Life of the Middle Class* (New York: Harper Perennial, 1990).

15. By conservative estimate, half of our annual GDP may be classified as waste: that is, as serving no useful function. When I say "conservative" I mean that those making that estimate counted about 70 percent of military expenditure as non-wasteful, and took only partial account of what has just been noted in the text. See my *Waste of Nations*, chap. 4.

16. A handy way to keep informed on all the third parties and related developments is by reading/subscribing to NationAlert, 72 Fifth Avenue, New York, NY 10011 ($18 annual sub.). You can also Interlink them—e-mail nation@igc.apc.org— and get your bulletin thataway (as we used to say in the old days).

17. Read Erich Fromm's *Escape from Freedom* (New York: Avon Books, 1982; originally 1941).

18. From "September 1, 1939" in *Selected Poems* (New York: Random House, Vintage Books, 1989).

19. Erich Fromm, again. In his *The Art of Loving* (New York: Harper & Row, 1956), Fromm is squarely concerned with "love" in the sense in which it is being used in the text. He writes lucidly and briefly of the varieties of love—romantic, family, solidaristic—and of love as an attitude and set of feelings dependent upon and generating concern, understanding, and respect, not just for those around one, but for those also whom one does not and probably never will know: "strangers," as Ignatieff would have it.

20. See, for example, the recent books by a couple of incorrigible do-gooders: Milton Wolff, *Another Hill: An Autobiographical Novel of the Spanish Civil War* (Champaign, IL: Illinois University Press, 1994), and Dave Dellinger, *From Yale to Jail*. Wolff, whom I see once in a while in San Francisco, was the last Commander of the Abraham Lincoln Brigade which, in a failed "deal" to have the Italians and Germans pull out of the war, left Spain in late 1938. Tough as can be, he is also relentlessly cheerful.

INDEX